Small Business Financial Management Kit For Dummies®

Financial Management Tips for Small Business Owners/Managers

✔ To survive and thrive, you must earn profit consistently, generate cash flow from profit, and control your financial condition. A separate financial statement is prepared for each imperative:

- The **P&L Statement** (also called the *Income*, or *Earnings Statement*) summarizes revenue and expenses and reports your resulting profit or loss for the period.

- The **Statement of Cash Flows** begins by reporting the net increase or decrease in cash from your revenue and expenses during the period (which is a different amount than your profit or loss for the period); this statement also summarizes other sources of cash you tapped during the period, and what you did with your available cash.

- The **Balance Sheet** (also called the *Statement of Financial Condition*) summarizes your assets and liabilities at the close of business on the last day of the profit period and reports the sources of your owners' equity (assets less liabilities).

✔ **The information in your financial statements is no better than your accounting system.** Hire a competent accountant to design and run your accounting system. Your accountant can be a valuable helpmate in managing your financial affairs.

✔ **Know how to read and interpret your financial statements.** Not understanding your own business's financial statements puts you at a serious disadvantage in making good business decisions and in dealing with your lenders and owners.

✔ **Cash flow accounting doesn't tell you profit for the period, and accrual-basis profit accounting doesn't tell you cash flow for the period.** Credit sales are recorded as revenue before cash is received. Some expenses are recorded before cash is paid, and some are recorded after cash is spent. Depreciation expense is not a cash outlay in the period. Never confuse profit and cash flow. You need to look at your P&L for your profit, and you need to look at your Statement of Cash Flows for your cash flow.

✔ **Read the preceding tip again!** Deep down in your psyche you probably believe that profit equals cash flow. You may want to believe this, but it ain't so. Chapter 3 explains cash flow from making profit. You may want to read this chapter more than once to make certain that you have a firm grip on cash flow.

✔ **Use a compact profit model for decision-making analysis.** The P&L report is indispensable for controlling profit performance, but this profit performance report is too bulky for decision-making analysis. A compact profit model is better. The P&L statement is like a high-end digital SLR camera; a profit model is like a pocket-size digital camera that you carry around with you and is good enough for most uses. Chapter 8 demonstrates how to use a profit model.

✔ **Seemingly small changes in profit factors can cause staggering differences.** A small slippage in the ratio of margin on sales revenue can have a devastating impact on profit. A slight boost in sales price or a relatively modest increase in sales volume can yield a remarkable gain in profit. Small changes mean a lot.

✔ **Determine the sizes of assets you need to support the level of your annual sales revenue.** The amount of your total assets determines the amount of capital you have to raise, and capital has a cost. The more assets you have, the more capital you need. Downsize your assets as long as you don't hurt sales. Chapter 11 explains how to determine the proper sizes of your operating assets and liabilities.

Small Business Financial Management Kit For Dummies®

Cheat Sheet

Financial Management Tips for Small Business Owners/Managers (continued)

- ✔ **Don't rush into securing debt and equity capital without doing due diligence.** Many small businesses are desperate for capital. Carefully examine the true, total cost of the capital and scrutinize the potential for interference from capital sources in running your business.

- ✔ **Trust, but protect.** Business is done on the basis of mutual trust, but not everyone is trustworthy, even a longtime employee and a close relative. Enforce effective controls to minimize threats of theft and fraud against your business. An ounce of prevention is worth a pound of cure. See Chapter 5 for more details on controls.

- ✔ **Businesses that make profit generate taxable income.** Small business ("S") corporations, partnerships, and LLCs (limited liability companies) don't have to pay income tax. They are *pass-through tax entities*; so, their owners include their respective shares of the business's taxable income in their individual income tax returns. The profit of a pass-through business is taxed only once — in the hands of its owners. Cash dividends paid to stockholders by regular ("C") corporations from their after-tax profits are included in the individual income tax returns of their stockholders and are thus subject to a second tax in the hands of the stockholders.

- ✔ **Take the time to forecast, plan, and budget.** Of course you are very busy, but it pays to step back from the day-to-day affairs of your business and look down the road. Have your Controller (chief accountant) prepare the following pro forma (according to plan) financial statements:

  - **Budgeted P&L statement for the coming year.** Even if this budgeted P&L is abbreviated and condensed it plays an invaluable role. Provide your Controller your best estimates and forecasts for sales prices, costs, and sales volume during the coming year. From this information your accountant prepare a P&L that serves as your performance benchmark as you go through the year. Don't be afraid to change the budgeted P&L in midstream. Sometimes totally unpredictable events make your original P&L budget out of date.

  - **Budgeted Balance Sheet at end of coming year.** You don't necessarily need a detailed listing of every asset and liability one year off. But you definitely should look ahead to your general, overall financial condition one year later. It's better to spot problems earlier than later. Looking down the road at where your financial condition is heading can help you avoid major problems.

  - **Budgeted Statement of Cash Flows.** Preparing this budgeted financial statement is an excellent way to keep close tabs on your cash flow from profit (operating activities) and how you plan to use this cash flow. If you are planning major capital expenditures (new investments to replace, modernize, and expand your long-term operating asserts) a budgeted statement of cash flows is essential for making strategic decisions regarding how you will secure the cash for these expenditures.

- ✔ **Don't confuse your balance sheet with the market value of your business.** True, your balance sheet reports your assets and liabilities, and the difference equals the book value of your owners' equity. Keep in mind, however, that historical costs are the values for many assets, and the balance sheet does not report your profit performance over recent years. Yet, the market value of a business depends heavily on current replacement values of your assets and your recent profit performance. Chapter 14 explains the basic methods for putting a market value on a small business.

For Dummies: Bestselling Book Series for Beginners

Small Business Financial Management Kit

FOR

DUMMIES®

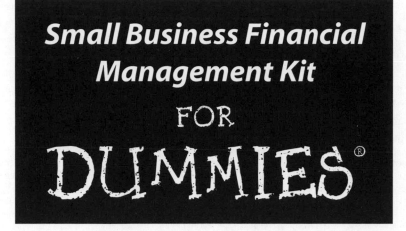

Small Business Financial Management Kit

FOR DUMMIES®

by Tage C. Tracy, CPA and John A. Tracy, CPA

BICENTENNIAL
1807
WILEY
2007
BICENTENNIAL

Wiley Publishing, Inc.

Small Business Financial Management Kit For Dummies®

Published by
Wiley Publishing, Inc.
111 River St.
Hoboken, NJ 07030-5774
www.wiley.com

Copyright © 2007 by Wiley Publishing, Inc., Indianapolis, Indiana

Published by Wiley Publishing, Inc., Indianapolis, Indiana

Published simultaneously in Canada

WILEY

About the Authors

Tage C. Tracy (Poway, California) is the principal owner of TMK & Associates, an accounting, financial, and strategic business planning consulting firm focused on supporting small- to medium-sized businesses since 1993. Tage received his baccalaureate in accounting in 1985 from the University of Colorado at Boulder with honors. Tage began his career with Coopers & Lybrand (now merged into PricewaterhouseCoopers). More recently, Tage coauthored with his father, John Tracy, *How to Manage Profit and Cash Flow*.

John A. Tracy (Boulder, Colorado) is Professor of Accounting, Emeritus, at the University of Colorado in Boulder. Before his 35-year tenure at Boulder, he was on the business faculty 4 years at the University of California at Berkeley. He served as staff accountant at Ernst & Young and is the author of several books on accounting and finance, including *Accounting For Dummies, Accounting Workbook For Dummies, The Fast Forward MBA in Finance, How to Read a Financial Report, and* coauthor with his son, Tage, of *How to Manage Profit and Cash Flow*. Dr. Tracy received his B.S.C. degree from Creighton University and earned his MBA and PhD degrees from the University of Wisconsin. He is a CPA (inactive) in Colorado.

Dedication

We dedicate this book to Edgar F. Jeffries, presently 96 years of age. Edgar is John's father-in-law and Tage's grandfather. In the midst of the Great Depression, Edgar and his father opened a small grocery store in Fort Dodge, Iowa. From scratch, they built Jeffries Grocery into a successful and respected institution. We quote Edgar more than once in this book.

Authors' Acknowledgments

We are deeply grateful to everyone at Wiley Publishing, Inc. who helped produce this book. Their professionalism and courtesy were much appreciated. First, we thank Mike Lewis, the acquisition editor. He stayed with us on developing the concept for the book. We appreciate his encouragement. Our editor, Kelly Ewing, was exceptional. It was a pleasure working with her. We owe Kelly a debt that we cannot repay. So, a simple but heartfelt "thank you" will have to do. We sincerely thank Wade Harb who reviewed our manuscript. He offered many helpful suggestions that made the book much better.

Publisher's Acknowledgments

We're proud of this book; please send us your comments through our Dummies online registration form located at www.dummies.com/register/.

Some of the people who helped bring this book to market include the following:

Acquisitions, Editorial, and Media Development

Project Editor: Kelly Ewing

Acquisitions Editor: Michael Lewis

General Reviewer: Wade Harb

Editorial Manager: Michelle Hacker

Editorial Assistants: Erin Calligan Mooney, Joe Niesen, Leeann Harney

Cartoons: Rich Tennant (www.the5thwave.com)

Composition Services

Project Coordinator: Patrick Redmond

Layout and Graphics: Carrie A. Foster, Brooke Graczyk, Stephanie D. Jumper, Heather Ryan, Alicia B. South

Anniversary Logo Design: Richard Pacifico

Proofreaders: Aptara, Cynthia Fields

Indexer: Aptara

Publishing and Editorial for Consumer Dummies

  Diane Graves Steele, Vice President and Publisher, Consumer Dummies

  Joyce Pepple, Acquisitions Director, Consumer Dummies

  Kristin A. Cocks, Product Development Director, Consumer Dummies

  Michael Spring, Vice President and Publisher, Travel

  Kelly Regan, Editorial Director, Travel

Publishing for Technology Dummies

  Andy Cummings, Vice President and Publisher, Dummies Technology/General User

Composition Services

  Gerry Fahey, Vice President of Production Services

  Debbie Stailey, Director of Composition Services

Contents at a Glance

Table of Contents

Introduction

● ●

A lot of small business owners/managers muddle through rather than knowingly manage the financial affairs of their business. They have a good overall business model and they manage other aspects of their business fairly well. But when you start talking about financial topics, they get sweaty palms. They do little more than keep tabs on their cash balance. That's no way to run a railroad!

This book, quite simply, explains the fundamentals of small business financial management. We explain the accounting reports — which are called *financial statements* or just *financials* — you need to understand in running your business. We discuss many other critical financial management topics, including raising capital, making smart profit decisions, and choosing the best form of legal entity for income tax.

About This Book

Business managers are busy people, and they have to carefully budget their time. Small business owners/managers are especially busy people; they have no time to waste. We promise not to waste your time in reading this book. In every chapter, we cut to the chase. We contain our discussions to fundamentals — topics you must know to handle the financial affairs of your business.

This book is not like a mystery novel; you can read the chapters in any order. Each chapter stands on its own feet. You may have more interest in one chapter than others, so you can begin with the chapters that have highest priority to you. Where a topic overlaps with a topic in another chapter, we provide a cross-reference.

By all means, use the book as a reference manual. Put the book on your desk and refer to it as the need arises. It's your book, so you can mark topics with comments in the margins or place sticky notes on pages you refer to often. This book isn't a college textbook. You don't have to memorize things for exams. The only test is whether you improve your skills for managing the financial affairs of your business.

Conventions Used in This Book

Throughout the book, we use financial statement examples. Many chapters use figures to demonstrate the financial statements that you work with in managing the financial affairs of your business. We explain what these financial statements mean and how to interpret the information.

The examples are as realistic as we can make them without getting bogged down in too many details. When, for example, we present an example of a P&L (profit and loss) statement, we make sure that its numbers make sense for actual businesses. The examples are not theoretical; the examples are from the real world.

In preparing financial statements, your accountant conforms to the *standardized formats and terminology* adopted by the accounting profession. In other words, your accountant adheres to the established protocols for presenting financial statements. These rules are the grammar for communicating information in financial statements. However, accounting comes across as a foreign language to many business managers, and we keep this point in mind on every page of the book. In Chapter 1, we begin by explaining the communication conventions of financial statements.

Speaking of accountants, we should distinguish between the *internal accountant,* who is an employee of your business, and the *outside, independent accounting professional* who advises you from time to time. A small business employs an accountant who is in charge of its accounting system. The employee's job title may be Controller, In-Charge Accountant, or Office Manager. In this book, the term *accountant* refers to the person on your payroll. We refer to your independent professional accountant as a CPA (certified public accountant).

What You're Not to Read

Not every topic may have you sitting on the edge of your seat. For example, if you're not a manufacturer, you may not be terribly interested in Chapter 13, and if you're not a service business, you may glance over Chapter 12 in a hurry. You can skip over topics that aren't immediately relevant or urgent. You won't hurt our feelings if you tread lightly on some topics.

We suspect that a few topics in the book are more detailed than you're interested in. You should refer the more technical aspects to your accountant and make sure that the accountant follows through on the assignment. A good example is Chapter 5 on *internal controls,* which refer to the procedures put in place to minimize errors and fraud. You should definitely understand the critical need for establishing and enforcing effective controls. But the implementation of internal controls is a job for your accountant.

Foolish Assumptions

In writing this book, we've done our best to put ourselves in your shoes as a small business manager. Of course, we don't know you personally. But we have a good composite profile of you based on our experience in consulting with small business managers and explaining financial issues to business managers who have a limited background in financial matters.

Perhaps you've attended a short course in finance for the nonfinance manager, which would give you a leg up for reading this book. We should mention that many of these short courses focus mainly on financial statement analysis and do not explore the broader range of financial management issues that small business owners/managers have to deal with.

We take nothing for granted and start our discussions at ground zero. We present the material from the ground level up. The more you already know about the topics, the quicker you can move through the discussion. Whether you're a neophyte or veteran, you can discover useful insights and knowledge in this book. If nothing else, the book is a checklist of the things you ought to know for managing the finances of a small business.

How This Book Is Organized

This book is divided into parts, and each part is divided into chapters. The following sections describe what you find in each part.

Part 1: Improving Your Profit, Cash Flow, and Solvency

In keeping your small business thriving and growing you encounter three financial imperatives: (1) making adequate profit consistently; (2) generating cash flow from profit for the needs of the business and its owners; and (3) controlling the financial condition of your business by keeping it healthy and avoiding insolvency. You receive a financial statement for each imperative. Part I explains these three financial statements and how to use this information for making a profit and controlling the cash flow and financial condition of your business.

Part II: Using Tools of the Trade

Part II explains basic small business financial management tools. It explores internal controls that minimize accounting errors and threats of fraud from within and without your business, as well as cost control, which goes beyond the simplistic notion of just minimizing costs. This part also covers practical budgeting and planning techniques for the small business and how to develop and use a _profit model_ for decision-making analysis.

Part III: Dealing with Small Business Financial Issues

In starting a business, the founders have to decide which type of legal entity to use. This part explains the alternative legal entities for carrying on business activities and what you should consider from the income tax point of view when you structure your business. This part also offers practical advice on how to raise the capital you need for your business.

Part IV: Looking at Service and Manufacturing Businesses

Part IV describes services businesses and how they differ from businesses that sell products, as well as how manufacturing businesses determine their product cost. Although you may not be a service business or a manufacturer, you can gain insights from this part.

Part V: Reaching the End of the Line

This part of the book has a special place in our hearts — not because we want you to go out of business, of course. But there may come a time when a successful business wants to cash in its chips and leave the game. You probably know of several entrepreneurs who decided to sell out and move on to new challenges. This part presents a concise explanation of small business valuation methods. It also walks you through the steps of liquidating assets, paying liabilities, and making final distributions to owners (assuming that some money is left after paying liabilities and the lawyers).

Part VI: The Part of Tens

The Part of Tens is a staple in every *For Dummies* book. These chapters offer pithy lists of advice that sum up the main points explained in the chapters. One chapter offers general management rules for the small business. First and foremost, you must be a good manager to make your small business venture a success. The second chapter focuses on ten important financial management rules and techniques.

About the CD

Every financial statement example in the book is on the CD that accompanies the book. We prepared all examples using the Excel spreadsheet program from Microsoft. Of course, you need to have Excel on your computer to open and use each example's worksheet.

You can use each example on the CD as a template, or pattern for your business situation or to explore alternative scenarios. For example, you can quickly analyze what would happen to profit if sales volume had been 10 percent higher or lower than in the example. To use the template for your business you need to replace the data in the example with the data for your business situation. You would probably assign this data entry process to your accountant, who should find the templates very useful. Your accountant can easily expand or modify the template to fit the particular circumstances of your business.

John, a coauthor of this book, has written *How To Read A Financial Report, The Fast Forward MBA in Finance*, and *How To Manage Profit and Cash Flow* with Tage, a coauthor of this book. (John Wiley & Sons is the publisher of all three books.) The books use financial statement examples that were prepared using Excel. John offers to e-mail the Excel worksheets to the reader. Literally hundreds and hundreds of readers have asked for the Excel worksheets. We thought it would be more convenient to provide the worksheets on the CD for this book. This book and its CD constitute an integrated kit.

Icons Used in This Book

Throughout this book, you see some little pictures in the margin. These icons highlight the following types of information:

This icon serves to remind you that the financial statement example is on the CD for the book. Each worksheet example is prepared as a template. You can open the figure with the Excel spreadsheet program and follow along on your computer screen each step in the explanation. This makes the explanation more live and real time. You can also change the data in the example to simulate outcomes for alternative scenarios, which is an effective learning method.

This icon asks you to keep in mind an important point that is central in the explanation of the topic at hand.

This icon highlights, well, *tips* for applying financial management techniques. These pointers and advisories are worth highlighting with a yellow marker so that you don't forget them. On second thought, this icon saves you the cost of buying a highlighter pen.

This sign warns you about speed bumps and potholes on the financial highway. Taking special note of this material can steer you around a financial road hazard and keep you from blowing a fiscal tire. You can save yourself a lot of trouble by paying attention to these warning signs.

Where to Go from Here

You may want to start with Chapter 1 and proceed through the chapters in order. If you're fairly familiar with the design of financial statements, start with Chapter 2, which explains how to read your P&L statement. If you already have a good handle on the P&L statement, you could start with Chapter 3 if you have questions about *cash flow* – and in our experience, small business managers have many questions on cash flow!

If your highest priority concerns are about income tax issues, you can jump into Chapter 9 right away. If you're having problems in raising capital for your business, you may want to start with Chapter 10. If you worry about fraud threats against your business, Chapter 5 is a good place to start.

Starting and managing a small business is a tremendously challenging undertaking, and we applaud you. You have a lot of guts. And you also need a lot of financial management savvy. We hope our book helps you succeed.

Part I
Improving Your Profit, Cash Flow, and Solvency

The 5th Wave   By Rich Tennant

"Business here is good, but the weak dollar is killing my overseas markets!"

In this part . . .

We begin with a general overview of what's involved in managing the financial affairs of the small business. Financial statements are the main source of information for carrying out your financial management functions. So, we carefully explain the conventions and customs accountants use in preparing financial statements.

The three primary financial imperatives of every business are to make profit, generate cash flow from making profit (which is not the same as making profit), and control financial condition and solvency. Accordingly, a separate financial statement is prepared for each purpose. We explain these three primary financial statements. Quite simply, you don't know what you're doing without a solid understanding of these financial statements.

Chapter 1

Managing Your Small Business Finances

---

*T*he small business manager has to be a jack-of-all-trades. You have to be good at sales and marketing. You have to be knowledgeable about hiring, training, and motivating employees. You have to understand production systems if you are in the manufacturing business. You have to be smart at purchasing. You should be aware of business law and government regulations. You have to figure out where you have an edge on your competitors. Equally important, you need good skills for managing the *financial affairs* of your business.

Identifying Financial Management Functions

Managing the finances of a small business is not just doing one or two things. Financial management is broader than you might think — it involves a palette of functions:

✔ Raising sufficient capital for the assets needed by your business

✔ Earning adequate profit consistently and predictably

✔ Managing cash flow from profit

✓ Minimizing threats of fraud and other losses

✓ Minimizing the income tax burden on your business and its owners

✓ Forecasting the cash needs of your business

✓ Keeping your financial condition in good shape and out of trouble

✓ Putting a value on your business when the time comes

When you grow your business to 50 or 100 million dollars annual sales — and we know you will someday — you can hire a chief financial officer (CFO) to manage the financial functions of your business. In the meantime these responsibilities fall in your lap, so you better know how to manage the financial affairs of your business.

The failure rate of new businesses is high. Many entrepreneurs would like to think that if they have a good business model, boundless enthusiasm, and work tirelessly they are sure to succeed. The evidence speaks otherwise. Many embryonic businesses hit financial roadblocks because the owner/ manager does not understand how to manage the financial affairs of his or her business.

To press home our point we ask an embarrassing question: do you really have the basic skills and knowledge for managing the financial affairs of your business? Are you really on top of the financial functions that keep your business on course and out of trouble for achieving your financial objectives? Our book helps you to answer yes to these questions.

Tuning In to the Communication Styles of Financial Statements

We should be upfront about one thing: as a small business manager you must have a solid understanding of your *financial statements*. You can't really manage the financial affairs of your business without having a good grip on your financial statements. There's no getting around this requirement.

We could beat around the bush and suggest that you might be able to get along with only a minimal grasp on your financial statements. This would be a risky strategy, however. Most likely you'd end up wasting time and money. You'd have to spend too much time asking your Controller or your CPA to explain things. A CPA doesn't come cheap. (Check with Tage, the coauthor of this book, regarding his hourly rate for advising small business clients.)

TIP

Financial statements are prepared according to established, or one could say entrenched *conventions*. Uniform *styles and formats* for reporting financial statements have evolved over the years and become generally accepted. The conventions for financial statement reporting can be compared to the design rules for highway signs and traffic signals. Without standardization there would be a lot of accidents.

It would be confusing if each business made up its own practices for presenting its financial statements. If your financial statements did not abide by these rules they would look suspect to your lenders, owners, and anyone else who sees the financials. They might question whether your accountant is competent. They may wonder what you are up to if your financial statements don't conform to the established rules of the game.

We present many financial statements and accounting reports throughout the book. Therefore, at this early point in the book we explain the communication styles and conventions of financial statements. To illustrate these customary formats of presentation we use the *P&L (profit and loss) statement* shown in Table 1-1 for a business. *Note:* This business example is organized as a pass-through entity for income tax purposes and, therefore, does not itself pay income tax. (We discuss pass-through entities in Chapter 9.)

Table 1-1	P&L Statement for Year	
Sales revenue		$5,218,000
Cost of goods sold expense		$3,267,000
Gross margin		$1,951,000
Sales and marketing expenses	$397,000	
Administrative and general expenses	$1,087,000	$1,484,000
Operating profit		$467,000
Interest expense		$186,000
Net Income		$281,000

The following financial statement conventions may seem evident, but then again you might not be aware of all of them:

✔ You read a financial statement from the top down. *Sales revenue* is listed first, which is the gross (total) income from the sale of products and services before any expenses are deducted. If the main revenue stream of the business is from selling products the first expense deducted from sales revenue is *cost of goods sold,* as in this example.

Deducting cost of goods sold expense from sales revenue gives *gross margin* (also called *gross profit*). The number of other expense lines in a P&L statement varies from business to business. Before interest expense is deducted the standard practice is to show *operating profit* (also called *operating earnings*), which is profit before interest expense.

✔ The sample P&L statement includes two columns of numbers. Note that the $1,484,000 total of the two operating expenses (that is, sales and marketing expenses plus administrative and general expenses) in the left column is entered in the right column. Some financial statements display all figures in a single column.

✔ An amount that is deducted from another amount — such as the cost of goods sold expense — may be placed in parentheses to indicate that it is being subtracted from the amount above it. Or, the accountant who prepared the financial statement may assume that you know that expenses are deducted from sales revenue, so no parentheses are put around the number. You see expenses presented both ways in financial reports, but you hardly ever see a minus (negative) sign in front of expenses — it's just not done.

✔ Notice the use of dollar signs in the P&L statement example. In the illustration all amounts are have a dollar sign prefix. However, financial reporting practices vary quite a bit on this matter. The first number in a column always has a dollar sign but from here down it's a matter of personal preference.

✔ To indicate that a calculation is being done, a single underline is drawn under a number, as you see under the $3,267,000 cost of goods sold expense number in the P&L statement example. This means that the expense amount is being subtracted from sales revenue. The number below the underline, therefore, is a *calculated* amount.

✔ Dollar amounts in a column are always aligned to the right, as your see in the P&L statement example. Trying to read down a column of numbers that are not right aligned would be asking too much; the reader might develop vertigo reading down a jagged column of numbers.

✔ In the sample P&L statement dollar amounts are rounded to the nearest thousand for ease of reading, which is why you see all zeros in the last three places of each number. Really big businesses round off to the nearest million, and drop the last six digits. The accountant could have dropped off the last three digits in the P&L statement, but probably wouldn't in most cases.

Many accountants don't like rounding off amounts reported in a financial statement — so you see every dollar amount carried out to the last dollar, and sometimes even to the last penny. However, this gives a false sense of precision. Accounting for business transactions cannot be accurate down to the last dollar; this is nonsense. A well-known economist once quipped that accountants would rather be precisely wrong than approximately correct. Ouch! That stings because there's a strong element of truth behind the comment.

✔ The final number in a column usually is double underlined, as you see for the $281,000 bottom-line profit number in the P&L statement. This is about as carried away as accountants get in their work — a double underline. Instead of a double underline for a bottom-line number, it may appear in **bold.**

The accounting terminology in financial statements is mixed bag. Many terms are straightforward. If you have business experience you should understand most terms. But, like lawyers and doctors, accountants use esoteric terms that you don't see outside of financial statements. Accounting is often called the language of business, but it's a foreign language to many business managers.

Look once more at the terminology in the P&L statement example. You probably know what the terms mean, don't you? Nevertheless, we must admit that accountants use jargon more than they should. In some situations accountants resort to arcane terminology to be technically correct, like language used by lawyers in filing lawsuits and drawing up contracts. Your accountant should prepare financial statements that are as jargon-free as possible. Where we have to use jargon in the book we pause and clarify what the terms mean in plain English.

Previewing What's Ahead

To give you an idea of what's coming down the pike in the book, we pose questions about small business financial management and tell you the chapters in which you can find the answers:

✔ What are the key reasons why cash flow deviates from bottom-line profit for the year? See Chapter 3

✔ How do you tell whether your business is dangerously close to insolvency? See Chapter 4

✔ How do you protect your business against accounting errors and fraud? See Chapter 5

✔ Which is better for profit an increase in sales volume or an equal percent increase in sales price? See Chapter 8

✔ What information do you need for controlling costs? See Chapter 6

    ✔ How large should your assets be relative to your sales revenue and expenses? See Chapter 11

    ✔ What is the best legal organization form for your business from the income tax point of view? See Chapter 9

    ✔ What are the sources of capital for your business? See Chapter 10

    ✔ How do you put a value on your business if you're thinking of selling? See Chapter 14

    ✔ How do you terminate a business, financially and legally? See Chapter 15

Chapter 2

Understanding Your P&L and Profit Performance

. . . .

In This Chapter

▶ Getting better acquainted with your P&L

▶ Matching up the P&L with your business model

▶ Being clear on profit and loss issues

▶ Analyzing profit performance

▶ Exploring ways of improving your profit performance

. . . .

Small business owners and managers must know whether they're earning a profit. You need to make a steady profit to survive and thrive. So, you'd think that the large majority of small business owners/managers would be pretty good at understanding and analyzing their profit performance. The evidence suggests just the opposite. They generally know that profit information comes out of their accounting system. But accounting reports are in a foreign language to many small business owners/managers. They don't do much more than glance at the bottom line. A quick peek at the bottom line is no way for keeping your business profitable and growing your business.

Profit is a financial measure for a period of time — one quarter (three months) and one year are the two most common periods for which profit is determined, At the end of the period, your accountant (Controller) prepares a financial statement, known as the *P&L (profit and loss)* statement that reports the amount of profit or loss you made and the components of your profit or loss. A good part of this chapter explains this profit performance financial statement. You should thoroughly understand this accounting report. You can't afford to be fuzzy on this financial statement. Believe us, there's no other way to know your profit performance and understand how to improve your profit.

You can't look at your cash balance to track profit performance. Your cash balance may be going down even though you're making a profit. Or, your cash balance may be going up even though you're suffering a loss. You can't smell profit in the air; you can't feel it in your bones. You have to read the newspaper to learn the news. You have to read your P&L report to discover your profit news.

In this chapter, we concentrate on the fundamentals of profit accounting and the basic design of the financial statement that reports your profit performance.

Getting Intimate with Your P&L (Profit and Loss) Report

One main function of accounting is to measure your periodic profit or loss and to prepare a financial statement that reports information about how you made a profit or loss. *Periodic* means for a period of time, which can be one calendar quarter (three months), one year, or some other stretch of time.

Inside most businesses, this key financial statement is called the *P&L report*. In the formal financial statements released outside the business (to creditors and nonmanagement owners), it's called the *income statement, earnings statement,* or *operating statement.* The P&L report is also called a *statement,* or sometimes a *sheet.* (We suppose because it's presented on a sheet of paper.) These days, a business manager may want it displayed on his computer screen.

Your Controller is the profit and loss *scorekeeper* for your business, although managers generally have a lot to say regarding the methods and estimates used to measure profit and loss.

Your business sells products, which are also known as *goods* or *merchandise.* Your basic business model is to sell a volume of products at adequate markups over their costs to cover operating expenses so that you generate a satisfactory profit after your interest and income tax expenses. As a matter of fact, this basic business model fits a wide variety of businesses that sell products — from Wal-Mart to your local bookstore or shoe store.

The information content and layout of your P&L report should follow your business model. Figure 2-1 presents an illustrative P&L report that reflects your business model. The P&L statement is designed so that you can see the actual results of your business model for the period. Hypothetical dollar amounts are entered in this illustrative P&L report to make calculations easy to follow.

Your Business Name P&L Report For Year Ended December 31, 2008			Source
Sales revenue		$1,000,000	Account(s)
Cost of goods sold expense		$600,000	Account(s)
Gross margin		$400,000	Calculation
Operating expenses:			
Salaries, wages, commissions and benefits	$185,000		Account(s)
Advertising and sales promotion	$30,000		Account(s)
Depreciation	$35,000		Account(s)
Other expenses	$35,000		Account(s)
Total operating expenses		$285,000	Calculation
Operating profit		$115,000	Calculation
Interest expense		$30,000	Account(s)
Earnings before income tax		$85,000	Calculation
Income tax expense		none	Not applicable
Net income		$85,000	Calculation

Figure 2-1: Presenting an illustrative small business P&L report.

On the CD accompanying this book, we provide P&L report templates for every figure in the chapter. You and your accountant can use these templates for your business situation. Basically, the spreadsheet template provides a quick means to simulate profit under different conditions. It's a great way to analyze past profit performance and to plan profit improvements.

Here are important points to keep in mind when you read a P&L report, such as the one presented in Figure 2-1:

✔ **Where the information comes from:** The Source column on the right side of Figure 2-1 isn't really part of the P&L report; only what's inside the box is in a P&L report. We include the source column in Figure 2-1 to call your attention to where the dollar amounts come from. Account(s) means that the dollar amount for this line of information comes from one or more accounts maintained in the business's accounting system. For example, the business keeps several accounts for recording sales revenue. These several sales accounts are added together to get the $1,000,000 total sales revenue amount reported in the P&L.

✔ **Amounts from accounts versus amounts from calculations:** Several dollar amounts in a P&L aren't from accounts; rather, these figures are *calculated amounts.* For example, the P&L statement reports *gross margin,* which is equal to sales revenue less cost of goods sold expense. (This important number is also called *gross profit.*) In Figure 2-1, the $400,000 gross margin amount is calculated by deducting the $600,000 cost of goods sold expense amount from the $1,000,000 sales revenue amount. A business doesn't keep an account for gross margin (or for any of the calculated amounts in the P&L report).

✔ **The business entity and income tax:** Note the income tax expense line in the P&L (see Figure 2-1). In the source column, you see *not applicable.* What's this all about? Figure 2-1 is for a business entity that doesn't pay income tax itself as a separate entity. The business is organized legally as a so-called *pass-through* entity. Its annual taxable income is passed through to its owners, and they include their proportionate share of the business's taxable income in their income tax returns for the year. (We explain different legal types of business entities in Chapter 9.)

✔ **GAAP assumption:** GAAP stands for *generally accepted accounting principles.* GAAP refers to the body of authoritative accounting and financial reporting standards that has been established by the accounting profession over many years. Today, the main source of new pronouncements on GAAP is the Financial Accounting Standards Board (FASB). The GAAP rulebook has become exceedingly complex, and some persons compare it with the Internal Revenue Code and Regulations. Presently, the FASB is looking into giving small businesses some relief from its more technical pronouncements, but don't hold your breath.

In short, these accounting standards should be used by all businesses no matter their size. Unless a financial statement makes clear that different accounting methods are being used, the reader is entitled to assume that GAAP are used to measure profit and to present financial condition. You should assume that the business is using *accrual-basis accounting,* not a cash-basis method. See the sidebar "A quick primer on accrual-basis accounting" for more information.

✔ **Markup in the P&L:** The first step in your business model is to sell a lot of products at adequate markups over their costs. The first three lines in the P&L provide feedback information on how well you did in this regard. In the example shown in Figure 2-1, sales generated $1,000,000 *revenue,* or total income, total inflow, or total increases of assets, during the year. Cost of goods (products) sold is $600,000, so the business's total markup for the year is $400,000, which is reported on the third line in the P&L. This amount is called *gross margin* (or *gross profit.*)

In P&L reports, accountants don't use the term *markup.* Gross margin equals profit before other expenses are taken into account. In accounting, the word *gross* simply means before other expenses are deducted. Indeed, your profit or loss depends on the size of the other expenses:

✔ **Reporting operating expenses:** Practices aren't uniform regarding how many operating expense lines are reported in P&L statements — except that interest and income tax expenses are almost always reported on separate lines. Even a fairly small business keeps more than 100 expense accounts. In filing its annual federal income tax return, a business has to disclose certain expenses (advertising, repairs and maintenance, salaries and wages, rents, and so on.) Of course, a business should keep these basic expense accounts. But this categorization isn't necessarily ideal for reporting operating expenses to business managers. (By the way, it's not a bad idea for the small business owner/manager to read the first page of the annual federal income tax return of the business, which is the P&L reported to the IRS.)

In Figure 2-1, we show four operating expense lines below the gross margin profit line. Operating expenses encompass the various costs of running a business. Typically salaries, wages, and commissions (plus benefits) make up the lion's share of operating expenses. Many small businesses have substantial advertising and other sales promotion costs. The cost of using its long-term operating assets (building, machines, trucks, and equipment) is recorded as depreciation expense. This particular expense is usually reported in a P&L (though not always).

The various operating costs that aren't included in the first three expenses just explained are collected in a catchall expense account. Total operating expenses are $285,000 in the example shown in Figure 2-1. This total is deducted from gross margin to arrive at the $115,000 *operating profit* amount. (This measure of profit is also called *operating earnings* or *earnings before interest and income tax*.)

✔ **Interest expense:** This expense is separated from operating expenses because it's a financial cost that depends on the amount of debt used by the business (and interest rates, of course). In the P&L statement shown in Figure 2-1, the business uses a fair amount of debt because its interest expense is $30,000 for the year. Assuming an annual interest rate of 8 percent, its interest expense amount indicates that the business used $375,000 interest-bearing debt during the year:

$375,000 debt × 8%= $30,000 interest

✔ **Income tax expense (maybe):** A business may be organized as an entity that is subject to paying federal income tax. If so, the amount of its income tax is reported as the last expense in its P&L report, after interest expense. Interest is deductible to determine annual taxable income (just like other business expenses). Thus, it makes sense to put income tax expense below the interest expense line. In contrast, many small businesses are organized as a pass-through entity that doesn't pay income tax itself. Instead, this type of business entity passes through its taxable income for the year to its owners. In the example shown in Figure 2-1, the business is a pass-through tax entity, so it has no income tax expense. Nevertheless, we show the income tax expense line in the illustrative P&L to show how it would be reported.

A quick primer on accrual-basis accounting

Simple cash-basis service businesses may use *cash-basis accounting,* which means they don't do much more bookkeeping than keeping a checkbook. If a business sells products, however, cash-basis accounting isn't acceptable and, in fact, this method of accounting isn't permitted for income tax purposes. A business that sells products must keep track of its inventory of products and can't record the cost of products to expense until the products are actually sold to customers. Until sold, the cost of products is recorded in an asset account called *inventory.* This is one basic element of *accrual-basis accounting.*

Accrual-basis accounting can be viewed as economic reality accounting. Businesses that sell products (and hold an inventory of products awaiting sale), sell on credit, make purchases on credit, and own long-lived operating assets (buildings, trucks, tools, equipment, and so on) use accrual-basis accounting to measure their profit and to record their assets and liabilities. Basically, accrual-basis accounting recognizes the assets and liabilities of selling and buying on credit and spreads the cost of long-term operating assets over the years of their useful lives, which is called *depreciation.*

What's the bottom line? This question refers to the last, or "bottom" line of the P&L report, which is called *net income.* It is also called *net earnings,* or just *earnings.* The term *profit* is generally avoided. The business earned $85,000 net income for the year. So, the business model was executed successfully: The business made sales that generated enough gross margin to cover its operating expenses and had $85,000 profit after interest expense (see Figure 2-1).

You may very well ask how successful was the business's profit performance. This question crosses the border from the accounting function to the financial management function. Accountants provide information; managers interpret and judge the information and take action for the future. As the owner/manager, would you be satisfied with the profit performance for the business example presented in Figure 2-1?

Measuring and Reporting Profit and Loss

In our experience, many small business owners/managers read their P&L reports at a superficial level. They don't have a deep enough understanding of the information presented in this important financial statement. One result is that they make false and misleading interpretations of the information in the P&L report. For example, they think sales revenue equals cash inflow from customers during the period. However, if the business sells on credit (typical for business to business sales), actual cash collections from customers during the year can be significantly lower than the sales revenue amount reported in the P&L statement.

Furthermore, many small business managers tend to think that an expense equals cash outflow. But, in fact, the cash payment for an expense during the year can be significantly more (or less) than the amount of the expense in the P&L statement. The confusion of amounts reported in the P&L with cash flows is such a common blunder that we devote Chapter 3 to explaining differences between revenue and expenses and their cash flows.

In addition to the confusion over the cash flows of revenue and expenses, small business managers should be aware of several other issues, outlined in the following sections, in measuring and reporting profit.

Accounting for profit isn't an exact science

Many estimates and predictions must be made in recording revenue and expenses. Most are arbitrary and subjective to some degree. For one example, a business has to estimate the useful lives of its *fixed,* or long-term, operating assets in order to record depreciation expense each year. Predicting useful lives of fixed assets is notoriously difficult and ends up being fairly arbitrary.

Here's another example. At the end of the year, a business may have to record an expense caused by the loss in value of its inventory because some of its products will have to be sold at a price below cost, or the products may not be salable at all. Determining the loss in inventory value is notoriously difficult. Inventory write-down is subject to abuse by businesses that want to minimize their taxable income for the year.

Your accounting records may have errors

The financial statements prepared from the accounting records of a business, including the profit performance statement (P&L) of course, are no better than the accounting system that generates the information for the financial statements. The reliability of your accounting system depends first of all on hiring a competent accountant to put in charge of your accounting system. Bigger businesses have an advantage on this score. They hire more experienced and generally more qualified accountants.

We recommend that you hire a trained and competent *accountant* to put in charge of your accounting system. This person is typically given the title *Controller,* assuming that she has adequate accounting education and experience. To save money, many small businesses hire a *bookkeeper* who knows recordkeeping procedures but whose accounting knowledge is limited. If you employ a bookkeeper (instead of a better educated and more experienced accountant), you should consider using an independent CPA to periodically review your accounting system. We don't mean a formal audit; we mean using the CPA to critically review the adequacy of your accounting system and appropriateness of your accounting methods.

Additionally, every business should enforce internal accounting controls to prevent or at least minimize errors and fraud. (We explain these important controls in Chapter 5.) As a practical matter, errors can and do sneak into accounting records, and employees or others may have committed fraud against the business. In order to conceal theft or embezzlement, they prevent the recording of the loss in your accounting records.

Ideally your accounting system should capture and record all your transactions completely, accurately, and in a timely manner. Furthermore, any losses from fraud and theft should be rooted out and recorded. You have to be vigilant about the integrity of your accounting records. Our advice is to avoid taking your accounting records for granted; use good internal accounting controls; and be ever alert for possible fraud. Trust, but verify.

Someone needs to select the accounting methods for recording revenue and expenses

Sales revenue can be recorded sooner or later, and likewise expenses can be recorded sooner or later. Some accounting methods record revenue and expenses as soon as possible; alternative methods record these profit transactions as late as possible. *Remember that profit is a periodic measure.* Expenses for the period are deducted from sales revenue for the period to measure profit for the period. This state of affairs is like having different speed limits for a highway. How fast do you want to drive?

In short, accounting standards permit different methods regarding when to record revenue and expenses. Take cost of goods sold expense, for example (one of the largest expenses of businesses that sell products). You can use three alternative, but equally acceptable, methods. Someone has to decide which method to use. You should take the time to discuss the selection of accounting methods with your Controller. As the owner/manager, you can call the shots. You shouldn't get involved in all the technical details, but you should decide whether to use conservative (slow) or liberal (fast) methods for recording revenue and expenses.

Once the die is cast — in other words, after you have decided on which specific accounting methods to adopt — you have to stick with these methods year after year. For all practical purposes, accounting methods have to be used consistently and can't be changed year to year. For one thing, the IRS insists on this consistency in filing your annual income tax returns. (A pass-through business tax entity must file an information return with the IRS.) For management purposes, a business should keep its accounting methods consistent. Otherwise, it would be next to impossible to compare profit performance one year to the next.

Recording unusual, nonrecurring gains and losses

The P&L report focuses on the regular, recurring sales revenue and expenses of your business. In addition to these ongoing profit-making activities, most businesses experience certain types of gains and losses now and then, which are incidental to their normal operations. For example, your business may sell a building you no longer need at a sizable gain (or loss). Or, you may lose a major lawsuit and have to pay substantial damages to the plaintiff. These special, nonrecurring events are called *extraordinary gains and losses*. They're reported separately in the P&L. You don't want to intermingle them with your regular revenue and expenses.

Keeping the number of lines in your P&L relatively short

For all practical purposes, you need to keep a P&L report on one page — perhaps on one computer screen. By its very nature, the P&L is a *summary-level* financial statement. Figure 2-1, for example, includes only one line for all sales. As the owner/manager, you're very interested in the total sales revenue. You also want to know a lot more information about your sales — by customers, by products, by locations (if you have more than one), by size of order, and so on. The best approach is to put detailed information in separate schedules. Our advice: Use supporting schedules for further detail and don't put too much information in the main body of your P&L.

The P&L is just the headline page of your profit story. You need to know more detailed information about your sales and expenses than you can cram into a one-page P&L report. For example, you need to know the makeup of the total $30,000 advertising and sales promotion expense (see Figure 2-1). How much was spent on each type of advertising? How much was spent on special rebates? You need to keep on top of many details about your expenses. The place to do so is not in the main body of the P&L but in supporting schedules. In short, the P&L gives you the big picture. Reading the P&L is like reading the lead paragraph in a newspaper article. For details, you have to read deeper.

Remembering that many business transactions are profit neutral (don't affect revenue and expenses)

Many business transactions don't affect revenue or expenses: you probably already know this fact, but it's a good point to be very clear on. Only transactions that affect profit — in other words, that increase revenue or expense — are reported in the P&L. A business carries on many transactions over the course of the year that aren't reported in its P&L.

For example, during the year, the business shown in Figure 2-1 borrowed a total of $450,000 from its bank and later in the year paid back $100,000 of the borrowings. These borrowings and repayments aren't reported in the P&L — although the interest expense on the debt is included in the P&L. Likewise, the business invested $575,000 in long-term operating assets (land and building, forklift truck, delivery truck, computer, and so on). These *capital expenditures* aren't reported in the P&L — although, the depreciation expense on these fixed assets is included in the P&L report.

The business shown in Figure 2-1 purchased $630,000 of products during the year. This cost was recorded in its inventory asset account at the time of purchase. When products are sold, their cost is removed from the inventory asset account and recorded in cost of goods sold expense. The business started the year with a stock of products (inventory) that cost $120,000. Therefore, the cost of products available for sale was $750,000. The total cost of goods sold during the year is $600,000 (see Figure 2-1). Therefore, the cost of unsold inventory at the end of the year is $150,000. This additional information about beginning inventory, purchases, and ending inventory is not presented in the P&L report (Figure 2-1), but it may be, as the next section explains.

Including more information on inventory and purchases

Traditionally, internal P&L reports and external income statements include for the following information (using the business example presented in Figure 2-1):

Beginning inventory	$120,000	
Purchases	$630,000	
Available for sale	$750,000	
Ending inventory	$150,000	
Cost of goods sold expense		$600,000

The P&L report presented in Figure 2-1 includes only the cost of goods sold expense line. You can ask your accountant to include all the preceding information, but do you really need this additional information in your P&L report?

You can easily find the beginning and ending inventory balances in your *balance sheet.* This financial statement is a summary of your assets and liabilities at the beginning and end of the period. The only real gain of information is your total purchases during the year. Do you want/need to know this amount? This question reveals the core issue in preparing the P&L and other financial statements. The question is this: What information should be included in the statement? What does the business manager need to know from each financial statement? Basically, this answer is your call; you should tell your Controller what you want in your financial statements.

For internal reporting, managers can ask for as much or as little information as they need and want. A business manager has only so much time to read and ponder the information in the financial statements he receives. So, the accountant should keep in mind how long the manager has available to digest information included in the P&L and other financial statements. The financial statements included in external financial reports that circulate outside the business are bound by standards of minimum disclosure. For example, in Chapter 3, we present a formal balance sheet that follows the rules of disclosure for external financial reporting.

Presenting the P&L Report for Your Business

Small business owners/managers have certain questions on their minds after the close of the year. How did I do during the year just ended? Did I do better or worse than last year? Did I make a profit or a loss? Sounds odd, doesn't it, to say, "make a loss," but that's what happens. Figure 2-2 presents a comparative P&L for the year just ended (December 31, 2008) and the preceding year (December 31, 2007). We use the same format we used for Figure 2-1. However, we modified the P&L format slightly to omit the income tax expense line, and we added the *Change* column. Recall that this business is organized legally as a pass-through entity for income tax. (We explain different business legal entities in Chapter 9.)

Your bottom line for 2007 reveals a $166,270 loss for the year. A loss is not good news of course. But it doesn't necessarily mean that you're on the edge of bankruptcy and will have to shortly terminate the business. In fact, you made improvements and your bottom line for the year just ended shows $95,651 profit — see Figure 2-2. This is a $261,921 improvement!

Your Business Name
P&L Report
For Year Ended December 31

	2007	2008	Change
Sales revenue	$2,286,500	$2,920,562	27.7%
Cost of goods sold expense	$1,411,605	$1,693,926	20.0%
Gross margin	$874,895	$1,226,636	40.2%
Operating expenses:			
Salaries, wages, commissions and benefits	$624,590	$662,400	6.1%
Advertising and sales promotion	$158,900	$192,550	21.2%
Depreciation	$93,250	$88,950	-4.6%
Other expenses	$116,800	$137,079	17.4%
Total operating expenses	$993,540	$1,080,979	8.8%
Operating profit (loss)	($118,645)	$145,657	$264,302
Interest expense	$47,625	$50,006	5.0%
Net income (loss)	($166,270)	$95,651	$261,921

Figure 2-2: Presenting your P&L report for year just ended and preceding year.

By the way, you should notice one thing in the Change column in Figure 2-2. A change from a negative number (the loss in 2007) to a positive number (the profit in 2008) can't be expressed as a percent. Therefore, the dollar amounts of the changes in operating profit and the bottom line are given in Figure 2-2.

Maintaining *solvency* (being able to pay liabilities on time) is a distinct financial function. You have to control your solvency in order to keep your business afloat and free from interruptions by your creditors. We discuss solvency management — in good times and in bad times — in Chapter 4. Solvency depends in part on cash flow from profit or loss. We explain the important topic of cash flow from profit or loss in Chapter 3. Chapter 4 covers the broader function of managing solvency in.

When you get the P&L report (see Figure 2-2), what should you do? Well, obviously, you didn't panic and start firing employees and slashing expenses following your loss in 2007. This reaction would have only worsened your situation. You should analyze the main reasons for your turnaround from a loss last year to a respectable profit in 2008. Maybe you could do more of the same and improve profit in 2009.

Here are a few questions to ask yourself:

✔ **What about your salary?** Notice the $624,590 salaries, wages, commissions and benefits expense for 2007 in your P&L (Figure 2-2). Your salary and benefits are included in this amount. Our first question is this: is your salary included in this amount and if so is your salary a reasonable amount? Of course the bottom line depends on the size of expenses deducted from sales revenue. Small businesses are unusual in one particular respect. The owner/manager sets his or her salary with little or no overview by anyone else. Suppose your salary and benefits were $350,000 for the year (don't you wish). In this case the loss for the year is due to your lofty compensation. Or putting it another way, your sales revenue was not enough to justify this level of compensation.

Of course the small business owner/manager deserves a reasonable compensation for his or her time, talents, and capital invested in the business. There's no debate about this. But, what exactly is a *reasonable* amount of compensation? There's no clear-cut way to answer this question. You could attempt to compare your compensation with other small business owners/managers but this information is hard to come by.

Perhaps you have joined a national trade association that compiles compensation information on the owners and principal managers of their members, which you could use as a benchmark. You could troll through government statistics for small businesses put out by the Department of Commerce and the Internal Revenue Service. You could ask your CPA or banker for general compensation guidelines for small business owners/managers. These are helpful sources of information. But in the end the compensation you decide on is a fairly arbitrary amount. In many cases the person starting up a new business venture limits his or her compensation until the business turns the profit corner. In the example presented here we assume that your compensation is reasonable in amount. We can't be more specific than that.

✔ **Are you cheating in any way?** Many small businesses are pretty much under the control of one person — the owner/manager of the business. We don't mean to accuse *you,* of course. Rather, we simply mean to acknowledge that many small businesses engage in dishonest or illegal activities that distort the P&L report. Some of these nefarious tactics include the following: (*Note:* the "you" in the following points is someone else because we assume that you would never think of doing any of the following things.)

  • **Sales skimming:** Instead of recording sales and putting the money in the business's cash account, you put the money directly in your pocket and don't record the sales. Diverting sales revenue directly to you rather than letting it flow through the business is called *skimming.* However, the cost of products (goods) sold is paid by the business. The result is that the sales revenue amount in the P&L is too low. The expense of the products sold is included in cost of goods sold. Therefore, gross margin is too low, and all the profit lines below gross margin are too low. People skim sales revenue to make income that they don't report on their income tax returns, to evade income tax. Be advised that the IRS is very aware that sales skimming goes on.

- **Expense padding:** Many small business owners/managers use the business to pay their personal expenses, which aren't expenses of the business. For example, the business pays the monthly lease for the auto driven by the spouse of the owner/manager. The car is never used for business, but the business absorbs the cost of the auto. The owner/manager takes a personal pleasure trip and conducts no business while on the trip, yet the business pays for the trip. Often, the spouse goes along on the trip. The owner/manager may have substantial repairs and improvements done on her private residence and runs the cost through the business as repair and maintenance expense.

  We could go on and on with examples of how expenses are padded, but we're sure you get the point. The result is that the expenses of the business are too high, and profit is too low.

- **Income shifting:** In many cases, the owner/manager of a small business has other business interests and investments. Suppose, for example, that you own a building and your business signs a lease agreement with the landlord (you). You could set the monthly rent too high or too low so as to shift income between your building investment and your business. Setting the rent too high makes the return on your building investment look better. But your business's profit ends up being too low because its rent is artificially high. Being the landlord of the building your business rents space in is but one example of how revenue and expenses can be shifted between the different business interests of a person.

- **Patently illegal activities:** To reduce expenses, a business (small or large) may knowingly pay employees less than the amounts they're legally entitled to under minimum wage laws or overtime laws. To save building maintenance costs, a business may violate building safety codes. You may bribe the building inspector. We can cite many more examples of illegal activities. The number of laws and regulations affecting every business — small and large — is truly staggering. It's one thing to unknowingly violate an obscure law or a highly technical regulation. It's quite another thing to be aware of a major law or regulation and knowingly disregard it.

Illegal behavior has a way of eventually catching up with a business. You've heard the expression of "keeping one step ahead of the law." This approach seems to be the strategy of unethical businesses. The eventual costs of illegal activities are impossible to account for as the business goes along — and generally aren't recorded until the day of reckoning. In summary, your P&L doesn't include the potential fines and other costs that may eventually result from illegal activities.

In the rest of the chapter, we assume that you don't skim sales revenue, you don't pad expenses, you don't shift income from or to your business, and you don't engage in illegal activities. Therefore, the revenue and expense amounts in your P&L report (see Figure 2-2) are fair and square and aren't misleading. We realize that, as economists are fond of saying, that this assumption may be heroic. In other words, our working assumption may not be entirely realistic. But we have no other choice.

Figuring out the reasons for your profit improvement

If this were our business and Figure 2-1 was our P&L, we'd definitely want to know the main reasons for a big improvement from the loss in 2007 to the profit in 2008. We'd build on these factors for trying to improve profit in 2009. No obvious answers jump off the page and grab you by the throat. A glib answer is that your sales revenue increased more than your expenses for the year. This is just another way of saying that your profit improved $261,921; it offers little insight regarding what caused the profit increase and how you can improve things to make a bigger profit next year.

You should notice the 27.7 percent increase in sales revenue compared with the 20 percent increase in cost of goods sold expense (see Figure 2-2). Therefore, your 2008 gross margin benefited — jumping 40.2 percent over 2007. You increased your markups on product costs in 2008, which helps gross margin and bottom-line profit of course.

You should also notice the changes in expenses in 2008 over 2007. Are your expenses under control? We assume that you were reasonably careful, maybe downright tight-fisted with your expenses. It's possible that you were careless about your costs, but we assume not. You didn't put your brother-in-law on the payroll with nothing to do, just to help the family. You didn't spend any more on your computer system than you really needed. You didn't spend too much on rent or advertising. In short, there's really no flab in any of your expenses — although it's always a good idea to scrutinize all your costs to make sure.

Looking at the sales capacity provided by operating expenses

A very useful way to look at operating expenses is that these costs provide *sales capacity*. For example, you rent a building for your retail, warehouse, and office space. Your retail space is 12,000 square feet. For your line of products, one square foot of retail space can accommodate $300 sales per year. (You can find benchmark information for sales in publications of trade associations, state business agencies, and university business research bureaus.) Thus, your annual sales capacity based on your retail space is $3,600,000:

12,000 square feet retail space × $300 annual sales per square foot = $3,600,000 annual sales

Your $2,920,562 sales revenue for 2008 (see Figure 2-2) falls short of this standard for retail sales space. However, the shortfall indicates that you have enough retail space to accommodate an increase in sales next year.

Looking at sales revenue needed per employee

Here's another dimension that illustrates how operating expenses provide sales capacity. You employ ten full time people — salespersons, yourself, office staff, a warehouse worker, and a truck driver. Your workforce provides the people power to make and support sales. In your line of business, you need at least $300,000 annual sales per employee — not just sales employees, but all employees. Sales revenue pays the costs of your employees. This point goes back to your basic business model — to sell a volume of products at high enough markups over cost to cover your operating costs.

Your basic pricing policy is to mark up product cost to earn 45 percent gross margin on sales revenue. For $100 sales revenue, you aim for $45 gross margin on product cost of $55. (Your markup on cost is about 82 percent: ($45 markup ÷ $55 product cost = 81.1% markup on product cost.) Using this benchmark, $300,000 annual sales yields $135,000 gross margin per employee ($300,000 sales × 45 percent gross margin rate on sales = $135,000 gross margin). Out of this $135,000, you have to pay the employee's salary or wages, employment taxes, workers' compensation insurance, and benefits. Also, you have a lot of marketing and business overhead costs to pay, not to mention interest expense.

In summary, you need $3,000,000 total annual sales revenue to support ten employees: $300,000 per employee × 10 employees = $3,000,000 sales revenue. Your actual $2,920,562 sales revenue for 2008 (see Figure 2-2) is close to this sales benchmark for sales per employee. The small gap between your benchmark annual sales revenue and your actual annual sales revenue could signal that stepping up sales volume next year means that you may have to hire another person or two.

You may ask where we got the two benchmarks just explained — *annual sales per square foot of retail space* and *annual sales per employee.* You better darn well know these two benchmarks for your line of business. You can find this information from trade association publications for your industry, from talking with bankers, CPAs, and business consultants, and from statistics for small businesses published by the Department of Commerce. You can talk with other business owners in the same line of business at weekly service club meetings and at local Chamber of Commerce meetings.

Looking at marketing expenses

We now focus on the advertising and sales promotion expense in your P&L report (see Figure 2-2). How much sales bang should you get for your marketing buck? This question isn't easy to answer. There are no handy yardsticks you can easily refer to. Nevertheless, you should try to develop a benchmark to judge this expense. We suggest that you look to data published by the trade associations and talk with other business managers in your line of business. A colleague that taught advertising used to say that half of advertising expense is wasted, but the trouble is that business managers don't know which half. There's a lot of truth in this comment.

This book isn't on advertising and sales promotion — far from it. But you don't have to be a rocket scientist to see that a small business manager should develop techniques for tracking the sales effects of advertising and sales promotion costs. Customers often indicate whether they have responded to your advertising and sales promotions. You can watch the sales response to special advertising and promotion campaigns. You might even hire a marketing consultant.

Knowing how your expenses behave

There's an undercurrent below the water line of the expenses reported in the P&L statement (see Figure 2-2). In analyzing profit, you should understand how expenses behave relative to sales revenue. Some expenses are higher when sales are higher and lower when sales are lower. These are called *variable* expenses. In the business example (see Figure 2-2), you pay your sales staff 5 percent commission on sales its make. The sales commission is a good example of a variable expense. Packing and shipping costs vary with the total quantity of products sold.

On the other hand, many expenses are relatively fixed in amount for the year. These costs remain the same whether sales are high or low. As you may guess, these expenses are *fixed*. For example, you sign a building lease for the coming year; the monthly rents are a fixed expense. You buy a computer system. The annual depreciation charged off is a fixed expense. Most employees are paid a fixed amount of wages or salaries. Employee compensation is a fixed cost for the year, unless you lay off someone or change the number of hours worked. The annual fixed expenses of many small businesses are a large part of their total operating expenses.

In a P&L statement for a business that sells products, the cost of goods sold expense is the first expense deducted from sales revenue, to determine gross margin. (Refer to the P&L report in Figure 2-2 again.) Cost of goods sold expense varies with sales revenue. In other words, when sales go up, this expense goes up; when sales go down, this expense goes down. However, cost of goods sold doesn't necessarily move in strict lock step with changes in sales revenue.

In the example in Figure 2-2, you were able to increase sales prices in 2008, even though your product costs per unit didn't increase. (Of course, product costs don't always stay the same from year to year.) Selling additional units at the higher sales prices pushed up your sales revenue by a larger percent than the increase in cost of goods sold (at the same product costs). Alternatively, a business may have to reduce its markups by cutting sales prices even though its product costs remain the same. Selling additional units at the lower markups would cause sales revenue to increase by a smaller percent than the increase in cost of goods sold.

Your Controller can put your operating expenses in two piles — *fixed* and *variable.* Depreciation expense is a fixed cost; a certain amount of depreciation expense is recorded each year regardless of the actual sales volume in the year. The annual compensation of the janitor is a fixed cost. Sales commissions are a prime example of a variable cost. The segregation between fixed and variable costs is important in analyzing past profit performance and in developing plans for improving profit in the future.

The P&L report presented in Figure 2-2 shows the typical format, or configuration, of this profit performance financial statement. If you visited 100 businesses and looked at their quarterly and annual P&L reports, the large majority of the profit reports would look pretty much like Figure 2-2. The number of expense lines would vary from business to business. Otherwise, we'd be surprised to find significant deviations from the basic format shown in Figure 2-2.

The standard format of the P&L has one flaw, or perhaps we should say one limitation — it does not differentiate between variable and fixed operating expenses. You can ask your accountant to prepare a second version of the P&L that does classify between fixed and variable operating expenses. (As a matter of fact, preparing a second version of the P&L isn't difficult; you can export the original P&L to an Excel spreadsheet and then rearrange the data.)

Figure 2-3 presents an alternative format for your P&L that classifies operating expenses between fixed and variable. Of course, your bottom-line profit (or loss) for each year is the same as in Figure 2-2. Notice the *contribution margin* line in this alternative format P&L report. Contribution margin equals sales revenue minus all variable expenses. In other words, contribution margin is profit before fixed expenses are deducted. In this example, the contribution margin equals 33.3 percent of sales revenue in 2007 and 37 percent in 2008. In other words, in 2008, you had 37 cents from each dollar of sales for covering your fixed expenses, compared with only 33.3 cents per dollar in 2007.

Your Business Name
P&L Classified By Expense Behavior
For Years Ended December 31

	2007		2008	
Sales revenue	$2,286,500	100.0%	$2,920,562	100.0%
Variable expenses:				
Cost of goods sold	$1,411,605		$1,693,926	
Operating costs	$114,325		$146,028	
Total variable expenses	$1,525,930	66.7%	$1,839,954	63.0%
Contribution margin	$760,570	33.3%	$1,080,608	37.0%
Fixed expenses:				
Operating costs	$879,215		$934,951	
Interest	$47,625		$50,006	
Total fixed expenses	$926,840		$984,957	
Profit (Loss)	($166,270)		$95,651	
Breakeven sales revenue =	$2,786,357		$2,662,046	

Figure 2-3:
Presenting
your P&L
that
separates
fixed and
variable
expenses.

Breaking Through the Breakeven Barrier

One way to explain your profit improvement in 2008 over 2007 (see Figure 2-3) is that you broke through your breakeven barrier in 2008, which you failed to do in 2007.

You probably have heard about *breakeven*. It's the mythical sales level at which your bottom line is exactly zero — no profit and no loss. We say *mythical* for two reasons. First, a business doesn't try to just break even, of course. Second, the breakeven point is just an *estimate* of what would happen if sales revenue were a certain amount and expenses behaved exactly as predicted. Nevertheless, the breakeven point is a valuable point of reference for profit analysis.

Determining the breakeven point requires that you, or more accurately that your Controller, distinguish between your fixed and variable operating expenses. Cost of goods sold is a variable expense. Generally, interest expense is treated as a fixed expense for purposes of breakeven analysis.

To illustrate the application of breakeven analysis, assume that your accountant determines that in 2007, your $993,540 total operating expenses (see Figure 2-2) were as follows: fixed operating expenses = $879,215; and, variable operating expenses = $114,325. (Don't take these two amounts as precise numbers; your Controller takes some expedient shortcuts in coming up with these numbers.)

Your breakeven sales level for 2007 is $2,786,357 (see Figure 2-3). The 2007 breakeven point is computed as follows:

> $926,840 total fixed expenses for year ÷ 33.3% contribution margin on sales = $2,786,357 breakeven sales revenue

Your actual sales for 2007 were lower than your breakeven sales level, so you had a loss (see Figure 2-3). You needed about $500,000 additional sales in 2007 just to hit your breakeven point. Alternatively, you needed a contribution margin ratio higher than 33.3 percent.

In 2008, you made a profit for the year, so you know that you exceeded your breakeven sales level for the year. Pay close attention to your contribution margin ratio as a percent of sales revenue for 2008. Your contribution margin ratio in 2008 improved to 37 percent, which is a marked improvement over the 33.3 percent in 2007 — see Figure 2-3.

Why did your contribution margin ratio increase in 2008? You were able to improve your markup. Notice from Figure 2-2 that your sales revenue increased 27.7 percent but your cost of goods sold increased only 20 percent. Your product costs per unit remained the same in 2008 (which isn't always true in many situations, of course). This news is really good. You sold 20 percent more volume at higher sales prices, which is no small accomplishment. (Perhaps you had underpriced your products in 2007 and remedied this problem in 2008.)

Breakeven analysis is important because it focuses attention on the *incremental*, or *marginal* profit earned by additional units sold. For example, if you had sold more units and sales revenue had been $100,000 higher in 2008, you would have increased your bottom line $37,000, which is a substantial gain over your actual profit for the year (see Figure 2-3):

> $100,000 additional sales revenue × 37.0% contribution margin ratio on sales = $37,000 additional profit

Breakeven analysis offers another important advantage. It focuses attention on fixed expenses, which are like an albatross hanging around the neck of your business. Your 2007 fixed operating expenses were $879,215 (see Figure 2-3), which is a big chunk of change. The bulk of these fixed operating costs are salaries and wages. This amount also includes depreciation, rent, licenses and fees, and several other costs. Interest is a fixed expense. Sometimes, the total amount of fixed expenses for the year is called "the nut" of the business, and it's a tough nut to crack. On the other hand, fixed costs buy sales capacity — the space and workforce to make sales.

Improving Profit

Yes, you did earn a profit in 2008, but you shouldn't be satisfied with your profit performance. For one thing, in the example in Figure 2-2, your 2008 profit is only 3 percent of annual sales revenue, and the normal profit for your industry is in the 7.0 to 10 percent range. For another thing, your relatively small profit for the year severely limited the amount of cash distribution from profit to you and the other owners of the business. Therefore, assume that you set a goal of earning at least $250,000 profit next year. Now comes the hard part: How are you going to improve profit next year?

Basically, your options for improving profit boil down to four areas:

- ✔ **Increase the markup ratio on sales revenue:** Through a combination of sales price increases, product cost decreases, and a richer mix of sales, improve your overall markup ratio on sales revenue.

- ✔ **Increase sales volume:** Sell new products and sell more units of old products.

- ✔ **Reduce variable costs:** Scale down the cost per dollar or the cost per unit of making sales.

- ✔ **Tighten down fixed costs:** Downsize fixed costs to match the sales capacity you actually need (which means eliminating the costs related to idle capacity you're not using), and lower other fixed costs if you can.

The most realistic ways to improve profit are found mainly in the first two options — increasing markup and sales volume. Most operating costs are victims of irresistible cost inflation pressures. Small business managers can't do much about general cost inflation trends. It goes without saying that a small business manager should ruthlessly scrutinize all operating costs and weed out wasteful expenditures. In our experience, most small business managers (though not all) are pretty good at expense control. Furthermore, they don't take on more fixed operating costs than are justified by their level of sales — though you should always be alert for the cost of idle sales capacity that you don't need.

Therefore, we concentrate on improving your markup and increasing sales volume. These two paths are most realistic for stepping up your profit performance.

A very useful technique for analyzing profit-improvement alternatives is to prepare *what-if scenarios* for next year. What if you sell 10 percent more volume next year? What if your markup ratio improves to 40 percent next year? This approach is quite practical using the Microsoft Excel spreadsheet program. Using a spreadsheet program takes the drudgery out of the process. Your 2008 profit performance is the point of reference for testing different scenarios for improving profit next year.

Improving markup

Recall that your basic business model is to sell a volume of products at adequate markups over their costs to cover your marketing and operating expenses in order to generate satisfactory profit after interest expense. In 2008, your markup (gross margin) equals 42 percent (refer to Figure 2-2 for data):

> $1,226,636 gross margin ÷ $2,920,562 sales revenue = 42% markup ratio on sales

Recall that your objective is to set sales prices high enough so that you earn a 45 percent markup on sales. Therefore, you fell short of this goal in 2008. During the year, you made price concessions on some sales; you didn't always hold to list prices that are based on your 45 percent markup rule. In other words, you discounted sales prices for certain customers. A logical what-if profit scenario to look at is one in which you hadn't discounted any sales prices.

To earn 45 percent gross margin on sales revenue, your cost of goods sold expense has to be 55 percent of sales revenue. Holding cost of goods sold the same, your sales revenue for 2008 should have been $3,079,865, which is calculated as follows (see Figure 2-3 for data):

> $1,693,926 cost of goods sold ÷ 55% cost of goods sold as percent of sales revenue = $3,079,865 sales revenue needed to earn 45% gross margin on sales

Figure 2-4 shows the what-if scenario for the case in which you can set sales prices higher so that you'd earn gross margin equal to 45 percent of sales revenue. In this scenario, sales volume isn't changed; only sales prices are higher. Also, all other factors are held the same. In other words, we isolate on the sales price factor; this is the only profit factor that is changed in the what-if scenario.

Your Business Name
P&L Comparing Actual With Higher Sales Prices Scenario
For Year Ended December 31, 2008

	Actual 2008		Higher Sales Prices	
Sales revenue	$2,920,562	100.0%	$3,079,865	100.0%
Variable expenses:				
Cost of goods sold	$1,693,926		$1,693,926	
Operating costs	$146,028		$153,993	
Total variable expenses	$1,839,954	63.0%	$1,847,919	60.0%
Contribution margin	$1,080,608	37.0%	$1,231,946	40.0%
Fixed expenses:				
Operating costs	$934,951		$934,951	
Interest	$50,006		$50,006	
Total fixed expenses	$984,957		$984,957	
Profit	$95,651		$246,989	

Figure 2-4:
P&L showing the what-if scenario for higher sales prices.

In the higher sales prices scenario (see Figure 2-4), notice that the variable operating costs increase in proportion with the sales revenue increase. You pay your sales staff 5 percent commissions on sales, so the larger amount of sales revenue makes this expense larger. The cost of goods sold expense and your fixed expenses remain the same in this scenario, and sales volume (the total number of products sold) doesn't change.

The higher sales prices would have improved your profit significantly, from $95,651 to $246,989 (see Figure 2-4). Increasing your sales prices 5.5 percent (from $2,920,562 total sales revenue to $3,079,865 total sales revenue) would have resulted in a very large percent increase in profit. This example illustrates the power of even relatively small changes in sales prices on the bottom line. If you could have sold products for just 5.5 percent higher prices than you actually did in 2008, your profit would have been almost $250,000.

We recognize, of course, that in many cases customers are very sensitive to sales prices. Even a seemingly small sales price increase could lead to a serious decline in demand. You, the owner/manager of the small business, have the difficult job figuring out the reaction of your customers to sale price increases and decreases. Our purpose in showing the higher sales prices scenario is to demonstrate the powerful effect of increasing sales prices on the bottom line.

Improving sales volume

Suppose that you had sold 10 percent more volume in 2008 than you actually sold. For every 100 units actually sold, what if you had sold 110 units? (Presume that your *sales mix,* the proportion of each product sold in total sales volume, would have been the same.) How much higher would your profit be in this scenario? Can you hazard a guess? Well, not really; you have to crank the numbers.

Figure 2-5 presents the P&L for the 10 percent higher sales volume scenario in 2008. Sales revenue, cost of goods sold expense, variable operating expenses, and contribution margin all increase 10 percent. The additional amount of sales revenue causes sales commissions expense to increase proportionally, which is the only variable operating cost in the business example shown in Figure 2-5. (A business may have other variable operating costs that depend on the number of units sold: examples are delivery costs and packing and shipping costs.)

Your Business Name
P&L Comparing Actual With Higher Sales Volume Scenario
For Year Ended December 31, 2008

	Actual 2008		Higher Sales Volume	
Sales revenue	$2,920,562	100.0%	$3,212,618	100.0%
Variable expenses:				
Cost of goods sold	$1,693,926		$1,863,319	
Operating costs	$146,028		$160,631	
Total variable expenses	$1,839,954	63.0%	$2,023,950	63.0%
Contribution margin	$1,080,608	37.0%	$1,188,669	37.0%
Fixed expenses:				
Operating costs	$934,951		$934,951	
Interest	$50,006		$50,006	
Total fixed expenses	$984,957		$984,957	
Profit	$95,651		$203,712	

Figure 2-5: P&L showing the what-if scenario for 10 percent higher sales volume.

So, contribution margin is 10 percent higher in the 10 percent higher sales volume scenario (data from Figure 2-5):

$1,188,669 contribution at higher sales volume - $1,080,608 contribution at actual sales level = $108,061 contribution margin increase

$108,061 increase ÷ $1,080,608 contribution at actual sales level = 10% increase

At this juncture, we encounter a serious question: Would your fixed expenses be higher at the 10 percent higher sales volume level? They might. Suppose that your actual 2008 sales volume stretched your sales capacity to the limit. Additional sales volume may require renting larger retail space or hiring more employees. We can't offer a general answer to this question. Figure 2-5 shows results based on the assumption that your fixed costs remain the same at the higher sales volume. But, your fixed costs may have to be higher, and you should keep this point in mind.

In any case, notice that the profit improvement in the 10 percent higher sales volume scenario is less — that's right is *less* — than in the 5.5 percent higher sales prices scenario shown in Figure 2-4. Sales price increases generally are more powerful than sales volume increases for improving profit. On the other hand, increasing sales volume may be the only avenue for increasing profit when you can't really bump up sales prices.

Chapter 3

Getting Up to Speed on Cash Flow from Profit

· ·

In This Chapter

▶ Knowing your sources of cash

▶ Differentiating cash flow and bottom-line profit

▶ Deciding how you want cash flow from profit information reported to you

▶ Running down the balance sheet from the cash flow viewpoint

▶ Exploring the statement of cash flows

· ·

Suppose that your business earned $250,000 net income for the year just ended. How do you know this fact? You read your P&L statement. The P&L reports sales revenue and expenses for the year, leading down to $250,000 bottom line profit (also called net income and earnings). Chapter 2 explains the P&L statement in detail. Now, a different question: What's your *cash flow* for the year from the $250,000 profit you earned?

You had other sources of cash during the year. You increased the amount borrowed from the bank, and the owners (including you) invested additional capital in the business. Our question focuses only on profit, not your other sources of cash during the year.

Did your cash balance increase $250,000 because of your profit for the year? The answer is no: The amount of cash flow from profit is almost certainly higher or lower than the amount of profit. For the large majority of businesses, profit and cash flow from profit are virtually never the same amount.

Your Controller (the chief accounting officer of your business) prepares a *statement of cash flows* that summarizes your cash sources and uses for the period. The first section reports cash flow from profit, which is called *cash flow from operating activities*. Unfortunately, the design of the first section isn't particularly user-friendly. Even CPAs can have trouble reading this section. It's far too technical. Therefore, we don't start this chapter with the statement of cash flows. We present this financial statement later in the chapter. First, we offer a more user-friendly explanation of cash flow from profit.

Sorting Out Your Sources of Cash

One immutable law for keeping a business going is *thou shall not run out of cash*. If your cash balance drops to zero, you can't meet your payroll or pay creditors on time. Your employees may quit, and your creditors may pull the plug on your business. You simply can't afford cash flow surprises. Quite clearly, you (or someone in your business) has to manage cash flows. You can't put cash flows on automatic pilot.

To start a business, you need to raise money to invest in the assets needed to support sales and to carry on day-to-day operations. Making profit starts with making sales, and making sales requires investing in a variety of assets. Every business needs some assets, and many businesses need a lot of assets to make sales and carry on operations. Usually, a business taps both debt and equity (ownership) sources of capital for money needed to get the business up and running. (We explore raising capital from different sources in Chapter 10.)

An ongoing business needs ongoing capital to finance its operations — both equity and debt capital (unless the business eschews borrowing money). And, an ongoing business depends on a third source of cash flow — *profit*. Profit is called an *internal source* of capital because the business doesn't have to go to outside, external sources of capital for this money. Profit is one of the three main tributaries of a business's cash flow river.

Cash flow from profit is the source for making distributions to owners. These distributions compensate the owners for their capital investment in the business. As you know, interest is compensation for the use of debt capital. In like manner, cash distributions from profit to owners provide compensation, or payment, for the use of owners' equity capital.

Instead of making distributions to owners, you can retain cash flow from profit and keep it in the business. To grow the sales of your business, you usually have to expand the assets you need to operate at the higher level of activity — you need higher levels of receivables and inventory, for example. You use the cash flow from profit plus money provided from debt and equity sources of capital to expand the assets of the business. See Figure 3-3 (a balance sheet example), later in this chapter, for the types of assets you need to operate a business.

Speaking very broadly — and we mean as wide as the Mississippi — making a profit generates positive cash flow (and making a loss causes negative cash flow). However, cash flows run on a different timetable than recording revenue and expenses. When you sell on credit, the actual cash inflow takes place weeks after recording the sales revenue. The actual payments of many expenses don't happen until weeks after recording the expenses (like when you use a credit card for your personal expenses). Furthermore, some costs are paid before being recorded as expenses.

Avoiding Confusion Between Profit and Its Cash Flow

Business managers don't think like accountants (and many argue that's a good thing). Say "sales revenue" to a business manager, and he thinks of collecting money from customers. Say "expenses" to a business manager, and she thinks of writing checks for the costs of operating the business. In short, business managers are cash flow thinkers. So, when business managers read their P&L reports, they tend to think they're reading cash flow information. However, the sales revenue and expense information in the P&L statement has been recorded on the accrual-basis of accounting. The sales revenue amount in your P&L statement is different than the total cash collections from customers during the year (unless you make only cash sales). And, the expense amounts in your P&L statement are different than the total amounts actually disbursed for these costs during the year.

In short, when discussing profit and cash flow from profit, you're talking about two different things — apples and oranges, as it were.

Here are two rather extreme examples that illustrate the divergence of cash flow and profit. Suppose that a business records $3,000,000 sales revenue and $2,750,000 total expenses for the year. So, its profit is $250,000 for the year.

- ✔ *Scenario 1:* Suppose that the business didn't collect a dime of its sales revenue; it extended long-term credit terms to its customers, and none of its customers made any payments to the business by the end of the year. Assume, however, that the business paid all its expenses during the year. Therefore, cash in equals zero, and cash out equals $2,750,000; cash flow from profit is a *negative* $2,750,000 for the year despite a profit of $250,000!

- ✔ *Scenario 2:* Suppose that the business collected all its sales revenue for the year. However, it didn't pay a dime of expenses; its vendors and suppliers, as well as its employees, agreed to wait for payment until next year (most unlikely, of course). Therefore, cash in equals $3,000,000, and cash out equals zero; cash flow from profit is a *positive* $3,000,000 despite profit of only $250,000!

Of course, you don't find such extreme examples in the real world of business. But the examples bring out a valid point: Cash flow from profit depends on when sales revenue is collected and when expenses are paid. When you ask about cash flow from profit, you're inquiring about whether cash collections from customers during the year are different than sales revenue and whether cash payments for expenses during the year are different than the expense amounts that are recorded to measure profit for the year.

A loss is bad news from the cash flow point of view. In most cases, a loss sucks money out of the business. There is no money to expand the business or to provide for cash distributions to owners (the shareholders or partners of the business who provide its owners' equity capital). The amount of cash drain caused by a loss can be significantly higher, or significantly lower, than the bottom line amount of loss reported in the P&L for the year. It's possible that a business could report a big loss in its P&L, and yet realize a *positive* cash flow from the loss. Isn't this an odd state of affairs? As we used to say in Iowa, how do you like them apples?

Deciding How to Have Cash Flow Information Reported to You

You can't afford to ignore cash flow from profit. Knowing your cash flow performance is as important as knowing your profit performance. There's no question that your accountant should determine the cash flow from profit (operating activities) for each quarter and for each year (perhaps monthly as well). But, there certainly is a question regarding how cash flow information should be reported to you, the owner/manager of the small business. In our view, your basic alternatives are the following three:

✔ **Report just cash flow:** Tell your Controller to include the amount of cash flow from profit for the period with your P&L. It's only one more line of information and can fit easily at the end of the statement. Just the amount of cash flow is reported, with no details indicating why it's more or less than profit for the period.

✔ **Report differences between cash flows and sales revenue and expenses in the P&L:** Tell your Controller to add an additional column of information in your regular P&L statement that reports the differences between cash flow and sales revenue and cash flows and expenses. You can skim over relatively minor differences and pay attention to significant variances between cash flow and your profit factors.

✓ **Try to read the first section of the statement of cash flows:** The statement of cash flows is one of the three primary financial statements that are prepared for external reporting to creditors and outside owners of a business. Because this cash flow statement has to be prepared anyway, use it for your cash flow information. In a sense, you get double duty out of the statement — for both external financial reporting and for internal managerial uses.

We like the middle option — including cash flow differences from sales revenue and expenses in the P&L statement. The first option doesn't give you much information. Reading the first section of the statement of cash flows is like reading the owner's manual that come with an electronic gadget. As the younger generation says, Don't go there. The decision is up to you. Next we discuss each of the three ways for having cash flow information reported to you. Remember, you're the boss; don't be intimidated by your Controller.

Appending cash flow to your P&L report

You may prefer not to analyze cash flow from profit in detail. In this case, you may decide on the first option mentioned in the preceding section: Just have the amount of cash flow from profit tacked on at the end of your P&L report without further details.

Figure 3-1 shows the 2008 P&L report of the business example we introduce in Chapter 2. (There's no point changing to a new business example.) In Chapter 2, we explain the P&L statement in detail. (See Figure 2-2 for its P&L statement.) You don't need to read Chapter 2 before this chapter, although you may want to refer to it if you don't have a basic understanding of the P&L statement.

In Figure 3-1, your eye is drawn to the difference between the business's $95,651 net income for the year and its $133,141 cash flow from profit. The business earned $95,651 profit for the year based on proper accounting methods. But, at the same time, the business had $133,141 net cash flow from its profit-making activities. Its cash increased $133,141 — not from increasing its debt and not from its owners investing more money in the business. This money was available for use as the owner/manager thinks is best for the business.

The rather obvious limitation of reporting only the final amount of cash flow from profit is that this one figure offers no clues regarding why the cash flow was more than profit. You're at a loss to know whether the excess of cash flow over profit is the normal state of affairs or not. Reporting only the final amount of cash flow from profit provides rather skimpy information, but it's better than no information at all.

Your Business Name
P&L Report Including Cash Flow From Net Income
For Year Ended December 31, 2008

	2008
Sales revenue	$2,920,562
Cost of goods sold expense	$1,693,926
Gross margin	$1,226,636
Operating expenses:	
Salaries, wages, commissions and benefits	$662,400
Advertising and sales promotion	$192,550
Depreciation	$88,950
Other expenses	$137,079
Total operating expenses	$1,080,979
Operating profit (loss)	$145,657
Interest expense	$50,006
Net income	$95,651
Cash flow from net income (operating activities)	$133,141

Figure 3-1:
Presenting a P&L report that also includes the cash flow from profit figure.

Reporting differences of cash flows from sales revenue and expenses in the P&L

We prefer including cash flow information with your P&L report. Figure 3-2 presents the business's P&L statement with additional cash flow statement for the year ending December 31, 2008. You'll notice the new column on the right side of the P&L statement that reports the negative or positive cash flow differences from sales revenue and expenses in the P&L statement.

In Figure 3-2, we separate depreciation expense from the total of other operating expenses. As an aside, we should mention that operating expenses are presented many different ways. Looking below the gross margin line in P&L reports, you'd see that expenses are reported in a variety of ways from business to business.

The purpose of combining the P&L and cash flow information (see Figure 3-2) is to call attention of the cash flow differences from sales revenue and expenses. In this example, cash collections from customers is $12,550 less than sales revenue for the year. Cash payments for products sold by the business were $50,555 more than cost of goods sold expense for the year. Both are negative cash flow factors. A negative cash flow difference means that cash inflow is less or cash outflow is more than the corresponding amount in the P&L statement.

Your Business Name
P&L Report and Cash Flow Differences
For Year Ended December 31, 2008

P&L		Cash Flow Difference*
Sales revenue	$2,920,562	($12,550)
Cost of goods sold expense	$1,693,926	($50,555)
Gross margin	$1,226,636	
Operating expenses:		
Salaries, wages, commissions and benefits	$662,400	
Advertising and sales promotion	$192,550	
Other expenses	$137,079	
Operating expenses excluding depreciation	$992,029	$10,380
Depreciation expense	$88,950	$88,950
Total operating expenses	$1,080,979	
Operating profit	$145,657	
Interest expense	$50,006	$1,265
Net income	$95,651	
Net cash flow difference		$37,490
Cash flow from profit (operating activities)	$133,141	

Figure 3-2:
Presenting a
P&L report
that
includes
cash flow
differences
from sales
revenue and
expenses.

* Positive = More cash inflow or less cash outflow than amount in P&L
   (Negative) = Less cash inflow or more cash outflow than amount in P&L

The combined P&L and cash flow information report shown in Figure 3-2 would be new to your Controller. Including cash flow information along with sales revenue and expenses isn't done in most businesses. You have to instruct your Controller to prepare this statement for you. Being a new report, your Controller would face a learning curve in getting up to speed on the report. Computer accounting programs don't include a module for generating a report like this one. Therefore, your Controller has to export data from your accounting database to an Excel spreadsheet to prepare the report. (Your accountant probably already uses this procedure in preparing other reports that aren't included in the computer accounting program.)

Here are brief explanations for each of the five cash flow differences reported in Figure 3-2:

✔ **Sales revenue:** You collected $12,550 less cash from customers during the year than the amount of sales revenue for the year, which appears as an increase in your *accounts receivable* asset account during the year.

✔ **Cost of goods sold expense:** You paid $50,555 more cash to vendors during the year than the amount of cost of goods sold expense for the year. You increased your store of products being held for sale, which is recorded in your *inventory* asset account, which is seen as an increase in your inventory asset account during the year. Also, you increased the amount you owe vendors, which is recorded in the *accounts payable* liability account, which is seen in the increase of your *accounts payable* liability account during the year. The net effect of increasing your inventory and accounts payable is that you wrote checks for $50,555 more than your cost of goods sold expense for the year.

✔ **Operating expenses (excluding depreciation):** Certain operating expenses (for example, insurance) are prepaid before being recorded as an expense; these advance payments are recorded in your *prepaid expenses* asset account. Other operating expenses are paid after being recorded as an expense; the liabilities for these expenses are recorded either in your *accounts payable* and *accrued expenses payable* liability accounts. The net cash flow effect is a positive $10,380 amount for the year. In other words, your actual cash payments were $10,380 less than the total amount of operating expenses (excluding depreciation). Your accountant uses changes in your prepaid expense asset account and the two liability accounts to determine the net cash flow effect.

✔ **Depreciation expense:** Over the years, you've invested in long-term operating assets, including land and a building, delivery trucks, computer system, office furniture, warehouse equipment, tools, and so on. Although these fixed assets last more than one year, they wear out or lose their economic usefulness over the years. Therefore, the cost of a fixed asset (except land) is allocated to each year of the estimated useful life of the fixed asset. Each year is charged with a certain amount of *depreciation expense*. Recording depreciation expense doesn't involve any further cash outlay. You already spent money when you bought the fixed assets. Therefore, depreciation expense is a positive cash flow difference. There was zero cash outlay for this expense during the year.

During the year, you collected most (though not quite all) your sales revenue in cash — total cash collections from customers during the year were just $12,550 less than your $2,920,562 sales revenue for the year (see Figure 3-2). Sales revenue reimburses the business for its expenses. In other words, the business sets sales prices high enough to recover its expenses and leave a little for profit. Most expenses are paid in cash sooner or later. But depreciation is unique. Depreciation expense is embedded in the cost of the fixed asset, and the cost is paid for when the business acquires the fixed asset. Therefore, the cash collections from sales each year pays back the business for the use of its fixed assets. In this way, depreciation generates cash flow to the business.

✔ **Interest expense:** You paid $1,265 less interest to the bank on your loans than the amount of interest recorded in the year. Interest expense is recorded as it accrues month to month, but typically interest is paid *in arrears,* or at the end of the period. The lag in paying interest is recorded in an accrued expense payable account. This liability account increased $1,265 during the year, which means you paid less cash than the amount of expense for the year.

The net cash flow difference from net income is $37,490 for the year — see Figure 3-2. The cash flow from depreciation is the biggest positive factor. The cash flow for building up your inventory is the biggest negative factor. Did you really need to build up your inventory? Assuming that you did, you should definitely understand that doing so required a $50,555 cash outlay.

The $133,141 cash flow from profit (net income) for the year, plus your other sources of cash during the year was the total amount of cash at your disposal. Presumably, you made good use of this money. Usually, a business faces several demands on its available cash — in particular, for growing the business and for making distributions from profit to owners.

Introducing the Statement of Cash Flows

An external financial report of a business to its creditors and shareowners includes three primary *financial statements:*

✔ **Income statement:** *Income statement* is the name for the P&L statement when it's reported outside the business. It's not called a P&L statement outside the business; it may be called the *earnings statement* or *operating statement.* Its purpose is to summarize the sales revenue (and other income) and the expenses (and losses) of the business for a period of time, and ends with the net income (or net loss) for the period. (Public corporations also report earnings per share in their income statements.)

✔ **Balance sheet:** This statement presents the assets, liabilities, and sources of owners' equity of the business at the close of business on the last day of the income statement period. It's also called the *statement of financial position* or *statement of financial condition.* It allows the reader to examine the composition of the business's assets, compare its liabilities against its assets, and evaluate profit performance relative to the total capital invested in assets that is being used to make profit.

✔ **Statement of cash flows:** This statement is prepared for the same period of time as the income statement. It summarizes the sources and uses of cash during the period so that the reader can determine where the business got its cash during the period and what it did with the money. For example, you can see whether the business distributed some of its profit to owners during the year.

To get a complete financial picture of a business, you have to read all three of its financial statements. One tells you whether it made a profit or not, one tells you about its financial condition at the end of the profit period, and the third tells you about its cash flows during the period.

Figure 3-3 presents the business's balance sheets at the end of 2007 and 2008. The changes in the business's assets, liabilities, and owners' equity accounts are the building blocks of its statement of cash flows.

Your Business Name
Balance Sheet
At December 31

	2007	2008	Changes
Assets			
Cash	$347,779	$584,070	$236,291
Accounts receivable	$136,235	$148,785	$12,550
Inventory	$218,565	$250,670	$32,105
Prepaid expenses	$65,230	$61,235	($3,995)
Total current assets	$767,809	$1,044,760	
Property, plant and equipment	$774,600	$896,450	$121,850
Accumulated depreciation	($167,485)	($256,435)	($88,950)
Cost less depreciation	$607,115	$640,015	
Total assets	$1,374,924	$1,684,775	
Liabilities and Owners' Equity			
Accounts payable	$286,450	$261,430	($25,020)
Accrued expenses payable	$67,345	$81,565	$14,220
Short-term notes payable	$100,000	$200,000	$100,000
Total current liabilities	$453,795	$542,995	
Long-term notes payable	$300,000	$400,000	$100,000
Owners' equity:			
Invested capital	$500,000	$525,000	$25,000
Retained earnings	$121,129	$216,780	$95,651
Total owners' equity	$621,129	$741,780	
Total liabilities and owners' equity	$1,374,924	$1,684,775	

Figure 3-3: Presenting the balance sheet for business example.

Running down the balance sheet from the cash flow point of view

Your business sells products both at retail to consumers and to other businesses. You extend short-term credit to your business customers. Over the years, you have invested in various long-term operating assets (called *fixed assets*) that you need to conduct the activities of the business — a parcel of land and a building, computers, trucks, office furniture, cash registers, and so on. Your business borrows money from two banks. Yours is not the only business model in the world of course. But it's a good comprehensive model to look at; one that captures most cash flow factors.

Here's a rundown on the items reported in your balance sheet (see Figure 3-3), paying particular attention to cash flow aspects:

- ✔ **Cash:** This item includes cash on hand (coins and currency) and money on deposit in checking accounts. Sooner or later, every transaction goes through the cash account, and it's the *sooner or later* that you should understand.

- ✔ **Accounts receivable:** You extend credit to your business customers; this asset account holds the amount of customers' receivables that should be collected in the near term. The balance of this account is the amount of money not yet collected from customers. It's been recorded as sales revenue, but it hasn't been received in cash as of the balance sheet date.

- ✔ **Inventory:** You stockpile products and hold them for sale and make immediate delivery to customers when sold; this asset account holds the cost of goods not yet sold, but that should be sold in the near term. The balance is your inventory asset account is the cost value of products held for sale. This amount has not been recorded as expense yet.

- ✔ **Prepaid expenses:** You prepay some expenses, such as insurance, property taxes, a store of office and shipping supplies, and so on. This asset account holds the cost of these prepaid costs that will not be charged to expense until time passes. You've paid cash for these things, but their cost hasn't yet been recorded to expense.

- ✔ **Property, plant, and equipment (fixed assets):** The balance in this account is the cost of long-term operating resources your business has bought. Acquiring these assets required major cash outlays, most of which occurred in previous years.

✓ **Accumulated depreciation:** This *contra account* is deducted from the original cost of your property, plant, and equipment asset account; the recording of depreciation expense each year increases the balance in this account, thus decreasing the *book value* of your fixed assets. Recording depreciation expense doesn't involve a cash outlay. The cash outlay was made when the fixed assets were bought.

✓ **Accounts payable:** You purchase products for inventory and buy many things on credit, which means that their costs aren't paid immediately. This liability account holds the total cost of these credit purchases until the amounts are paid. No cash has been paid out yet for these purchases. Of course, that's why they're a liability at the end of the year.

✓ **Accrued expenses payable:** Before being paid, certain expenses are recorded based on calculations and estimates of costs as they accrue, or accumulate, during the period. Examples include accrued vacation pay, property taxes to be paid later, and accrued interest on notes payable. This liability account holds the costs of the expenses until they're paid. Like accounts payable, no cash has been paid out yet for these liabilities.

✓ **Notes payable:** The amount of money borrowed from your banks is reported in this liability account. Actually, the total amount borrowed is divided into the current (short-term) portion, and the remainder is put in the long-term category (see Figure 3-3). Debt is a major source of money to most businesses.

✓ **Owners' equity — invested capital:** The amount of money invested in the business by its owners is recorded in this account. The exact title of the account depends on how the business entity is organized legally. For example, a business corporation issues capital stock shares to its owners, so the account is called *capital stock*. Owners' equity is a major source of money to a business.

✓ **Owners' equity — retained earnings:** The amount of annual profit earned by a business is recorded in this account to recognize the increase in owners' equity and to separate this source of owners' equity from money invested in the business by the owners. The balance in this account equals the cumulative total of annual profits over the years, minus any annual losses that occurred, and minus distributions to owners from profit.

Doing a quick calculation of cash flow from profit

In the sample business's two-year balance sheet (see Figure 3-3), note that its short-term and long-term notes payable increased $200,000 during the year, which provided $200,000 cash to the business. Also, note that Owners' equity — invested capital increased $25,000; the owners put $25,000 additional money in the business during the year.

So, the business raised $225,000 from debt and equity sources during the year. It spent $121,850 on capital expenditures (see Figure 3-3) for purchases of fixed assets. The net increase in cash from securing $250,000 from debt and equity sources less the $121,850 capital expenditures is, therefore, $103,150:

> ($225,000 from debt and equity - $121,850 capital expenditures = $103,150 cash increase

The business's balance sheet reports that its cash balance increased $236,291 (see Figure 3-3). So, there's another $133,141 of cash increase to explain:

> ($236,291 increase in cash balance during year - $103,150 net cash increase explained by debt and equity sources minus capital expenditures = $133,141 to be explained)

There's only one other source of cash — *profit*. Therefore, the cash flow from profit for the year is a positive $133,141. After you account for increases in cash from debt and equity sources during the year and deduct the amount spent on capital expenditures, the remaining amount of the cash increase during the year must be attributable to cash flow from profit.

Classifying cash flows in the statement of cash flows

In the statement of cash flows, a business's flows of money during the year are classified into three types: *operating* activities, *investing* activities, and *financing* activities. Note the *changes* column in the balance sheet (see Figure 3-3). Each change is put into one of the three categories — except the increase in cash itself. One purpose of the statement of cash flows is to explain the reasons for the increase (or decrease) of cash during the year. The broader purpose is to present an overview of the business's cash flows, which are separated into three classes of activities.

The term *operating activities* refers to making sales and incurring expenses, or in other words the transactions a business engages in to make profit. The term *investing activities* refers to making expenditures for the long-term operating assets (long-lived tangible and intangible resources). Investments in new long-term operating assets are also called *capital expenditures,* to emphasize the investment of capital in these assets for relatively long periods. This category includes proceeds from the disposal of previously owned fixed assets. In the example, the business didn't dispose of any fixed assets during the year.

The term *financing activities* refers to borrowing and repaying money from debt sources of capital. Financing activities also includes raising capital from equity sources of capital and distributions from profit to them, as well as the return of capital to them. In the example, the business increases its short-term and long-term debt during the year, which are positive cash flows. Also, its owners invested additional equity capital in the business during the year. The business didn't make any distributions from profit to its owners during the year (though it probably could have).

Presenting the statement of cash flows

The Financial Accounting Standards Board (FASB) is the authoritative body that makes pronouncements on *generally accepted accounting principles* (GAAP) in the United States. For many years, the accounting profession had been criticized for not requiring disclosure of cash flows in business financial reports. Finally, in 1975, the FASB issued an edict regarding how to report cash flow information. It decided on a basic format for the statement of cash flows. Accordingly, the 2008 statement of cash flows for the business example is presented in Figure 3-4.

The first section in the statement of cash flows begins with the business's $95,651 net income for the year — see Figure 3-4. Following net income, positive and negative adjustments are made to net income to determine the $133,141 cash flow from operating activities — see Figure 3-4 again. (We prefer the term *cash flow from profit* instead of the official phraseology *cash flow from operating activities.*) For example, the increase in accounts receivable during the year is a negative adjustment to net income. The depreciation expense amount is a positive adjustment to net income.

The first section of the statement of cash flows has proven difficult for non-accountants to understand. Frankly, this part of the statement seems designed for other accountants rather than for business managers and other users of financial reports. As the younger generation would say, the section sucks.

Your Company Name
Statement of Cash Flows
For Year Ending December 31, 2008

Cash Flow From Operating Activities

Net income from income statement		$95,651	
Accounts receivable increase	($12,550)		
Inventory increase	($32,105)		
Prepaid expenses decrease	$3,995		
Depreciation	$88,950		
Accounts payable decrease	($25,020)		
Accrued expenses payable increase	$14,220	$37,490	$133,141

Cash Flow From Investing Activities

Expenditures for property, plant and equipment	($121,850)

Cash Flow From Financing Activities

Increase in short-term debt	$100,000	
Increase in long-term debt	$100,000	
Additional capital invested by owners	$25,000	$225,000

Increase in cash during year	$236,291
Cash balance at start of year	$347,779
Cash balance at end of year	$584,070

Figure 3-4:
Presenting the statement of cash flows for business example.

As we show in Figure 3-2, including cash flow differences from sales revenue and expenses in the regular P&L report seems a more user-friendly way to present cash flow information to business managers (and probably to investors and creditors as well). Most accountants probably would think that we're out in left field on this point. In any case, we encourage you to instruct your Controller to report information on cash flow from profit to you in the most understandable way and not to be constrained in the GAAP straitjacket. Remind your Controller that GAAP were developed for *external* financial reporting, and that these rules don't govern the reporting of financial information inside a business.

Small business owners/mangers should find easier going in reading the investing and financing sections of the statement of cash flows — in most cases. Please read these two sections in Figure 3-4. We bet that you understand the information in these two parts of the statement for this business example. However, reading the investing and financial sections in of many businesses (especially large companies) can be a real challenge.

Financing activities can be quite complicated (stock options, financial derivatives, and so on). A business can have many purchases, construction projects, and disposals of fixed assets in the year. Summarizing all these investing activities in the statement of cash flows can be a bit much. A business may have extraordinary (nonrecurring) losses and gains during the year that add further detail to the statement. The upshot is that the statement of cash flows often is crowded with many details, which works against the readability of the financial statement of course. Many public companies report 40 to 50 lines of information in their statement of cash flows, if you can believe it.

Summing Up the Critical Importance of Cash Flow from Profit

The financial sustainability of a business depends foremost on its ability to generate a steady stream of cash flow from profit. Without a doubt, you should have a good grip on the factors that drive cash flow from profit. Profit is the mainstream of cash for every business. You should be very clear on the factors that control cash flow from profit. Financial and investment analysts pay a great deal attention to cash flow from profit, for good reason.

Generally, the big three factors governing cash flow from profit are changes in accounts receivable and inventory and depreciation. Changes in accounts payable and other short-term operating liabilities are important factors in some situations — but first look to the big three factors.

Suppose that you forecast minor changes in your accounts receivable and inventory for the coming year. In this case, you can simply add depreciation to profit for the coming year, which gives a good estimate of cash flow. On the other hand, when your business is growing or if your business is in a cyclical industry, you should forecast changes in your accounts receivable and inventory for the coming year. These changes will have a definite impact on cash flow from profit for the year.

Projecting cash flow from profit for the coming year is the critical first step in developing your master financial plan for the coming year. You start with how much internal cash you'll generate during the coming year from making profit, and then you build your overall financial plan based on this foundation. A successful business plan includes a carefully thought-out forecast of cash flow from profit. Budgeting cash flow from profit is a big plus in securing loans from banks and raising equity capital. In fact, if you don't include a convincing projection of cash flow from profit, it will appear that you don't know what you're doing.

Chapter 4

Keeping Your Business Solvent

In This Chapter

▶ Understanding liquidity and business solvency

▶ Measuring business solvency and liquidity

▶ Watching for liquidity traps

▶ Tapping sources of liquidity for your business

▶ Keying in on financial leverage

A ll businesses, at one point or another, have most likely experienced some sort of financial pain when it comes to keeping the doors open and the bills paid. From suppliers demanding payments on outstanding invoices to customers providing every excuse in the book as to why they need extended payment terms, businesses must constantly manage financial resources to ensure that capital is readily available to support their ongoing operations.

The concept of keeping a business solvent, on the surface, would appear to be relatively simple from the standpoint of making sure that enough capital is available to meet its current obligations and commitments. While this statement isn't entirely untrue, the problem with business solvency isn't so much based in managing short-term financial issues and obligations but rather managing a long-term business plan and making sure that the appropriate amount and type of capital is "readily" available. As most businesses will attest, economic as well as business cycles come and go, so the real key lies in being able to properly position your company during the cycles to always ensure that adequate solvency and liquidity are maintained.

When times are good, businesses tend to have more than enough capital available from both internal sources and external partners (for example, a bank providing a loan) because everyone wants to jump on the bandwagon and share in the success. It's when the times turn, profits suddenly become losses, and internal financial pressures mount that you find your financial partners may not be all they promised and begin to demand that "you perform before they commit." This situation, of course, represents the ultimate "Catch-22" because before your business can perform, you need them to commit. So remember, implementing proper business planning efforts becomes the foundation to ensuring that your business will always remain solvent and have ample liquidity to manage through both good times and bad.

This chapter focuses on providing a better understanding of business solvency and liquidity, as well as the necessary tools to properly measure it. It also covers helping your business avoid falling into liquidity traps, and if you do, what strategies, resources, and/or "tricks of the trade" may be available to assist you with getting out of a real mess.

Liquidity and Business Solvency

To truly understand if a business is solvent, the concept of liquidity must be addressed simultaneously. *Solvency* is best defined from a balance sheet perspective in terms of evaluating a company's assets and liabilities. If assets are greater than liabilities, then a business would appear to be solvent. If assets are less than liabilities, then a business would appear to be insolvent (as in theory, not enough assets are available to satisfy all liabilities). This rather simplistic definition represents a sound basis on which to evaluate a company's solvency, but you need to remember that you must look past just the balance sheet to gain a complete understanding of whether a business is really solvent.

Business solvency is best described by evaluating a business's financial position at a point in time. To illustrate the concept of liquidity versus solvency, Figure 4-1 summarizes the financial results of XYZ Manufacturing, Inc. during the past three years. By applying business solvency measurement tools (see the section "Business Solvency Measurement Tools," later in this chapter), you may conclude that XYZ, Manufacturing, Inc. is basically insolvent as of 12/31/06. The company's current ratio is less than one to one and stands at .68 to 1, only $118,000 of cash is available, the company realized a loss of $1,066,000 during the year, and only $335,000 of equity remains compared to total liabilities of $3,747,000. All are relatively poor signs (no doubt) to an external party attempting to understand the financial performance of the company and evaluate whether XYZ Wholesale, Inc. has a chance to survive.

But this type of situation is where business solvency measurements stop, and business liquidity measurements start. Business liquidity looks at not only the current financial position of a company (which looks bleak for XYZ Wholesale, Inc.) but captures financial information and data that isn't clearly presented in the basic financial statements. *Liquidity* is best defined by evaluating the total resources available to a company in relation to meeting its total obligations. A company may appear to be insolvent, but if resources are available to meet its obligations, then the business has enough liquidity to support its continued operations.

For XYZ Wholesale, Inc., the following additional company information needs to be evaluated to determine whether enough liquidity is available to survive:

✔ XYZ Wholesale, Inc. has structured a loan agreement that allows the company to borrow up to 80 percent of eligible trade receivables and 50 percent of inventory. As of 12/31/06, the company can borrow a total of roughly $1.4 million (80 percent of $1,272,000 of receivables plus 50 percent of $867,000 of inventory) compared to an outstanding balance of just $200,000 (the current balance outstanding on the line of credit borrowings). After subtracting the current amount of $200,000 borrowed from the total amount available to borrow of $1,400,000, an additional $1,200,000 of borrowing capacity remains to support the company's operations.

✔ XYZ Wholesale, Inc. has successfully secured extended payment terms with its vendors and suppliers. The primary shareholder of the company has provided a personal guarantee (see Chapter 10 for more on this topic) to key vendors and suppliers, which has allowed the company to move its payment terms for net 30 days to net 90 days. The personal guarantee was accepted by the vendors and suppliers due to the shareholder's high personal net worth. These terms can be extended to 120 days.

✔ XYZ Wholesale, Inc.'s financial performance for 2005 was negatively impacted by the company's decision to expand its product offerings into a high volume, low price/profitability product line. Although sales increased (but below management's expectations), gross margins suffered significantly because too much of the product was purchased and thus sold at discounted prices (to move the inventory). In addition, the company increased its sales, general, and administrative expenses too much in anticipation of supporting the higher sales volumes that did not materialize. By 2006, the company's "sins" finally were addressed by management as the product line was discontinued. This decision drove sales lower but allowed gross margin to recover from 21 percent to 25 percent (as well as reducing sales, general, and administrative expenses). However, the company had to take a one-time write-down of $1 million (reflected in other expenses) related to obsolete inventory with the product line that could not be sold. By cleaning house and refocusing the company's efforts in 2006, XYZ Manufacturing, Inc. had to sacrifice its current financial statements to position the company for future growth.

Although the company's struggles the last two years have negatively impacted its current business solvency, XYZ Wholesale, Inc. has secured additional capital to ensure that it has enough liquidity to survive and prosper in the coming years. Also, note that no income tax expense or benefit is present in 2006 because the company used up its income tax benefit from losses in 2005 by "carrying" them back to 2004 and receiving a refund for prior taxes paid. The company used up all of its income tax carry-back benefits in 2005, so nothing is left to be realized in 2006 (the bad news). The good news is that if the company can generate future profits, it will be able to carry forward roughly $1 million of losses to offset the future profits and reduce income tax liabilities.

XYZ WHOLESALE, INC.
UNAUDITED FINANCIAL STATEMENTS — COMPARISON

Summary Balance Sheet	Year End 12/31/04	Year End 12/31/05	Year End 12/31/06
Current Assets:			
Cash & Equivalents	$94,929	$123,214	$117,632
Trade Receivables, Net	$1,272,083	$1,743,750	$1,271,875
Inventory	$1,383,391	$1,916,381	$867,188
Total Current Assets	$2,750,403	$3,783,345	$2,256,695
Fixed & Other Assets:			
Property, Plant, & Equipment, Net	$1,250,000	$1,500,000	$1,750,000
Other Assets	$75,000	$75,000	$75,000
Total Fixed & Other Assets	$1,325,000	$1,575,000	$1,825,000
Total Assets	$4,075,403	$5,358,345	$4,081,695
Current Liabilities:			
Trade Payables	$1,037,543	$2,682,934	$2,601,563
Accrued Liabilities	$51,877	$134,147	$195,117
Line of Credit Borrowings	$0	$100,000	$200,000
Current Portion of Long-Term Liabilities	$300,000	$300,000	$300,000
Total Current Liabilities	$1,389,420	$3,217,080	$3,296,680
Long-Term Liabilities:			
Notes Payable, Less Current Portion	$900,000	$600,000	$300,000
Other Long-Term Liabilities	$125,000	$140,000	$150,000
Total Long-Term Liabilities	$1,025,000	$740,000	$450,000
Total Liabilities	$2,414,420	$3,957,080	$3,746,680
Equity:			
Common and Preferred Equity, $1 Per Share	$500,000	$500,000	$500,000
Retained Earnings	$750,000	$1,160,983	$901,265
Current Earnings	$410,983	($259,718)	($1,066,250)
Total Equity	$1,660,983	$1,401,265	$335,015
Total Liabilities & Equity	$4,075,403	$5,358,345	$4,081,694

Summary Income Statement	Year End 12/31/04	Year End 12/31/05	Year End 12/31/06
Revenue	$15,265,000	$16,740,000	$13,875,000
Costs of Goods Sold	$11,067,125	$13,140,900	$10,406,250
Gross Profit	$4,197,875	$3,599,100	$3,468,750
Gross Margin	27.50%	21.50%	25.00%
Selling, General, & Administrative Expenses	$3,001,000	$3,525,000	$3,060,000
Depreciation Expense	$250,000	$300,000	$350,000
Interest Expense	$72,000	$68,000	$75,000
Other (Income) Expenses	$212,000	$125,000	$1,050,000
Net Profit Before Tax	$662,875	($418,900)	($1,066,250)
Income Tax Expense (Benefit)	$251,893	($159,182)	$0
Net Profit (Loss)	$410,983	($259,718)	($1,066,250)

Figure 4-1:
Liquidity
versus
solvency.

Summary Cash Flow Statement	Year End 12/31/04	Year End 12/31/05	Year End 12/31/06
Operating Cash Flow:			
Net Income (Loss)	$410,983	($259,718)	($1,066,250)
Depreciation Expense	$250,000	$300,000	$350,000
Net Operating Cash Flow	$660,983	$40,282	($716,250)

Working Capital:			
(Increase) Decrease in Trade Receivables	($250,000)	($471,667)	$471,875
(Increase) Decrease in Inventory	($150,000)	($532,991)	$1,049,194
Increase (Decrease) in Trade Payables	$350,000	$1,645,391	($81,371)
Increase (Decrease) in Accrued Liabilities	$25,000	$82,270	$60,971
Increase (Decrease) in Current Debt	$0	$100,000	$100,000
Net Working Capital Cash Flow	($25,000)	$823,003	$1,600,668
Financing Capital:			
Equity Contributions	$0	$0	$0
Additions to Long-Term Debt	$0	$0	$0
Deletions to Long-Term Debt	($300,000)	($300,000)	($300,000)
Fixed Asset Additions	($500,000)	($550,000)	($600,000)
Change to Other Long-Term Assets	$0	$0	$0
Change to Other Long-Term Liabilities	$0	$15,000	$10,000
Net Financial Capital Cash Flow	($800,000)	($835,000)	($890,000)
Beginning Cash	$258,946	$94,929	$123,214
Ending Cash	$94,929	$123,214	$117,632

Figure 4-1: (continued)

You need to understand both business solvency and liquidity measurements concepts when managing your business. Solvency measurements, by themselves, don't often tell a company's entire story and whether it has the ability to survive. In Figures 4-1 through 4-3, the company appears to be insolvent. But upon review of the company's operations, we were able to determine that the company has additional liquidity to operate the business and has implemented operational changes to support its return to profitability. Conversely, we could have just as easily presented a company that is highly profitable with strong solvency measurements but, as a result of poor planning, has run out of cash (with no borrowing facilities structured to support continued growth) and has pushed its vendors and suppliers to the limit. Due to the lack of understanding of liquidity and poor planning, this company may even be at greater risk of failing (as the vendors and suppliers may cut off the flow of products to sell thus causing a chain reaction of events causing the company to implode).

Business Solvency Measurements Tools

Business solvency measurements tend to evaluate data as of a point in time, such as the fiscal year end. This data is then subjected to numerous analyses to evaluate how well a company is performing, as well as how strong financially it is (including measuring the businesses solvency). Figure 4-2 presents basic business solvency measurement tools that all business executives should clearly understand.

Needless to say, this list of business solvency measurements is by no means complete as the boys on Wall Street would attest. However, the following measurements represent the basics in understanding business solvency:

✔ **Net working capital:** Total current assets less total current liabilities equals the net working capital of a business. Generally speaking, a positive figure should be present for most businesses.

✔ **Current ratio:** Total current assets divided by total current liabilities equals a company's current ratio. A ratio of greater than one to one should be present.

✔ **Quick or acid-test ratio:** Total current assets is reduced by inventory and other current assets (such as prepaid expenses, deposits, and so on) and then divided by total current liabilities to produce the quick or acid-test ratio. The higher the ratio, the better, but having a ratio of less than one to one is often common, especially for companies with significant levels of inventory.

✔ **Debt-to-equity ratio:** Total debt (current and long term) divided by the total equity of the company equals the debt-to-equity ratio. Higher ratios indicate that the company has more financial leverage (see the last section of this chapter), which translates into more risk being present.

✔ **Days sales outstanding in trade accounts receivable:** Trade receivables divided by average monthly sales multiplied by 30 days produces the days sale outstanding in trade accounts receivable figure. Lower numbers with this calculation are usually positive because it indicates a company is doing a good job of managing this asset and not consuming excess capital.

Be careful when using average monthly sales because companies that are growing rapidly or that have significant seasonal sales will want to use an average monthly sales figure that is more representative of recent business activity.

✔ **Days costs of goods sold outstanding in inventory:** Inventory divided by average monthly costs of goods sold multiplied by 30 days produces the days costs of goods sold outstanding in inventory figure. Lower numbers with this calculation are usually positive because it indicates a company is doing a good job of managing this asset and not consuming excess capital.

Be careful when using average monthly costs of goods sold because companies that are growing rapidly or that have significant seasonal sales will want to use an average monthly costs of sales figure that is more representative of recent business activity.

✔ **Debt service coverage ratio:** Interest and depreciation expense are added back to the net income (or loss) of a company, which is then divided by the current _debt service_ (defined as interest expense plus the current portion of long-term debt plus any outstanding balance with a current line of credit facility termed out over a reasonable period) to produce the debt service coverage ratio. A ratio of greater than one to one is desired and indicates that a company generates enough free cash flow to cover its debt service.

XYZ WHOLESALE, INC.
BUSINESS SOLVENCY RATIO ANALYSIS

Ratio	Year End 12/31/04	Year End 12/31/05	Year End 12/31/06
Net Working Capital:			
Total Current Assets	$2,750,403	$3,783,345	$2,256,695
Total Current Liabilities	$1,389,420	$3,217,080	$3,296,680
Net Working Capital	$1,360,983	$566,265	($1,039,985)
Current Ratio:			
Total Current Assets	$2,750,403	$3,783,345	$2,256,695
Total Current Liabilities	$1,389,420	$3,217,080	$3,296,680
Current Ratio	1.98	1.18	0.68
Quick or Acid Test Ratio:			
Total Current Assets	$2,750,403	$3,783,345	$2,256,695
Less: Inventory & Other Current Assets	$1,383,391	$1,916,381	$867,188
Net Current Assets	$1,367,012	$1,866,964	$1,389,507
Current Liabilities	$1,389,420	$3,217,080	$3,296,680
Quick or Acid Test Ratio	0.98	0.58	0.42
Debt to Equity Ratio:			
Total Liabilities	$2,414,420	$3,957,080	$3,746,680
Total Equity	$1,660,983	$1,401,265	$335,015
Debt to Equity Ratio	1.45	2.82	11.18
Days Sales O/S in Trade Receivables:			
Total Trade Receivables	$1,272,083	$1,743,750	$1,271,875
Average Monthly Sales	$1,272,083	$1,395,000	$1,156,250
Days Sales O/S in Trade Receivables	30	37.5	33
Days Costs of Goods Sold O/S in Inventory:			
Total Inventory	$1,383,391	$1,916,381	$867,188
Average Monthly Costs of Sales	$922,260	$1,095,075	$867,188
Days Costs of Goods Sold O/S in Inventory	45	52.5	30
Debt Service Coverage Ratio:			
Net Income (Loss)	$410,983	($259,718)	($1,066,250)
Interest Expense	$72,000	$68,000	$75,000
Depreciation Expense	$250,000	$300,000	$350,000
Adjusted Debt Service Cash Flow	$732,983	$108,282	($641,250)
Interest Expense	$72,000	$68,000	$75,000
Note Payable Principal Payments Due, 1 Yr.	$300,000	$300,000	$300,000
Current Balance of Line of Credit, Due in 1 Yr.	$0	$100,000	$200,000
Total Debt Service Payments, 1 Yr.	$372,000	$468,000	$575,000
Debt Service Coverage Ratio	1.97	0.23	–1.12

Figure 4-2:
Basic business solvency measurement tools.

Liquidity Measurement Tools

Business liquidity measurements are meant to evaluate a business's total liquidity by using both data as presented at a point in time, as well as resources available to a business (but not necessarily presented in the basic financial statements) either today or in the future. Following are liquidity measurement tools (see Figure 4-3):

✔ **Available current working capital:** Takes the current net working capital of the company and adds available capital that can be accessed during the next 12 months. This figure then needs to be adjusted to account for any other factors, such as extended vendor terms that impact the company's liquidity.

In Figure 4-3, two points should be noted. First, in 2005, the available borrowing capacity was reduced to account for $1 million of obsolete inventory. In this example, the bank became concerned about the value of this inventory and decided to eliminate it from the company's ability to borrow. Second, in 2006, $1.5 million was added back to account for the fact that the company was able to secure extended payment terms from vendors for the coming year. In effect, the company has secured a "permanent" source of capital for the year from the vendors providing extended terms (and thus providing more capital to operate the business).

✔ **Cash burn rate:** Calculates the average *negative cash flow* (defined as net income or loss plus depreciation expense) the company is experiencing on a periodic basis (usually monthly). Burn rates represent key data points for investors attempting to understand how long a company will take until it becomes cash flow positive. This figure then drives how much capital is needed to support the company during the negative cash burn periods. For XYZ Wholesale, Inc., the company's cash burn rate was approximately $60,000 a month in 2006. The equation to calculate this would be to take the annual net loss of the company, add back depreciation expense, and then divide it by 12 to calculate the monthly burn rate.

✔ **Liquidity availability analysis:** The concept with this analysis is to calculate the potential available liquidity that can be tapped from company assets and compares it to the total current outstanding debt (secured with the assets). The idea is to evaluate whether any "untapped" sources of capital are available on the balance sheet. In Figure 4-3, roughly $1.5 million of potential and actual liquidity is available (even though the solvency measurements paint a much more difficult situation).

The three liquidity measurement tools provided represent just a small sample of the entire list of potential liquidity measurements tools available. Unlike the business solvency measurements noted in the preceding section, liquidity measurements tend to be customized for specific company and industry issues in order to properly manage and understand liquidity at any point in time. The key concept, however, remains the same because you must always have a clear understanding of what capital and liquidity is available to your company (at any time) in order to properly manage your business interests.

XYZ WHOLESALE, INC.
BUSINESS LIQUIDITY RATIO ANALYSIS

Ratio	Year End 12/31/04	Year End 12/31/05	Year End 12/31/06
Available Current Liquidity:			
Net Working Capital	$1,360,983	$566,265	($1,039,985)
Available Borrowing Capacity	$1,709,362	$1,753,191	$1,251,094
Extended Vendor Terms Benefit	$0	$0	$1,500,000
Available Current Liquidity	$3,070,345	$2,319,455	$1,711,109
Cash Burn Rate:			
Net Income (Loss)	$410,983	($259,718)	($1,066,250)
Depreciation Expense	$250,000	$300,000	$350,000
Monthly Cash Burn Rate	$55,082	$3,357	($59,688)
Liquidity Availability Analysis:			
Trade Receivables	$1,272,083	$1,743,750	$1,271,875
Borrowing Rate	80%	80%	80%
Available Liquidity	$1,017,667	$1,395,000	$1,017,500
Inventory, Net of Obsolete Items	$1,383,391	$916,381	$867,188
Borrowing Rate	50%	50%	50%
Available Liquidity	$691,695	$458,191	$433,594
Total Available Liquidity	$1,709,362	$1,853,191	$1,451,094
Current Borrowings — Line of Credit	$0	$100,000	$200,000
Net Available Liquidity	$1,709,362	$1,753,191	$1,251,094
Fixed Assets, @ Cost	$2,000,000	$2,550,000	$3,150,000
Maximum Loan Value Available	60%	40%	30%
Total Available Potential Liquidity	$1,200,000	$1,020,000	$945,000
Current Borrowings — Note Payable	$1,200,000	$900,000	$600,000
Potential Net Available Liquidity	$0	$120,000	$345,000
Total Potential & Actual Available Liquidity	$2,909,362	$2,873,191	$2,396,094
Total Borrowings, All Types	$1,200,000	$1,000,000	$800,000
Net Potential & Actual Available Liquidity	$1,709,362	$1,873,191	$1,596,094
Current Borrowing Utilization Rate	41%	35%	33%
Available Borrowing Capacity Rate	59%	65%	67%

Figure 4-3:
Liquidity
measure-
ment tools.

Liquidity Traps

Sometimes businesses get into trouble and unintentionally find themselves in liquidity traps. Liquidity traps come in a variety of shapes, sizes, and forms and, to a certain extent, result from business or industry-specific factors. However, when the liquidity traps are viewed from a generalized perspective, the primary sources (of liquidity traps) are centered in one of three areas, described in the following sections.

The volume and complexity of liquidity traps are extensive and vary from business to business. You'd be amazed at how many liquidity traps there are and how quickly they can consume your business. One day everything is fine, and then 180 days later, the markets turned, new product releases have been delayed, sales have softened, and the banks are all over you. To be quite honest, it's not a matter of if you will have to manage a liquidity trap but rather when, so the better prepared you are in dealing with liquidity traps (and understand the primary causes of the liquidity traps), the better you'll be at managing the problem.

Having access to capital (whether debt or equity) represents one of the most important elements of executing a business plan. This point especially holds true when a business is turning the corner and is ready to grow rapidly because that's when the demand for capital will be the greatest. As one of our business mentors constantly reminds us, "I don't need access to capital going into a recession or downturn but I sure as the hell need access to capital as I come out of a recession and begin to grow quickly again." Not managing liquidity traps and positioning a business to pursue new market opportunities often leads to one of the largest losses a company will ever realize (but never see): lost market opportunity!

Asset investment

As everyone knows, a company needs assets so that it can execute its business plan and generate revenue. Some assets are highly liquid and represent attractive vehicles on which to secure financing (think trade accounts receivables that a bank may use as collateral to extend a loan, new equipment that a leasing company may use as collateral to provide a long-term lease, and so on).

Other assets, however, such as certain inventory, prepaid expenses, intangible assets, and the like, aren't nearly as attractive to a lender because the lender can't liquidate the asset (and repay the loan) if the company can't survive. The more liquidation value the asset has, the more likely lenders will provide financing.

The following list of asset investment liquidity traps are examples of when "Good Assets Go Bad":

✔ **Trade receivables:** Trade receivables, in general, are usually very liquid assets that can be utilized to secure financing. Certain trade receivables, however, aren't as attractive to financing sources. For example, trade receivables that are 90 days past due will often be excluded by a lender from being able to borrow against because the age of the receivable "indicates" that the business is having trouble paying its bills. While this situation may or may not be the case, the lender usually assumes the worst and excludes the trade receivable from being able to borrow against.

In addition to old trade account receivables, other receivables can create problems, including receivables generated from foreign customers, governmental entities, and related parties/entities. Also (and as strange as it may sound), receivable concentration issues may produce problems; if too much of your company's trade receivables are centered in too few accounts, again the lender will get nervous (as its logic is now that if one big customer tanks, the entire company may go down).

Make sure that you have a complete understanding of what comprises your trade accounts receivable balance to have a clear understanding of what is available to borrow against at any point in time. While the balance sheet may state that your company has $1,000,000 (which the company can borrow 80 percent of, or $800,000), you may find that $400,000 of the receivables are "ineligible" — the receivables can't be borrowed against — which leaves only $600,000 of good receivables to borrow against (meaning only $480,000 of financing is available).

✔ **Inventory:** Similar to trade accounts receivables, inventory can often represent the basis of a sound asset on which to secure financing; if you already have a readily available market for a company's product, you should have no problem liquidating the products in case the worst should happen, right? No. Financing sources tend to be very nervous and skittish with lending against inventory because if the worst should happen, all kinds of problems are produced by taking possession of the inventory and then attempting to sell or liquidate it. Financing sources aren't prepared to handle this function. When all potential liquidation factors are considered with inventory, including identifying and disposing of obsolete items, paying a liquidator to sell the inventory, watching the market hammer the value of the inventory as it becomes available (for example, the going-out-of-business sale), the lender will be lucky to receive 40 to 50 percent on the dollar. Hence, lenders tend to shy away from extending loans against inventory, and when they do, lending rates are usually well below 50 percent.

Excessive inventory levels can create problems on numerous fronts. First, for every dollar of inventory increase, a lending source may only provide 40 percent of the cash necessary to support the added investment (leaving 60 percent to be supported by internal resources). Second, the risk of inventory obsolescence increases; the slower the inventory moves, the older it becomes, which generally forces the company into taking inventory write-off "hits" on the financial statements. As most business owners know, in today's rapidly changing market, inventory can become obsolete in as little as three months. And third, excessive inventory is expensive to maintain because it must be stored, insured, tracked, protected from theft, and so on. Quite often, inventory maintenance expenses can run up to 10 percent of the inventory's cost on an annual basis.

✔ **Property, equipment, and other fixed assets:** The concept of consuming liquidity in fixed assets is based on the same concept as when you purchase a new car (but even worse). That is, the day you purchase a new car and drive it off the lot, the car loses 25 percent of its value. For fixed assets, this concept also applies, but tends to be even more severe. Once new equipment, computers, furniture, fixtures, and so on are purchased, within 90 days, their value is now based on a "used" status (and you will be lucky to get 50 percent on the dollar). Compounding this problem is that if you do need to secure financing against the fixed assets (which are now used), the financing will be expensive (meaning higher interest rates) compared to acquiring the fixed assets when new.

The time to obtain financing with fixed assets is at the point of purchase when the asset value is the highest and the most financing sources are available to obtain competitive pricing and terms. Once the equipment becomes used, the market for financing sources becomes much more expensive, with far fewer choices available.

Inappropriate use of debt

The second major liquidity trap is centered in not keeping your balance sheet in balance. By not keeping your balance sheet in balance, we mean that short-term debt, such as a line of credit structured to support trade accounts receivables, is utilized to finance a purchase of a long-term asset. This scenario can create significant problems for a company.

For example, say that a company has structured a line of credit financing agreement or loan where it could borrow up to 80 percent of eligible or qualified receivables. The company is growing quickly and had increased its trade accounts receivables to roughly $2 million in total, of which 90 percent were eligible to borrow against. In total, the company borrowed $1.4 million, which was within the financing agreements limit ($2 million of total account receivables of which $200,000 where ineligible to borrow against leaving a net borrowing base balance of $1.8 million producing a total borrowing capacity of $1.44 million). Of the $1.4 million, $400,000 was used to purchase fixed assets and $1 million used to support the trade accounts receivables. Within six months, the company's trade accounts receivable decreased to $1.5 million while at the same time the ineligible percent increased to 20 percent (as a result of certain trade accounts receivables becoming 90 days past due). The change in accounts receivables reduced the company's ability to borrow to $960,000 ($1.5 million of trade accounts receivables times 80 percent eligible times 80 percent advance rate). Unfortunately, the company used the cash generated from the $500,000 decrease in trade accounts receivables to reduce trade payables and cover operating losses (as well as pay down the loan). The company was able to pay down the loan only by $200,000, leaving an outstanding balance of $1.2 million against a borrowing available of $960,000. Needless to say, the financing source requested the company "cure" this over-advanced position, which the company couldn't (leading to a very interesting round of discussions and additional financing source restrictions being placed on the company). By not properly financing the fixed asset purchase (which the financing source should little sympathy in addressing, especially given the losses the company had recently incurred), the company fell into a very common and painful liquidity trap.

The exact opposite can happen as well. For example, say that a loan payable, which has a repayment term of three years, is used to support a current asset (such as trade accounts receivables). While the asset (or trade accounts receivable) may be growing as a result of increased sales, the debt is being reduced over a three-year period. Just when the company needs capital to finance growth, capital is flowing out of the organization to repay debt.

It's imperative that a proper balance of capital to asset type is maintained to better manage the balance sheet. The following three simple rules can help you match capital or financing sources with asset investments:

✓ **Finance current assets with current debt.** Current assets, such as trade accounts receivable or inventory, should be financed with current debt, such as trade vendors or suppliers and a properly structured lending facility.

✓ **Finance long-term assets with long-term debt.** Fixed assets, such as equipment, furniture, computers, technology, and so on, should be financed with longer term debt, such as term notes payables (a five-year repayment period), operating or capital leases, and so. The general concept here is that a fixed asset will produce earnings or cash flow over a period of greater than one year, and as such, the cash flow stream should be matched with the financing stream.

✓ **Debt-financing sources provide capital for tangible assets and don't like to finance losses or "soft" assets.** Other asset types (including intangibles such as patents or trademarks, certain investments, and prepaid expenses) and company net losses need to be supported from equity capital sources including the internal earnings of the company.

Excessive growth rates

The most common, but least understood liquidity trap, is when your business experiences excessive growth rates. A rapidly growing business requires significant amounts of capital to support ongoing operations. As revenue (and hopefully profitability) levels grow, so will assets and the need to finance the assets.

The problems rapidly growing companies run into is that they get caught up in the fact that new market opportunities seem almost endless and, as such, the company "invests" earnings from profitable operations into the expansion of new operations (which tend to lose money during the startup phase). This strategy, if properly managed, can be very effective as long as management keeps a keen eye on the distribution of earnings between supporting new operations versus strengthening the balance sheet. While no set rule dictates how much of your earnings should be used to reinvest in new operations versus strengthening the balance sheet, the real key lies in the ability to keep your debt-to-equity ratio manageable so that if the company does hit a speed bump, resources are available through the difficult times.

Pushing your company to the limit by leveraging every asset with debt financing and reinvesting internal earnings in new operations is a recipe for failure. Businesses must constantly manage the growth versus available capital tradeoff issue to ensure that their interests aren't exposed to unnecessary risks that quite often carry extremely expensive outcomes.

Untapped Sources of Liquidity

If you've run out of cash and can't borrow anymore, it's up to the executive management team to identify sources of capital to work through the troubled times. Fortunately, potential capital sources are available, described in the following sections, which can assist your business in times of need.

Asset liquidations

Liquidating assets is often targeted by management as a quick and easy method to raise capital. This philosophy would appear to make sense as if a company has unneeded or underutilized assets; selling them may help ease a cash crunch.

Although liquidating assets does represent a viable alternative, be careful of the following pitfalls with this strategy:

- ✔ **Values received:** If you plan on moving older, slow-moving inventory in bulk or selling old, unused equipment, be prepared to sell the assets well below cost. While the cash received is great, remember that you'll have to explain the losses to investors, lending sources, and the like.

- ✔ **Collateral support:** Certain assets represent collateral for loans extended to the company. If you liquidate the assets, not only may you be violating your loan agreement, but you may also be reducing your ability to borrow (as the asset base is reduced, so will your borrowing capacity).

- ✔ **Future growth:** Liquidating assets that are unnecessary in the short term but that you'll eventually need can be very expensive.

- ✔ **Management time:** Liquidating assets often takes much more time and effort than anticipated, which means that the parties responsible for this function are distracted from their regular duties.

Lending sources

Your company's primary lending sources, such as banks, asset-based lenders, leasing companies, and the like, represent a potential source of quick capital if needed. The key in approaching these sources is to have solid information available for review and a clear action plan on how the capital will be repaid in a reasonable time frame. There is no question that these groups want to see your business survive, so being able to leverage the relationship can provide some added liquidity.

The following two examples demonstrate how you can squeeze capital from these sources:

✔ **Loan advance rates:** Lenders provide borrowing capacity based on the value of the asset they're secured by. For example, a bank may advance 80 percent on eligible trade account receivables. During a particular tight period, such as during increased seasonal demand, you may be able to get the lender to advance 85 to 90 percent of the eligible receivables so that you can free up capital.

If your bank doesn't want to work with you, then an asset-based lender may be a better financial partner. Asset-based lenders offer more aggressive loan facilities in exchange for higher rates and tighter reporting to compensate for the higher risk present. Asset-based lenders understand the importance of having access to capital in relation to businesses operating in challenging times.

✔ **Asset sale lease-back:** Although asset sales may represent a source of quick capital to your business (see the section earlier in this chapter), it comes with a number of potential problems. You may want to consider executing an *asset sale lease-back* where you sell the asset to a leasing company who in turn immediately leases it back to you. You achieve your goal of freeing up short-term liquidity, and the leasing company doesn't have to worry about finding a new lessee for the asset.

Similar to working with an asset-based lender, leasing companies that support these types of transactions will be more expensive.

✔ **Restructure notes payable:** You may want to consider restructuring any long-term notes payable with the lender to lengthen the repayment period (thus reducing the current monthly payment) or move it to an interest only note for a short period (for example, six months). The goal is to reduce the capital outflow with the note agreement to better match it with the ability for your company to generate internal cash flows to service the debt.

If you find your company has to work with financing sources that are more expensive than traditional banks and low-risk leasing companies, you can expect to be charged higher interest rates and more fees. While there are no set rules, on average you can expect to pay at least 3 percent more in overall interest costs (which can quickly reach 5 percent). If the bank is charging you Prime Rate plus 1 percent (which today would be approximately 9.25 percent), you can expect to pay at least Prime Rate Plus 4 percent (pushing your rate to 12.25 percent).

If the difference between your business making money and losing money is 3 percent points, then you probably have bigger problems than just a short-term liquidity squeeze. Access to the capital is the key, so paying 3 percent more on the capital should be far cheaper than the alternatives, which include lost business growth opportunities or, worse yet, a failed business.

Unsecured creditors

You can tap your vendors, suppliers, and yes, even your customers, from time to time to help manage potential liquidity issues. These parties are already in bed with you and stand to lose the most if your company fails. In addition, they stand to gain quite a bit if your business continues to grow and prosper (which means more business for everyone).

Having customers step up with an advance payment, deposit on a large project, and so on can help ease a liquidity squeeze. Also, you can provide customers with incentives, such as a 1 percent discount if paid within 10 days, to pay quicker). If a customer has ample cash resources available and it's earning a measly 4 percent, why not offer an incentive that provides a chance to save three times this much? Of course, this strategy has some pitfalls, but in certain situations, customers can be leveraged to accelerate payment delivery. An example of a pitfall is that certain large customers may still take the discount offered but not pay within the shorter time period. Although you could pursue the larger customer for the discount, you would then risk alienating the customer. Large companies tend to dictate payment terms based on their criteria and not yours.

In addition, vendors and suppliers offer a relatively cheap and easily accessible source of capital to your company. Various strategies are available and range from requesting extended payment terms during a high sales period to *terming out* a portion of the balance due the vendors to be repaid over a longer period — in other words, instead of paying the entire balance in 60 days, see whether you can pay it over 12 months in equal installments with a nominal interest rate attached.

When needed, you can also evaluate your internal employees to determine whether you can secure added liquidity. In tight times, you may ask your senior management team to defer a portion of their compensation, which will then be paid when the company hits certain milestones. If they're resistant to this suggestion, at least you know where they stand in terms of their commitment to the company. Also, if you have paid commissions on sales when they're booked, you may want to restructure this program to pay commissions when payment for sales are actually received (in cash) to better match cash outflows with cash inflows.

You must remember to be careful when using customers, vendors, and suppliers to provide additional capital resources. It's one thing to push these sources within the normal course of business, but you don't want to appear desperate. You may actually find that payment terms tighten up and customers get nervous (thus delaying orders), which then produces the exact opposite of what you were trying to achieve.

Equity and off-balance sheet sources

A number of external capital sources are also available to provide additional liquidity during a bind:

- ✓ **Owner personal financial strength:** Business owners and key executives have been asked (on more than one occasion) to step up and provide additional capital to support their business. If your lenders, vendors, suppliers, customers, and employees are all on board, why not the owners of the business? Business owners with ample personal wealth are often asked to pledge some of it for the benefit of the company.

- ✓ **Family, friends, and close business associates:** This group is a natural source to secure capital for a business, as well as during a liquidity squeeze when they may be able to provide a bridge loan to get the company through a tight period. While nobody likes to ask family members for money, when your business life depends on it, you may have no other choice.

- ✓ **Off-balance sheet assets:** You may have various assets that relate to the business, but aren't included in the balance sheet or are restricted in nature. For example, the building your company leases may actually be owned by a group of investors (including the owners of the company) with close ties to the company. Over a period of time, the building may have appreciated in value and may be refinanced with the proceeds then loaned to your company from the legal entity that owns the building. Conversely, if the legal entity that owns the building has the resources, the lease payments from your company may be reduced or deferred for a period of time to free up cash.

Business owners and key executive management team members have the most to gain if a business succeeds and the most to lose if it fails. Stepping up on the capital front provides for much more than simply helping with a liquidity squeeze. Rather, it displays creditability to other parties that the management team and business owners believe in the business and are willing to stand behind it (in good times and in bad).

Financial Leverage — the Good, the Bad, and the Ugly

Financial leverage is best measured by the business solvency debt-to-equity ratio (see the section "Business Solvency Measurement Tools"). That is, the higher the amount of debt your company has in relation to your equity, the higher the ratio will be that indicates your company is operating with a greater degree of financial risk. As such, financial leverage can be broken down into the Good, the Bad, and the (outright) Ugly:

- ✔ **The Good:** If properly managed, financial leverage can enhance your company's profitability and improve earnings per share. This approach allows the company to secure less equity-based capital (since the appropriate amount and type of debt-based capital is secured), providing the business owners with greater ownership control of the entity.

    To achieve the good, you must remember to keep the balance sheet in balance and avoid leveraging your assets too high. Companies always need to remember to keep a war chest available to manage both business problems and opportunities. The challenge is to find the ideal balance between equity and debt capital sources.

- ✔ **The Bad:** Financial leverage can often produce a certain amount of business and personal stress during the down times. The creditors of your company tend to be more interested in getting repaid during the down times instead of providing additional capital to support a new growth opportunity. Companies that have strong equity levels and who can afford some missteps along the way will have more leeway in pursuing new markets than companies operating under heavy debt loads. While you may survive a down period and manage to get your company's debt under control, a stronger competitor may have seized the moment and captured new market opportunities that you didn't have the resources to pursue.

✔ **The Ugly:** The ugly is when financial leverage is so excessive (or high), that you've tapped out every asset and have nothing left to work with or your debt financing sources push the company into bankruptcy or an involuntary liquidation (see Chapter 15). Basically, you reach a point of no hope of the company repaying the debt and turning around its operations. The remaining option is to lose control of your company and watch others dismantle it to settle the obligations due.

If we can leave you with one final thought, it's this quote from the late Ted Knight who played the ever popular Judge Smails in the movie *Caddyshack:*

"It's easy to grin when your ship comes in and you've got the stock market beat. But the man worthwhile is the man who can smile when his shorts are too tight in the seat"

Trust me when we say that it helps to remember this simple quote when dealing with liquidity and solvency squeezes. We have yet to see a small- to medium-sized business not have to deal with a major liquidity squeeze and place tremendous pressure on the management team.

Part II
Using Tools of the Trade

The 5th Wave   By Rich Tennant

"Sorry, Cedric the King cut my budget for additional fools. He said the project already had enough fools on it."

In this part . . .

Savvy managers use certain tools of the trade in managing the financial affairs of their small business. The four chapters in this part of the book explain these techniques and methods. Chapter 5 should convince you that every small business needs effective internal controls, which are procedures designed to minimize errors and prevent embezzlement and other kinds of fraud against the business.

Chapter 6 speaks from the podium on cost control, which we argue does not simply consist of minimizing costs. You need to get in the right frame of mind and judge costs relative to the revenue results of the costs. Chapter 7 demonstrates the value of financial planning and budgeting — yet many small business managers put budgeting on the back burner. Not developing a financial plan for the coming year is a serious mistake.

The P&L statement reports the profit performance of your business. This financial statement may seem to be just what you need for making profit decisions. Chapter 8 explains, however, that the P&L report is too bulky for strategic decision analysis. A compact profit model is a much more useful tool, which allows you to focus on the relatively few principal factors that drive profit without getting lost in a deluge of details.

Chapter 5

Protecting the Family Jewels

*Y*ou need to be confident and optimistic in starting and growing a business. At the same time, you shouldn't ignore the risks your small business faces. Customer demand may take sudden turns, vendors may fail to make deliveries on time, and a key employee may quit without warning. This chapter explains two business risks you should pay attention to, keeping in mind that you're probably already very busy in running the business and doing your best to cope with several other business risks.

A small business is a sitting duck for fraud and theft of all kinds — unless the business puts into place effective protections against these threats. These preventive procedures are called *internal controls*. These precautions don't automatically pop into place. You have to be proactive and implement definite internal control procedures to guard against fraud and theft that could cause serious losses. An ounce of prevention is worth a pound of cure.

A risk that small business owners and managers may overlook is that their accounting system may have serious errors. Your accounting system should include specific procedures called *internal accounting controls,* which are designed to prevent recordkeeping errors and to detect any errors that still might sneak into the accounting process. Accounting errors mean that your P&L reports (see Chapter 2) and your other financial statements (see Chapter 3) are wrong and misleading. It's hard enough running a small business with correct accounting information.

This chapter focuses mainly on internal controls to defend against fraud and theft. Small business managers should exercise these controls or delegate some of these controls to other managers and employees. We briefly discuss internal accounting controls, but we don't go into great detail. These controls are the responsibility of your chief accountant (Controller). Of course, the small business owner/manager should make sure that the Controller is using good internal accounting controls.

Recognizing the Need for Controls

John's father-in-law was a small business owner/manager for many years. He told him that based on his experience, there's a little bit of larceny in everyone's heart. Unfortunately, he was right. He could have added that there's a lot of larceny in the hearts of a few.

An unpleasant fact of business is that some customers shoplift, some vendors and suppliers overcharge and short-count on deliveries, some employees embezzle or steal assets, and some managers commit fraud against the business or take personal advantage of their position of authority in the business. None of this is news to you probably. But you may think your business is exempt from these risks; you feel that all your employees are honest and everyone you deal with is honest. If this is your attitude, we'd like to talk with you about buying a bridge in Brooklyn.

Preventing fraud and theft against your business

A small business is a natural target for fraudulent schemes, scams, employee embezzlement, pilferage, worker crime, and theft. Even a relatively small business handles a lot of money, holds valuable assets, and deals with a lot of people — a perfect mix for bad things to happen. To protect against these threats, a small business should put into place and vigorously enforce *internal controls*. For example, the simple practice of giving all customers a receipt to document their purchase is a good internal control because it forces the employee to ring up the sale on the cash register, and thereby all sales are recorded. Various precautions are established to prevent, or at least to minimize losses from all types of dishonesty against the business from within and without. Big business understands the critical importance of internal controls. You're preaching to the choir here. In contrast many small businesses are careless regarding internal controls, which is like leaving money on the counter for the taking.

Police look to motive and opportunity in solving a crime. In business, the motive is clear enough — to steal money or other assets without getting caught. Internal controls are designed first to minimize opportunities for people to steal from the business and second to detect theft quickly in order to stop the losses as soon as possible. *Deter* and *detect* are the twin objectives of internal controls. Every small business should establish and enforce internal controls. Indeed, what's the alternative? Well, you could trust everyone and hope no one takes advantage of your trust. This policy would be asking for trouble, of course.

Studies by experts in the field have found that business fraud and theft is in the range of 6 percent of annual sales revenue. Suppose that your profit is 10 percent of your annual sales revenue. You could boost your profit 60 percent (from 10 percent to 16 percent of annual sales revenue) by eliminating all fraud and theft against your business. Fraud researchers found that the average loss per incident was about $100,000. Could you slough off a $100,000 loss caused by just one case of fraud against your business? In short, outlining and enforcing internal controls is a good investment for the small business.

The logic for internal controls is persuasive. However, the devil is in the details. Which internal controls are most effective? Which internal controls give the most bang for the buck? Which internal controls are least intrusive to normal business operations? Which internal controls are acceptable to customers and employees, and which do they strongly resent? Also, you need to consider the time factor. Small business owners/managers are bombarded with many demands on their time. Quite rightly, they're concerned about how much time internal controls would impose on their workweek. Using a core set of effective internal controls is well worth your time and can prevent a major loss from fraud against your business.

Avoiding errors in your accounting system

Many small business owners/managers assume that because their books are in balance, the accounts have no errors. Well, as we use to say in Iowa, hold 'er down, Knute. Debits may equal credits, but this balance doesn't mean that the accounts don't contain errors — not by a long shot. (Debits and credits are labels for balances in accounts; the sum of accounts with debit balances should equal the sum of accounts with credit balances.) Some recordkeeping errors cause an imbalance of debits and credits, which signals an obvious error. However, when an entry isn't recorded that should be recorded, the accounts are still in balance. For example, suppose that an inventory loss from shoplifting or employee theft hasn't been recorded in your accounts (but should be, of course). Your accounts are in balance, but in error.

Your accounting records should be complete, accurate, and up to date — no ifs, buts, or ands. Every accounting system, without exception, needs strong internal accounting controls to guard against errors in capturing, processing, and storing financial information. Without these safeguards, errors would accumulate in your accounting records. Your profit reports, tax returns, payroll checks, financial statements, and payments to vendors would have errors. Every accounting system depends on its internal accounting controls to minimize bookkeeping errors and to correct any errors that may sneak into the accounting process.

As the owner/manager of a small business, you should understand the importance of internal accounting controls. These controls are the responsibility of your accountant. Your function is to make sure that your Controller is using adequate internal accounting controls to keep errors in your accounting records to an absolute minimum.

Clarifying Terminology

Often, the term *internal controls* is used broadly to include internal accounting controls, as well as controls designed primarily to prevent fraud and theft. The reason is that many fraud and theft internal controls use forms and procedures that are integrated into the accounting process. These forms and procedures are part and parcel of the accounting process of recording the transactions of the business. But the two types of controls have different purposes.

The term *internal accounting controls* refers to practices that are inserted in the accounting system to guard against specific data processing errors. Accountants have learned over many years of practicing accounting which errors are likely to happen and how to prevent these errors going undetected. Even a small business has a relatively large number of transactions and a mountain of data to process. Internal accounting controls are needed regardless of which fraud and theft controls are adopted by a business.

A much different term is *accounting fraud* (often used interchangeably with *financial reporting fraud*). This term refers to the *intentional* use of incorrect, indefensible, and misleading accounting methods to record revenue and/or expenses for the purpose of stage-managing reported profit. Accounting fraud is also done to hide liabilities of the business, or to overstate its assets. (Financial reporting fraud also includes the failure of a business to disclose significant events and developments that affect its financial situation.) Internal accounting controls, as such, aren't very effective in preventing accounting fraud. Accounting fraud is orchestrated by, or at least sanctioned by, the chief executive officer of a business. The CEO has the authority and power to compel the use of fraudulent accounting methods, in which case he would not leave his fingerprints on the accounting fraud. On the other hand, if the CEO is a very hands-off style of manager, he may not even be aware that accounting fraud is going on.

Large business organizations should put into place controls to protect against fraudulent accounting. They can have the internal auditors of the business report directly to the board of directors about any concerns they have about the accounting methods of the business. The board can delegate to its audit committee broad powers to question the accounting practices of the business. In contrast, a small business doesn't enjoy the luxury of having internal auditors and an audit committee. The principal manager of a small business has the responsibility to ensure that its accounting methods are proper. Your Controller should know which accounting methods are proper, of course, but you may want to ask an outside CPA for an evaluation of your accounting methods. The CPA can provide an independent review of whether your accounting methods are up-to-date and conform to present standards.

The principal manager of a small business may resort to *cooking the books.* The manager may use fraudulent accounting methods to evade income taxes, paint a rosier picture of the business's financial situation in securing a bank loan, or overstate profit performance in reporting to the outside owners in the business. Frankly, we don't know to what extent small businesses engage in accounting fraud. Undoubtedly, some accounting fraud goes on by small businesses. Both of us have experience with clients that engaged in accounting fraud. However, public records aren't compiled on accounting fraud by small (private) businesses.

Finally, you should distinguish accounting fraud, which is called cooking the books, and *massaging the numbers,* which refers to choosing among legitimate accounting methods to control when profit is recorded. Chapter 2 explains choosing accounting methods. Quoting John's father-in-law again, he called massaging the numbers fluffing the pillows, which isn't a bad way to put it. In massaging the numbers, you bend accounting rules to tilt one way or the other. In accounting fraud, you break the rules. When you massage the numbers, you push against the limit of what's acceptable, but you don't cross over the line. When you cook the books (commit accounting fraud), you cross the line. Legally speaking, you'd beat the rap if you do no more than massage the numbers, but if you were convicted of accounting fraud, you may have to serve time in the slammer.

Reporting on Internal Controls

The last three decades saw a surge of attention to internal controls. The large number of accounting and financial reporting fraud scandals involving top-level executives of public companies during this period put the spotlight on internal controls — or, we should say, the *lack* of internal controls.

Enron is a well-known example of accounting fraud, of course, but it's just one of many high profile scandals stretching back to the 1970s. Many companies were cooking their books (engaging in accounting fraud to overstate reported profit). In recent years, an astounding number of companies have restated their earnings for one or more prior years. (Even more astounding is that their CPA auditors didn't catch the accounting frauds, but that's another story.)

Reporting by public companies

The Sarbanes-Oxley Act of 2002 (SOX) was enacted to prevent accounting frauds — although it didn't help the thousands of investors who suffered huge losses. The thinking behind the act was that a breakdown of internal controls left the door open to fraudulent accounting and financial reporting. Among other provisions, SOX requires the CEO of the business and its auditor to provide assurances in the annual financial report regarding the effectiveness of the company's internal controls in preventing fraudulent accounting and reporting. Public companies had to expand and stiffen their internal controls to meet the requirements of SOX, and auditors had to do a lot more work in testing and evaluating the internal controls of their clients.

Figure 5-1 shows an example of a statement on internal controls by a CEO, which is from Microsoft's 2006 annual financial report filed with the Securities and Exchange Commission. Would you be comfortable signing such a statement without strong internal controls in place? We wouldn't, that's for sure!

In essence, the CEO and the auditor of a public company have to sign off on the internal controls of the business and say so clearly in its annual financial report. Recently, a growing backlash from the corporate community argues that SOX is too onerous and too costly. Internal control reporting rules may be relaxed in the future, but we don't see the rules being repealed any time soon — although you never know. You can keep up with developments on SOX in the financial/business section of your newspaper.

Accounting methods and disclosure requirements for financial reporting by businesses (large and small, public and private) are governed by *generally accepted accounting principles* (GAAP). These accounting and disclosure standards apply to all businesses in the United States. The CPA auditor explicitly states in the audit opinion whether the company's financial report is in accordance with United States GAAP. Under GAAP, a business isn't obligated to make comments in its financial reports about the effectiveness of its internal controls. The SOX internal control disclosure rules for public companies override GAAP in this respect — but only for companies that have issued equity and debt securities that are traded in public markets.

CERTIFICATIONS

I, Steven A. Ballmer, certify that:

1. I have reviewed this annual report on Form 10-K of Microsoft Corporation;

2. Based on my knowledge, this report does not contain any untrue statement of a material fact or omit to state a material fact necessary to make the statements made, in light of the circumstances under which such statements were made, not misleading with respect to the period covered by this report;

3. Based on my knowledge, the financial statements, and other financial information included in this report, fairly present in all material respects the financial condition, results of operations and cash flows of the registrant as of, and for, the periods presented in this report;

4. The registrant's other certifying officer and I are responsible for establishing and maintaining disclosure controls and procedures (as defined in Exchange Act Rules 13a-15(e) and 15d-15(e)) and internal control over financial reporting (as defined in Exchange Act Rules 13a-15(f) and 15d-15(f)) for the registrant and have:

a) Designed such disclosure controls and procedures, or caused such disclosure controls and procedures to be designed under our supervision, to ensure that material information relating to the registrant, including its consolidated subsidiaries, is made known to us by others within those entities, particularly during the period in which this report is being prepared;

b) Designed such internal control over financial reporting, or caused such internal control over financial reporting to be designed under our supervision, to provide reasonable assurance regarding the reliability of financial reporting and the preparation of financial statements for external purposes in accordance with generally accepted accounting principles;

c) Evaluated the effectiveness of the registrant's disclosure controls and procedures and presented in this report our conclusions about the effectiveness of the disclosure controls and procedures, as of the end of the period covered by this report based on such evaluation; and

d) Disclosed in this report any change in the registrant's internal control over financial reporting that occurred during the registrant's most recent fiscal quarter (the registrant's fourth fiscal quarter in the case of an annual report) that has materially affected, or is reasonably likely to materially affect, the registrant's internal control over financial reporting; and

5. The registrant's other certifying officer and I have disclosed, based on our most recent evaluation of internal control over financial reporting, to the registrant's auditors and the audit committee of registrant's Board of Directors (or persons performing the equivalent functions):

Figure 5-1:
Microsoft's
statement
on internal
controls by
its CEO in
its 2006
financial
report.

a) All significant deficiencies and material weaknesses in the design or operation of internal control over financial reporting which are reasonably likely to adversely affect the registrant's ability to record, process, summarize and report financial information; and

b) Any fraud, whether or not material, that involves management or other employees who have a significant role in the registrant's internal control over financial reporting.

August 25, 2006

/s/ Steven A. Ballmer

Steven A. Ballmer
Chief Executive Officer

Nonreporting by private companies

Privately owned businesses are outside the reach of SOX. Private businesses (large and small) aren't required to discuss internal controls in their financial reports to creditors and owners. When you go to your bank for a loan, it's very unlikely that the loan officer will ask you for a statement by you or your auditor about the internal controls you use, although, we suppose, banks could start asking for this statement in the future. The equity investors in your business don't expect any commentary on internal controls in your external financial reports.

Investors in private business are satisfied with the traditional financial report that includes the three primary financial statements — income statement, balance sheet, and statement of cash flows — plus footnotes, as well as a transmittal letter from the principal manager of the business. You could throw in some comments about internal controls in your annual financial report. The equity investors in your business would be surprised — but they would be reassured that you pay attention to internal controls. Frankly, if we were equity investors in your business, we'd prefer that you did include a few comments about the internal controls you're using to prevent fraud and theft against our business.

The requirements for commentary on internal controls by the CEO and the auditor, which are now mandated for public companies, could conceivably trickle down and eventually become a requirement for small (private) businesses. But we don't see this change on the horizon. There's no law prohibiting a private business discussing its internal controls in its financial reports. With all the attention to corporate accounting fraud in the financial press, we suppose that it's possible that debt and equity sources of capital to small businesses could start clamoring for commentary about internal controls. We don't hear such talk at the present time. However, you should know that small business has a history of getting caught up in the swirl of developments in the big business sector. Reporting on the internal controls would impose yet another cost on the small business, which most legislators would be sensitive to, we think.

Distinguishing Security and Safety Procedures from Internal Controls

The term internal controls generally doesn't refer to the security and safety procedures that a business employs. A business takes a wide range of steps to protect against physical and legal threats and to comply with safety laws and regulations. Examples of common security and safety procedures include the following:

- ✔ Using alarm systems to deter burglary and robbery

- ✔ Limiting access to warehouses and offices during working hours

- ✔ Putting cash in safes

- ✔ Hiring security guards

- ✔ Training employees on what to do during a hold up

- ✔ Requiring employees to wear protective clothing as required under Occupational Safety and Health Act (OSHA) and other laws and regulations

- ✔ Keeping fire extinguishers available where needed

- ✔ Offering safety training programs for employees

- ✔ Requiring employees to wear identification badges

- ✔ Correcting violations from building inspections

- ✔ Installing surveillance cameras

This list of security and safety procedures is only a sampling of security and safety procedures that a small business should consider.

Internal controls are different than security and safety procedures in one fundamental respect. Internal controls are implemented to protect against *violations of trust* by persons who should be, and largely are, trustworthy — employees, vendors, customers, and others the business deals with. On the one hand, business is conducted on the basis of mutual trust. On the other hand, a few rotten apples are always in the barrel. An inherent condition of employment is that you shouldn't steal from your employer. But some employees embezzle money or steal other assets. The purchasing officer of a business may agree to a higher a price from a vendor in exchange for a kickback or other payoff. Obviously, the purchasing officer is violating the terms of his or her employment by taking under-the-table payoffs. Salespersons shouldn't pad their expense reports, but some do just that.

Internal controls take aim at the very persons the business depends on to play fair with the business — its customers, vendors, and employees. In implementing internal controls, a business follows a key principle in politics: *Trust but verify.* Knowing that internal controls are in place is an efficient determent to those inclined to break the rules and take advantage of the business. In a friendly game of poker among friends, the players trust each other not to cheat, but they cut the deck before dealing the cards. And, keep in mind that a player other than the dealer is the one who cuts the deck.

Policing Internal Controls

As we explain in the earlier section "Avoiding errors in your accounting system," internal accounting controls are essential to ensure that a business's accounting records are complete, accurate, and up to date. The Controller is in charge of these accounting system controls, with general overview by the principal manager of the business. As boss, you don't have the time (or expertise) to get involved with these accounting system controls. Rather, you should make sure that the accountant is doing his or her job regarding these controls.

You should be alert for signals that your accounting system may have problems. For example, if employees complain that their payroll checks are wrong or if your vendors complain that they're not paid on time, your accounting system may be in trouble. Your regular P&L and other financial reports should arrive on your desk shortly after the close of the period. If not, ask your Controller for an explanation.

We know we sound like a stuck record on the point, but we say again that a small business should institute internal control procedures to deter and detect dishonesty by customers, employees, and vendors. The upside of these internal controls is that losses from fraud and theft are kept to a minimum. The downside is that most of the controls require additional forms and paperwork. Someone has to police whether forms are being filled out and the paperwork is being processed properly. Not a very glamorous job, but someone has to do it. The responsibility for compliance with internal control forms and paperwork falls in the lap of the accountant.

For example, a traveling salesperson's weekly expense report is submitted for reimbursement. The internal control procedure requires that these reports include copies of charge slips, hotel bills, client entertainment expenses, and so on. The accountant makes sure that all the paperwork is in order before sending it on to you or another manager for payment approval. Or, suppose that a past due customer receivable is being considered for write-off. Adequate documentation must be assembled by the Controller for the manager in deciding whether to write off the customer's balance. This documentation would include a history of sales to and collections from the customer (if any), and any other relevant information (such as a legal notice that the customer has declared bankruptcy).

In brief, your Controller is in charge of policing many internal controls. A good accountant needs a finely honed sense of professional skepticism and should constantly be on the lookout for errors and dishonesty. It's a nasty job, but someone has to do it. The owner/manager of a small business has to police the Controller. You have to supervise your accountant in helping you protect the family jewels. In a real sense, you are the internal control to make sure that your business's internal controls are working.

You should have the Controller develop a manual describing in reasonable detail your internal control procedures and policies. Your bookkeeper and other employees can refer to the manual when they have questions. The manual is a good reference for training new employees. If you have a financial report audit, the CPA would find the manual invaluable for testing compliance with your established internal controls. In short, the internal controls manual is a very useful reference.

Surveying Internal Controls for Small Businesses

There's no shortage of articles on internal controls — and many focus on the small business. One recent article we particularly recommend is by Joseph T. Wells in the March 2003 issue of the *Journal of Accountancy* (which you can access at the Web site www.aicpa.org/pubs/jofa/mar2003/wells. htm). Your Controller should be keeping up with developments on internal controls, especially the activities of COSO (the Committee of Sponsoring Organizations of the Treadway Commission, at www.coso.org). Your accountant can go to the Amazon and Borders Web sites for many books on internal controls. In short, there's a lot of reference material on internal controls. Nevertheless, one aspect of small business internal controls gets short shrift.

Finding time for internal controls

Most discussions of internal controls for the small business are, for lack of a better term, overenthusiastic. Most authors assume that all internal controls are created equal. The impression you get is that every internal control is of critical importance, and therefore your should use all of them. Well, this approach simply isn't realistic. Given the demands on their time, small business managers have to be very selective. They have to decide which internal controls are so important that they have to make time for doing them on a regular basis. Other controls may be useful if you had the time. But it's much better to carry out a relatively few critical internal controls very well, rather than do a large number of internal controls superficially.

The rest of the chapter explains internal controls that we rank high on the list — ones you should seriously consider doing yourself or having another manager in your business doing routinely. We understand that you (and the other managers) probably don't have the time for doing all the following internal controls. But we encourage you to give each one serious thought. If it were our business, we'd carefully consider each of the following internal controls.

An example of lack of internal controls

Recently, a local paper reported a case of business fraud that illustrates several key points. The police charged a young woman who worked as a hostess and who was in charge of a restaurant's cash register of with stealing $115,000 over a period of five years. The owner, who evidently wasn't on the premises most of the time, noticed that sales peaked during the two weeks that the woman took a vacation.

In the past, the owner had noticed that sales seemed to be lower during the shifts this particular employee worked. Some employees told the police that they had suspected her of not ringing up all sales and that she also was stealing tips. The police investigation found that the woman and her husband lived a lifestyle beyond their combined incomes. To top it off, the police found the woman had a rap sheet that included jail time for similar offenses.

Certain basic controls, had they been in place, would have prevented this fraud. First, the background of all new employees, especially those who will be handling money, should be checked to determine whether they have a criminal record. Second, every business should have in place strong controls over cash receipts because cash is the preferred asset to steal. Cash transactions are a high-risk area.

Some restaurants, for example, place a conspicuous sign near the cash register that your meal is free if you don't get a receipt. Prenumbered order forms should be used, and all numbers should be accounted for to make sure that all sales are rung up. A video surveillance camera could have been used to watch cash register activities. If the owner had some questions regarding the hostess, he could have had a friend or two eat at the restaurant and closely observe whether the hostess rang up their cash. The owner could have hired a private investigator to discreetly look into the situation.

The owner should have noticed early on the mismatch between the sales revenue and expenses in the monthly or quarterly P&L reports. A business owner/manager should develop a profit model for the business against which actual results are compared. For a certain level of sales revenue, the owner/manager should know how much expenses should be, at least within a few thousand dollars or so.

The restaurant owner comes off looking rather dim-witted or naïve in this case. On the other hand, you have to give the owner some credit for noticing the variation in sales when the hostess was on duty versus when she was off duty. Finally, one other possibility comes to mind. Perhaps the owner was also skimming some cash and not reporting all sales revenue in the income tax returns for the business and not in his tax returns. This scenario may help explain why the owner took five years to take action.

Thinking like a crook

John taught the auditing course in our accounting curriculum at the University of Colorado for many years. One of the first things he told the students is this: To be a good auditor, you have to _think like a crook_. Likewise, to understand internal controls, you have to think like a crook. Most people are honest and don't get out of bed each day thinking up schemes to steal money or to take advantage of their employers. But, then again, we know some people who do just that.

It helps to get into the mindset of a dishonest person. You have to ask, if I were a crook, how would I go about stealing from this business? For example, my grandson worked for a local Subway store that allowed eight different employees access to the cash register during the day. At the end of one day, the owner found that cash was short $300. Well, the owner shouldn't have been surprised. (He deducted an equal amount from every employee's payroll check to make up the loss, which probably wasn't legal.)

Looking at a study on business fraud

A fraud survey by the Big Four CPA firm KPMG in 2003 found the following types of fraud by the businesses surveyed in the study:

- Diversion of sales
- Duplicate billings
- Extortion
- False invoices and phantom vendors
- Inventory theft
- Kickbacks and conflicts of interest
- Loan fraud
- Theft of intellectual property

The main advice offered in publications on business fraud is to put into place and to vigilantly enforce preventive controls. The publications have considerably less advice to offer regarding what course of action managers should take once an instance of fraud is discovered, other than to say that the manager should plug the hole that allowed the fraud to happen. The KPMG Fraud Survey found that the companies in its survey (mainly larger businesses) took the following actions:

✓ Began an investigation

✓ Immediately dismissed employees who committed fraud

✓ Sought legal action

✓ Notified a government regulatory agency or law enforcement.

Presenting Internal Control Guideposts for Small Business Managers

A small business has a large repertoire of internal controls to choose from. We remind you that this book is directed to small business managers, not to accountants. Therefore, we don't delve into the details of internal accounting controls. Rather, we offer general guideposts for managing internal controls that apply to most small businesses.

Identify high-risk areas

Strong and tight controls are needed in high-risk areas. Managers should identify which areas of the business are the most vulnerable to fraud and theft. The most likely fraud points in a business usually include the following areas (some businesses have other high-risk areas, of course):

✓ Cash receipts and disbursements

✓ Payroll (including workers' compensation insurance fraud)

✓ Customer credit and collections, and writing off bad debts

✓ Purchasing and storage of inventory

Without doubt, cash collections and cash disbursements are the highest risk areas for most businesses. The small business should make sure that all checks mailed to the business and cash collected at the point of sale is recorded in its cash account. For this reason, many small business owners/managers open their mail each day and count the money in their cash registers at the end of each day. They make deposits in their bank accounts themselves. You may or not have time to take this action. If you don't, it's best to have someone other than your Controller take on this responsibility — someone who does not have access to the cash register.

The person opening the mail that includes cash collections from customers and the person counting money in cash registers should not be the accountant who records the entries in your cash account. Assign someone other than an accountant (or bookkeeper) the responsibility for opening the mail and counting cash in the sales registers.

On the other hand, the accountant is generally given the responsibility for preparing the required forms and paperwork that are presented to managers for payment approval. But the accountant should not be given the authority to sign checks, and someone other than the accountant should mail checks. You can't be too careful about cash collections and disbursements.

Consider legal considerations

Pay careful attention to the legal aspects of internal controls and enforcing the controls. For example, controls shouldn't violate the privacy rights of employees or customers. Needless to say, a business should be very careful in making accusations against an employee suspected of fraud.

At the other extreme, the absence of basic controls possibly can expose a manager to legal responsibility on grounds of reckless disregard for protecting the company's assets. A legal opinion may be needed on your internal controls, just to be safe.

Separate the duties of employees with an eye on internal control

Where practical, two or more employees should be involved in the authorization, documentation, execution, and recording of transactions — especially in the high-risk areas. The idea behind this *separation of duties* is to force collusion of two or more persons to carry out and conceal a fraud.

For example, two or more signatures should be required on checks over a certain amount. For another example, the employee preparing the receiving reports for goods and materials delivered to the company should not have any authority for issuing a purchase order and should not make the accounting entries for purchases. Instead of the concentration of duties in the hands of one person, duties should be divided among two or more employees, even if some loss of efficiency occurs.

Make surprise audits and inspections

Make use of surprise counts, inspections, and reconciliations that employees can't anticipate or plan for. Of course, the persons doing these surprise audits should be independent of the employees who have responsibility for complying with the internal controls.

For example, a surprise count and inspection of products held in inventory may reveal missing products, unrecorded breakage and damage, products stored in the wrong locations, mislabeled products, or other problems. Such problems tend to get overlooked by busy employees. More important, the inventory errors may be evidence of fraud or theft. Many of these errors should be recorded as inventory losses, but may not be found out unless you order surprise audits. It may look sneaky, but surprise audits and inspections are very useful.

Encourage whistle blowing

Encourage ell employees to report suspicions of fraud by anyone in the business (which has to be done anonymously, in most situations). Admittedly, this tactic is tricky. You're asking people to be whistleblowers. Employees may not trust management; they may fear that they will face retaliation instead of being rewarded for revealing fraud. Employees generally don't like being spies on each other, but on the other hand, they want the business to take action against any employees who are committing fraud.

Employees will not blow the whistle unless they're convinced that they'll remain anonymous and unidentified. So, you must come up with some way to make sure that a report of suspicious activity can't be traced to its source. One possibility is to use a third party who your employees trust. The third party would pass along the message and provide a barrier to anyone's attempt to identify the whistleblower.

Leave audit trails

Insist that good audit trails be created for all transactions. The documentation and recording of transactions should leave a clear path that can be followed back to source documents. Supporting documents should be organized in good order and should be retained for a reasonable period of time. The IRS publishes recommended guidelines for records retention, which are a good point of reference for a business; have your accountant go to www.irs.gov/formspubs. In particular, your accountant should look in Publication 583, *Starting a Business and Keeping Records.*

Limit access to accounting records and end-of-year entries

Access to all accounting records should be strictly limited to accounting personnel, and no one other than the accounting staff should be allowed to make entries or changes in the accounting records of the business. Also, managers are well advised to keep a close eye on end-of-year accounting entries to close the books for the period. Managers provide critical information for these entries, which may have a large effect on the amount of profit recorded for the period. (Providing the information to their accountants for these entries provides the managers with the opportunity to massage the financial statement numbers, which Chapter 2 explains.)

Perform new employee background checks

Thorough background checks should be made on all employee applicants, especially those that will handle money and work in the high-risk fraud areas of the business. Letters of reference from previous employers may not be enough. A business may have to consider more extensive background and character checks when hiring managers. Studies have found that many applicants falsify their resumes and list college degrees that they, in fact, have not earned. Databases are available to check on a person's credit history, and his or her driving record, criminal record, workers' compensation insurance claims, and life insurance rejection record. The problem is locating the various databases, judging how reliable and up-to-date they are, and knowing how to interpret the information in the database. In most cases, you probably should consider hiring a private firm, such as a private investigator, that specializes in background checks on job applicants.

Order periodic audits of your internal controls

Consider having an independent assessment done on your internal controls, by a CPA or other professional fraud specialist. This audit may reveal that critical controls are missing or, conversely, that you're wasting money on ineffectual controls. If your business has an annual financial statement audit, the CPA evaluates and tests your business's internal controls. But, you may need a more extensive and critical evaluation of your internal controls that looks beyond just the accounting oriented controls.

Do regular appraisals of key assets

You should schedule regular checkups of your business's key assets — receivables, inventory, and fixed assets. Over time, these assets develop problems that aren't dealt with in the bustle and day-to-day pressures on managers and other employees. Receivables may include seriously past due balances, but these customers' credit may not yet have been suspended, so business would be throwing good money after bad. Some products in inventory may not have had a sale in months. Some items in fixed assets may have been abandoned or sold off for scrap value, yet the assets are still on the books and are being depreciated.

Discuss computer controls with your chief accountant (Controller)

Computer hardware and software controls are extremely important, but most managers don't have the time or expertise to get into this area of internal controls. Obviously, you should use passwords and firewalls, and managers know about the possibility of hackers breaking into their computers, as well as the damage that viruses can cause. Every business has to adopt internal controls over e-mail, downloading attachments, updating software, and so on.

There is one good piece of news. Small business accounting software packages today generally have strong security features — but you can't be too careful.

Don't believe that you're too small for effective internal controls

The lament of many small business owners/managers is, "We're too small for internal controls." This complaint isn't true. Even a relatively small business can enforce certain internal controls that are very effective. Among these are the following:

✔ **The owner/manager should sign all checks, including payroll checks.** This practice forces the owner/manager to keep a close watch on the expenditures of the business. Under no conditions should an accountant, a bookkeeper, or the Controller of the business be given check-signing authority. This person can easily conceal fraud if he or she has check-writing authority.

✔ **In high-risk areas (generally cash receipts and disbursements, receivables, and inventory), require that employees working in these operating areas take vacations.** Furthermore, make sure that another employee carries out their duties while there're on vacation. By doing the same job, the fill-in employee serves as a check on whether the regular employee is doing things correctly and according to the rules.

✔ **Although separation of duties on a full-time basis may not be practical, consider the job-sharing approach.** In *job sharing,* two or more employees are regularly assigned to one area of the business on alternate weeks or some other schedule. Each employee acts as a check on the other so that both use established methods and procedures. When a second employee shares the job, embezzlement is more difficult to conceal, unless the two persons collude.

✔ **Without violating their privacy, keep watch on the lifestyles of your employees.** If your bookkeeper buys a new Mercedes every year and frequently is off to Monte Carlo, you may ask where the money is coming from. You know the salaries of your employees, so you should be able to estimate what sort of lifestyles they can afford.

Talk with other small business managers about internal controls

Many businesses, especially smaller companies, adopt the policy that some amount of fraud and theft simply has to be absorbed as a cost of doing business, and that it's not worth the time and cost of enforcing internal controls. This sort of attitude reflects the fact that business, by its very nature, is a risky venture. Despite taking precautions, you can't protect against every risk a business faces. On the other hand, a business invites trouble and becomes an attractive target if it doesn't have basic internal controls.

It's very difficult to estimate how many instances of fraud are prevented by the internal controls used by a business, and the damage that would have been done by the frauds. Where do managers look for information about fraud, then? Well, for one thing, they read articles in newspapers about frauds. Also, managers trade information with business associates. Business trade associations provide information about frauds in the industry. At regional and national meetings, managers swap stories about fraud.

Learn from fraud cases that come to your attention

We read about cases of fraud all the time. One thing never ceases to amaze us. You wouldn't think the perpetrators of some frauds could have gotten away with the fraud so long, or have stolen such a large amount without being noticed. We remember newspaper stories years ago reporting that a long-time, trusted bookkeeper had stolen virtually half the assets of a small bank in the Midwest. As we recall, this scenario happened to more than one bank as a matter of fact. The bookkeeper realized that many of the bank's savings accounts by older depositors were inactive, and the bookkeeper also knew the bank officers never took a close look at these accounts.

So, the bookkeeper withdrew money from these savings accounts, but sent monthly statements to the depositors that reported their original balances. Because the bookkeeper prepared the depositor statements, it was easy to falsify the balances. The simple internal control of separating the duty of preparing depositor statements from the duty of recording deposits and withdrawals in the accounts would have prevented the fraud (unless the two employees collude). Of course, the bank's officers should have been held accountable for not keeping a close eye of inactive savings accounts. They should have recognized that the inactive accounts are at higher risk for embezzlement than active accounts.

As John recalls, the owner of one of the inactive savings accounts with a large balance died, and the executor of that person's estate wanted to distribute the money in the savings account to the heirs. This request caused the bank to take a closer look at the savings account balance, which in turn revealed the missing money. Most fraud schemes aren't foolproof. Even carefully crafted embezzlement schemes can't anticipate every eventuality. Many fraud schemes collapse from their own weight as the fraud gets bigger and bigger over time.

Keep in mind the costs and limits of internal controls

Internal controls aren't free. Internal controls take time and money to design, install, and use. It's difficult to measure or estimate the costs of an internal control, or of a related group of related internal controls in one area of the business, such as purchasing, cash collections, payroll, or customer credit. Well, if you buy fidelity insurance on certain employees, you know the cost of the premiums, of course. The employee(s) covered by a fidelity insurance policy are said to be *bonded*. A *fidelity insurance policy* reimburses a business (up to the limits of the policy) for a loss due to embezzlement or other type of fraud against the business by an employee. One reason for buying fidelity insurance is that the insurance company (called the underwriter) does a thorough background check on the employee(s) being insured.

Furthermore, some internal controls can have serious side effects. Customers may resent certain internal controls, such as checking backpacks before entering a store, and take their business elsewhere. Employees may deeply resent entry and exit searches, which may contribute to low morale.

Internal accounting controls are not 100-percent foolproof. A disturbing amount of fraud still slips through these preventive measures. How are these frauds found out? The 2003 fraud study by KPMG reports that common ways for uncovering frauds include the following:

- ✔ Internal controls
- ✔ Internal audits
- ✔ Notification by an employee
- ✔ Accident
- ✔ Anonymous tip
- ✔ Notification by customer
- ✔ Notification by regulatory or law enforcement agency
- ✔ Notification by vendor
- ✔ External audit

Small businesses don't have internal auditors. But the other ways of finding out about fraud apply to small, as well as big, businesses. Sometimes the guilty party simply makes a dumb mistake. Our favorite story along this line is the case of the office manager who set up a bogus office-supplies store and then sent bills to the business for non-existent purchases of office supplies. He kept the purchases to fairly small amounts, so as not to attract the attention of anyone. The office manager approved these bills and forwarded them to the accountant who prepared the paperwork that was sent to the manager for payment approval. This strategy worked like a charm for several years. The office manager had the checks sent to his home address, which would have worked because no one in the business thought to check the address of the office-supplies vendor in the yellow pages. But then the office manager made a stupid mistake. He sold his house to a fellow employee and forgot to change the address of his bogus office-supplies vendor. The next check came to his old home address. Fortunately, the new homeowner thought it was suspicious and notified the manager of the business. Who knows how long this ruse might have gone on if the office manager had not sold his house to a fellow employee?

One test of a good internal control is that it will quickly detect a fraud if it fails to prevent it. Of course, finding out about fraud after it has already occurred is like closing the barn door after the horse has escaped. Still, it's very important to discover what fraud has happened and record the loss. As a matter of fact, the purpose of internal controls is to make concealment of fraud as difficult as possible. The logic is to send a clear message to potential fraudsters: You may be able to steal, but you will be found out in quick order.

In some cases, internal controls are established by a small business, but they're not carried out contentiously, or internal control procedures are done in a perfunctory manner. In theory, managers should not tolerate such a lackadaisical attitude toward internal controls by employees. A manager may intervene and override an internal control, which may set a very poor example for employees. In fact, overriding an established internal control may be evidence of fraud by the manager.

Understand the psychology of fraudsters

An easy and quick answer to why people commit fraud is for the money. However, this answer doesn't always get to the root causes why people commit fraud. How do they rationalize stealing money? Do they not think it's stealing? Do they need the money that bad? Don't they see the risks of getting caught? Don't they see the shame and dishonor getting caught will bring down on their family and their good name?

Well, for one thing, many people seem to think that business is a fair target because businesses rip them off every day. Or, they may do it to get back at the owner of a business. John was passing through the Omaha airport a few years ago to attend his father's funeral in Iowa. He was waiting for his oldest son (not the coauthor on this book) to fly into the airport so that we could travel together to the funeral. He went into the bookstore in the airport. (He wanted to know whether the bookstore had any of his books on the shelves.) It was a slow day, so the clerk struck up a conversation with him and asked what he did. John told him he was a professor of accounting, and that he had written books on accounting and financial management. Well, they got to talking, and he told John that he had served time in the state penitentiary for embezzlement. He was quite willing to talk about this experience, which is unusual.

He told me that he had been the accountant for a business. He said that the owner of the business was arrogant and treated him with contempt. So, to get even (as he put it) and to prove that he could do it, he embezzled $300,000 over a period of years. However, he was caught and convicted and served hard time in prison. He didn't go into details regarding how he was caught. Ironically, he had just returned from being a guest speaker at a national convention of forensic accountants and fraud specialists. (He showed me the permission letter signed by his parole officer to travel to Los Angeles for his talk.) John thinks he did it for the money. (He suspected he had a drug habit.) But the other factors he mentioned probably motivated his fraud. Perhaps just the thrill and excitement of doing it was a factor. Who knows?

How do people that commit fraud rationalize or justify their actions in their minds? Fraud usually involves a variety of financial, personal, emotional, and other factors that can push even the most honest, hard-working person over the limit. Fraud driven by the need to survive probably is more commonplace and represents a much greater risk to the average business than fraud driven by greed alone. For example, we know of cases where a business owner went way over the line. The business owner viewed his company as a part of his family. The owner was willing do anything to ensure the survival of the business, which would be his legacy to his family.

Businesses should know that its employees and managers will sometimes have problems paying their bills on time, to say nothing about all the other financial pressures caused by divorce, health problems, medical emergencies, college-bound kids, drug addiction, and on and on. You can make a good argument that business is responsible for have good internal controls that prevent its employees and managers from committing fraud. Indeed, you can make a good case that a business has a social responsibility for exercising good internal controls.

Insist on internal control information with your accounting reports

All too often we have found that small managers do not ask their accountants to include internal control information with their regular P&L and other financial reports. If inventory shrinkage is a problem in your business, for example, insist on regular reports on inventory shrinkage every period. Don't let your Controller bury this information out of sight in your P&L. Suppose that your business makes a lot of cash sales. You should get information on abnormal discrepancies between daily sales and the cash counts at the end of each day.

The type of internal control information you need depends on the particular characteristics of your business. For example, sales returns may be a significant factor in a retail clothing business. So, sales return information should be in your P&L reports. For auto dealers, in contrast, sales returns aren't a problem. They're more concerned with warranty work done after the sale.

You should sit down with your Controller and explain the types of internal control information you want in your regular accounting and flash reports. This two-way discussion can give your Controller a better understanding of the business and how you operate. Encourage your Controller to make suggestions about possible internal control problems. Maybe you should send your Controller to a workshop on fraud in the small business.

Make yourself the centerpiece internal control

The starting and ending point in effective internal controls is you — the owner/manager of the small business. It begins and ends with you. We don't mean that you have to do every internal control procedure every day. Rather, we mean the attitude and seriousness that you exhibit about internal controls — especially to your employees, your vendors, your customers, and to everyone else with which you have business relationships.

In the accounting articles and books on big business internal controls, one point is mentioned over and over — the *tone at the top*. Tone at the top means that the business's top-level managers take internal controls seriously and put into practice what they preach.

Don't pay lip service to internal controls. Your employees quickly figure out whether or not you take internal controls seriously.

Remember that your P&L and balance sheet may not recognize unrecorded losses from fraud and theft

Finally, keep in mind that there's a chance that your business has suffered a loss from undiscovered fraud, which therefore hasn't been recorded and reported in your P&L and balance sheet. The threat of an unrecorded loss from fraud hangs over your financial statements. Good internal controls reduce this threat to a minimum. You don't want to suffer losses from fraud and theft, of course. But when fraud has happened, you need to record the loss as soon as possible. Otherwise, your financial statements are misleading.

Chapter 6

Scrutinizing Your Costs

．．

In This Chapter

▶ Getting the right perspective on controlling costs

▶ Analyzing the costs in your P&L line by line

▶ Paying particular attention to cost of goods sold and depreciation expense

▶ Comparing your P&L with your balance sheet

▶ Focusing on profit centers

．．

*W*hat's the first thing that comes to mind when we say *cost control?* We bet you think of cutting costs, don't you? Well, it may come as a surprise, but slashing costs is not the main theme of this chapter. Cost control is just one element in the larger playing field of profit management. The best, or optimal, cost is not always the lowest cost.

A knee-jerk reaction is that costs should be lower. Don't rush to judgment. In some situations, increasing costs may be the best path to increasing profits. It's like coaching sports: You have to play both defense and offense. You can't play on just one side of the game. Making sales is the offense side of business; defense is keeping the costs of making sales and operating the business less than sales revenue.

Getting in the Right Frame of Mind

Of course, you shouldn't waste money on excessive or unnecessary costs. If possible, you should definitely save a buck here and there on expenses. There's no argument on this point. In our experience, small business owners/managers don't particularly need tutorials on shaving costs. Rather, they need to stand back a little and rethink the nature of costs and realize that costs are pathways to profit. If you had no costs, you'd have no revenue and no profit. You need costs to make profit. You have to spend money to make money.

The crucial test of a cost is whether it contributes to generating revenue. If a cost has no value whatsoever in helping a business bring in revenue, then it's truly money down the rat hole. The key management question about costs is whether the amounts of the costs are in alignment with the amount of revenue the business is generating. A business manager should ask: Are my expenses the appropriate amounts for the revenue of my business?

Getting Down to Business

Controlling costs requires that you evaluate your costs relative to your sales revenue. Suppose that your business's salaries and wages expense for the year is $425,000. Is this cost too high? There's no way in the world you can answer this question, except by comparing the cost against your sales revenue for the year. The same goes for all your expenses.

In an ideal world, your customers are willing to pay whatever prices you charge them. You could simply pass along your costs in sales prices and still earn a profit. Your costs would be under control no matter how high your costs might be. Because you earn a profit, your costs are under control and need no further attention.

The real world is very different, of course. But this ideal world teaches a lesson. Your costs are out of control when you can't set sales prices high enough to recover your costs and make a profit.

It's hardly news to you that small businesses face price resistance from their customers. Customers are sensitive to sales prices and changes in sales prices for the products and services sold by small businesses. In setting sales prices, you have to determine the maximum price your customers will accept before turning to lower price alternatives, or not buying at all. If the price resistance point is $125 for a product, you have to figure out how to keep your costs below $125 per unit. In other words, you have to exercise cost control.

Putting cost control it its proper context

Cost control is part of the larger management function of revenue/cost/profit analysis. So, the best place to focus is your P&L report. (Chapter 2 explains the P&L report.) This profit performance statement summarizes your sales revenue based on the sales prices in effect during the year and your expenses for the year based on the amounts recorded for the expenses. (There are some issues regarding the accounting methods for recording certain expenses, which we discuss later in the chapter — see the section "Selecting a cost of goods sold expense method.")

Say that you're the principal manager of a business. The business is a pass-through income tax entity, which means that it doesn't pay income tax itself but passes its taxable income through to its shareholders, who then include their shares of the business's annual taxable income in their personal income tax returns for the year.

Figure 6-1 presents the P&L report of your business for the year just ended and includes the prior year for comparison (which is standard practice). This P&L report includes the percents of expenses to sales revenue. It also breaks out and *facilities expense* — the cost of the space used by the business — and reports it on a separate line.

Facilities expense includes expenditures for leases, building utilities, real estate taxes, and insurance on your premises. Depreciation isn't included in facilities expense; depreciation is an unusual expense and it's best to leave it in an expense by itself (see Figure 6-1).

In this case, the business moved out of the red zone (loss) in 2007 into the black zone (profit) in 2008 – see Figure 6-1. Making a profit, however, doesn't necessarily mean that your costs are under control. Dealing with the issue of cost control requires closer management analysis.

Your Business Name
P&L Report
For Years Ended December 31

	2007 % of Sales Revenue	2007	2008 % of Sales Revenue	2008	Change Over 2007 Amount	Change Over 2007 %
Sales revenue		$2,286,500		$2,920,562	$634,062	27.7%
Cost of goods sold expense	61.7%	$1,411,605	58.0%	$1,693,926	$282,321	20.0%
Gross margin	38.3%	$874,895	42.0%	$1,226,636	$351,741	40.2%
Operating expenses:						
Salaries, wages, commissions and benefits	27.3%	$624,590	22.7%	$662,400	$37,810	6.1%
Advertising and sales promotion	6.9%	$158,900	6.6%	$192,550	$33,650	21.2%
Depreciation	4.1%	$93,250	3.0%	$88,950	($4,300)	–4.6%
Facilities expense	3.9%	$89,545	3.2%	$94,230	$4,685	5.2%
Other expenses	1.2%	$27,255	1.5%	$42,849	$15,594	57.2%
Total operating expenses	43.5%	$993,540	37.0%	$1,080,979	$87,439	8.8%
Operating profit (loss)	–5.2%	($118,645)	5.0%	$145,657	$264,302	
Interest expense	2.1%	$47,625	1.7%	$50,006	$2,381	5.0%
Net income (loss)	–7.3%	($166,270)	3.3%	$95,651	$261,921	

Figure 6-1: Your P&L report for cost control analysis.

You can attack cost control on three levels:

✔ Your *business as a whole* in its entirety

✔ The separate *profit centers* of your business

✔ Your specific costs item by item

Figure 6-1 is the P&L for your business as a whole. At this level, you look at the forest and not the trees. It's helpful to divide your business into separate parts called *profit centers*. Basically, a profit center is an identifiable, separate stream of revenue to a business. At this level, you examine clusters or stands of trees that make up different parts of the forest.

For example, Starbucks sells coffee, coffee beans, cup ware products, food, and other products. Each is a separate profit center. For that matter, each Starbucks store is a separate profit center, so you have profit centers within profit centers. Last, you can drill down to particular, individual costs. At this level, you look at specific trees in the forest.

Beginning with sales revenue change

You increased sales $634,062 in 2008 — see Figure 6-1. This is good news for profit, but only if costs don't increase more than sales revenue, of course. For revenue/cost/profit analysis, it's extremely useful to know how much of your sales revenue increase is due to change in volume (total quantity sold) versus changes in sales prices. Unfortunately, measuring sales volume can be a problem.

An auto dealer can keep track of the number of vehicles sold during the year. A movie theater can count the number of tickets sold during the year, and a brewpub can keep track of the number of barrels of beer sold during the year. On the other hand, many small businesses sell a very large number of different products and services. And we mean a large number! A local hardware store in Boulder says it sells more than 100,000 different items, which we don't doubt. A clothing retailer may sell several thousand different items.

Exactly how your business should keep track of sales volume depends on how many different products you sell and how practical it is to compile sales volume information in your accounting system. In many situations, a small business can't do more than keep count of its sales transactions — number of sales rung up on cash registers, number of invoices sent to customers, customer traffic count, or something equivalent. If nothing else, you should make a rough count of the number of sales you make during the year.

In the example portrayed in Figure 6-1, you increase sales volume 20 percent in 2008 over the prior year, which is pretty good by any standard. You made much better use of the sales capacity provided by your workforce and facilities in 2008. You increased sales per employee and per square foot in 2008 — see the later sections "Analyzing employee cost" and "Looking at facilities expense." The 20 percent sales volume increase is very important in analyzing your costs in 2008. A key question is whether changes in your costs are consistent with the sales volume increase.

The example portrayed in Figure 6-1 is for a situation in which product costs remain the same in both years. Therefore, cost of goods sold expense increases exactly 20 percent in 2008 because sales volume increases 20 percent over the previous year. (Of course, product costs fluctuate from year to year in most cases.)

Sales revenue, in contrast, increases more than 20 percent because you were able to increases sales prices in 2008. In Figure 6-1, note that sales revenue increases more than the 20 percent sales volume increase. Ask your accountant to calculate the average sales price increase. In the example, your sales prices in 2008 are 7.7 percent higher than the previous year. (Trust us on this calculation; we're accountants.)

You did not increase sales prices exactly 7.7 percent on every product you sold; this situation would be quite unusual. The 7.7 percent sales price increase is an average over all the products you sold. You should know the reasons for and causes of the average sales price increase. The higher average sales price may be due to shift in your sales mix toward higher priced products. (Sales mix refers to the relative proportions that each source of sales contributes to total sales revenue.) Or, perhaps your sales mix remained constant and you bumped up prices on most products.

In any case, what's the bottom line (or should we say the top line because we're talking about sales revenue)? In 2008, you had $634,062 additional sales revenue to work with compared with the prior year. More than half of the incremental revenue is offset by increases in costs. But $261,921 of the additional revenue ended up in profit. How do you like that? More than 41 percent of your additional revenue goes toward profit (see Figure 6-1 for data):

> $261,921 profit increase ÷ $634,062 additional sales revenue = 41.3% profit from additional revenue

This scenario may seem almost too good to be true. Well, you should analyze what happened to your costs at the higher sales level to fully understand this profit boost. Could the same thing happen next year if you increase sales revenue again? Perhaps, but maybe not.

Focusing on cost of goods sold and gross margin

For businesses that sell products, the first expense deducted from sales revenue is *cost of goods sold*. (You could argue that it should be called cost of products sold, but you don't see this term in P&L statements.) As we explain in Chapter 2, this expense is deducted from sales revenue to determine *gross margin* (see Figure 6-1). Gross margin is also called *gross profit;* it's profit before any other expense is deducted from sales revenue. Cost of goods sold is a *direct variable* expense, which means it's directly matched against revenue and varies with sales volume.

This expense may appear straightforward, but it's more entangled than you may suspect. It's anything but simple and uncomplicated. In fact, a later section ("Looking into Cost of Goods Sold Expense") in the chapter explains this expense in more detail. For the moment, we step around these issues and focus on the basic behavior of the expense. In the example in Figure 6-1, your business's product costs are the same as last year. Of course, in most situations, product costs don't remain constant very long. But it makes for a much cleaner analysis to keep product costs constant at this point in the discussion.

The 20 percent jump in sales volume increases your cost of goods sold expense 20 percent — see Figure 6-1 again. Pay special attention to the change in your gross margin ratio on sales. Chapter 2 explains that your basic sales pricing strategy is to mark up product cost to earn 45 percent gross margin on sales. For example, if a product cost is $55, you aim to sell it for $100 to yield $45 gross margin. However, your gross margin is only 42.0 percent in 2008. You gave several customers discounts from list prices. But you did improve your average gross margin ratio over last year, which brings up a very important point.

How is it that your sales volume increases 20.0 percent and your sales prices increase 7.7 percent in 2008, but your gross margin increases 40.2 percent? The increase in gross margin seems too high relative to the percent increases in sales volume and sales prices, doesn't it? What's going on? Figure 6-2 presents the analysis of how much of the $351,741 gross margin gain is attributable to higher sale prices and how much to the higher sales volume.

Figure 6-2:	**2007**		**Change in 2008**		
Analyzing your gross margin increase.	$2,286,500	Sales revenue ×	7.7%	Sales price increase =	$176,762
	$874,895	Gross margin ×	20.0%	Sales volume increase =	$174,979
				Total increase in gross margin =	$351,741

In Figure 6-2, note that the 7.7 percent increase in sales prices causes more gross margin increase than the 20.0 percent sales volume increase. This is because of the *big base effect;* the smaller sales prices percent increase applies to a relatively large base (about $2.3 million) compared with the volume gain that is based on a much smaller amount (about $.9 million).

Suppose that you want to increase gross margin $100,000 next year. Assume that your 42.0 percent gross margin ratio on sales remains the same. If sales prices remain the same next year, then your sales volume would have to increase 8.15 percent:

> $100,000 gross margin increase goal ÷ $1,226,636 gross margin in 2008 = 8.15% sales volume increase

If your sales volume remains the same next year, then your sales prices on average would have to increase just 3.42 percent:

> $100,000 gross margin increase goal ÷ $2,920,562 sales revenue in 2008 = 3.42% sales price increase

In short, a 1 percent sales price increase has more profit impact than a 1 percent sales volume increase.

Analyzing employee cost

As the owner/manager of a small business, your job is to judge whether the ratio of each expense to sales revenue is acceptable. Is the expense reasonable in amount? Your salaries, wages, commissions, and benefits expense equals 22.7 percent of sales revenue in 2008 (see Figure 6-1). In other words, your employee cost absorbs $22.70 of every $100.00 of sales revenue. This expense ratio is lower than it was last year, which is good, of course. But the fundamental question is whether it should be an even smaller percent of sales. This question strikes at the essence of cost control. It's not an easy question to answer. But, as they say, that's why you earn the big bucks — to answer such questions.

It's tempting to think first of reducing every cost of doing business. It would have been better if your employee cost had been lower — or would it? Could you have gotten by with one less employee? One less employee may have reduced your sales capacity and prevented the increase in sales revenue. In the example, you have ten full-time employees on the payroll both years. Chapter 2 explains that for your line of business, the benchmark is $300,000 annual sales per employee. In 2008, your sales per employee is $292,056 (see Figure 6-1 for sales revenue):

> $2,920,562 annual sales revenue ÷ 10 employees = $292,056 sales revenue per employee

A speech to students on business success

The methods for cutting costs can be ruthless, or at least seem to be — which reminds me of a true story. At the time, John was a junior professor at Berkeley. One of his duties was to serve as the faculty sponsor of the local chapter of the National Honor Society of accounting majors.

At the spring initiation banquet, the custom was to invite a distinguished speaker. We invited a well-known CPA and financial executive who had just retired. He was introduced to the audience, which included the students and

their proud mothers and fathers on this gala occasion.

John will never forget the speaker's opening comment after saying he appreciated the nice introduction. He said that to succeed in business, you had to be a *ruthless sob*. (He didn't say sob, he used the actual term.) Both his comment and his language came as a shock to the students, their parents, and John. But the more John reflected on it, the more he thinks the speaker did the right thing — give the students a dose of reality that they didn't see in their textbooks.

Summing up, your employee cost looks reasonable for 2008, assuming that your sales per employee benchmark is correct. This doesn't mean that you couldn't have squeezed some dollars out of this expense during the year. Maybe you could have furloughed employees during the slow time of year. Maybe you could have fired one of your higher paid employees and replaced him or her with a person willing to work for a lower salary. Maybe you could have cut corners and not have paid overtime rates for some of the hours worked during the busy season. Maybe you could have cut health-care and vacations benefits during the year.

Business managers get paid to make tough and sometimes ruthless decisions. (See the sidebar "A speech to students on business success" for a story that illustrates this point.) This is especially true in the area of cost control. If your sales prices don't support the level of your costs, what are your options? You can try to get more sales out of your costs. In fact, you did just this with employee costs in 2008 compared with 2007 — see Figure 6-1 again. Your sales revenue per employee increased significantly in 2008. But you may be at the end of the line on this course of action. You may have to hire an additional employee or two if you plan to increase sales next year.

Analyzing advertising and sales promotion costs

The total of your advertising and sales promotion costs in 2008 is just under 7 percent of sales revenue, which is about the same it was in 2007 (see Figure 6-1 again). As you probably have observed, many retail businesses depend heavily on advertising. Others don't do more than put a sign on the building and rely on word of mouth. This book isn't on marketing, advertising, and sales promotion — which ought to be rather obvious. (You can refer to *Small Business Marketing For Dummies*, 2nd Edition, by Barbara Findlay Schenck.) You can advertise and promote sales a thousand different ways. Maybe you give away free calendars. You can put an insertion in the yellow pages. You can place ads in local newspapers. Maybe you make a donation to your local public radio or television station. Or perhaps you place ads on outdoor billboards or bus benches.

Like other costs of doing business, you need a benchmark or reference point for evaluating advertising and sales promotion costs. For the business example, we set the ratio at around 7 percent of annual sales. This ratio is in the typical range of the advertising and sales promotion expense of many small businesses. Of course, your business may be different. Retail furniture stores, for example, spend a lot more than 7 percent of sales revenue on advertising. Locally owned office-supply stores, in contrast, spend far less on advertising.

Although we're not marketing experts, it's fairly clear that you should keep watch on which particular advertisements and sales promotions campaigns work best and have the most impact on sales. The trick is to find out which ads or promotions that your customers respond to and which they don't. Keeping the name of your business on the customer's mind is a high marketing priority of most businesses, although measuring how your name recognition actually affects customers' purchases is difficult to track. Nevertheless, you should develop some measure or test of how your marketing expenses contribute to sales.

Of course, you can keep an eye on your competitors, but they aren't likely to tell you which sales promotion techniques are the most effective. You increased your advertising and sales promotion costs more than $30,000 in 2008, which is more than 20 percent over last year (see Figure 6-1). Sales revenue went up by an even larger percent, so the ratio of the expense to sales revenue actually decreased. Nevertheless, you should determine exactly what the extra money was spent on. Perhaps you bought more newspaper ads and doubled the number of flyers distributed during the year.

Appreciating depreciation expense

Depreciation expense is the cost of owning fixed assets. The term *fixed assets* includes land and buildings, machinery and equipment, furniture and fixtures, vehicles and forklift trucks, tools, and computers. These long-term operating resources aren't held for sale; they're used in the day-to-day operations of the business. Except for land, the cost of these long-term operating resources is allocated over the estimated useful lives of the assets. (Land is viewed as a property right that has perpetual life and usefulness, so its cost is not depreciated; the cost stays on the books until the land is disposed of.)

As a practical matter, the useful life estimates permitted in the federal income tax law are the touchstones used by most small businesses. Instead of predicting actual useful lives, businesses simply adopt the useful lives spelled out in the income tax law to depreciate their fixed assets. The useful life guidelines are available from the IRS; go to the IRS web site (www.irs.gov/publications). Probably the most useful booklet is Publication 946 (2005), *How To Depreciate Property*. Your Controller should know everything in this booklet.

You should understand the following points about the depreciation expense:

✔ The two basic methods for allocating the cost of a fixed asset over its useful life are the *straight-line method* (an equal amount every year) and an *accelerated method* by which more depreciation expense in recorded in the earlier years than in the later years; the straight-line method is used for buildings, and either method can be used for other classes of fixed assets.

✔ Businesses generally favor an accelerated depreciation method in order to reduce *taxable income* in the early years of owning fixed assets; but don't forget that taxable income will be higher in the later years when less depreciation is recorded.

✔ In recording depreciation expense, a business *does not set aside money* in a fund for the eventual replacement of its fixed assets restricted only for this purpose. (A business could invest money in a separate fund for this purpose, of course, but we've never seen one that does.)

✔ Recording depreciation expense *does not require a decrease to cash* or an increase in a liability that will be paid in cash at a later time; rather the fixed asset accounts of the business are written down according to a systematic method of allocating the original cost of each fixed asset over its estimated useful life. (Chapter 3 explains the cash-flow analysis of profit.)

✔ Even though the *market value of real estate* may appreciate over time, the cost of a building owned by the business is depreciated (generally over 39 years).

✔ The *eventual replacement costs* of most fixed assets will be higher than the original cost of the assets due to inflation; depreciation expense is based on original cost not on the estimated future replacement cost.

✔ The *estimated useful lives of fixed assets for depreciation are shorter* than realistic expectations of their actual productive lives to the business; therefore, fixed assets are depreciated too quickly, and the book values of the assets in the balance sheet (original cost less accumulated depreciation to day) are too low.

✔ Depreciation expense is a real cost of doing business because fixed assets wear out or otherwise lose their usefulness to the business — although, a case can be made for not recording depreciation expense on a building whose market value is steadily rising. Generally accepted accounting principles require that the cost of all fixed assets (except land) must be depreciated.

We should mention in passing that one technique used in the fields of investment analysis and business valuation focuses on EBITDA, which equals earnings before interest, tax (income tax), depreciation, and amortization. *Amortization* is similar to depreciation. Amortization refers to the allocating the cost of *intangible* assets over their estimated useful lives to the business. By and large, small businesses do not have intangible assets, so we don't discuss this topic. Chapter 14 explores small business valuation.

One last point about depreciation expense: Note in Figure 6-1 that your depreciation expense is lower in 2008 than the prior year. Yet sales revenue and all other expenses are higher than the prior year. The drop in depreciation expense is an aberrant effect of accelerated depreciation; the amount of depreciation decreases year to year. You have a year-to-year built-in gain in profit from because depreciation expense drops year to year. The aggregate effect on depreciation expense for the year depends on the mix of newer and older fixed assets. The higher depreciation on newer fixed assets is balanced by the lower depreciation on older fixed assets. One advantage of the straight-line method is that the amount of depreciation expense on a fixed asset is constant year to year, so you don't get fluctuations in depreciation expense year to year that are caused by the depreciation method being used.

Request your Controller to explain the year-to-year change in depreciation expense in your annual P&L. In particular, ask your accountant whether a decrease in the depreciation expense is due to your fixed assets getting older, with the result that less depreciation is recorded by an accelerated depreciation method.

Looking at facilities expense

The P&L report presented in Figure 6-1 includes a separate line for facilities expense. In Chapter 2, we argue that you should definitely limit the number of expense lines in your P&L. But in our view, this particular expense deserves separate reporting. Basically, this expense is your cost of physical space — the square footage and shelter you need to carry on operations plus the costs directly associated with using the space. (You may prefer the term *occupancy expense* instead.)

Most of the specific costs making up facilities expense are *fixed commitments* for the year. Examples are lease payments, utilities, fire insurance on contents and the building (if owned), general liability insurance premiums, security guards, and so on. You could argue that depreciation on the building (if owned by the business) should be included in facilities expense. However, it's best to put depreciation in its own expense account.

In this example, your business uses 12,000 square feet of space, and you've determined that a good benchmark for your business is $300 annual sales per square foot. Accordingly, your space could support $3,600,000 annual sales. In 2008, your annual sales revenue is short of this reference point. Therefore, you presumably have space enough for sales growth next year. These benchmarks are no more than rough guideposts. Nevertheless, benchmarks are very useful. If your actual performance is way off base from a benchmark, you should determine the reason for the variance. Based on your own experience and in looking at your competitors, you should be able to come up with reasonably accurate benchmarks for sales per employee and sales per square foot of space.

In the business example portrayed in Figure 6-1, you use the same amount of space both years. In other words, you did not have to expand your square footage for the sales growth in 2008. The relatively modest increase in facilities expense (only 5.2 percent, as shown in Figure 6-1) is due to inflationary cost pressures. Sooner or later, however, continued sales growth will require expansion of your square footage. Indeed, you may have to relocate to get more space.

Looking over or looking into other expenses

In your P&L report (see Figure 6-1 again), the last expense line is the collection of residual costs that aren't included in another expense. A small business has a surprising number of miscellaneous costs — annual permits, parking meters, office supplies, postage and shipping, service club memberships, travel, bad debts, professional fees, toilet paper, signs, to name just a handful. A business keeps at least one account for miscellaneous expenses. You should draw the line on how large an amount can be recorded in this catchall expense account. For example, you may instruct your Controller that no outlay over $250 or $500 can be charged to this account; any expenditure over the amount has to have its own expense account.

The cost control question is whether it's worth your time to investigate these costs item by item. In 2008, these assorted costs represented only 1.5 percent of your annual sales revenue. Most of the costs, probably, are reasonable in amount – so, why spend your valuable time inspecting these costs in detail?

On the other hand, these costs increase $15,594 in 2008 (see Figure 6-1), and this amount is a relatively large percent of your profit for the year:

$15,594 increase in other expenses ÷ $95,651 net income for year = 16.3% of profit for year

If this were our business, we'd ask the accountant to list the two or three largest increases. You may see some surprises. Perhaps an increase is one-time event that will not repeat next year. You have to follow your instincts and your experience in deciding how deep to dive into analyzing these costs. If your employees know you never look into these costs, they may be tempted to use one of these expense accounts to conceal fraud. (Chapter 5 discusses internal controls against fraud.) So, it's generally best to do a quick survey of these costs, even if you don't spend a lot of time on them. It's better to give the impression that you're watching the costs like a hawk, even if you're not.

Running the numbers on interest expense

Interest expense is a financial cost — the cost of using debt for part of the total capital you use in operating the business. It's listed below the operating profit line in the P&L report (see Figure 6-1). Putting interest expense below the operating profit line is standard practice, for good reason. *Operating profit* (also called *operating earnings,* or *earnings before interest and income tax*) is the amount of profit you squeeze out of sales revenue before you consider how your business is financed (where you get your capital) and income tax.

Obviously, interest expense depends on the amount of debt you use and the interest rates on the debt. Figure 6-3 presents the balance sheets of your business at the end of the two most recent years. At the end of 2007, which is the start of 2008, you had $400,000 of interest bearing debt ($100,000 short-term and $300,000 long-term). Early in 2008, you increased your borrowing and ended the year with $600,000 debt ($200,000 short-term and $400,000 long-term). Based on the $600,000 debt level, your interest expense for the year is 8.3 percent.

Because you negotiated the terms of the loans to the business, you should know whether this interest rate is correct. By the way, the interest expense in your P&L may include other costs of borrowing such as loan origination fees and other special charges in addition to interest. If you have any question about what's included in interest expense, ask your Controller for clarification.

Your Business Name
Balance Sheet
At December 31

	2007	2008
Assets		
Cash	$347,779	$584,070
Accounts receivable	$136,235	$148,785
Inventory	$218,565	$250,670
Prepaid expenses	$65,230	$61,235
Total current assets	$767,809	$1,044,760
Property, plant and equipment	$774,600	$896,450
Accumulated depreciation	($167,485)	($256,435)
Cost less depreciation	$607,115	$640,015
Total assets	$1,374,924	$1,684,775
Liabilities and Owners' Equity		
Accounts payable	$286,450	$261,430
Accrued expenses payable	$67,345	$81,565
Short-term notes payable	$100,000	$200,000
Total current liabilities	$453,795	$542,995
Long-term notes payable	$300,000	$400,000
Owners' equity:		
Invested capital	$500,000	$525,000
Retained earnings	$121,129	$216,780
Total owners' equity	$621,129	$741,780
Total liabilities and owners' equity	$1,374,924	$1,684,775

Figure 6-3:
Presenting
your year-
end balance
sheets.

Comparing your P&L with your balance sheet

We highly recommend one last step in your revenue/cost/profit analysis: You should compare your P&L numbers with your balance sheet numbers. Basically, you should ask whether your sales and expenses for the year are in agreement with your assets and liabilities. Every business, based on its experience and its operating policies, falls into ruts as it were regarding the sizes of its assets and liabilities relative to its annual sales revenue and expenses. If one of these normal ratios is out of kilter, you should find out the reasons for the deviation from normal.

The ratios between assets and liabilities and their corresponding sales revenue and expense is a main theme of John's book, *How To Read A Financial Report*, 6th edition (Wiley). You may want to take a look at this book. In any case, the small business manager should definitely know the proper sizes of assets and liabilities relative to the sizes of the business's annual sales revenue and expenses.

Three critical tie-ins between the P&L and balance sheet are the following:

- *Accounts receivables/Sales revenue from sales on credit:* Your ending balance of accounts receivable (uncollected credit sales) should be consistent with your credit terms. So, if you give customers 30 days credit, then your ending balance should equal about one month of credit sales.

- *Inventory/Cost of goods sold expense:* Your ending inventory depends on the average time that products spend in your warehouse or on your retail shelves before being sold. So, if your inventory turns six times a year (meaning products sit in inventory about two months on average before being sold), your ending inventory should equal about two months of annual cost of goods sold.

- *Operating liabilities/Operating costs:* Your ending balances of accounts payable and accrued expenses payable should be consistent with your normal trade credit terms from vendors and suppliers and the time it takes to pay accrued expenses. So, if your average credit terms for purchases are 30 days, your ending accounts payable liability balance should equal about 30 days of purchases.

You should instruct your accountant to do these calculations and report these P&L/balance sheet ratios so that you can keep tabs on the sizes of your assets and liabilities.

A business can develop solvency problems. One reason is that the manager keeps a close watch on the P&L but ignores what was going on in the balance sheet. Assets and liabilities were getting out of hand, but the manager thought that everything was okay because the P&L looked good. We discuss solvency problems and cures in Chapter 4.

One additional purpose for comparing your P&L with your balance sheet is to evaluate your profit performance relative to the amount of capital you're using to make the profit. Your 2008 year-end balance sheet reports that your owners' equity is $741,780 (see Figure 6-3). This amount includes the capital the owners put in the business (invested capital), plus the earnings plowed back into the business (retained earnings). Theoretically, the owners could have invested this $741,780 somewhere else and earned a return on the investment. For 2008, your business earned 12.9 percent return on owners' equity:

$95,651 net income for 2008 ÷ $741,780 2008 year-end owners' equity = 12.9% return on owners' equity capital

Keep in mind that the business is a pass-through tax entity. So, the 12.9 percent return on capital is before income tax. Suppose that the average income tax bracket of the owners is 25 percent (it may very well be higher). Taking out 25 percent for income tax, the return on owners' equity is 9.7 percent. You have to decide whether this percentage is an adequate return on capital for the owners. And, don't forget that the business did not pay cash dividends during the year. All the profit for the year is retained; the owners did not see any cash in their hands from the profit.

Looking into Cost of Goods Sold Expense

Business managers have a tendency to take cost amounts reported by accountants for granted — as if the amount is the actual, true, and only cost. In contrast, business managers are pretty shrewd about dealing with other sources of information. When listening to complaints from employees, for example, business managers are generally good at reading between the lines and filling in some aspects that the employee is not revealing. And then there's the legendary response from a customer who hasn't paid on time: The check's in the mail. Business managers know better than to take this comment at face value. Likewise, you should be equally astute in working with the cost amounts reported for expenses.

Everyone agrees that there should be uniform accounting standards for financial reporting by businesses. Yet, the accounting profession hasn't reached agreement on the best method for recording certain expenses. We explain in the earlier section "Appreciating depreciation expense" that a business can choose between a straight-line and an accelerated method for recording depreciation expense. And, a business can choose between two or three different methods for recording cost of goods sold expense.

Selecting a cost of goods sold expense method

The cost of goods sold expense is the largest expense of businesses that sell products, typically more than 50 percent of the sales revenue from the goods sold. In the business example, cost of goods sold is 58 percent of sales revenue in the most recent year (refer to Figure 6-1). You would think that the accounting profession would have settled on one uniform method to record cost of goods sold expense. This isn't the case, however. Furthermore, the federal income tax law permits different cost of goods sold expense methods for determining annual taxable income. A business has to stay with the same method year after year (although a change is permitted in very unusual situations).

This book is directed to small business managers, not accountants. There's no reason for a small business manager to get into the details of the alternative cost of goods sold expense methods. Your time is too valuable. Like other issues that you deal with in running a small business, the basic question is What difference does it make? Generally, the method doesn't make a significant difference in your annual cost of goods sold expense — assuming that you don't change horses in the middle of the stream (in other words, that you keep with the same method year after year). Our advice is to instruct your Controller to give you a heads up if your accounting method causes an unusual, or abnormal impact, on cost of goods expense for the year.

Your cost of goods sold expense accounting method affects the *book value of inventory,* which is the amount reported in the balance sheet. Under the *first-in, first out* (FIFO) accounting method, the inventory amount is based on recent costs. For example, refer to the balance sheet in Figure 6-3. Inventory at year-end 2008 is reported at $250,670. Under the FIFO method, this amount reflects costs of products during two or three months ending with the balance sheet date. Instead of using FIFO or LIFO, a business can split the difference as it were and use the *average cost* method. The average cost accounting method reaches back a little further in time compared to the FIFO method; the cost of ending inventory is based on product costs from throughout of the year under the average cost method.

If you use the last-in, first-out (LIFO) accounting method the cost value of your year-end inventory balance could reach back many years, depending on how long your have been using this method and when you accumulated your inventory layers. For this reason, businesses that use the LIFO method disclose the current replacement cost of their ending inventories in a footnote to their financial statements to warn the reader that the balance sheet amount is substantially below the current cost of the products.

Which cost of goods sold expense method should you use, then? Our advice is to start by looking at your sales pricing policy. What do you do when a product cost goes up? Do you wait to clear out your existing stock of the product before you raise the sales price? If so, we recommend the first-in, first-out (FIFO) method, because this method keeps product costs in sync with sales prices. On the other hand, sales pricing is a complex process, and sales prices aren't handcuffed with product cost changes. To a large extent, your choice of accounting method for cost of goods sold expense depends on whether you prefer a conservative, higher cost method (generally LIFO) — or a liberal, lower cost method (generally FIFO).

Dealing with inventory shrinkage and inventory write downs

Deciding which cost of goods sold expense accounting method to use isn't the main concern of many small businesses that carry a sizable inventory of products awaiting sale. The more important issues to them are losses from *inventory shrinkage* and from *write downs of inventory* caused by products that they can't sell at normal prices. These problems are very serious for many small businesses.

Inventory shrinkage is caused by theft by customers and employees, damages caused by the handling, moving, and storing of products, physical deterioration of products over time, and errors in recording the inflow and outflow of products through the warehouse. A business needs to take a *physical inventory* to determine the amount of inventory shrinkage. A physical inventory refers to inspecting and counting all items in inventory, usually at the close of the fiscal year. This purpose is to discover shortages of inventory. The cost of the missing products is removed from the inventory asset account and charged to expense. This expense is painful to record because the business receives no sales revenue from these products. A certain amount of inventory shrinkage expense is considered to be a normal cost of doing business, which can't be avoided.

Also, at the close of the year, a business should do a *lower of cost or market test* on its ending inventory of products. Product costs are compared against the current replacement costs of the products and the current market (sales) prices of the products. This is a two-fold test of product costs. If replacement costs have dropped or if the products have lost sales value, your Controller should make a year-end adjusting entry to write down your ending inventory to a lower amount, which is below the original costs you paid for the products.

Recording inventory shrinkage expense caused by missing products is cut and dried. You don't have the products. So, the cost of the products is removed from the asset account — that's all there is to it. In contrast, writing down the costs of damaged products (that are still salable at some price) and determining replacement and market values for the lower of cost or market test is not so clear-cut.

A business may be tempted to write down its inventory too much in order to minimize its taxable income for the year. We know a business that knocks down its ending inventory much more than can be justified by actual inventory shrinkage and lower replacement and sales values of its products. You're on thin ice if you do this, and you better pray that the IRS won't audit you.

In recording the expense of inventory shrinkage and inventory write down under the lower of cost of market test, your accountant has to decide which expense account to charge and how to report the loss in your P&L. Generally, the loss should be included in your cost of goods sold expense in the P&L because the loss is a normal expense that sits on top of cost of goods sold. However, when an abnormal amount of loss is recorded, your accountant should call the loss to your attention — either on a separate line in the P&L report or in a footnote to the statement.

Focusing on Profit Centers

A business consists of different revenue streams, and some are more profitable than others. It would be very unusual if every different source of sales were equally profitable. A common practice is to divide the business into separate *profit centers,* so that the profitability of each part of the business can be determined. For example, a car dealership is separated into new car sales, used car sales, service work, and parts sales. Each profit center's sales revenue may be further subdivided. New vehicle sales can be separated into sedans, pick up trucks, SUVs, and other models. In the business example we use in this and other chapters, you sell products both at retail prices to individual consumers and at wholesale prices to other businesses. Quite clearly, you should separate your two main sources of sales and create a profit center for each.

Determining how to partition a business into profit centers is a management decision. The first question is whether the segregation of sales revenue into distinct profit centers helps you better manage the business. Generally, the answer is yes. The information helps you focus attention and effort on the sources of highest profit to the business. Comparing different profit centers puts the spotlight on sources of sales that don't generate enough profit, or even may be losing money.

Generally, a business creates a profit center for each major product line and for each location (or territory). There are no hard and fast rules, however. At one extreme, each product can be defined as a profit center. As a matter of fact, businesses keep records for every product they sell. Many managers want a very detailed report on sales and cost of goods sold for every product they sell. This report can run many, many pages. A hardware store in Boulder sells more than 100,000 products. Would you really want to print out a report that lists the sales and cost of goods of more than 100,000 lines? The more practical approach is to divide the business into a reasonable number of profit centers and focus your time on the reports for each profit center.

A profit center is a fairly autonomous source of sales of a business, like a tub standing on its own feet. For example, the Boulder hardware store sells outdoor clothing, which is quite distinct from the other products it sells. Does the hardware store make a good profit on its outdoor clothing line of products? The first step is to determine the gross margin for the outdoor clothing department. The cost of goods sold is deducted from sales revenue for the outdoor clothing line of products. Is outdoor clothing a high gross margin source of sales? Frankly, we don't know, but the manager of the hardware store certainly should know!

The report for a profit center doesn't stop at the gross profit line. One key purpose of setting up profit centers is, as far as possible, to match direct operating costs against the sales revenue of the profit center. *Direct operating costs* are those that can be clearly assigned to the sales activity of the profit center. Examples of direct operating costs of a profit center are the following:

- Commissions paid to salespersons on sales of the profit center
- Shipping and delivery costs of products sold in the profit center
- Inventory shrinkage and write downs of inventory in the profit center
- Bad debts from credit sales of the profit center
- The cost of employees who work full-time in a profit center
- The cost of advertisements for products sold in the profit center

Assigning direct operating costs to profit centers doesn't take care of all the costs of a business. A business has many *indirect* operating costs that benefit all, or at least two or more profit centers. The employee cost of the general manager of the business, the cost of its accounting department, general business licenses, real estate taxes, interest on the debt of the business, and liability insurance are examples of general, business-wide operating costs. Accountants have come up with ingenious methods for allocating indirect operating costs to profit centers. In the last analysis, however, the allocation methods have flaws and are fairly arbitrary. The game may not be worth the candle in allocating indirect operating costs to profit centers. Generally, there is no gain in useful information. You have all the information you need by ending the profit center report after direct operating costs.

The bottom line of a profit center report is a measure of profit before general business operating costs and interest expense (and income tax expense, if applicable) are taken into account. The bottom line of a profit center is more properly called *contribution* toward the aggregate profit of the business as a whole. The term profit is a commonly used label for the bottom line of a profit center report, but keep in mind that it doesn't have the same meaning as the bottom line of the P&L statement for the business as a whole.

Reducing Your Costs

This section covers a few cost reduction tactics that we have observed over the years. It's not an exhaustive list, to be sure. But you may find one or two of these quite useful.

✔ Have your accountant alert you to any expense that increases more than a certain threshold amount, or by a certain percent.

✔ Hire a cost control specialist. Many of these firms work on a contingent fee basis that depends on how much your expense actually decreases. These outfits tend to specialize in certain areas such as utility bills and property taxes, to name just two.

✔ Consider outsourcing some of your business functions, such as payroll, security, taking inventory, and maintenance.

✔ Put out requests for competitive bids on supplies you regularly purchase.

✔ Make prompt payments of purchases on credit to take advantage of early payment discounts. Indeed, offer to pay in advance if you can gain an additional discount.

✔ Keep all your personal and family costs out of the business.

✔ Keep your assets as low as possible so that capital you need to run the business is lower, and your cost of capital will be lower.

✔ Set priorities on cost control, putting the fastest rising costs at the top.

✔ Ask your outside CPA for cost control ideas she or he has observed in other businesses.

Chapter 7

Practical Budgeting Techniques for Your Business

---

*T*hroughout this book, we harp on the concept of planning. The planning process includes numerous elements ranging from obtaining current market information to evaluating personnel resources to preparing budgets or forecasts. This chapter focuses on one of the most critical elements of the planning process: preparing a budget.

Budgets aren't based on the concept of "How much can I spend in my division this year?" Rather, budgets are more comprehensive in nature and are designed to capture all relevant and critical financial data including revenue levels, costs of sales, operating expenses, fixed asset expenditures, capital requirements, and the like. All too often, budgets are associated with expense levels and management, which represent just one element of the entire budget.

The budgeting process doesn't represent a Chicken and the Egg riddle. From a financial perspective, the preparation of budgets, forecasts, projections, proformas, and the like represent the end result of the entire planning process. Hence, you must first accumulate the necessary data and information on which to build a forecasting model prior to producing projected financial information (for your company). There is no point in preparing a budget that does not capture your company's true economic structure.

Deciding Where the Budgeting Process Starts

As John has pointed out on many occasions (and in numerous books he has published), accounting represents more of an art than a science. This concept also holds true with the budgeting process as it helps to be creative when preparing projections. Before creating your first budget, you should prepare by taking the following four steps:

1. **Delve into your business's financial history.**

   To start, you should have a very good understanding of your company's prior financial and operating results. This history may stretch back three months, one year, five years, or longer, but the key concept is that sound information not only should be readily available but it should be clearly understood. There is no point in attempting to prepare a budget if the party completing the work doesn't understand the financial information.

   Remember that while the history of a company may provide a basic foundation on which to develop a budget, it by no means is an accurate predictor of the future.

2. **Involve your key management.**

   The budgeting process represents a critical function in most companies' accounting and financial departments and rightfully so as these are the people that understand the numbers the best. Although the financial and accounting types produce the final budget, they rely on data that comes from numerous parties such as marketing, manufacturing, and sales. You must ensure that all key management team members are involved in the budgeting process, covering all critical business functions, to produce a reliable projection. Just as you wouldn't have a regional sales manager prepare a fixed asset schedule (tracking all asset additions, disposals, and depreciation expenses), you wouldn't have your accountant estimate sales volumes by product line during the holiday season (and what prices the products may fetch). Critical business data comes from numerous parties, all of which must be included in the budgeting process to produce the most reliable information possible.

3. **Gather reliable data.**

   The availability of quality market, operational, and accounting data represents the basis of the budget. A good deal of this data often comes from internal sources. For example, when a sales region is preparing a budget for the upcoming year, the sales manager may survey the direct sales representatives on what they feel their customers will demand as far as products and services in the coming year. With this information, you can determine sales volumes, personnel levels, wages rates, commission plans, and so on.

While internal information is of value, it represents only half the battle because external information and data is just as critical to accumulate. Having access to quality and reliable external third-party information is absolutely essential to the overall business planning process and the production of reliable forecasts. Market forces and trends may be occurring that can impact your business over the next 24 months but aren't reflected at all in the previous year's operating results.

4. Coordinate the budget timing.

From a timing perspective, most companies tend to start the budgeting process for the next year in the fourth quarter of their current calendar year. This way, they have access to recent financial results on which to support the budgeting process moving forward. The idea is to have a sound budget to base the next year's operations on. On the timeline front, the following general rule should be adhered to: The nearer the term covered by the projection means more detailed information and results should be produced. That is, if you're preparing a budget for the coming fiscal year, then monthly financial statement forecasts are expected (with more detailed support available). Looking two or three years out, you could produce quarterly financial statement projections (with more summarized assumptions used).

The concept of "garbage in, garbage out" definitely applies to the budgeting process. If you don't have sound data and information, the output produced will be of little value to the management team. The data and information used to prepare your company's budgets must be as complete, accurate, reliable, and timely as possible. While you can't be 100 percent assured that the data and information accumulated achieves these goals (as, by definition, you're attempting to predict the future with a projection), proper resources should be dedicated to the process to avoid getting bit by large information black holes.

Finally, keep in mind that the projections prepared must be consistent with the overall business plans and strategies of the company. All too often, we come across budgets and forecasts that were prepared based on an outdated business economic model. While management has put forth the effort to restructure the company's operations in a changing market environment, an old projection model that doesn't capture the essence of the new economic realities is used. Remember, the budgeting process represents a living, breathing thing that constantly must be updated, adapted, and so on to changing market conditions. What worked two years ago may not provide management with the necessary information today on which to make appropriate business decisions.

Honing in on Budgeting Tools

After you have solid historical data in hand (see preceding section), you're ready to produce an actual projection model. To help start the process, three simple acronyms have been provided that can be used as tools to accumulate the necessary information to build the projection model.

Complete, Accurate, Reliable, and Timely

Complete, Accurate, Reliable, and Timely (CART) applies to all the data and information you need to prepare for the projection model. It doesn't matter where the information is coming from or how it's presented; it just must be complete, accurate, reliable, and timely:

- **Complete:** Financial statements produced for a company include a balance sheet, income statement, and a cash flow statement. All three are needed in order to understand the entire financial picture of a company. If a projection model is incorporating an expansion of a company's manufacturing facility in a new state, for example, all information related to the new facility needs to be accumulated to prepare the budget. This data includes the cost of the land and facility, how much utilities run in the area, what potential environmental issues may be present, whether a trained workforce is available, and if not, how much will it cost to train them, and so on. While overkill is not the objective, having access to all material information and data is.

- **Accurate:** Incorporating accurate data represents the basis for preparing the initial budget. Every budget needs to include the price your company charges for the goods or services it sells, how much you pay your employees, what the monthly office rent is, and so on. The key to obtaining accurate information is ensuring that your accounting and financial information system is generating accurate data.

- **Reliable:** The concept of reliability and accuracy are closely linked but also differ as well. It may be one thing to obtain a piece of information that is accurate, but is it reliable? For example, you may conduct research and find that the average wage for a paralegal in San Diego is $24 per hour. While this figure may sound accurate, you may need a specialist paralegal who demands $37 per hour.

- **Timely:** The information and data accumulated must be done in a timely fashion. It's not going to do a management team much good if the data and information that is needed is provided six months after the fact. Companies live and die by having access to real-time information on which to make business decisions and change course (and forecasts) if needed.

Keep It Simple Stupid

Used in the marketing world for years, the concept of Keep it Simple Stupid (KISS) also applies to the budgeting process every bit as much. Because those involved in the budgeting process come from a variety of backgrounds and probably aren't well educated in accounting and finance jargon, your goal is to provide guidance and support that allows them to accumulate the information in their world.

For example, large staffing companies often operate in multiple regions and have multiple divisions. One division may provide staffing services to the legal community, whereas another may target general, clerical, and administrative services. Each division speaks a different language, operates with different cost structures, and, as such, focuses on unique market characteristics. Rather than bury the division managers with requests for every piece of information it takes to support their operation, you could simply request the following (summarized) information from the division managers:

Average weekly temporary hours realized (by quarter):

1st Qtr. _____ 2nd Qtr. _____ 3rd Qtr. _____ 4th Qtr. _____

Average pay rate per temporary hour realized (by quarter):

1st Qtr. _____ 2nd Qtr. _____ 3rd Qtr. _____ 4th Qtr. _____

Average bill rate per temporary hour realized (by quarter):

1st Qtr. _____ 2nd Qtr. _____ 3rd Qtr. _____ 4th Qtr. _____

Average monthly permanent placements realized (by quarter):

1st Qtr. _____ 2nd Qtr. _____ 3rd Qtr. _____ 4th Qtr. _____

Please complete the following schedule related to the number of staff you require (by primary staff function) and the average compensation level expected:

Operations Manager(s), # needed by quarter 1st __, 2nd __, 3rd __, 4th __, Average Annual Compensation Level $_____.

Business Dev. Rep(s), # needed by quarter 1st __, 2nd __, 3rd __, 4th __, Average Annual Compensation Level $_____.

Staffing Coordinator(s), # needed by quarter 1st __, 2nd __, 3rd __, 4th __, Average Annual Compensation Level $_____.

The goal of accumulating these critical data points is to have the division managers' focus on the information they had the most knowledge with and control over, which also represents the critical economic data points at the base of their operations. By responding to these five simple questions, you can prepare a basic budget for each division and then roll them up into one larger, company-wide budget with all divisions and branches. You don't need to ask the division managers to attempt to forecast every type of expense, such as detailed travel, lodging, and auto expenses, that they may incur to support their operation. Rather, if their operation was going to produce X amount of revenue and Y amount of gross profit dollars, then they should incur only T amount of travel and transportation expenses, A amount of advertising expenses, and so on. The accounting department can then accumulate the remainder of the information required from the key data points provided.

Strengths, Weaknesses, Opportunities, and Threats analysis

Don't be afraid to utilize a Strengths, Weaknesses, Opportunities, and Threats (SWOT) analysis, which is an effective planning and budgeting tool used to keep businesses focused on key issues. The simple SWOT analysis (or matrix) in Figure 7-1 shows you how this process works.

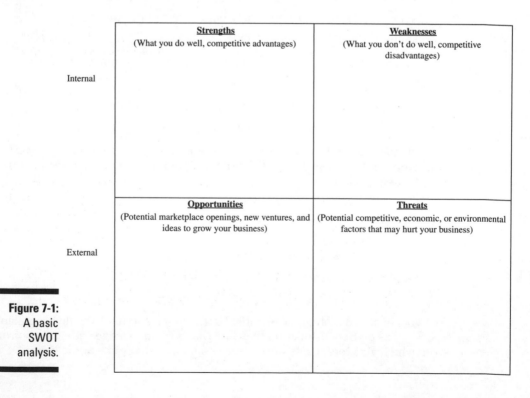

	Strengths (What you do well, competitive advantages)	**Weaknesses** (What you don't do well, competitive disadvantages)
Internal		
	Opportunities (Potential marketplace openings, new ventures, and ideas to grow your business)	**Threats** (Potential competitive, economic, or environmental factors that may hurt your business)
External		

Figure 7-1:
A basic
SWOT
analysis.

A SWOT analysis is usually broken down into a matrix containing four segments. Two of the segments are geared toward positive attributes, such as your strengths and opportunities, and two are geared toward negative attributes, such as your weaknesses and threats. In addition, the analysis differentiates between internal company source attributes and external, or outside of the company source attributes. Generally, division managers or directors prepare the SWOT analysis to ensure that critical conditions are communicated to management for inclusion in the budget.

If used correctly, a SWOT analysis not only can provide invaluable information to support the budgeting process but, more importantly, can help identify what type of management you have in place. The responses you receive provides invaluable information as to whether the party completing the SWOT analysis is nothing more than a front-line manager (a captain needing direction) or a bonafide business person (the colonel leading the charge).

You can't see the forest through the trees! We're sure you've heard this comment numerous times as people struggle with business concepts and ideas. As an executive or owner of a business, you must be able to understand the big picture and your company's key economic drivers in order to prepare proper business plans, strategies, and ultimately, forecasts. The ability to understand and positively affect the key economic drivers of your business and empower the management team to execute the business plan represents the end game. Getting lost in the forest of "Why did you spend an extra $500 on the trip to Florida?" is generally not the best use of senior management's time.

Flash reports

Flash reports represent nothing more than a quick snapshot of critical company operating and financial data, which is then used to support the ongoing operations of the business. All types of flash reports are used in business, and they range from a printed circuit board manufacturing company evaluating its book-to-bill ratio on a weekly basis to Wal-Mart reporting daily sales activity during the holiday season to an auto manufacturer evaluating weekly finished goods inventory levels.

The goal with all flash reports remains the same in that critical business information is delivered to management for review much more frequently. As such, flash reports tend to have the following key attributes present:

- ✔ **Flash reports tend to be much more frequent in timing.** Unlike the production of financial statements (which occurs on a monthly basis), flash reports are often produced weekly and, in numerous cases, daily. In today's competitive marketplace, management is demanding information be provided more frequently than ever to stay on top of rapidly changing markets.

- ✔ **Flash reports are designed to capture critical operating and financial performance data of your business or the real information that can make or break your business.** As a result, sales activities and/or volumes are almost always a part of a businesses' flash reporting effort. Once management has a good handle on the top line, the bottom line should be relatively easy to calculate.

- ✔ **Flash reports aren't just limited to presenting financial data.** Flash reports can be designed to capture all kinds of data, including retail store foot volume (or customer traffic levels), labor utilization rates, and the like. While the president of a division may want to know how sales are tracking this month, the manufacturing manager will want to keep a close eye on labor hours incurred in the production process.

- ✔ **Flash reports obtain their base information from the same accounting and financial information system that produces periodic financial statements, budgets, and other reports.** While the presentation of the information may be different, the source of the information should come from the same transactional basis (of your company).

- ✔ **Flash reports are almost exclusively used for internal management needs and are rarely delivered to external parties.** The information contained in flash reports is usually more detailed in nature, tends to contain far more confidential data than, say, audited financial statements, and are almost never audited.

- ✔ **Flash reports are closely related to the budgeting process.** For example, if a company is experiencing a short-term cash flow squeeze, management will need to have access to a rolling 13-week cash flow projection to properly evaluate cash inflows and outflows on a weekly basis. Each week, the rolling 13-week cash flow projection is provided to management for review in the form of a flash report, which is always being updated to look out 13 weeks.

Flash reports should act more to "reconfirm" your company's performance rather than representing a report that offers "original" information. Granted, while a flash report that presents sales volumes for the first two weeks of February compared to the similar two-week period for the prior year is reporting new sales information, the format of the report and the presentation of the information in the report should be consistent. Thus, management should be able to quickly decipher the results and determine whether the company is performing within expectations and what to expect on the bottom-line for the entire month.

Budgeting Resources

The budgeting process is much easier to undertake (and ultimately understand) if the majority of the relevant data needed to complete company forecasts is accumulated before hand (see preceding sections). After you have your data in hand, you need to identify and secure the appropriate resources to prepare a company forecast. The resources we're talking about are the personnel that will be assigned the task of completing the budget and the software needed to prepare flexible and adaptable projection models. On the personnel front, the budgeting task tends to fall on the accounting and finance department because these are the people in the organization that seem to work best with "the numbers."

The accounting and finance department may prepare the actual budget, but the base information required for completion of the budget comes from all critical departments of the organization.

On the software front, you have two choices readily available to complete company projections:

- ✓ **The ever popular software program known as Excel:** Part of the Microsoft line of software products, Excel is very flexible and relatively easy to use for both nonfinancial and financial types. Excel is extremely versatile and is used in companies as small as the local deli to billion-dollars-a-year organizations.

- ✓ **The budgeting component of the software you use for accounting purposes:** Most accounting software packages (such as QuickBooks, Great Plains, and others) include a budgeting module to support this function, but, in general, these modules aren't as flexible as Excel (and are a little more difficult to use).

Most accounting software packages easily interface with Excel, so you can create the base projection model in Excel and import the results into your accounting software module.

Preparing an Actual Budget or Forecast

The best way to dive into preparing a budget, once all the necessary information has been accumulated, is to begin by building a draft of the budget that is more summarized in nature and is focused on the financial statement, which is most easily understood and widely used. The reason more summarized budgets are developed at first is to create a general format or framework that captures the basic output desired by the parties using the budget.

Offering a summarized visual version of the budget allows for management reviews and edits to be incorporated into the forecasting model before too much effort is expended in including detail that may not be needed. Once the desired output reports and data points of the budget are determined, it can be expanded and adjusted to incorporate the correct level of detail. The best way to prepare a summarized budget that is both flexible and adaptable is to build the forecasting model in software such as Excel, which is relatively easy to use and widely accepted by most businesses.

On the financial statement front, for most companies, the forecasting process tends to starts with producing a projected income statement for three primary reasons. First, this financial statement tends to be the one that is most widely used and easily understood by the organization. Questions such as how much revenue can the company produce, what will our gross margin be, and how much profit will be generated are basic focal points of almost every business owner, executive, and manager. The balance sheet and cash flow statements aren't nearly as easy to understand and produce.

Second, the income statement often acts as a base data point to produce balance sheet and cash flow statement information. For example, if sales volumes are increasing, it's safe to say that the company's balance in trade accounts receivable and inventory would increase as well.

And third, the majority of the information and data accumulated to support the budgeting process is generally centered in areas associated with the income statement such as how many units can be sold, at what price, how many sales persons will we need, and so on.

Remember also that most budgets are prepared in a consistent format with that of the current internally produced financial statements and reports utilized by your company. This achieves the dual goal of information conformity (for ease of understanding) and capturing your businesses' key economic drivers. To illustrate, Figure 7-2 presents a summarized budget for XYZ Wholesale, Inc. for the coming year.

Figure 7-2 represents a budget for the year ending 12/31/07 for XYZ Wholesale, Inc. The basic budget shown in Figure 7-2 is fairly simplistic but also very informative. It captures the macro level economic structure of the company in terms of where it is today and where it expects to be at the end of next year. When reviewing the figure, notice the following key issues:

> ✔ **The most recent year-end financial information has been included in the first column to provide a base reference point to work from.** Gaining a thorough understanding of your company's historical operating results to forecast into the future is important. Also, by having this base information, you can develop a consistent reporting format for ease of understanding.

XYZ WHOLESALE, INC.
UNAUDITED FINANCIAL STATEMENT — QUARTERLY PROJECTIONS

Summary Balance Sheet	Actual Year End 1/1/11	Forecast Quarter End 4/1/11	Forecast Quarter End 7/1/11	Forecast Quarter End 10/1/11	Forecast Quarter End 1/1/12	Forecast Year End 1/1/12
Current Assets:						
Cash & Equivalents	$117,632	$11,364	$26,263	$38,200	$24,313	$24,313
Trade Receivables, Net	$1,271,875	$1,213,333	$1,646,667	$2,253,333	$1,610,000	$1,610,000
Inventory	$867,188	$886,667	$1,132,400	$1,248,000	$856,800	$856,800
Total Current Assets	$2,256,695	$2,111,364	$2,805,330	$3,539,533	$2,491,113	$2,491,113
Fixed & Other Assets:						
Property, Plant, & Equipment, Net	$1,750,000	$1,725,000	$1,700,000	$1,675,000	$1,650,000	$1,650,000
Other Assets	$75,000	$75,000	$75,000	$75,000	$75,000	$75,000
Total Fixed & Other Assets	$1,825,000	$1,800,000	$1,775,000	$1,750,000	$1,725,000	$1,725,000
Total Assets	$4,081,695	$3,911,364	$4,580,330	$5,289,533	$4,216,113	$4,216,113
Current Liabilities:						
Trade Payables	$2,601,563	$2,340,800	$2,547,900	$2,808,000	$1,965,600	$1,965,600
Accrued Liabilities	$195,117	$234,080	$254,790	$280,800	$196,560	$196,560
Line of Credit Borrowings	$200,000	$500,000	$1,000,000	$1,100,000	$250,000	$250,000
Current Portion of Long-Term Liabilities	$300,000	$300,000	$300,000	$300,000	$300,000	$300,000
Total Current Liabilities	$3,296,680	$3,374,880	$4,102,690	$4,488,800	$2,712,160	$2,712,160
Long-Term Liabilities:						
Notes Payable, Less Current Portion	$300,000	$225,000	$150,000	$75,000	$0	$0
Other Long-Term Liabilities	$150,000	$150,000	$150,000	$150,000	$150,000	$150,000
Total Long-Term Liabilities	$450,000	$375,000	$300,000	$225,000	$150,000	$150,000
Total Liabilities	$3,746,680	$3,749,880	$4,402,690	$4,713,800	$2,862,160	$2,862,160
Equity:						
Common and Preferred Equity, $1 Per Share	$500,000	$500,000	$500,000	$500,000	$1,000,000	$1,000,000
Retained Earnings	$901,265	($164,985)	($164,985)	($164,985)	($164,985)	($164,985)
Current Earnings	($1,066,250)	($173,531)	($157,375)	$240,719	$518,938	$518,938
Total Equity	$335,015	$161,484	$177,640	$575,734	$1,353,953	$1,353,953
Total Liabilities & Equity	$4,081,695	$3,911,364	$4,580,330	$5,289,534	$4,216,113	$4,216,113

Summary Income Statement	Actual Year End 1/1/11	Forecast Quarter End 4/1/11	Forecast Quarter End 7/1/11	Forecast Quarter End 10/1/11	Forecast Quarter End 1/1/12	Forecast Year End 1/1/12
Revenue	$13,875,000	$2,800,000	$3,800,000	$5,200,000	$4,200,000	$16,000,000
Costs of Goods Sold	$10,406,250	$2,128,000	$2,831,000	$3,744,000	$3,024,000	$11,727,000
Gross Profit	$3,468,750	$672,000	$969,000	$1,456,000	$1,176,000	$4,273,000
Gross Margin	25.00%	24.00%	25.50%	28.00%	28.00%	26.71%
Selling, General, & Administrative Expenses	$3,060,000	$700,000	$800,000	$900,000	$750,000	$3,150,000
Depreciation Expense	$350,000	$100,000	$100,000	$100,000	$100,000	$400,000
Interest Expense	$75,000	$20,531	$27,844	$32,906	$22,781	$104,063
Other (Income) Expenses	$1,050,000	$25,000	$25,000	$25,000	$25,000	$100,000
Net Profit Before Tax	($1,066,250)	($173,531)	$16,156	$398,094	$278,219	$518,938
Income Tax Expense (Benefit)	$0	$0	$0	$0	$0	$0
Net Profit (Loss)	($1,066,250)	($173,531)	$16,156	$398,094	$278,219	$518,938

Summary Cash Flow Statement	Actual Year End 1/1/11	Forecast Quarter End 4/1/11	Forecast Quarter End 7/1/11	Forecast Quarter End 10/1/11	Forecast Quarter End 1/1/12	Forecast Year End 1/1/12
Operating Cash Flow:						
Net Income (Loss)	($1,066,250)	($173,531)	$16,156	$398,094	$278,219	$518,938
Depreciation Expense	$350,000	$100,000	$100,000	$100,000	$100,000	$400,000
Net Operating Cash Flow	($716,250)	($73,531)	$116,156	$498,094	$378,219	$918,938
Working Capital:						
(Increase) Decrease in Trade Receivables	$471,875	$58,542	($433,333)	($606,667)	$643,333	($338,125)
(Increase) Decrease in Inventory	$1,049,194	($19,479)	($245,733)	($115,600)	$391,200	$10,388
Increase (Decrease) In Trade Payables	($81,371)	($260,763)	$207,100	$260,100	($842,400)	($635,963)
Increase (Decrease) In Accrued Liabilities	$60,971	$38,963	$20,710	$26,010	($84,240)	$1,443
Increase (Decrease) In Current Debt	$100,000	$300,000	$500,000	$100,000	($850,000)	$50,000
Net Working Capital Cash Flow	$1,600,668	$117,263	$48,743	($336,157)	($742,107)	($912,257)
Financing Capital:						
Equity Contributions	$0	$0	$0	$0	$500,000	$500,000
Additions to Long-Term Debt	$0	$0	$0	$0	$0	$0
Deletions to Long-Term Debt	($300,000)	($75,000)	($75,000)	($75,000)	($75,000)	($300,000)
Fixed Asset Additions	($600,000)	($75,000)	($75,000)	($75,000)	($75,000)	($300,000)
Change to Other Long-Term Assets	$0	$0	$0	$0	$0	$0
Change to Other Long-Term Liabilities	$10,000	$0	$0	$0	$0	$0
Net Financial Capital Cash Flow	($890,000)	($150,000)	($150,000)	($150,000)	$350,000	($100,000)
Beginning Cash	$123,214	$117,632	$11,364	$26,263	$38,200	$117,632
Ending Cash	$117,632	$11,364	$26,263	$38,200	$24,312	$24,312

Figure 7-2:
A quarterly forecast.

✔ **The projections are "complete" from a financial statement perspective.** That is, the income statement, balance sheet, and statement of cash flows have all been projected to assist management with understanding the entire financial picture of the company. The forecasts prepared for XYZ Wholesale, Inc. indicate that the line of credit will be used extensively through the third quarter to support working capital needs. By the end of the fourth quarter, borrowings on the line of credit are substantially lower as business slows and cash flows improve (used to pay down the line of credit).

✔ **The projections have been presented with quarterly information.** We'd normally recommend that projections for the next fiscal year be prepared on a monthly basis to provide management with more frequent information. However, for this book, we prepared quarterly information.

✔ **The projections have been prepared and presented in a "summary" format.** That is, not too much detail has been provided, but rather groups of detail have been combined into one line item. For example, sales may originate from ten different company divisions or branches. Individual budgets are prepared to support each division or branch, but when a company-wide forecast is completed, all the sales are rolled up onto one line item. Budgets prepared in a summary format are best suited for review by external parties and top company executives.

✔ **Certain key or critical business economic drivers have been highlighted in the projection model.** First, the company's gross margin has been called out as it increases from 24 percent in the first quarter to 28 percent in the first half of the year. The increase was the result of the company moving older and obsolete products during the first six months of the year to make way for new merchandise and products to be sold at higher prices starting in the third quarter (and then accelerating in the 4th quarter during the holidays). Second, the company's pretax net income, for the entire year, has improved significantly. This increase occurred because the company's fixed overhead and corporate infrastructure (expenses) did not need to increase nearly as much to support the higher sales (as a result of realizing the benefits of economies of scale). In addition, the company didn't have to absorb an inventory write-off of $1 million (as with 2006).

✔ **A couple of very simple, but extremely important, references are made at the top and bottom of the projections.** At the top, the company clearly notes that the information prepared is confidential in nature. At the bottom, the company notes that the information is unaudited. In today's business world, information that is both confidential and that hasn't been audited by an external party should clearly state so.

The best way to prepare your first budget is to simply dive in and give it a go. There is no question that your first draft will undergo significant changes, revisions, and edits but it's much easier to critique something that already exists than create it from scratch. The hard part is preparing the first budget. After that, the budget can then be refined, expanded, and improved to provide your organization an even more valuable tool in managing everyday challenges, stress, and growing pains.

Understanding Internal Versus External Budgets

Information prepared for and delivered to external users (a financing source, taxing authorities, company creditors, and so on) isn't the same as information prepared for and utilized internally in the company. Not only does this fact apply to historically produced information, but it applies to financial information you forecast as well. The following examples show how a business can basically utilize the same information, but for different objectives:

✔ **The internal sales-driven budget:** To date, we have yet to see a budget prepared based on sales and marketing information that is more conservative than a similar budget prepared based on operations or accounting information. By nature, sales and marketing personnel tend to be far more optimistic in relation to the opportunities present than other segments of the business (which, of course, includes the ultra-conservative nature of accountants). So rather than attempt to have these two groups battle it out over what forecast model is the most accurate, simply prepare two sets of projections. Companies often have more than one set of projections completed. You can use the marketing and sales based projection as a management and motivational tool to push this group but use a more conservative projection for delivery to external financing sources, which provides a "reasonable" projection so that the company isn't under enormous pressure to hit aggressive plans. Granted, this strategy has to be properly managed (and kept in balance) because one forecast shouldn't be drastically different than another.

✔ **Drilling down into the detail:** When information is delivered to external parties, the level of detail is far less than what is utilized internally by management on a daily basis. This concept holds true for the budgeting process as well. The level and amount of detail that is at the base of the projection model will often drill down to the core elements of your business. For example, the summary projected in Figure 7-2 displays corporate overhead expenses as one line item. This one line item could, in fact, be the summation of more than 100 lines of data and capture everything from the cost of personnel in the accounting department to the current year's advertising budget (for the company). Again, an outside party should not (and does not want) to see that level of detail because it tends to only confuse them and lead to more questions being asked than is needed. However, by being able to drill down into the detail at any given time (and provide real support for financial information presented in the budget), you can kill two birds with one stone. Internally, you have the necessary detail to hold management team members responsible for expense and cost control. Externally, you can provide added confidence and creditability to your partners (e.g., a financing source) that the business is being tightly managed.

Creating a Living Budget

A *living budget* is based on the idea that in today's fiercely competitive marketplace, business models change much quicker than they did a decade ago. While the budget prepared in the fourth quarter of the previous year looked good, six months later the story may change. Any number of factors, such as losing a key sales executive, having a competitor go out of business, or experiencing a significant increase in the price of raw materials to produce your products, may cause the best prepared budgets to be useless by midyear. So you may want to keep in mind the following terminology when preparing budgets to ensure that the process doesn't become stagnant during the year:

✔ **What ifs:** A *what-if analysis* is just as it sounds. That is, if this happens to my business or in the market, what will be the impact on my business? If I can land this new account, what additional costs will I need to incur and when to support the account? Utilizing what-if budgeting techniques is a highly effective business management strategy that you can apply to all levels of the budgeting process, from a single division to the company as a whole. Figure 7-3 presents a company's original budget along side two other scenarios, one of which is a low-case scenario and the other a best-case scenario. By completing what-if budgeting, XYZ Wholesale, Inc. has provided itself with a better understanding of what business decisions need to be made in case either the low-case or high-case scenarios are realized.

XYZ WHOLESALE, INC.
UNAUDITED FINANCIAL STATEMENT — COMPARATIVE

Summary Balance Sheet	Actual Year End 1/1/11	Forecast — Low Year End 1/1/12	Forecast — Med Year End 1/1/12	Forecast — High Year End 1/1/12
Current Assets:				
Cash & Equivalents	$117,632	$56,515	$24,313	$48,265
Trade Receivables, Net	$1,271,875	$1,550,000	$1,610,000	$2,000,000
Inventory	$867,188	$825,000	$856,800	$1,000,000
Total Current Assets	$2,256,695	$2,431,515	$2,491,113	$3,048,265
Fixed & Other Assets:				
Property, Plant, & Equipment, Net	$1,750,000	$1,600,000	$1,650,000	$1,700,000
Other Assets	$75,000	$75,000	$75,000	$75,000
Total Fixed & Other Assets	$1,825,000	$1,675,000	$1,725,000	$1,775,000
Total Assets	$4,081,695	$4,106,515	$4,216,113	$4,823,265
Current Liabilities:				
Trade Payables	$2,601,563	$1,900,000	$1,965,600	$1,750,000
Accrued Liabilities	$195,117	$190,000	$196,560	$210,000
Line of Credit Borrowings	$200,000	$700,000	$250,000	$550,000
Current Portion of Long-Term Liabilities	$300,000	$300,000	$300,000	$300,000
Total Current Liabilities	$3,296,680	$3,090,000	$2,712,160	$2,810,000
Long-Term Liabilities:				
Notes Payable, Less Current Portion	$300,000	$0	$0	$0
Other Long-Term Liabilities	$150,000	$150,000	$150,000	$150,000
Total Long-Term Liabilities	$450,000	$150,000	$150,000	$150,000
Total Liabilities	$3,746,680	$3,240,000	$2,862,160	$2,960,000
Equity:				
Common and Preferred Equity, $1 Per Share	$500,000	$1,000,000	$1,000,000	$1,000,000
Retained Earnings	$901,265	($164,985)	($164,985)	($164,985)
Current Earnings	($1,066,250)	$31,500	$518,938	$1,028,250
Total Equity	$335,015	$866,515	$1,353,953	$1,863,265
Total Liabilities & Equity	$4,081,695	$4,106,515	$4,216,113	$4,823,265

Summary Income Statement	Actual Year End 1/1/11	Forecast — Low Year End 1/1/12	Forecast — Med Year End 1/1/12	Forecast — High Year End 1/1/12
Revenue	$13,875,000	$14,250,000	$16,000,000	$18,500,000
Costs of Goods Sold	$10,406,250	$10,687,500	$11,727,000	$13,597,500
Gross Profit	$3,468,750	$3,562,500	$4,273,000	$4,902,500
Gross Margin	25.00%	25.00%	26.71%	26.50%
Selling, General, & Administrative Expenses	$3,060,000	$3,000,000	$3,150,000	$3,250,000
Depreciation Expense	$350,000	$350,000	$400,000	$450,000
Interest Expense	$75,000	$81,000	$104,063	$74,250
Other (Income) Expenses	$1,050,000	$100,000	$100,000	$100,000
Net Profit Before Tax	($1,066,250)	$31,500	$518,938	$1,028,250
Income Tax Expense (Benefit)	$0	$0	$0	$0
Net Profit (Loss)	($1,066,250)	$31,500	$518,938	$1,028,250

Summary Cash Flow Statement	Actual Year End 1/1/11	Forecast — Low Year End 1/1/12	Forecast — Med Year End 1/1/12	Forecast — High Year End 1/1/12
Operating Cash Flow:				
Net Income (Loss)	($1,066,250)	$31,500	$518,938	$1,028,250
Depreciation Expense	$350,000	$350,000	$400,000	$450,000
Net Operating Cash Flow	($716,250)	$381,500	$918,938	$1,478,250

Figure 7-3:
What-if
forecasts.

Working Capital:				
(Increase) Decrease in Trade Receivables	$471,875	($278,125)	($338,125)	($728,125)
(Increase) Decrease in Inventory	$1,049,194	$42,188	$10,388	($132,813)
Increase (Decrease) in Trade Payables	($81,371)	($701,563)	($635,963)	($851,563)
Increase (Decrease) in Accrued Liabilities	$60,971	($5,117)	$1,443	$14,883
Increase (Decrease) in Current Debt	$100,000	$500,000	$50,000	$350,000
Net Working Capital Cash Flow	$1,600,668	($442,617)	($912,257)	($1,347,617)
Financing Capital:				
Equity Contributions	$0	$500,000	$500,000	$500,000
Additions to Long-Term Debt	$0	$0	$0	$0
Deletions to Long-Term Debt	($300,000)	($300,000)	($300,000)	($300,000)
Fixed Asset Additions	($600,000)	($200,000)	($300,000)	($400,000)
Change to Other Long-Term Assets	$0	$0	$0	$0
Change to Other Long-Term Liabilities	$10,000	$0	$0	$0
Net Financial Capital Cash Flow	($890,000)	$0	($100,000)	($200,000)
Beginning Cash	$123,214	$117,632	$117,632	$117,632
Ending Cash	$117,632	$56,515	$24,312	$48,265

Figure 7-3: Continued.

✔ **Recasts:** When you hear the term *recast,* it generally means a company is going to update its original budgets or forecasts during some point of the year to recast the information through the end of the year. Companies are constantly under pressure to provide updated information on how they think the year will turn out. Everyone wants updated information, so at the end of select periods (for example, month end or quarter end), the actual results for the company through that period are presented with recast information for the remainder of the year to present recast operating results for the entire year (a combination of actual results and updated projected results). Having access to this type of information can greatly assist business owners and managers so that they can properly direct the company and adapt to changing conditions, not to mention provide timely updates to key external parties (on how the company is progressing).

Nobody likes surprises (especially bad ones), and nothing will get an external party, such as a bank or investor, more fired up than management not being able to deliver information on the company's performance.

✔ **Rolling forecasts:** *Rolling forecasts* are similar to preparing recast financial results with the exception that the rolling forecast is always looking out over a period of time (for example, the next 12 months) from the most recent period end. For example, if a company has a fiscal year end of 12/31/07 and has prepared a budget for the fiscal year end 12/31/08, an updated rolling 12-month forecast may be prepared for the period of 4/1/08 through 3/31/09 once the financial results are known for the first quarter ending 3/31/08. This way, management always has 12 months of projections available to work with.

Rolling forecasts tend to be utilized in companies operating in highly fluid or uncertain times that need to always look out 12 months. However, more and more companies are utilizing rolling forecasts to better prepare for future uncertainties.

Using the Budget as a Business Management Tool

The real key to a budget lies in management being able to understand the information and then acting on it. This section reviews some of the most frequently relied upon outcomes from the budgeting process.

The *variance report* is nothing more than taking a look at the budget and comparing it to actual results for a period of time. Figure 7-4 presents a variance report for XYZ Wholesale, Inc. and compares the budgeted results for the quarter ending 3/31/07 against the company's actual results.

XYZ WHOLESALE, INC.
UNAUDITED FINANCIAL STATEMENT — VARIANCE ANALYSIS

Summary Income Statement	Forecast Qtr. End 4/1/11	Actual Qtr. End 4/1/11	Variance Qtr. End 4/1/11
Revenue	$2,800,000	$2,865,000	$65,000
Costs of Goods Sold	$2,128,000	$2,018,500	$109,500
Gross Profit	$672,000	$846,500	$174,500
Gross Margin	24.00%	29.55%	
Selling, General, & Administrative Expenses	$700,000	$705,000	($5,000)
Depreciation Expense	$100,000	$100,000	$0
Interest Expense	$20,531	$20,000	$531
Other (Income) Expenses	$25,000	$18,500	$6,500
Net Profit Before Tax	($173,531)	$3,000	$172,469
Income Tax Expense (Benefit)	$0	$0	$0
Net Profit (Loss)	($173,531)	$3,000	$172,469

Figure 7-4:
Variance analysis.

Of keen importance is the increase in the company's gross margin, which helped the company break even during the quarter compared to a projected loss of $174,000. Obviously, management needs to understand what caused the gross margin to increase. Was it from higher sales prices or lower product

MDOR or MDA

MDOR stands for the management discussion of operating results, and MDA stands for the management discussion and analysis. Both are essentially the same document and serve the same purpose: They provide a written narrative of how the company's performing that translates financial information, results, and numbers into written words, strategies, plans, and events. While this type of documentation sounds relatively easy to complete, the MDOR and MDA can be difficult to prepare because the translation process can be very difficult.

At the base of the MDOR and MDA, when explaining actual results versus planned, is a well-developed budget that provides a clear road map to understanding operating result variances. We bring up the issue of the MDOR and MDA for two reasons:

✔ If you present financial information without being able to explain it, readers (whether internal or external) will often come to their own conclusion on why the company is performing a certain way. More times than not, their conclusions are incorrect, which may lead to adverse decisions being made that negatively impact your business. Remember, the more you can do to eliminate assumptions from being made, the better.

✔ By being able to clearly relay your company's financial results, key parties (whether internal or external) will gain more confidence in your management abilities, which should lead to additional credibility. This may not sound like much, but believe us when we tell you that management integrity and credibility has saved more than a few businesses. For financing sources, credit decisions are easy and tend to be based on the financial information. But when a business decision needs to be made, management integrity and credibility rise to the surface.

costs? Of more importance, however, is that management needs to act on the information. If the market is supporting higher prices in general, then the company may want to revisit pricing strategies for the second through fourth quarters to take advantage of conditions that may allow it to further improve the company's annual financial performance.

Another use of the budget is to support the implementation of specific plans and action steps. For example, if a new production distribution facility is set to open in the third quarter of the year, then you need to secure the staff to support this facility in the middle of the second quarter and then train them to ensure that they're ready when the new facility opens. Yes, all this data should have been accumulated and incorporated into the original budget prepared for the new facility, but the idea is to turn the budget into a proactive working document (easily accessible for reference) rather than a one-time effort left on the shelf to die.

Using Budgets in Other Ways

When preparing budgets, you must remember that you can use the base data and information accumulated to support other business planning and management functions as well. For example, you can use a well-developed budget to not only prepare forecast financial statements but to prepare the estimated taxable income or loss of a company. Chapter 9 discusses why taxable income differs from book income. For some companies, the difference between book and tax income is small. However for others, the difference can be significant, as the following example displays:

A large provider of personnel services elects to implement a strategy to self-fund its worker's compensation insurance costs. The preliminary analysis indicates that an average annual savings of 30 percent or more can be achieved if properly managed. At the end of the third year of the self-funded worker's compensation insurance program, the company had established an accrued liability for more than $1 million to account for potential future claims (to properly reflect the fact that claims made under the program through the end of the year would eventually cost the company $1 million). For book purposes, the $1 million represented an expense recorded in the financial statements, which resulted in the company producing net income of roughly zero dollars. For tax purposes, the IRS would not allow the expense until the claims were actually paid, so the taxable income of the company was $1 million (resulting in a tax liability of $400,000). If the company didn't properly budget for this business event, it may have been in for a rude surprise as, per the books, the company made nothing yet owed $400,000 in taxes. You can be assured that this is not the type of surprise an executive wants to experience on short notice.

Budgets also play a critical role in developing a business plan, especially when a company is attempting to secure capital to execute its strategy. Financial forecasts act as a visual or numeric display of management's vision and outlook of where the company is headed. Effectively presented, financial forecasts can enhance the creditability of the management team and basis of the business plan, which, in turn, provides for fewer barriers to acceptance from potential funding sources. In effect, the financial forecasts must clearly present the "story" of the business.

You can also use the budget for other purposes as well, such as preparing information for specialized needs from external parties to training a new division manager on the basic economics of how his division should perform to ensuring that the vision of the company is properly aligned with the direct action of management.

The better a budget is designed and structured from the beginning, the more uses and value it will provide your business down the road.

Chapter 8

Making Decisions with a Profit Model

....

In This Chapter

▶ Demonstrating the decision-making uses of a profit model

▶ Analyzing effects of sales volume and price changes

▶ Keeping fixed costs aligned with sales

▶ Trading off sales price and volume

▶ Looking into reasons for cost changes

....

*T*he P&L report is like a large suitcase, but all you really need is a satchel for thinking out profit decisions. The full-blown P&L report is a rather heavy and bulky tool for profit decision-making analysis — like using a sledgehammer to drive a nail. The P&L report is indispensable for management control after decisions have been made and implemented. But for decision-making analysis, the P&L is a lot to lug around. A better decision-making tool is a compact model, or schematic of profit — one you can do quick calculations with and readily determine the main effects of changes in profit variables. This chapter demonstrates the decision-making uses of a profit model.

Introducing the Profit Model

Business managers face constant change — in particular, the factors that drive profit change frequently. Some changes are external and beyond the control of the business, and some changes are initiated by managers themselves. Many management decisions are triggered by changes. Indeed, business managers are characterized as *change agents*.

The costs of the products sold by the business may increase. The company may raise wages for some or all of its employees, or wage rates may actually decrease due to employee give-backs. The landlord may raise the rent. Competitors may drop their sales prices, and the business has to decide whether to follow them down. Or managers may decide that they have to raise sales prices to keep up with cost inflation. Changes set in motion a new round of decisions.

After changes happen, you need to reexamine your new profit environment. The best course of action to take for maintaining and improving your profit performance is not obvious in most situations. Often, you have to compare alternatives. And, usually, you have to make decisions in a hurry. A good profit model is very helpful.

The *profit model* is like a miniature P&L (see Chapter 2 for more on the P&L). The P&L itself provides essential feedback information for *management control* of profit — to monitor progress and spot any problems that are brewing. On the other hand, for a profit model, the P&L report is stripped down to its bare bones. Reading a P&L report is like looking under the hood of your auto; reading a profit model is like looking at the dashboard. Not to stretch this figure of speech too far, but a good profit model starts you off in the right direction to reach your profit destination.

Figure 8-1 presents a profit model. Five key profit factors appear in bold; the other lines are different measures of profit. The dollar amounts in the profit model example are in the range of many small businesses. Of course, your business may be larger or smaller. We round off dollar amounts in the example to keep calculations easier to follow.

Net Sales Revenue	$3,000,000
Product Costs	($1,650,000)
Variable Operating Costs	($450,000)
Margin	$900,000
Fixed Operating Costs	($750,000)
Operating Profit	$150,000
Interest Expense	($48,000)
Profit Before Income Tax	$102,000

Figure 8-1: The profit model.

The following sections briefly explain the five key factors that drive profit. Chapters 2 and 6 offer more extensive explanations of revenue, costs, and cost control.

Net sales revenue

The starting point in the profit model is *net sales revenue,* which equals the total volume (quantity) of all products sold times their *net sales prices.* The net sales price of a product is its list sales price less any discounts and allowances given to the customer, and less variable costs that can be directly matched against the sale.

A manufacturer's suggested retail price (MSRP), or sticker price, is an example of a *list price.* The sales prices printed in its catalogs and price sheets by a business are its list prices. The shelf prices of the products sold by retailers are list prices. As you probably know, list prices aren't always the actual amount of sales revenue received by a business. The list price on the gas pump is the actual price you pay per gallon, but for many products, list prices are just the point of departure.

Actual prices are less than list prices for many reasons. Many factors drive down the actual sales revenue received by the business. For example, retailers accept credit cards, such as VISA, MasterCard, Discover, American Express, and Diners Club. The credit card sales invoices are deposited with the participating bank. The bank discounts a certain percent from the amount of the sale and credits the balance in the business's checking account. Discount rates vary between 2 to 4 percent (sometimes lower or higher). So, the business nets only 98¢ to 96¢ from each dollar of a credit card sale.

The credit-card discount comes right off the top of each sales dollar. The business avoids the expenses of extending and administering credit directly to its customers. Many retailers accept debit cards. The discounts and fees charged to the business by the bank that issues a debit card may be more favorable than traditional credit cards.

Sales commissions are another common example of an expense that comes right off the top of sales revenue. As you probably know, many businesses pay their sales staff on a commission basis, which usually is a certain percent of the total sales amount. If the sales commission is, say, 5 percent, the business nets only 95 cents on a dollar of sales.

In selling to other businesses, a company usually extends short-term credit, called *trade credit.* No matter how carefully customers are screened before they're extended credit, a few never pay what they owe the business. Eventually, after making repeated collection efforts, the business ends up writing off these uncollectible receivable balances. These losses are called *bad debts* and are a normal expense of doing business on credit. Based on its experience and credit policies, a business can estimate the percent of its credit sales that will end up being written off as bad debts. For example, for every $10,000 of sales revenue (net of discounts), a small business manager may expect that $250 will not be collected despite its best efforts to screen customers.

Another example of an expense that is a direct offset against sales revenue is one you may not think of — *rent.* A small business may sign a lease agreement that calls for rental amounts based on gross sales. The lease calls for a certain base amount, or fixed minimum monthly rent. In addition, the lessee pays a variable amount equal to a percent of total sales revenue. Paying a variable component on top of the fixed minimum amount of rent is common for retailers renting space in shopping centers. The *franchise fee* paid by a franchisee is typically based on gross sales, which is another example of a direct deduction from sales revenue.

A business may offer its credit customers *prompt payment discounts* from list prices if they pay within ten days of the sale. Some businesses offer *quantity discounts* to customers if they buy a case of products (such as a wine retailer offering 10 percent off the price per bottle). Many businesses give nonprofit customers *special discounts* from list prices. Businesses sometimes negotiate price reductions, called *allowances,* after the time of sale. Mail-in rebates have become very popular in recent years. Auto dealers give you money back when you buy a new auto or pick up truck (which they really don't of course, but we don't discuss this sales tactic).

In summary, the profit model starts with *net* sales revenue to the business, which is less than the amount of sales revenue at list prices. The sales revenue figure in the profit model is net of discounts from list prices, sales commissions, sales price allowances, and direct variable costs based on sales revenue. Suppose in the example that after deducting discounts, sales commissions, allowances, and direct costs of making sales your net sales revenue is only 85 percent of list sales prices. At list prices, sales revenue would have been more than $3,500,000. But, as you see in Figure 8-1, net sales revenue is $3,000,000, which is the actual revenue you have to work with to recover your costs and to provide profit.

Product costs and variable operating costs

The product costs line in the profit model (see Figure 8-1) includes losses from inventory shrinkage and inventory write-downs caused by declines in the replacement and sales values of products. (We explain these losses in Chapter 6.) Generally these losses run parallel with your cost of goods sold expense. The $1,650,000 product costs in Figure 8-1 includes $82,500 loss from inventory shrinkage and write-downs, which is 5 percent of the total product costs. Of course, some businesses experience higher rates of inventory shrinkage, and some lower.

Variable operating costs (see the next line in Figure 8-1) are those that depend mainly on sales volume. Packaging, shipping, and delivery costs are prime examples. For example, at stores, customers' purchases are put in plastic bags and paper sacks, and this cost depends on the number of products sold. The size of variable operating costs relative to sales varies from business to business. In the profit model example, this cost is high enough to hold your interest.

Deducting product costs and variable operating costs from net sales revenue gives the all-important figure called *margin.* Margin is the measure of profit before fixed costs are deducted. (Accountants also call this *contribution margin;* the idea is that margin contributes toward covering fixed costs.) In Figure 8-1, you earn $900,000 margin, which is calculated by deducting $1,650,000 product costs and $450,000 variable operating costs from the $3,000,000 net sales revenue. Basically, *margin is revenue minus variable costs.*

Fixed operating costs

Every business is saddled with *fixed operating costs.* Your company's fixed operating costs are $750,000 for the year, which includes depreciation expense on your fixed assets. The amount of depreciation expense recorded in the year is a fixed amount regardless of whether the long-term operating assets are used heavily or lightly during the period. Chapter 6 explains that the depreciation expense amount recorded annually depends on the choice of accounting method. In contrast, a business doesn't have a choice of accounting methods for recording its other fixed operating costs — although a business does have some latitude in making estimates for some fixed costs and in the precise timing for recording certain fixed costs.

Fixed means that these operating costs, for all practical purposes, are locked in for the year. Your fixed operating costs are the same whether your sales are higher or lower than actual sales for the year. Examples of fixed costs are employees paid fixed salaries, building rent, many types of insurance, and your annual CPA fee. Property taxes and vehicle licenses are fixed amounts for the year. Once spent, advertising is a fixed cost.

Fixed costs are like the old joke about hell: It's easy to get in, but very hard to get out. For all practical purposes, you can't change fixed costs over the short run. The longer the time horizon, however, the more you can adjust fixed costs up or down. It takes a relatively long time to get out from fixed cost obligations. Once you've made these commitments, you can only hope that your actual sales will be high enough to justify your fixed operating costs.

Fixed operating costs can't be scaled down over the short run — unless the business takes drastic action, such as breaking contracts, firing employees, or delaying payment of property taxes. For all practical purposes, fixed operating costs are locked in place for the year. Fixed operating costs are called *overhead costs* because these costs hang over the head of the managers running the business like an albatross. Fixed costs are also called the *nut* of the business, and a tough nut to crack.

Why would any rational manager commit to fixed overhead costs? The short answer is that fixed operating costs provide *sales capacity*. These costs make available the people and facilities to carry on sales activity and the operations of the business. Fixed costs are incurred to provide the needed space, equipment, and personnel to sell products and to carry on the operating activities of the business. By committing to these costs, the business acquires a certain amount of capability of making sales.

A small business manager should estimate the sales capacity of the business — the maximum sales volume provided by the fixed operating costs of the business. Estimating sales capacity is not all that precise. But you can make a reasonable, ballpark estimate. The manager can start by asking whether a 10 percent sales volume increase would require an increase in the business's fixed costs. Your business may have a sizable amount of unused sales capacity. Perhaps your sales could grow 10, 20, or 30 percent before you'd need to rent more space, hire more employees, or purchase more equipment. Sizing up the unused sales capacity of your business is especially important in planning ahead and in analyzing the profit impact of changes in the key factors that drive profit.

One bit of advice: The term *fixed* should be used with some caution. True, the fixed operating costs of a business for the year are largely unchanging and inflexible — but not down to the last penny. The main point about fixed costs is that they're insensitive to the number of units sold during the period. You can adjust many fixed costs if sales drop off precipitously or surge ahead rapidly. For example, suppose that your sales take a sudden and unexpected downturn. You could sublet part of the space you rent, reduce your insurance policy limits, or sell some real estate you own. On the other hand, if sales spurted up suddenly, you could ask employees to work overtime hours. The term *fixed* really means that these costs remain largely constant over a range of sales activity that may be 10 or 20 percent lower or higher than your actual sales volume.

Managers should be equally vigilant and hard-nosed about their fixed operating costs as they are about their product costs and variable operating costs (see preceding section). Managers should take a close look at their fixed costs even when sales are good. All too often, it takes a steep nosedive in sales to get managers to scrutinize their fixed costs. Reducing fixed costs require tough decisions. You may have to lay off employees, sell off surplus assets, and rent smaller quarters. But if you're not utilizing the full potential of your fixed operating costs and if you don't predict much future sales growth, you should bite the bullet and get to work downsizing your fixed operating costs.

In the profit model example (see Figure 8-1), the $750,000 fixed operating costs are deducted from the $900,000 margin to determine your $150,000 *operating profit,* which also is called *operating earnings,* or *earnings before interest and income tax* (EBIT). Don't forget that to make profit, you need assets, and to finance your assets, you probably use some debt capital.

Interest expense

In Chapters 3 and 6, we explain the balance sheet of a business. On one side of the balance sheet are your assets. On the other side are the sources of your assets, which consist of three basic types — operating liabilities, interest-bearing debt, and owners' equity. Accounts payable and accrued expenses payable are the two main kinds of operating liabilities. Debt is classified as either short term (maturity dates of one year or shorter) or long term (maturity dates more than one year out).

The business shown in Figure 8-1 has $1,500,000 total assets. This amount of total assets is not atypical for a business that has $3,000,000 annual sales. The total of its operating liabilities (mainly accounts payable and accrued expenses payable) is $300,000. These non-interest bearing liabilities arise in the normal course of operations, in particular from making purchases on credit and not paying certain expenses immediately. Subtracting operating liabilities from total assets gives $1,200,000, which is the amount of capital that your business has raised. One-half, or $600,000 of your capital, is from interest-bearing debt. Your interest expense for the year is $48,000 (see Figure 8-1). Thus, your annual interest rate is 8 percent:

$48,000 annual interest expense ÷ $600,000 debt = 8% annual interest rate

The mix of debt to equity, or debt to equity ratio, varies from business to business, and interest rates vary, of course. Using debt for half of your capital is fairly aggressive. Many businesses are more conservative and prefer to keep their debt level less than half of total capital. The main point is that you should have a clear idea of the amount of assets you need to support your level of sales and how much of the capital for your total assets is supplied from interest-bearing debt. As the owner/manager of the business, you make this critical decision regarding how to finance the business. (Chapters 4 and 10 explain raising capital and making sure that your business is able to pay liabilities on time.)

Stopping at Profit Before Income Tax

Deducting $48,000 interest expense from $150,000 operating profit gives $102,000 profit — before income tax is considered, roughly speaking, and we're as rough as sandpaper when we say that the taxable income of a business equals operating profit minus interest expense. As you know, income tax is a very complicated topic even for a small business. Most small businesses use a tax professional to determine their annual taxable income, as well they should.

Because of the complexity of income tax and because many small businesses don't pay income tax themselves as a separate entity, we stop the profit model at profit before income tax. Keep in mind, however, that there is an income tax liability hovering over the $102,000 profit line in the profit model. Chapter 9 explains income tax and the small business.

Improving Margin

Business managers are under constant pressure to improve profit performance. Before going into profit improvement analysis, we have a hypothetical question for you. Suppose that you could have one or the other but not both: Would you prefer a 10 percent sales *volume* increase or a 10 percent *sales price* increase? There is a huge profit difference between the two, everything else being equal.

Marketing managers would quickly argue that higher sales volume would increase market share, and in the long run, a larger market share leads to more control over sales prices. In any case, we suggest that you make a mental note of your tentative answer. The next two sections examine the effects of increasing sales volume and then increasing sales prices. One is definitely better than the other.

Increasing sales volume

Business managers, quite naturally, are sales oriented. No sales, no business — it's as simple as that. As they say in marketing "Nothing happens until you sell it." Many businesses don't make it through their startup phase because it's very difficult to build up and establish a customer base. Customers have to be won over. Once established, sales volume can never be taken for granted. Sales are vulnerable to competition, shifts in consumer preferences and spending decisions, and general economic conditions.

Thinking more positively, sales volume growth is the most realistic way to increase profit. Sales price increases are met with some degree of customer resistance in most cases, as well as competitive response. Indeed, demand may be extremely sensitive to sales prices. Cost containment and expense control are important, to be sure, but they're more in the nature of defensive tactics and don't constitute a sustainable profit growth strategy.

Suppose that you could increase sales volume 10 percent and that your variable cost factors remain the same as given in the profit model example. Figure 8-2 shows the impacts of increasing sales volume 10 percent, with some question marks.

	Profit Model Example	Ten Percent Sales Volume Increase Scenario	Changes
Net Sales Revenue	$3,000,000	$3,300,000	+ 10.0%
Product Costs	($1,650,000)	($1,815,000)	+ 10.0%
Variable Operating Costs	($450,000)	($495,000)	+ 10.0%
Margin	$900,000	$990,000	+ 10.0%
Fixed Operating Costs	($750,000)	?	
Operating Profit	$150,000	?	
Interest Expense	($48,000)	?	
Profit Before Income Tax	$102,000	?	

Figure 8-2: The 10 percent sales volume increase scenario.

The 10 percent increase in sales volume increases net sales revenue, product costs, and variable operating costs 10 percent. So, margin increases 10 percent, or $90,000 in the example shown in Figure 8-2. But now you have to answer some interesting questions. Would your fixed operating costs increase with 10 percent more sales volume? Would your interest expense increase? We can't offer general answers that fit all situations.

First of all, do you have some sales capacity slack hidden in the $750,000 fixed operating costs? In other words, do you have some unused, idle sales capacity such that you could take on 10 percent more volume without having to increase your fixed costs? Perhaps your fixed costs would increase only slightly at the higher sales level (maybe some overtime hours, for example). Many businesses have surplus sales capacity. A relatively modest increase in sales volume doesn't increase their fixed operating costs. Assume, therefore, that fixed operating costs don't increase (or that the increase is relatively minor).

What about your interest expense? The size of your interest expense is explained in the earlier section "Interest Expense." Recall that the ratio of annual net sales revenue to total assets is 2 to 1:

> $3,000,000 annual net sales revenue ÷ $1,500,000 total assets = 2 times, or 2 to 1 ratio

This ratio of sales to assets is called the *asset turnover ratio*. Some businesses are asset heavy, or capital intensive. They need a lot of assets relative to their sales, which means that they have relatively low asset turnover ratios. Other businesses don't need a lot of assets to support their sales; they have high asset turnover ratios. In any case, the profit model builds on a 2 to 1 asset turnover ratio. Therefore, the additional $300,000 net sales revenue (see Figure 8-2) would drive up total assets $150,000:

> $300,000 net sales revenue increase ÷ 2 times asset turnover ratio = $150,000 total assets increase

In the example, operating (non-interest bearing) liabilities equal 20 percent of total assets. So only 80 percent of the increase in assets, or $120,000, would come from an increase in capital. Debt supplies half of capital, so debt increases $60,000 at the higher sales volume level. Your interest rate is 8 percent per year, so interest expense would increase $4,800 at the higher sales volume:

> $60,000 increase in interest-bearing debt at higher sales volume level × 8.0% annual interest rate = $4,800 interest expense increase

It's tempting to ignore the change in assets caused by an increase in sales volume, but it would cause you to overlook the interest expense increase caused by the increase in interest-bearing debt needed at the higher level of assets. Higher sales volume generally requires higher levels of assets (inventory, accounts receivable, and so on). Even if you don't do a precise calculation based on your asset turnover ratio, we recommend that you make a reasonable guess for the interest expense increase.

Assume that fixed operating costs don't increase at the higher sales volume because you have enough slack, or unused sales capacity, to handle the sales volume increase (which may not be true in some situations, of course). Deducting the $4,800 interest expense increase from the $90,000 margin increase gives the $85,200 boost to the bottom line (profit before income tax), resulting in an 83.5 percent increase in profit:

> $85,200 increase in profit before income tax ÷ $102,000 profit at present sales volume = 83.5% increase in profit at 10% higher sales volume level

This percentage gain in profit is impressive, to say the least. But don't forget that it's based on the critical assumption that fixed operating costs don't increase at the higher sales volume level. If you had to increase your fixed costs to support the higher sales volume level, the increase in profit would be much smaller, of course. Indeed, it could be that you'd have to increase fixed operating costs more than the $90,000 margin increase to support a 10 percent jump in sales volume — which should give you second thoughts about increasing sales volume, of course. But if your fixed operating costs can support a higher sales volume, then the profit payoff is quite handsome.

By the way, the 83.5 percent gain in profit versus the much smaller 10 percent increase in sales volume (in this example) is referred to as the *operating leverage* effect. In other words, you're getting better leverage out of your fixed costs by selling more units. You're spreading your fixed operating costs over a greater number of units.

An experienced business manager would raise some very pertinent questions about an increase in sales volume. How are you going to increase sales volume? Would your customers buy 10 percent more units without any increase in advertising, or without sales price incentives, or without product improvements, or without other inducements? Increasing sales volume usually requires some stimulant, such as more advertising, that would increase your fixed operating costs. Improving product quality would increase product cost. If you increase sales by opening another location, your fixed costs would definitely increase. These are good points to keep in mind.

Looking at a sales volume decline

Suppose that things don't look good for next year; you forecast that you'll sell 10 percent fewer units next year, and perhaps even worse. You'd be very much concerned, of course, and probe into the reasons for the decrease. More competition? Are people switching to substitute products? Are hard times forcing customers to spend less? Is the location deteriorating? Has customer service slipped?

A sales volume decline is one of the most serious problems confronting any business. Unless the decline is quickly reversed, you'll have to make extremely wrenching decisions regarding how to downsize the business. These decisions usually involve laying off employees, selling off fixed assets, shutting down locations, and so on. The profit impact of a sales volume decrease depends heavily on whether you can reduce your fixed operating costs in order to adjust to the lower sales volume.

Suppose that your sales volume drops 10 percent, and you're not able to decrease fixed operating costs. Your margin would drop $90,000. (See Figure 8-2 for dollar amounts, keeping in mind that we're talking about a *negative* change in sales volume.) Because you don't reduce fixed operating costs, your operating profit would drop $90,000. Your assets would fall at the lower level of sales. Supposedly, you could decrease your debt load at the lower level of assets, in which case your interest should fall somewhat. But any way you slice it, suffering a 10 percent drop in sales volume wipes out most of your profit.

The moral is that if you suffer decline in sales volume and can't reverse the decline, then you must reduce your fixed operating costs. But, to be frank, this step is no more than bailing water out of the lifeboat. If sales continue to decline, you have to seriously consider throwing in the towel and getting out of business. We discuss the end stage of a business in Chapter 15.

Raising sales prices

Setting sales prices is one of the most perplexing decisions facing business managers. Competition normally dictates the basic range of sales prices. But usually you have some room for deviation from your competitors' prices because of product differentiation, brand loyalty, location advantages, and quality of service — to cite just some of the reasons that permit higher sales prices than your competitors.

In any case, the purpose here is to look at the effects of higher sales prices while holding sales volume constant. Suppose that your net sales prices had been 10 percent higher than in the profit model example, shown in Figure 8-1. Of course, a 10 percent increase in net sales prices is very significant. Customers would probably react to a sales price increase of this magnitude — well, except for increases in gas prices at the pump, it seems.

Figure 8-3 shows the profit factor changes if sales prices had been 10 percent higher. Basically, net sales revenue increases 10 percent, or $300,000, and only your interest expense would go up with the higher sales prices. Because you sell the same volume of products, your product costs and variable operating costs would not change, and your fixed operating costs should not change at the higher sales prices. You would generate more sales revenue, so your total assets and debt would increase. Your interest would increase $4,800 at the higher debt level. (The earlier discussion in the section "Increasing sales volume" explains this amount.)

Figure 8-3 shows that profit would increase almost four times, from about $100,000 to about $400,000. Quite clearly, a 10 percent sales price increase is far superior to 10 percent sales volume increase. Two main reasons result in the relatively large gain in profit from the sales price increase:

✓ The incremental $300,000 net sales revenue is *pure margin;* product costs and variable operating costs don't increase at the higher sales prices, so the entire increase in net sales revenue benefits margin.

✓ Fixed operating costs aren't affected by the higher sales prices; the fact that you're moving more sales dollars through the business at the higher prices should not cause any of your fixed costs to change.

	Profit Model Example	Ten Percent Sales Price Increase Scenario	Changes
Net Sales Revenue	$3,000,000	$3,300,000	$300,000
Product Costs	($1,650,000)	($1,650,000)	no change
Variable Operating Costs	($450,000)	($450,000)	no change
Margin	$900,000	$1,200,000	$300,000
Fixed Operating Costs	($750,000)	($750,000)	no change
Operating Profit	$150,000	$450,000	$300,000
Interest Expense	($48,000)	($52,800)	($4,800)
Profit Before Income Tax	$102,000	$397,200	$295,200

Figure 8-3: The 10 percent sales price increase scenario.

Now, you may be thinking that the 10 percent higher sales prices scenario shown in Figure 8-3 is too good to be true. You know the first principle in economics is that there is no such thing as a free lunch. So, what's the catch? Well, the main caveat is that in most cases it's extremely difficult to raise sales prices 10 percent. As you know, customers generally are very sensitive to sales prices, and pushing through a sales price increase of this magnitude would be very difficult in most situations. On the other hand, your sales prices may be too low, and your customers may not bolt to a competitor if you raised prices 10 percent. In any case our purpose is to demonstrate the *profit power* of increasing sales prices versus increasing sales volume.

We can demonstrate the relative advantage of sales price increases over sales volume increases in another manner. In the 10 percent sales volume increase scenario, profit increases $85,200, from $102,000 to $187,200 (assuming that fixed operating costs don't increase at the higher sales volume level). By what percent would you have to increase net sales prices to increase profit the same amount?

Remember that interest expense increases as net sales revenue increases. In Figure 8-3, interest expense equals 1.6 percent of net sales revenue. This ratio is based on the business's asset turnover ratio of 2 to 1, the proportion of its debt to total capital, and the interest rate. The following calculations show that interest equals 1.6 percent of net sales revenue (see Figure 8-3 for data):

> $48,000 interest expense ÷ $3,000,000 net sales revenue = 1.6% in profit model example

> $52,800 interest expense ÷ $3,300,000 net sales revenue = 1.6% in higher sales price scenario

In other words, interest expense absorbs 1.6 percent of the increase in net sales revenue. Therefore, to increase profit $85,200, you have to increase net sales revenue a little more, or $86,585, to be precise:

> $85,200 ÷ 98.4% profit after interest expense increase = $86,585 net sales revenue increase to cover interest expense increases

The $86,585 increase in net sales revenue would require a 2.9 percent increase in sales prices:

> $86,585 increase in net sales revenue ÷ $3,000,000 net sales revenue = 2.9 percent increase in sales prices

Less than a 3 percent sales price increase would produce the same profit gain as a 10 percent sales volume increase. Given your druthers, you should look first to the possibility of increasing sales prices. But, in many situations, you can't boost sales prices, so your only option is to increase sales volume. Or, perhaps you could do some of both. In passing, we should mention that in most cases, certain products and product lines have higher margins than others, and increasing sales volume in these areas would be better than in the lower margin areas.

Looking at a sales price decrease

It's no secret that a small business may be forced to cut sales prices in some situations. You don't like taking this step, of course, but you should at least have a clear idea of how bad a profit hit you'd take from cutting sales prices. If we were the owners/managers of a business, we'd definitely make a quick calculation of the profit damage from cutting sales prices — rather than waiting for the sad results to show up in our next P&L report. Indeed, the analysis is very helpful in deciding just how far you can go in slashing sales prices without courting disaster.

Even a seemingly minor sales price decrease can wipe out profit. Suppose that your business comes under competitive pressure and you're thinking of lowering your sales prices by, say, 5 percent. You plan to offer special rebates and bigger quantity discounts. List prices will not be reduced, but the effect will be to reduce the net sales prices of the products you sell by 5 percent. A 5 percent sales price cut may not seem too bad on the surface. But you better do some quick calculations to be sure about this. The profit model is the best tool for this analysis.

In the example, you're seriously considering cutting net sales prices 5 percent. Hopefully, this tactic is temporary. You hope that you'll be able to raise sales prices back to their normal levels before too long. Keep in mind, however, that once you lower sales prices, you may see a ratchet effect. Your customers may get used to the lower prices and resist any attempt to raise prices back up to their previous levels. So, be very cautious about cutting sales prices.

Suppose that the lower sales prices continue for one year, and that other factors in the profit model don't change. In other words, product costs, as well as variable and fixed operating costs, don't change during the year (which may not be the case of course). Figure 8-4 presents the results for a 5 percent decrease in sales prices.

The $150,000 slump in net sales revenue (see Figure 8-4) causes your margin to plunge from $900,000 to $750,000. This is very bad news. Your fixed operating costs are $750,000, so at the lower sales prices, operating profit is zero. (Accountants call this situation the *breakeven point.*) By cutting sales prices 5 percent, you're giving away all your operating profit. Your interest expense would drop a little because net sales revenue drops, so your total assets and debt should go down. You end up with $45,600 loss (before income tax) in this scenario.

What's the moral of the story? Profit is very sensitive to changes in sales prices. As the example demonstrates, a 5 percent decline in sales prices can wipe out operating profit. Profit performance swings wildly with changes in sales prices, much more so than an equal percent change in sales volume. This lesson is extremely important for keeping your business in the profit column.

	Profit Model Example	Five Percent Sales Price Decrease Scenario	Changes
Net Sales Revenue	$3,000,000	$2,850,000	($150,000)
Product Costs	($1,650,000)	($1,650,000)	no change
Variable Operating Costs	($450,000)	($450,000)	no change
Margin	$900,000	$750,000	($150,000)
Fixed Operating Costs	($750,000)	($750,000)	no change
Operating Profit	$150,000	$0	($150,000)
Interest Expense	($48,000)	($45,600)	$2,400
Profit Before Income Tax	$102,000	($45,600)	($147,600)

Figure 8-4: The 5 percent sales price decrease scenario.

Using the Profit Model for Trade-off Analysis

You can use the basic profit model (see Figure 8-1) for any number of decision-making situations. It's not limited to changing just one factor at a time. A classic use of the model is for trade-off analysis.

Cutting prices to gain volume

Your sales manager has put forth a proposal to decrease sales prices 5 percent. He predicts that this sales price reduction would increase sales volume 10 percent, maybe more. On the surface, this one-for-two trade-off appears to be a good move. Giving up 5 percent of sales prices for 10 percent more sales volume appears to be a no-brainer. Before cranking the numbers, however, you should think about several nonquantitative aspects of making a radical change in your business's profit strategy.

Your competition may follow you down in price, so your sales volume may not increase. On the other hand, your competitors may not follow you down on sales prices. Your products are differentiated from your competitors' products. And your products have stronger brand names. For several years, there have been sales price spreads between your products and those offered by the competition. In your opinion, a 5 percent price cut probably would not trigger price reductions by your competitors. Even if the competition followed you down in sale prices, the market-wide demand for these types of products may increase at lower sales prices.

One reason for seriously considering the proposal is that your business isn't selling up to capacity, which isn't an unusual situation. Many businesses have some slack, or unused capacity, that is provided by their fixed operating costs. Your present level of fixed operating costs provides enough space and personnel to handle a sizable increase in sales volume, 20 percent or more according to your best estimate. Therefore, the sales manager's proposal to increase sales volume is attractive. You can spread fixed costs over a larger sales volume, which reduces the fixed cost per unit sold. Surely a lower average fixed cost per unit improves profit, doesn't it? You'd better check the numbers to be sure.

Of course, customers may not respond to the sales price reductions as much as your sales manager predicts. Or sales volume may increase more than 10 percent. In any case, if you go ahead and cut sales prices, you should definitely keep a close eye on the reaction of customers. One serious risk is that if sales volume doesn't increase, you may not be able to reverse directions. You may not be able to roll back the sales price decreases. Customers may see only the reversals and perceive that you are raising prices. But, putting your concerns aside, you and the sales manager are of the opinion that lower prices would induce customers to buy more products.

Figure 8-5 presents the full year results for the scenario in which you cut sales prices 5 percent, which triggers a 10 percent gain in sales volume. You may be surprised to see that your margin falls $75,000 in this scenario, and your profit would go down even more because interest expense would expand a little at the higher net sales revenue level. Also keep in mind that this scenario assumes that your fixed operating costs don't change.

	Sales price decrease =	5%		
	Sales volume increase =	10%		

		Profit Model Example	Sales Price/ Sales Volume Trade-Off Scenario	Changes
	Net Sales Revenue	$3,000,000	$3,135,000	$135,000
	Product Costs	($1,650,000)	($1,815,000)	($165,000)
	Variable Operating Costs	($450,000)	($495,000)	($45,000)
	Margin	$900,000	$825,000	($75,000)
	Fixed Operating Costs	($750,000)	($750,000)	no change
	Operating Profit	$150,000	$75,000	($75,000)
	Interest Expense	($48,000)	($50,160)	($2,160)
	Profit Before Income Tax	$102,000	$24,840	($77,160)

Figure 8-5: The sales price decrease/ sales volume increase scenario.

Quite clearly, the 5 percent sales price decrease and 10 percent sales volume trade-off would be a poor decision, despite looking attractive at first glance Why?

To answer the question, suppose that you sell 1,000 units of one product. Dividing the total amounts in Figure 8-5 by 1,000 gives the per unit amounts. Margin per unit is $900. (See Figure 8-5 for data and remember to divide by 1,000 units to get the per unit amounts.)

> ($3,000 sales price – $1,650 product cost per unit – $450 variable operating costs per unit) = $900 margin per unit

Cutting sales price 5 percent decreases your margin per unit $150 ($3,000 sales price × 5 percent sales price reduction = $150). Based on the 1,000 units sales volume, your margin would drop $150,000. You have to sell a lot more units just to offset the drop in margin. Each unit you sell at the lower sales price contributes $750 margin per unit ($900 margin per unit before sales price reduction – $150 sales price decrease = $750 margin per unit). Just to earn the same margin, you have to sell 200 additional units ($150,000 reduction in margin at the lower sales price ÷ $750 margin per unit = 20,000 additional units). A 10 percent, or 100 units, increase in sales volume doesn't cut the mustard.

By cutting sales prices, you sacrifice margin that you're already earning on your present sales. You have to sell a lot more units just to compensate for the margin you give up at the lower sales prices. To actually increase margin (and profit) you have to sell even more units. Is this likely? You have to be the judge and jury on this question.

Just to keep profit before income tax the same, you'd have to increase sales volume 21 percent — see Figure 8-6 for this answer. To solve for this sales volume change percent, we kept changing the percent until profit was the same for both scenarios (see Figure 8-6). The CD supplied with the book provides the spreadsheet template you can use to do this simulation for the circumstances of your particular decision situation. Doing such realistic simulations is a huge advantage of a computer-based spreadsheet program. (Microsoft's Excel is the most widely used spreadsheet program, as you probably know.)

Once a spreadsheet template is prepared, you can analyze and compare all sorts of alternative scenarios. Spreadsheets do all the calculations for you. (But remember the first rule of computer programming — *garbage in, garbage out;* if the data input or formulas are wrong, the results are wrong.) For example, you could budget a profit increase of, say, $100,000, and change sales prices or sales volume, or a mix of both to see what it would take to reach your new profit goal.

If you don't have time (or don't like using computers), have your Controller do the number crunching. If your Controller doesn't know how to use the Excel spreadsheet program, you should tell him to get up to speed in a hurry. These days, knowing how to use Excel is just as essential as knowing how to use a ten-key calculator was when John went into public accounting in 1956. (In those days, we used worksheets, which were the forerunners of today's computer-based spreadsheets.)

		Profit Model Example	Sales Price/ Sales Volume Trade-Off Scenario	Changes
Sales price decrease =		5%		
Sales volume increase =		21%		
Net Sales Revenue		$3,000,000	$3,447,189	$447,189
Product Costs		($1,650,000)	($1,995,741)	($345,741)
Variable Operating Costs		($450,000)	($544,293)	($94,293)
Margin		$900,000	$907,155	$7,155
Fixed Operating Costs		($750,000)	($750,000)	no change
Operating Profit		$150,000	$157,155	$7,155
Interest Expense		($48,000)	($55,155)	($7,155)
Profit Before Income Tax		$102,000	$102,000	($0)

Figure 8-6: Sales volume increase needed to counter-balance sales price decrease.

Sacrificing volume for higher prices

An idea has been floating around in the back of your head. Why not *increase* sales prices in order to improve margin? Sure, sales volume probably would fall off. But you think the sales volume decrease wouldn't be too drastic. Furthermore, at the lower sales volume, you'd be able to downsize fixed operating costs.

Your sales manager doesn't think along these lines. Sales managers generally are opposed to giving up sales volume. They argue that the loss of market share is hard to recapture later. Any decision that deliberately decreases sales volume should be considered very carefully. You can use the profit model to analyze the consequences of deliberately boosting sales prices knowing that sales volume will suffer.

You're thinking of raising sales prices 10 percent. Most certainly, your sales volume would fall off; you predict that sales volume will drop 20 percent. In this case, would margin decrease, or would it increase? Fixed operating costs are considered later. (These costs certainly wouldn't increase at the lower sales volume level.) Figure 8-7 shows the results of this scenario (holding fixed operating costs the same.) Margin would increase $60,000, or about 7 percent — before savings in fixed operating costs are considered. This tradeoff provides a very nice profit boost— see Figure 8-7.

Nevertheless, many business managers in this situation would decide *against* raising sales prices — even though the numbers show an excellent gain in profit. By and large successful companies have built their success on getting, keeping, and expanding a base of loyal and satisfied customers who make repeat purchases. Furthermore, few businesses are voluntarily willing to give up market share. When a business has a significant market share it is a major player and dominant force in the marketplace, which provides very impor-tant competitive advantages.

In short, there is a heavy bias against giving up sales volume. Also, many business mangers argue that cutting sales prices is the classic mistake of thinking only in the short-run. From the long-run point of view many man-agers doubt that a business can maintain its sales prices higher than the competition for any length of time.

To be more conservative in your analysis you could assume a 25 or larger percent decrease in sales volume from increasing sales prices. You can use the profit model template (Figure 8-7) on the CD supplied with the book to determine the exact percent that sales volume would have to decrease in order to keep profit the same amount. (Your sales volume would have to fall about 26 percent to keep profit the same.)

	Sales price increase =	10%	
	Sales volume decrease =	20%	

	Profit Model Example	Sales Price/ Sales Volume Trade-Off Scenario	Changes
Net Sales Revenue	$3,000,000	$2,640,000	($360,000)
Product Costs	($1,650,000)	($1,320,000)	$330,000
Variable Operating Costs	($450,000)	($360,000)	$90,000
Margin	$900,000	$960,000	$60,000
Fixed Operating Costs	($750,000)	($750,000)	no change
Operating Profit	$150,000	$210,000	$60,000
Interest Expense	($48,000)	($42,240)	$5,760
Profit Before Income Tax	$102,000	$167,760	$65,760

Figure 8-7: The sales price increase/ sales volume decrease scenario.

Predicting how sales demand would respond to a sales price increase is very difficult, particularly if your competitors don't raise their sales prices. A 10 percent sales price increase for most products is a big chunk of change. If new auto prices jumped 10 percent, for example, sales demand would fall off significantly. On the other hand, increasing sales prices may actually stimulate demand for some products. The higher prices may enhance the prestige or premium image of the company's products and attract a more upscale clientele who are quite willing to pay higher prices. Some businesses carve out a relatively small market niche and build their profit performance on low sales volume at premium prices. Or, the business may provide its customers better service than its competitors, and the customers are willing to pay for. In any case, the analysis just explained demonstrates the profit logic of the niche strategy, which is built on high margin that makes up for smaller sales volume.

On balance, the majority of business managers probably would rather keep their market share and not give up any sales volume, even though profit could theoretically be increased in the short run with a higher sales price/lower sales volume mix. Protecting sales volume and market share is deeply ingrained in the thinking of most business managers, for good reasons.

Pushing Cost Increases Through to Prices

One basic function of business managers, not discussed that much, is raising sales prices in order to pass along to customers increases in product costs and operating costs of the business caused by inflation. Managers must get customers to pay higher prices to cover the higher costs of the business, which is not an easy task, to say the least. The main purpose is not to improve profit performance as such, but simply to increase sales prices to pay for cost increases.

The costs of the large majority of products (with some notable exceptions) tend to rise over time. Customers generally accept higher sales prices if they perceive that the company is operating in an inflationary environment. In their minds, everything is going up. A particular product doesn't cost more relative to price increases of other products they purchase, and hopefully their wages or other incomes are going up at about the same rate as inflation. (This assumption isn't true for people on fixed incomes, of course.)

Higher sales prices may not adversely affect sales volume in a market with an inflation mentality. Assuming that competitors also face general cost inflation, a company's sales volume may not suffer from passing along product cost increases in higher sales prices — the competition is doing the same thing. On the other hand, if customers' incomes aren't rising in proportion with sales price increases, demand will likely fall off at higher sales prices.

Getting Behind the Reasons for Cost Changes

General price level inflation throughout the economy pushes up the expenses of a business like a rising tide that lifts all boats. The defining characteristic of inflation is that the actual quality and quantity (or size), of an economic good doesn't change, but its price increases. Inflation-driven cost increases are quite distinct from deliberate cost increases a business makes to improve its sales volume or, as strange as it may sound, to improve its margins by increasing sales prices more than the increases in costs. These *strategic cost changes* should be distinguished from general inflation cost changes.

Looking into reasons for fixed costs increases

Most fixed operating costs increase over time. This fact is hardly new to the small business manager. General inflationary pressures may drive up these costs. For example, utility bills, real estate taxes, and insurance premiums drift relentlessly upward and seem hardly ever to go down. You don't find very many fixed costs that follow a steady downward trend line.

When fixed operating costs increase due to general inflationary trends, no change occurs in a company's warehouse and retail space, the appearance (attractiveness) of the retail space the number of employees, and so on. As far as customers can tell, they see no changes that would benefit them. A business has to increase its sales prices to pass through the increase in its fixed costs.

On the other hand, fixed operating costs may be deliberately increased (over and above inflation-driven increases) to expand sales capacity. A business may rent a larger space or hire more employees on fixed salaries to provide for a larger sales capacity. A manufacturer may expand its plant, facilities, and workforce to provide greater production capacity. Over time, a business has to keep its capacity (and thus its fixed operating costs) in alignment with its sales volume. In any one year, a business may have a certain amount of idle, or unused, capacity. But the business has to plan carefully to keep its capacity consistent with sales volume.

Instead of expanding capacity, fixed costs may be increased by a business to improve demand for its products and the customer traffic of its present location. For example, a business could invest in better furnishings and equipment.

Looking into reasons for variable costs increases

Consider the cost of a product that a business manufactures or purchases. An inflation-driven cost increase means that the product remains the same, but now costs more per unit. In contrast, a strategic cost increase improves the quality or size of the product; the product itself is changed. Inflation is external to a business — these cost increases are driven by outside forces over which the business has little or no control. Strategic cost increases are internal to a business. They're the result of deliberate decisions by a business to change its products or operating practices as part of an overall plan to improve sales volume or sales prices, or both.

Inflation is one thing; quite another is when a business makes changes to deliberately increase the costs of its products. The quality of the products is improved to make them more attractive to customers. Making product improvements is a common marketing strategy, designed to give customers a better product at the same sales price in order to stimulate demand and increase sales volume. At the same sales price, customers would buy more — perhaps a lot more.

Also, a business may increase its variable operating costs to improve the quality of the service to customers. For example, a business may use faster delivery methods, such as overnight Federal Express or UPS, even though it would cost more than traditional truck and rail delivery methods. These changes would increase variable operating costs. A business may increase the percentage of sales commissions to improve the personal time and effort the sales staff spends with each customer.

Distinguishing Cost Decreases: Productivity Gains Versus Cutting Quality

Suppose that you lower your product costs and variable operating costs. Good for you, well, *maybe* good for you — it depends. On the one hand, cost savings may be true efficiency and productivity gains. Sharper bargaining may reduce purchase costs. Wasteful costs may be identified and eliminated. Labor productivity gains reduce unit product costs of manufacturers.

If a business can lower its costs and still deliver the same product and identical quality of service, then sales volume should not be affected. Customers should see no differences in products or service. The cost savings would improve margin and profit would increase accordingly. Suppose that you could lower product costs 2 percent in the profit model example shown in Figure 8-1 because of true efficiency and productivity gains that don't cause any degradation of the products you sell.

We don't present the complete picture for this scenario. You can easily see that reducing product costs 2 percent would improve your margin $33,000: ($1,650,000 product costs × 2.0% reduction in product cost = $33,000). This result would be a significant improvement on your $102,000 profit (over one-third). Paying attention to cost efficiencies has it rewards.

A key question regarding a cost reduction is whether products remain the same and whether the quality of service to customers remains the same. Maybe so, maybe not. Product cost decreases may be due to quality degradations or may result from reducing sizes (such as smaller candy bars or fewer ounces in breakfast cereal boxes). Reducing variable operating costs may adversely affect the quality of service to customers — for example, spreading fewer sales personnel over the same number of customers.

Managers know very well that product quality and the quality of service to customers are absolutely critical, though sometimes they lose sight of this in the pursuit of short-term profits through ill-advised cost reductions. Cost savings can cause degradation in the quality of products or service to customers. As the result, sales volume may decrease. On the one hand, cost reductions improve margin, but on the other hand, the resulting decrease in sales volume hurts margin. The lost customers may never return.

Part III

Dealing with Small Business Financial Issues

The 5th Wave   By Rich Tennant

"Here's what I think happened: He was wounded by Schedule A and B; then he was hit by Schedule D, which brought him to his knees. Then, as he was crawling to reach his calculator, he gets it square in the pocketbook by Schedule C, and that's what finally did him in."

In this part . . .

This part of the book examines three critical aspects of managing the financial side of your small business — *income taxes*, *raising capital*, and *controlling your financial condition*. Every small business has to deal with federal income tax issues, including which type of legal entity is best for your business. Income tax is not the end of the story. Like all businesses, small businesses are hit with payroll and many other taxes.

We present a down-to-earth, street-level discussion of the sources of capital a small business can tap and we explain successful strategies and techniques for raising capital for starting and growing a business. Small business managers should not overlook the balance sheet — the summary of the assets and liabilities of the business. We explain how to analyze the sizes of your assets and operating liabilities. Investing more in assets than is truly needed wastes capital and causes other serious problems as well.

Chapter 9

Jumping Through Tax Hoops

. . . .

In This Chapter

▶ Choosing a business legal structure from an income tax point of view

▶ Understanding how taxable income is calculated

▶ Managing payroll taxes

▶ Looking at other types of business taxes

▶ Lifting the rug to find hidden taxes

. . . .

*B*enjamin Franklin made the famous statement that ".... In this world nothing can be said to be certain except death and taxes." Most people would agree that this statement is not only one of the most widely known and referenced but in addition, extremely accurate. In this chapter, we focus on business taxation and regulatory mandated costs burdening businesses today.

Thinking about Business Taxes

Two general thoughts should be kept in mind with business taxes:

✔ **Identifying and securing the appropriate taxation professional counsel can be worth its weight in gold.** The volume and complexity of business taxation issues has exploded during the past 20 years to the point where it has become almost impossible to stay in 100 percent compliance with every taxing and regulatory authority. Given this environment, it's important to remember that a business is both a taxpayer and tax collector for foreign, federal, state, and local governments. If there ever has been a business management function that requires and/or can benefit from external professional counsel, taxation is it. By professional counsel, we either mean an accounting professional, CPA, or, if needed for more complex issues, a tax attorney.

✔ **Tax planning and compliance represent an essential element of a successful business plan requiring proactive management.** A business owner or manager must understand what triggers tax compliance and obligation requirements in addition to the different types of business taxes present. Executing a business decision as simple as expanding the company's geographical market by adding a new sales representative in a new state is often much easier said than done. This decision can carry with it a requirement to comply with a series of new licensing, taxation, and regulatory mandated costs that may erode profits and consume expensive management time and resources. By establishing the presence of a business operation in a new legal jurisdiction, a company's tax compliance requirements often grow exponentially.

When the term *nexus* is used, it generally refers to the fact that a business has established a legal operating presence within a specific geographical location or governmental jurisdiction. Nexus can be established by the simple act of having one sales representative employed or by having a small branch office operating (in a state). Once nexus has been established, the tax floodgate opens wide. The jurisdictions of the taxing authorities that your business is subject to represent the starting points for evaluating whether your business must comply with the variety of state, county, city, and/or local taxing regulations that will most likely be present.

Coming to Terms with Income Taxation and the Business Legal Structure

A business's legal structure can influence the type and amount of capital raised (see Chapter 10). Furthermore, the legal structure of a business also has a significant effect on income taxation issues based on one simple concept: Is the legal entity responsible to pay the income taxes, or are the owners of the legal entity responsible to pay the income taxes?

When you hear the term *pass-through entity* used in a taxation context, it's referring to the fact that the business entity will pass its taxable profits (and losses) on to the owners of a business who then must pay taxes on the net profits or losses allocated to them. As a result, the individual shareholders — not the legal entity — are responsible for calculating, reporting, and remitting the income taxes due.

Understanding the different types of legal structures available to form a business and their related impact on income taxes is important when it comes to tax planning:

✔ **Regular C corporation:** A regular C corporation is not a pass-through entity. Generally speaking, the income tax rates for a regular C corporation are basically the same as the high-end income tax rates for individuals (with top federal tax rates of roughly 35 percent), so the overall income tax the federal government receives (from either source) is about the same. However, a regular C corporation has a significant tax disadvantage because of *double taxation* —the profits generated from a regular C corporation are taxed first at the corporate legal entity level. Then, if the corporation declares a dividend payable to the shareholders of the company, the dividend is subject to income taxes at the individual level (with potentially favorable lower income tax rates being applied using long-term capital gains rates). Figure 9-1 provides an example of how the double taxation impacts a regular C corporation and its shareholders.

✔ **Subchapter S corporation:** A subchapter S corporation is a pass-through entity, which means that its taxable profits and losses are transferred to the individual owners of the legal entity. The good news with a subchapter S corporation is that the company's profits are only taxed once at the individual level. In addition, if a subchapter S corporation generates a loss, the loss is passed through to the owners of the company; the loss may be able to be used against other compensation earned by the owners from sources other than the company. However, a subchapter S corporation does have a couple of disadvantages. First, certain benefits, such as health insurance, paid to more than 2 percent of the owners are restricted in terms of the deductions realized by the owner on their individual returns. Second, the income taxes owed represent a personal obligation and not a corporate obligation. In a regular C corporation, the income taxes represent an obligation of the legal entity — it protects the shareholders' assets if the income taxes aren't paid. In a subchapter S corporation, income tax obligations are personal — if they're not paid, the taxing authority can pursue personal assets to collect the balance due.

✔ **Limited Liability Company (or LLC):** A limited liability company can elect to be treated as a pass-through entity. An LLC is similar to a subchapter S corporation in that it provides legal protection for business related matters to the owners of the LLC while passing through the taxable profits or losses to the owners. However, LLCs have additional advantages in relation to how taxable profits or losses are distributed. In a subchapter S corporation, the profits and losses must be distributed in relation to the proportionate ownership held by each shareholder. For example, if John Tracy owns 35 percent of a subchapter S corporation, then John Tracy will be allocated 35 percent of the profits or losses for the year. In an LLC, the distribution of earnings can be allocated in a disproportionate manner to the ownership controlled by each member. While one member may own 50 percent of the LLC, this member may receive only 25 percent of the profits or losses (to recognize a reduced management role within the company). This type of flexibility can greatly assist with the proper structuring of an LLC in terms of providing different "incentives" to the investors and executive management team of the LLC.

✔ **Partnerships (general and limited) & sole proprietorships:** Generally speaking, partnerships and sole proprietorships are usually reserved for the smallest of business entities with only very few owners (for example, one to three). Partnerships and sole proprietorships are pass-through entities. For partnerships, a separate federal income tax return is completed, whereas for sole proprietorships, the revenues and expenses of the business are completed on Schedule C of an individual tax return. Although certain tax disadvantages are present similar to a subchapter S corporation, the biggest single drawback with a partnership or sole proprietorship is the lack of liability shield. With a regular C corporation, subchapter S corporation, and LLC, a liability shield is present between the legal entity and the owners that can limit (but not in all cases) a claim against the legal entity to just being able to pursue the assets of the legal entity (and not pursue the individual assets of the owners). For partnerships and sole proprietorships, personal assets can be exposed to business claims and obligations.

	XYZ, Inc. Subchapter S Corporation Year End	XYZ, Inc. Regular C Corporation Year End
Income Statement Summary	12/31/06	12/31/06
Revenue	$15,265,000	$15,265,000
Costs of Goods Sold	$11,503,000	$11,503,000
Gross Profit	$3,762,000	$3,762,000
Gross Margin	24.64%	24.64%
Selling, General, & Administrative Expenses	$3,251,000	$3,251,000
Other (Income) Expenses	$212,000	$212,000
Net Profit Before Tax	$299,000	$299,000
Income Tax Expense	$0	$113,620
Net Profit	$299,000	$185,380
Allocation of Earnings to Personal		
Tax Returns		
Owner A, 55% Ownership	$164,450	$0
Owner B, 25% Ownership	$74,750	$0
Owner C, 20% Ownership	$59,800	$0
Total	$299,000	$0
Distribution of Earnings to Cover Personal		
Income Tax Liabilities		
Owner A, 55% Ownership	$62,491	$0
Owner B, 25% Ownership	$28,405	$0
Owner C, 20% Ownership	$22,724	$0
Total	$113,620	$0
Net Profit Retained — Before Extra Distributions & Dividends	$185,380	$185,380
Extra Distribution Declared	$75,000	$0
Income Tax Obligation Due on the Distribution	$0	$0
Dividend Declared	$0	$75,000
Income Tax Obligation Due on the Dividend	$0	$18,750
Total Income Taxes Paid — Individual & Business	$113,620	$132,370

Figure 9-1: Taxation of a pass-through subchapter S corporation versus a regular C corporation.

Shareholder, partner, and membership agreements

Generally speaking, most businesses are formed on the basis that multiple owners will be present regardless if the business is structured as a corporation, partnership, or LLC. The shareholder, partnership, or membership agreement is a critical business formation and management issue that all business owners need to proactively manage and document. Unfortunately, this agreement tends to be overlooked.

These agreements clearly and concisely define, in a predetermined and agreed upon fashion, how various business issues, transactions, and events will be resolved (by and between the owners of the business). For example, if a business has four equal owners and one of the owners dies, this agreement clearly spells out how the deceased owner's business interest will be valued and eventually purchased (from the deceased owner's estate).

When structuring these agreements, remember to incorporate the following critical issues into the agreement:

- ✔ **Use professional counsel, such as a business attorney or qualified accountant, to draft and finalize the document.** Professional counsel not only has significant experience in preparing these types of agreements but can offer an independent perspective to support treating all the owners in a fair manner.

- ✔ **Protect minority owners' interests.** For example, if a business has one party that owns 60 percent of the company and two other parties that own 20 percent each, the minority owners will want to ensure that the 60 percent owner can't "bully" them (with his 60 percent ownership control). Hence, you often see provisions incorporated into these agreements that require 75 percent owner approval for transactions that are "material" in nature, such as year-end bonuses, authorization of borrowing levels, large capital assets or acquisitions, and the like.

- ✔ **Determine clear exit strategies for the owners.** Whether an owner dies, becomes disabled, or simply wants out, an agreed-upon path needs to provide an efficient method to execute this type of transaction. The last thing a business wants or needs is a distraught wife becoming involved or a disinterested owner sticking around. Trust us when we say that these types of owners can create major operating and management headaches. Businesses often use life insurance policies to assist with death and disability issues as well as structuring notes payable to establish a set repayment term to buyout the departed owner's interests (as rarely can a company afford to just write a check to cover the purchase price).

- ✔ **Agree to a widely accepted and commonly used business valuation method in case new owners are added or existing owners exit the company.** Chapter 14 discusses two commonly used business valuation methods that you can use as a basis to value the business but that are generally customized to account for company specific issues. For example, if a founding partner of a public relations firm is retiring and you risk losing various customers, the value calculated for the retiring partner's interest will most likely be based on an adjusted cash flow figure that takes into consideration the impact of future lost business (thus driving the business's value lower).

- ✔ **Incorporate independent third-party involvement to assist with problem or dispute resolution.** Independent arbitrators, legal counsel, and/or similar service providers can act as an intermediary to support the inevitable problems that arise but that nobody saw coming. Rather than reaching the point of a deadlock that may cripple the business, independent third parties can facilitate resolutions and settlements if required.

A distribution of earnings is not a taxable event. The term *distribution* here means the allocation, or apportionment of the earnings of the business entity among its owners; it does *not* mean the actual payment of money to the owners. A distribution of taxable profits or losses as reported on a Schedule K-1 is a taxable event. In Figure 9-1, owner A receives a distribution (allocation) of taxable profits of $164,650 (which is reported on form K-1). Owner A is responsible to pay income taxes, which have been estimated at $62,491. If the company elects to actually pay Owner A $100,000 with a check on December 31, 2006, Owner A doesn't pay taxes on this distribution of cash. Rather, the payment of $100,000 represents a portion of the total $164,650 taxable profits distributed on schedule K-1. Owner A could then use $62,491 of the cash received from the business entity to pay the income tax obligation and retain the remaining $37,509 with no further tax obligations present. Trust us when we say that this issue confuses more than a few business owners as it seems counter-intuitive to receive a cash distribution with no tax obligation produced from the distribution. The key to understanding this important point is to distinguish between the distribution (allocation) of profit among the owners and the actual distribution (payment) of cash to the owners.

When thinking about income tax and business entities, also keep the following tips in mind:

✔ **Income tax returns/forms:** Separate federal income tax returns/forms are used for a regular C corporation (form 1120), a subchapter S corporation (a form 1120S), and a partnership (form 1065). An LLC generally uses a partnership return for federal income tax reporting purposes. A sole proprietorship uses schedule C of an individual income tax return (form 1040) to report revenues and expenses.

Even though pass-through entities don't have federal income tax obligations, they must prepare informational income tax returns on an annual basis that are filed with the IRS. Just because income taxes aren't due doesn't mean a tax return isn't filed as all businesses must stay in compliance with income tax reporting requirements. In addition, every pass-through entity (with the exception of the sole proprietorship) will produce a form K-1 to be sent to each owner of the legal entity. The form K-1 reports the owners' proportionate shares of the total annual profit or loss of the business, specialized gains and losses (for example, long-term capital gains), passive income and expenses (such as interest income), and other requirements.

✔ **Income tax reporting methods:** The IRS generally recognizes two basic methods to report income taxes. The first is a modified accrual method, which, for lack of a better description, is based on GAAP or generally accepted accounting principles. The second is the cash method, which is based on recording revenue when cash is received and recording expenses when cash is disbursed. Both methods employ certain modifications that are designed to:

- Reduce or eliminate perceived tax abuses

- Encourage certain economically beneficial transactions by providing tax incentives

The cash method is usually reserved for smaller businesses that don't have complex accounting issues. The cash method offers a significant cash flow advantage in that tax liabilities (whether at the corporate level or passed through to the owners) aren't generated until net cash profits are received. Thus, cash is available to cover tax liabilities on a real-time basis. If the accrual method is used and generates a profit (but with no cash available as it has been used to finance trade accounts receivables), a company may have to borrow money to cover tax obligations. Using the cash method of accounting to report taxable income offers a strategic cash flow planning tool.

✔ **State income tax reporting:** In general, most states attempt to follow federal taxation guidelines, but almost all states have some type of variance. For example, some states have a separate tax form available for LLCs to file their returns, whereas others use a partnership return. In California, the state charges most subchapter S corporations a *franchise tax* of $800 or 1.5 percent on net pretax profits (whichever is greater), even though it's a pass-through entity. In other states (such as Nevada), no state income tax is imposed. Rather than attempt to even begin to delve into this subject, let me save you the trouble by offering one simple piece of advice — retain qualified SALT (State and Local Taxation) professionals.

✔ **Other taxes:** All businesses should keep in mind the absolute critical necessity of complying with a long list of other taxes, including payroll, property, and sales/use (all discussed in this chapter). Businesses tend to get into far more trouble with the mismanagement of these types of taxes as not only can they be very complex to understand, but they also carry personal financial risks. (For more on this topic, see the upcoming section "Managing Payroll Taxes.")

✔ **Shareholders versus members versus partners:** In a corporation, the owners are appropriately referred to as shareholders or stockholders (as they own stock shares of the company). In an LLC, the owners are referred to as members (as they own membership interests in the LLC). Likewise in a partnership, the owners are referred to as partners (as they are a part owner of the company). You should make sure that you clearly understand the terminology used for each type of owner in each type of legal entity.

✔ **Legal agreements:** For a corporation, both Articles of Incorporation and Corporate By-Laws need to be prepared to form the entity. For an LLC, you need to prepare a membership agreement, and for a partnership, a partnership agreement is necessary. Not only do these agreements provide the basis for the legal formation of the entity (which almost all states require to be filed with the states respective regulatory body), but, more importantly, they document how the legal entity will be governed between the owners. It is of critical importance that management, officers, and board of directors' roles and responsibilities be clearly defined from day one to avoid potentially disastrous disputes down the road. You'll be doing yourself a big favor by securing the appropriate professional counsel (for example, attorneys) to properly form and structure the initial creation of your business.

Filing Annual Income Tax Returns

Big or small, foreign or domestic, public or private, for profit or not, all entities that carry on business activities must file annual income tax returns regardless of the type of legal business entity and whether it made a profit. The first step in managing business income taxation issues is to understand the type of business legal entity is being used (see preceding section). Figure 9-1 displays a simplified example of the income statement for XYZ Wholesale, Inc. It illustrates the difference in taxation principles between two types of business entities, a subchapter S corporation and a regular C corporation. In the end, the various taxing authorities still get their income taxes with the only real difference being who (a business or an individual) actually forwards the money.

Even though the subchapter S corporation has no income tax obligation (at the corporate level) in Figure 9-1, the three individual owners of the company must report ordinary taxable income ranging from $164,450 to $59,800 on their personal returns. Assuming that each owner is subject to a marginal tax rate of 38 percent (combined federal and state), income tax liabilities ranging from $62,491 to $22,724 are present individually or $113,620 in total. Hence, the subchapter S corporation will most likely want to make a cash distribution from earnings to the owners in the amount of at least $113,620 (in total) to ensure that they have enough funds available to cover their personal tax liabilities. A common tax planning strategy is to make periodic distributions of earnings to coincide with when the individual income tax obligations are due. That is, if quarterly estimated tax payments are due from the owners of the company, quarterly cash distributions of earnings are made to ensure that the owners of the company have enough cash to cover their income tax obligations.

Furthermore, if the company then elects to declare an extra cash distribution (for a subchapter S corporation) or declare an extra dividend (for a regular C corporation), keep in mind the following tax effects:

✔ For the subchapter S corporation, no additional taxes are due because the $75,000 additional cash represents a distribution of previously taxed income.

✔ For the regular C corporation, additional taxes of $18,750 are due by the recipients of the dividend, assuming that each recipient is in a marginal tax bracket of 25 percent (federal and state). The relatively low marginal tax bracket of 25 percent is based on the assumption that the dividend will be subject to long-term capital gains tax rates by the IRS. Recent legislation enacted by the IRS provides for a comparable tax treatment between investments held long term (greater than one year) and dividends received from investments held long term. The primary objective of the IRS is to provide additional tax incentives to encourage long-term investments (which benefits the overall economy), whether in the form of buying and selling long-term investments or realizing dividends/earnings from long-term investments.

The example in Figure 9-1 presents a situation where the taxing authorities basically receive the same amount of income taxes from either entity (prior to a dividend being declared), just in a different form. So this begs the question, why use an S corporation over a C corporation or vice versa? The answer lies in the ability to utilize proper tax planning techniques to manage potential income tax obligations over the long term:

✔ If earnings are generated and can be passed through to owners at a lower marginal income tax rate (by utilizing a pass-through entity), then tax dollars are saved and capital retained in the business, which can be used to finance business growth. In addition, if the subchapter S corporation generates a loss that can be passed through to the owners of the company and offset against other individual earned income, then tax liabilities can be reduced on the other individual earned income. In certain cases, owners may have other earned income from outside of the business, including interest or dividend income generated from investment portfolios, real estate rental income, and other sources. In other cases, the owner may not have any other earned income. The ability to utilize pass-through losses is dependent on each owner's personal tax situation.

✔ As Figure 9-1 illustrates, earnings from a pass-through entity are only taxed once, whereas in a C corporation, earnings are taxed at the corporate level and then again at the personal level if any distribution of earnings are made in the form of a cash dividend (producing a double taxation environment). While double taxation may benefit the United States government (with higher tax receipts), the ultimate effect on the business and its shareholders isn't as positive.

The list of technical tax differences between the two types of business entities is extensive and goes well beyond the scope of this book. However, you need to understand the pros and cons of each business type (from a taxation perspective) when establishing and operating a business. Business planning should definitely incorporate how different legal entities may benefit a business from all angles, including taxation, raising capital, and ownership incentives.

Understanding How Taxable Income Is Calculated

The majority of financial statements prepared for external distribution are based on accrual-basis generally accepted accounting principles (GAAP), and many businesses have their financial statements audited by an independent CPA. However, the IRS has established its own set of principles, guidelines, and rules for businesses to follow when calculating annual taxable income. The primary differences between determining annual taxable income for the IRS and GAAP-based financial statements can be broken down into two areas: permanent versus timing differences.

Permanent differences

Permanent differences relate to those transactions that under the Internal Revenue Code aren't allowed to be recorded as either income or expense in the determination of annual taxable income. Needless to say, most permanent differences relate to expense deductions, which are disallowed by the IRS when calculating taxable income. One of the most widely recognized disallowed expenses relates to meals and entertainment expense. The basic rule is that you can deduct only 50 percent of expenses incurred for meals and entertainment. So if a business incurred $100,000 of meals and entertainment expenses during the year, for tax purposes, it can deduct only $50,000. A number of other types of permanent differences are present, including certain penalties/late fees, life insurance premiums (depending on how the beneficiary is established), and others.

Timing differences

Timing differences relate to those transactions that the IRS requires to be recorded when calculating taxable income. However, the period in which the expense or income is recorded differs from the GAAP-based financial statements. The following examples reveal some of the most frequently incurred timing differences:

✔ **Depreciation expense:** For GAAP purposes, a company may elect to use the straight-line method of depreciation and expense certain capital assets over a 60-month period in equal monthly charges. For tax purposes, the IRS lets you accelerate the depreciation to expense more of the asset in the first two or three years of its use, which gives the business a tax incentive.

✔ **Bad debt expense:** For tax purposes, the IRS generally only allows the so-called direct write-off method. Bad debt expense can only be deducted when the specific receivables deemed uncollectible are actually written off (reduced to a zero value in the accounts) because no future collection is expected. For GAAP purposes, companies often utilize the allowance for doubtful accounts method to record bad debt expense by estimating how many receivables will become worthless. For example, if a company had $5,000,000 of trade receivables of which $100,000 was estimated to be uncollectible, the company would record an expense of $100,000 on its GAAP-based income statement to properly reflect this cost of conducting business. If no receivables were actually written off, then the company could not record an income tax deduction of $100,000. If during the next year, $75,000 of receivables were actually written off, the company would get a tax deduction of $75,000 even though the GAAP deduction of $100,000 was recorded the prior year.

✔ **Deferred compensation:** Companies often use deferred compensation plans and programs to provide additional earning potential to employees with pretax dollars. That is, employees can set aside certain earnings in these deferred compensation programs, and these earnings aren't subject to personal income taxes. While these programs are a great deal for the employee, the employer often isn't allowed to deduct the deferred compensation contribution currently but rather must wait until the employee actually receives the earnings and records it as taxable income (in the year of receipt).

✔ **Cash basis of reporting:** The most common timing difference between GAAP and taxable income relates to qualified companies being able to utilize the cash method of reporting for income taxes. The cash method of reporting taxable income provides for revenue not to be recorded until the cash is received (even though the company has generated a valid trade receivable) and the expense not to be realized until the cash is actually disbursed (even though the company has incurred a valid trade payable).

This next statement may sound far-fetched, but we're going to go out on a limb anyhow in saying that the volume and complexity of income tax permanent and timing differences are extensive. (Translation: The IRS has killed more than a few trees in producing the complete tax code.) The following list contains the key points regarding business income taxation:

✔ Know what type of entity is being used for income taxation purposes.

✔ Understand the basic concept of how taxable income is calculated, including timing versus permanent differences between GAAP and taxable income.

✔ Comply with all the various authorities requiring income tax returns to be completed, including federal, state, local, and if applicable, foreign.

✔ Produce and maintain a sound set of GAAP-based financial statements, which represents the starting point for properly managing income tax issues and generating the information required to prepare various income tax returns.

✔ Don't be afraid to ask for help and/or retain professional assistance to manage income tax issues. There is almost no way for a business owner today to stay on top of the multitude of foreign, federal, state, and local income tax issues and still operate a business.

✔ Realize that income tax obligations aren't due unless a taxable profit (as defined by the various rules and regulations established) is present. When due, remember that income tax obligations are usually paid in quarterly installments over the tax period.

Managing Payroll Taxes

As the old saying goes, the three most important success factors of investing in real estate are location, location, and location. When operating a business, the three most important rules for managing tax issues are pay your payroll taxes; pay your payroll taxes; and pay your payroll taxes. Although relatively simple to manage and understand in relation to the complexities associated with income taxes, the risks of not properly managing payroll taxes (to the business and its principal owners) can be far greater.

Payroll taxes represent withholdings of employee earnings that must be remitted to various federal, state, and local governmental agencies on a periodic basis. In almost all cases, wages paid to employees are subject to payroll taxes based on established guidelines, tables, and formulas as determined by various governmental agencies. Unlike income taxes, which are only due and payable if the business has generated taxable profits, payroll taxes are due when wages (including salaries, hourly compensation, bonuses, commissions, *spiffs* [special performance incentives], and other forms of compensation reported as W-2 earnings per the IRS) are paid to an employee. And once again, the various taxing authorities at the federal, state, and local levels all seem to have their hand in the pot.

The federal government imposes four primary payroll taxes: Social Security, Medicare, individual income, and unemployment (a form of insurance). The first three of these taxes are paid by the individual and are withheld from each employee's wages. The fourth, federal unemployment tax, isn't a burden on the individual, but rather the employer. Thus, no tax is withheld from the employee's wages for this particular tax.

Social Security and Medicare taxes tend to be the most burdensome; not only are these taxes withheld from the employee's wages, but the employer must match, dollar for dollar, the amount withheld and periodically remit the payroll taxes to the IRS. Figure 9-2 provides an example of how payroll taxes are calculated for three employees (at different wage levels) from both the employee and employer perspective.

At the state level, two types of payroll taxes are generally present: personal income and unemployment. Personal income taxes are withheld from the employee's wages. Similar to the federal unemployment insurance, the state unemployment tax represents just the obligation of the employer. Other forms of mandatory withholdings are also present at the state level, including local taxes, disability insurance, and others. However, these taxes vary significantly on a state-by-state basis.

When reviewing Figure 9-2, note the following key issues related to each payroll tax type:

- ✔ Social Security taxes (used to fund the United States national retirement and social security program) are applied at a rate of 6.2 percent on the first $97,500 of wages earned in 2007, which is slightly higher than the 2006 limit. The IRS raises this figure annually to account for inflation and other factors. A business is responsible for not just withholding the Social Security taxes amount from the employee's wages, but it also must match the amount and remit the total to the IRS. This matching requirement represents an expense to the company.

- ✔ Medicare taxes (used to fund the United States national healthcare system for qualified parties) are applied at a rate of 1.45 percent of all employee earnings. Similar to Social Security, the business must match the amount withheld and remit it to the IRS on a periodic basis. However, unlike the Social Security component, the Medicare tax component has no limit or cap as it's applied to all wages earned, including commissions, bonuses, salaries, hourly wages, and the like. This matching requirement also represents an expense to the company.

Employee	Brian S.	Rich E.	Dennis B.
Annual Wages/Earnings — 2007	$124,000	$74,500	$24,500
Payroll Tax Withholdings, Employee:			
Social Security	$6,045	$4,619	$1,519
Medicare	$1,798	$1,080	$355
Federal Personal Income Tax	$31,000	$14,900	$2,450
State Personal Income Tax	$7,440	$2,980	$245
Federal Unemployment Insurance	$0	$0	$0
State Unemployment Insurance	$0	$0	$0
Total Withholdings, Employee	$46,283	$23,579	$4,569
Payroll Tax Expense, Employer:			
Social Security	$6,045	$4,619	$1,519
Medicare	$1,798	$1,080	$355
Federal Personal Income Tax	$0	$0	$0
State Personal Income Tax	$0	$0	$0
Federal Unemployment Insurance	$56	$56	$56
State Unemployment Insurance	$245	$245	$245
Total Expense, Employer	$8,144	$6,000	$2,175
Payroll Tax Withheld Plus Tax Paid By Employer			
Social Security	$12,090	$9,238	$3,038
Medicare	$3,596	$2,161	$711
Federal Personal Income Tax	$31,000	$14,900	$2,450
State Personal Income Tax	$7,440	$2,980	$245
Federal Unemployment Insurance	$56	$56	$56
State Unemployment Insurance	$245	$245	$245
Total Obligation, Employer	$54,427	$29,580	$6,745
Summary:			
Total Expense (Wages & Taxes), Employer	$132,144	$80,500	$26,675
Net Wages Earned, Employee	$77,717	$50,921	$19,931
Total Tax Obligation, Employer	$54,427	$29,580	$6,745
Tax Ratio to Total Employer Expense	41.19%	36.74%	25.28%

Figure 9-2:
Employment taxes for different wage earners.

✔ Federal personal income taxes are withheld just from the employee's wages as the company isn't required to match it. The federal government collects these taxes based on what it estimates the individual will owe in federal personal income taxes at the end of the year. The federal government provides tables to assist employers for calculating how much federal personal income tax should be withheld, depending on the employee's individual tax reporting status, which considers marital status, number of children/exemptions, and other personal factors. The IRS provides the W-4 form (completed by all employees at the time of initial employment) to assist with determining what the proper personal income tax withholdings should be.

✔ Federal unemployment taxes (used to support the unemployment insurance payment programs administered by the states to provide supplemental income to unemployed workers) represent an expense of the company as no withholdings are present from the employee's wages. Currently, the federal government requires .8 percent of an employee's first $7,000 in annual wages to be remitted. For anyone who struggles with math, this amounts to a whopping $56. Unemployment taxes tend to be paid during the first two quarters of each year as once the employee exceeds the base wage level, no further tax is due. However, it is extremely important to note that the wage base level applies on a company identification basis and not to the employee. Hence, if you hire an employee in midyear at which time they've already earned in excess of $7,000 (with their previous employer), the unemployment tax will be due again as the new company hasn't paid any wages to the employee.

✔ At the state level, generally only personal income tax and unemployment taxes are present. Similar to federal personal income taxes, a state collects these taxes based on what it estimates the individual will owe in personal income taxes at the end of the year. Tables are established by the state and provided to employers so that the appropriate amount of taxes can be withheld from the employee's wages and remitted to the state periodically. State unemployment taxes operate in much the same fashion as federal unemployment taxes as a rate is established and applied to a base amount of wages earned by each individual. The base amount is determined by each state and may be consistent with the federal $7,000 level, or it may be higher or lower. The company absorbs the expense because no withholdings are made from the employee's wages. The main difference between federal and state unemployment taxes is based in the rates used and the wages subject to the rate. Most states use a rate well in excess of .8 percent and wage levels of above $7,000. Hence, the bite of $56 at the federal level is much smaller than the amount at the state level.

Pass-through tax entities often use a rather unique and aggressive tax strategy in relation to the compensation paid to the owners of the corporation. For example, say that the architectural firm of Howey, Buildem, and Win is formed as an LLC and has four equal owners/members who each own 25 percent of the company. Each owner is provided a base salary of $75,000 per year, which is treated as regular W-2 type earnings. At the end of the year, the company shows a profit of $1,000,000 before compensating the owners. Figure 9-3 shows the total net tax effect of each owner given this criteria compared to if each owner was paid $200,000 per year (which would consume most of the profits).

Description	Low Wage Scenario #1	High Wage Scenario #2
Net Profit Before Owner W-2 Wages	$1,000,000	$1,000,000
Gross W-2 Owner Wages	$300,000	$800,000
Net Company Profit, Before Payroll Taxes	$700,000	$200,000
Total Payroll Tax Obligation:		
Social Security Taxes, Employee	$18,600	$24,180
Medicare Taxes, Employee	$4,350	$11,600
Social Security Taxes, Employer	$18,600	$24,180
Medicare Taxes, Employer	$4,350	$11,600
Federal Unemployment Taxes	$224	$224
State Unemployment Taxes	$980	$980
Total Payroll Tax Obligation	$47,104	$72,764
Net Company Profit, After Payroll Taxes	$675,846	$163,016
Gross W-2 Owner Wages	$300,000	$800,000
Total Individual Taxable Income	$975,846	$963,016
Marginal Tax Bracket/Tax Rate	38%	38%
Total Income Taxes Due	$370,821	$365,946
Total Payroll Tax Obligation:	$47,104	$72,764
Total Tax Obligation, Payroll & Income	$417,925	$438,710
Total Tax Savings		$20,785

Figure 9-3:
Wage level strategies for 2007.

The reason total tax savings are present is based in the treatment of earnings of the company. In the low wage scenario, the emphasis is placed on maximizing company earnings and minimizing wages earned. This strategy allows for the company to reduce the total amount of payroll taxes realized as a result of Social Security and Medicare. Lower W-2 earnings results in lower Social Security and Medicare taxes (at both the employee and employer level). And because income tax rates applied to either W-2 wages or the distribution of company profits are the same (as both types of earnings will flow through to the individual's personal tax return), the total income tax due is approximately the same.

Before you attempt to go out and implement this strategy, you need to know that the IRS has begun to focus on this area as a tax strategy that is being abused. Companies that artificially deflate W-2 wages to avoid paying Social Security and Medicare taxes can open themselves up to IRS audits, which may bring penalties and interest charges. The key to using this strategy is that the W-2 wages paid to the owners of the company must be reasonable given the industry the company operates within, its geographical location, historical operating performance levels, and so on. If an attorney is paying himself $45,000, living in San Francisco, when his company is making $1 million a year, and attorneys performing similar services make $250,000 annually, a problem is present. Again, proper planning represents the basis of managing owner compensation levels.

If you remember just one thing about payroll taxes, remember this point: Payroll taxes are held in trust for the employee by the withholding party (in other words, the business). As such, if the payroll taxes aren't paid, taxing authorities will not only pursue the business in their attempt to secure funds for payment, but they'll also pierce whatever legal business form is present to collect the taxes (including a corporation). Hence, the officers, board members, check signers, senior managers, and/or any other party aware of the deficiency or who was responsible for remittance of the payroll taxes can be pursued individually to collect the outstanding obligation. Tax collection tactics include attaching to personal assets, such as homes, retirement accounts, college funds, savings, and/or just about any other type of personal asset. Needless to say, businesses don't want to find themselves in trouble for unpaid payroll taxes.

Beyond the all-important concept of paying your payroll taxes, keep in mind the following:

✔ A number of external payroll services, including ADP, Paychexs, and other organizations, are available to assist in managing payroll tax issues. These organizations are cheap and reliable, provide quality services, and are one of the best outsourcing values a business can invest in.

The list of services provided by these organizations goes well beyond just managing payroll taxes because they also process the payroll checks or direct deposits, prepare management reports, support various human resource functions, and so on. For smaller businesses, these organizations offer a highly reliable and inexpensive solution with supporting the payroll processing function.

✔ Payroll taxes are remitted to the various taxing authorities on a periodic basis depending upon the dollar amount of the payroll tax obligation. The larger the periodic amount, the more frequent the business will be required to remit payroll taxes (including being required to transfer funds electronically).

✔ Payroll tax compliance reporting is essential and is usually completed on both a quarterly and annual basis (at both the federal and state levels). These reports reconcile the amount of payroll taxes withheld and owed against the amount paid to ensure employers are remitting their obligations in a timely manner.

✔ For every dollar of payroll and payroll taxes paid, from 25 to more than 40 percent, is remitted to various governmental agencies. This point is extremely important to understand as the nation continues to evolve into more of an employee-based service orientated economy from a production/manufacturing basis. Effective management of payroll taxation issues can improve bottom-line performance.

Remembering Other Types of Business Taxes (The Fun Is Just Starting)

The third major area of taxation covers everything else. It's almost impossible to address and cover every other type of taxation due to the volume of federal, state, and local enacted legislation, which is often focused on vertical markets/industries. For example, the hotel/hospitality industry is subject to a room tax passed through to the end customers. For communities' dependent on tourism, such as San Diego, Las Vegas, and New York, the room tax represents a significant governmental revenue source. In the oil and gas industry, federal and state excise taxes significantly raise the price per gallon of gas a typical motorist pays.

It's really not a matter of who pays the ultimate tax, but rather where the tax is applied and how it's administered. In the hospitality field, the hotel charges the customer the tax and remits it (with a clear reference to the tax on the customer's bill). In the oil and gas industry, the wholesale distributor charges the retail outlet the tax and remits it to the various authorities. (The end customer never sees the tax component of each gallon of gas purchased.)

Sales and use taxes

First on the list are the ever-popular sales and use taxes. We start with this tax because basically every consumer in this country has paid it. *Sales taxes* are generally produced from the sale of tangible personal property, from automobiles to zippers. For example, a retail store that sells jewelry is required to collect sales tax from the customer purchasing a product and remit it (periodically) to the appropriate taxing authority. Sales tax rules, regulations, and rates are established at the state, local, and city levels, depending on the need for these jurisdictions to generate revenue.

In some instances, no sales tax is due as the specific jurisdiction has opted not to impose a sales tax. (For example, the state of Oregon does not have a sales tax.) However, not applying sales tax tends to be the exception rather than the rule as almost every state in the country has some form of sales tax in place. Sales tax rates can also be a function of multiple government entities as the state, county, city, and other local organizations (such as a metropolitan transit authority) all may have a need to generate revenue. Although the state sales tax rate may be 6 percent, the actual rate charged for a local purchase may be 8 percent to account for the other governmental agencies, such as the city or county.

Accompanying the sales tax is its close cousin the *use tax*. Use taxes are similar to sales taxes (and often administered at the same rates), but are applied to the organization consuming and/or using the tangible personal property. *Consumption* is the key word here as property purchased and subsequently resold is not subject to sales or use taxes (for example, inventory purchases made by a wholesale operation that sells it to a retail store). The importance of the distinction between sales and use tax lies not in the tax rate applied, but who is responsible for paying the tax.

The best way to illustrate this point resides in how a number of catalog companies sell their goods. For example, a customer in California orders a piece of clothing from a catalog company located in Maine, pays for the purchase with a credit card, and then receives the product via the United States Postal Service. Because the catalog company in Maine hasn't established nexus in the state of California, they're not required to collect and remit sales tax. Rather, the end user or consumer of the product is obligated to remit a use tax to the governmental agency where the product is consumed (and we all know how often this occurs). This loss of sales/use tax revenue by various governmental entities has been an issue for a number of years and is being amplified by the proliferation of purchases over the Internet using e-commerce.

For consumers, the potential risk of not paying use tax on a $100 out-of-state clothes purchase is minimal. For businesses, the story is different as they must understand the importance of properly accounting for and complying with use tax rules and regulations. Purchases of items consumed in the normal course of business (ranging from office supplies to tools used in a manufacturing process) that were obtained without paying sales tax must be reported to the appropriate taxing authority for assessment. If a business fails to do so, the taxing authority can audit the business, which would trigger not only the use tax due but penalty and interest charges as well. It goes without saying that businesses are much easier and bigger targets for the taxing authorities to pursue and collect tax receipts due.

Most states have different taxing authorities administering the different taxes. For example, in California, The Franchise Tax Board administers state income tax requirements, the Employment Development Department administers state and local payroll taxes, and the State Board of Equalization administers state and local sales and use taxes. These different authorities have become wise to the means in which businesses attempt to lower overall tax obligations, and they often communicate with one another in terms of making another taxing authority aware of a business's presence in the state (and the need to report and pay various taxes). You can pretty much be assured that if one taxing authority becomes aware of your presence in a state, then others will eventually follow. So rather than attempt to "beat the odds" and hope the tax man doesn't catch up with you, complying with all taxing authorities within a jurisdiction can limit major headaches down the road.

Property taxes

Property taxes represent nothing more than a tax assessed on the value of tangible/real property owned. For most people, the most prevalent form of property tax is based on the value of real estate owned (in other words, your primary residence), which is paid either direct or included with a normal monthly mortgage payment (and paid through an escrow account). For businesses, property taxes are most often assessed annually and based on the value of the tangible/real property owned by a company.

Businesses are required to complete an annual property tax return that identifies all the assets owned, leased, and/or in its possession summarized by date of purchase, amount, and type of asset, such as computer equipment, office furniture, and production tools. This return is then forwarded to the various taxing authorities for review and assessment. Then a property tax bill is forwarded to the company. Generally speaking, property taxes are administered and managed by county tax assessors as opposed to income, payroll, and sales/use taxes, which are federal and state responsibilities.

Other business taxes

Beyond sales, use, and property taxes lay a series of other taxes, which are widely utilized but not nearly as well known and/or understood. Rather than attempt to list and explain every potential tax, we provide the following examples:

- ✔ **Unclaimed property:** Property in the possession of a business that rightfully belongs to another party but hasn't been claimed must be turned over to the appropriate authority for administration. States have enacted so called *escheatment laws* requiring that ownership to property that has remained unclaimed for a certain period of time reverts to the state. For example, a business doesn't get to keep the money owed to a former employee who never cashed her payroll check. Rather, an unclaimed property tax return needs to be completed with the money owed turned over to the taxing authority for eventual distribution to the rightful owner. You can argue that this is not a tax as such, but escheatment laws impose responsibilities on businesses to turn over property that doesn't rightly belong to them.

- ✔ **Head taxes:** A *head tax* is a periodic tax applied based on the number of employees present. For example, a state may assess a $25 per head per quarter tax on the number of employees working. If a company has 100 full-time employees, a $2,500 tax is due. The state of Nevada utilized a head tax until 2003, at which time the state abolished this tax and replaced it with a modified business tax based on the gross wages paid over a quarter — different name with the same concept.

- ✔ **Excise and "sin" taxes:** These taxes come in all shapes, sizes, and forms and are applied on everything from fuel to liquor/tobacco to the rendering of certain services, such as personnel staffing. Certain taxes are called *sin taxes* because the products being taxed are viewed as immoral by some (alcohol and tobacco being the two main examples). Excise taxes, in contrast, are taxes on economic activities that government has a legitimate interest in regulating and protecting the public interest.

- ✔ **Incentive tax credits:** Amazingly enough, not all taxes represent the outflow of money from businesses. Various federal, state, and local tax laws and regulations provide tax credits as incentives to pursue certain business strategies. Some of the most common incentive tax credits reside in hiring qualified employees (from certain economic classes) and using environmentally friendly energy sources. A dollar of tax credit offsets a dollar of income tax that otherwise would be payable.

Discovering Hidden Taxes

As much fun as we've had in attempting to discuss the plethora of business taxation issues, it pales in comparison to the sheer enjoyment (you may detect a little sarcasm here) of discussing other governmentally mandated costs, which, for lack of a better term represent, hidden taxes. This cost area within a business has become one of the most problematic for employers to manage and only looks to get worse as federal, state, and local governments attempt to fix problems by burdening companies with more and more responsibilities. The good news, however, lies in the fact that this cost area represents a significant opportunity for employers to proactively manage risks within the organization to reduce expenses and gain competitive advantages.

Workers' Compensation Insurance

Workers' compensation insurance is basically required in every state of the country. This form of mandated insurance is charged to the employer to cover potential employee injuries, accidents, and similar types of events. Workers' compensation insurance is designed to cover both medical-related costs, such as a worker falling and breaking his ankle at work, as well as lost wages/earnings (for example, while the same worker is laid up for two weeks unable to work). In addition, workers' compensation insurance premiums also cover the administrative costs associated with managing this form of insurance, as well as potential other costs, such as legal fees.

State laws, rules, and regulations dictate the types of benefits provided to the injured worker and typically govern workers' compensation insurance coverage levels. The actual workers' compensation insurance premium charged to the employer is generally based on the level of risk its employees are undertaking as they work. For example, a construction worker operates in a much higher risk environment than an accountant pushing paper. Although both may earn $20 per hour, the workers' compensation insurance premium for the construction worker may average 15 percent of this hourly rate (for example, $3 per hour), whereas the premium for the accountant may be only 1 percent of the hourly rate (20 cents per hour).

Because states mandate that the employer carry workers' compensation insurance, state-operated programs are available to employers to secure coverage. A business basically has the option of either securing workers' compensation insurance coverage from a quasi governmental agency, such as the State Compensation Insurance System in California, or going to the open market and obtaining insurance from carriers willing to extend these types of coverages. In some states, carriers openly provide quotes and aggressively pursue business, as state laws tend to be employer friendly.

In other states, carriers apply strict underwriting criteria and guidelines. Needless to say, the difference between state coverage levels can vary widely as a workers' compensation insurance claim in one state may run $2,000, whereas the same claim in another state may reach $10,000 plus.

It's not too hard to figure out why businesses locate certain operations, such as a manufacturing plant, in one state over another given the potential added workers' compensation insurance expenses present. Business-friendly states that offer relatively low worker's compensation insurance rates, reduced state income tax rates, and provide affordable living environments are continually pursuing companies for relocation from high-cost states.

Business owners and managers should keep three key issues in mind with workers' compensation insurance:

- If you don't have the coverage, penalties assessed by the states can be severe and actually may include criminal charges in certain situations (against the officers/owners of the business).

- State-operated and supported workers' compensation insurance programs are often inefficient, expensive, and burdensome. If your company has the ability, resources, and size, pursue private coverage. If you can't obtain private coverage, state programs often act as a final safety net or can be used as the insurer of last resort, which is often the case for smaller businesses that aren't attractive to the private insurance market.

- Properly and proactively managed workers' compensation insurance programs can provide your business with a competitive weapon. Investing internally in the needed corporate infrastructure and staff to aggressively manage workers' compensation claims generally lead to a better resolution of the claim and lower total costs.

Health/medical insurance

Beyond workers' compensation insurance, health/medical insurance represents the next most pressing potential regulatory mandated business cost. We use the term *potential* because health/medical insurance is still generally provided to employees at the option of the employer. However, California is pushing this issue with the introduction of a bill that would charge a 4 percent payroll tax to fund a state-administered health/medical insurance plan to ensure that every person living in the State of California is provided basic health/medical insurance coverage.

Clearly, states are experiencing significant economic discomfort from the past years of annual double-digit increases in health/medical costs, which show no signs of abating soon. States once again are looking to pass the economic burden of rising expenses on to businesses rather than attempt to manage the issue internally with limited/inadequate resources. Business owners and managers need to stay on top of this issue in the years to come because absorbing medical/health insurance costs, which can easily exceed 10 percent of an employees base compensation, internally can significantly change economic operating models.

Business licenses, permits, and fees

Businesses must obtain various *fees, licenses,* and *permits* to operate in certain local jurisdictions, such as cities and unincorporated county locations. If a business has established nexus in a local jurisdiction, chances are that a periodic license, permit charge, or fee will be due. This fee can range from a one-time annual flat fee that varies depending on the number of employees a company has to a fee based on the amount of receipts generated within that jurisdiction (sounds like another tax).

The easiest rule to apply here is really quite simple: If you have a business presence in a local jurisdiction, assume that you need to obtain and pay for a license, fee, and/or permit to legally operate.

Chapter 10

Raising Capital for Your Business

Years ago, industry giants such as Hewlett Packard, Yahoo!, Microsoft, Intel, and the like launched the technology industry, driving it into the mainstream of the United States economy. As difficult as it may be to imagine, these companies were all at one time or another small startup enterprises struggling like most other businesses with managing their business interests and developing economically sustainable models. The ultimate successes of the companies are (needless to say) well known and have been documented countless times.

At the root of their success, however, was the ability to secure all the essential ingredients needed to build a business, including leadership, vision, talent, planning, determination, and so on, at the most opportune time, with a little luck, combined with the all important element of securing the proper amount and type of capital to support the business concept. Big or small, public or private, foreign or domestic, one month new or 20 years old, it really doesn't matter. Securing and managing capital resources represents the lifeline of any company looking to operate in today's challenging economic climate.

Securing capital for a company represents one of the most painstaking and time-consuming efforts a business will undertake. It's one thing to get a party interested in providing capital to your organization, but it's an entirely different event to actually receive the commitment and secure the capital. Securing capital represents a full-time job requiring the undivided attention of a company's senior management team and, ultimately, the CEO.

Getting the Scoop on Capital

When implementing a new business concept, only one definition captures the real essence of capital: "It takes money to make money." From the aspiring entrepreneur designing a new software product in a home office to an executive of a multinational corporation looking to expand foreign distribution channels for new product introductions, launching any new business concept requires capital, or money, as a basis to execute the business plan. One of the most common reasons businesses fail is due to a lack of or inappropriately structured capital resources.

For the sake of simplicity, capital is the amount of financial resources needed to implement and execute a business plan. Before a business sells its first product or delivers a service to the market, it needs financial resources for product development, sales, marketing and promotional efforts, administrative support, the company's formation, and countless other critical business functions.

Capital should not be perceived as just the amount of "cash on hand" but rather the amount of financial resources available to support the execution of a business plan.

While financial resources come in countless forms, types, and structures, two main basic types of financial resources are available to most businesses: debt and equity.

- **Debt** represents a liability or obligation of a business. Debt is generally governed by mutually agreed upon terms and conditions as provided by the party extending credit. For example, a bank lends $2 million to a company to purchase additional production equipment to support the expansion of a manufacturing facility. The bank establishes the terms and conditions of the debt agreement including the interest rate, repayment term, the periodic payment, collateral required, and other elements of the agreement. These terms and conditions must be adhered to by the company, or it runs the risk of default.

- **Equity** represents an investment in the business, usually doesn't have set repayment terms, but does have a right to future earnings. Unlike debt, equity investments aren't subject to set repayment terms, but the owners of the equity investments may be paid dividends or distributions if profits and cash flows are available. For example, a software technology company requires approximately $2 million in capital to develop and launch a new Internet-based software solution. A niche venture capitalist group invests the required capital under the terms and conditions present in the equity offering, including what their percentage ownership in company will be, rights to future earnings, representation on the board of directors, preferred versus common equity status, conversion rights, antidilution provisions, and so on. Under this scenario, the company isn't required to remit any payments to the capital source per a set repayment agreement but has given up a partial right to ownership (which can be even more costly).

Of course, many variations, alternatives, subtypes, and classifications are present within each type of capital. If it were as easy as debt versus equity, there wouldn't be much of a need for bankers, accountants, investment bankers, venture capitalists, and the like (which, of course, to most business owners would be a welcome change).

You may be wondering whether debt or equity capital is best suited for a company. Well, this decision really depends on the company's stage in terms of its operating history, industry profile, profitability levels, asset structure, future growth prospects, and general capital requirements, as well as where the sources of capital lie.

Debt

Debt is best evaluated by understanding its two most important characteristics:

- **Maturity** refers to the length of time the debt instrument has until repayment. In the case of trade accounts payable, vendors often extend payment terms of net 30 to their customers, which requires repayment within 30 days of receipt of the product or service. Any debt instrument requiring repayment within one year or less is classified as current or short term on the balance sheet. Logic then dictates that long-term debt is any obligation present with a repayment due date of one year or greater. For example, mortgages provided by banks for real-estate purchases are often structured over a 30-year period and are considered long-term in nature.

- **Security** refers to the type of asset the debt is supported by or secured with. If a bank lends $2 million to support the expansion of a manufacturing facility, the bank takes a *secured position* in the assets acquired for the $2 million loan. That is, the bank issues a public notice that it has lent money to the manufacturing company and that it has a first right to the equipment financed in the case of a future default. This notice provides the bank with additional comfort that if the company can't cover its debt service obligations, it actually has a tangible asset that it can attach to and liquidate if it needs to cover the outstanding obligation. Other forms of security also include intangible assets, such as a patent or rights to intellectual property, inventory, trade accounts receivable, real estate, and future cash flow streams, such as a future annuity payment stream that guarantees *X* dollars to be paid each year.

> You may assume that most companies that provide credit to businesses would prefer to be in a secured status to reduce the inherent risks present. However, this scenario is logistically almost impossible due to the nature of how most businesses operate on a day-to-day basis. Hence, secured creditors tend to be associated with credit extension agreements that are both relatively large from a dollars committed standpoint and cover longer periods of time.

On the opposite end of secured lenders are the *unsecured creditors.* This type of creditor tends to be the mass of vendors that provide basic goods and services to a company for general operating requirements. Examples of these vendors are professional service firms, utility and telecommunication companies, material suppliers, general office services, and so on. Unsecured creditors obviously take on more risk in that a specific company asset is not pledged as collateral to support the repayment of the obligation. This risk is mitigated by the fact that unsecured creditors tend to extend credit with shorter repayment terms (for example, the invoice is due on net 20 day terms) and in lower dollar amounts. In addition, if unsecured creditors are concerned about getting paid, then they can use other strategies, such as requiring a deposit or a prepayment.

Beyond the maturity and security elements of debt are a number of additional attributes:

- ✔ *Personal guarantees,* where a party outside of the company guarantees the repayment of a debt similar to how a cosigner works. Personal guarantees are often required by the owners of the business due to their relatively high net worth status but also to display a willingness to stand behind their business.

- ✔ *Priority creditors,* where business creditors achieve a priority status due to the type of obligation present, such as payroll taxes withheld for the IRS.

- ✔ *Subordination agreements,* where a creditor specifically takes a secondary position to a secured lender.

- ✔ *Default provisions,* where, in the event of a loan default, the remedies of the parties involved are specified.

- ✔ *Lending agreement covenants,* where the company must perform at a certain level to avoid triggering a default.

For a more complete discussion of these debt attributes, refer to Chapter 15.

Equity

Equity is best evaluated by understanding its two most important characteristics:

- ✔ **Preference** refers to the fact that certain types of equity have preferences to earnings and, if needed, company assets over other forms of equity. For example, a series A preferred stock may be issued to investors that have an interest in making an equity investment but want to protect or prioritize their investments in relation to the common shareholders or another series of preferred stock. A series B preferred stock may hold a lower preference to the series A preferred stock in terms of asset liquidations, but may have a slightly higher dividend yield attached or offered with a warrant that allows it to purchase common shares at a later date at a favorable price.

  The features built into preferred stock are almost endless and can create a large number of different types of preferred stock. For common equity, so, too, can preferences exist. Common stock type A may have full voting rights and dividends (after the preferred shareholders receive their dividend), whereas a common stock type B may have only rights to dividends but can't vote.

  Equity investors will attempt to secure as many preferences and features that protect their interests as possible. While this situation may be good for them, it may not be in the best interests of the company and can restrict its ability to operate farther down the road.

- ✔ **Management influence** is centered in the fact that when equity capital is raised, the provider of the capital is considered an owner or shareholder of the company. By its very nature, this ownership entitles the shareholder to have a say in the company's operations (unless otherwise restricted) with the ability to vote for the board of directors and on other critical matters, such as approving the company's external auditor. This management influence can be extended significantly when preferences are factored into the equation. It's very common for early stage equity investors to secure the right to influence the board of directors more actively. For example, if a company has determined that five board members are needed, the early stage investors may carve out the right to elect two of these board members and the other investors the remaining three. This right provides the early stage equity investors with additional management control of the business during its critical formation years.

If you remember one thing when raising equity capital, it should be this: Be prepared to co-manage the business with your new best friends as your dictatorship will give way to a democracy (hopefully).

Developing a Business Plan

The starting point for raising or securing capital resides in one simple document: the *business plan*. This document represents management's foundation and justification for birthing, growing, operating, and/or selling a business based on the economic environment present. Without a business plan, management is left to operate a business in the dark, attempting to guess or use its intuition on the best course of action to pursue. Companies all too often proceed with strategies of "We've always done it like that" or "This is how the industry has operated for the past up-teen years" rather than really evaluating and investigating the economic markets in which they operate.

Business plans come in a variety of shapes, sizes, forms, and structures and often take on the characteristics and traits of the business founder(s). Different sections of the business plan may be developed in more depth, while other sections are presented in a quasi summary format because the needed data, information, or knowledge isn't readily available for presentation. For example, a founder of a fledging new software company may be able to provide a complete analysis on the software product developed, underlying code used, and even how the product will be packaged. However, when asked about the real market demand for the product, distribution channels available, competition present, and/or the best method to price the product, the founder may struggle with providing solid, third-party corroborated information.

The business plan should be built from the outside looking in so that any reasonable party can clearly, concisely, and efficiently understand the business concept.

Although business plans come in many different formats, every business plan should include four main sections:

- ✔ **Executive summary:** The executive summary represents a brief overview of the business concept in terms of the market opportunity present, the operational logistics required to bring a product and/or sevice to market, the management team that is going to make it happen, and the eventual potential economic return available, including the amount of capital needed to execute the plan. This section of the business plan is really nothing more than a condensed summary of the entire business concept presented in a neat and tidy overview that's usually not more than five pages (and hopefully shorter).

Although the meat of the business plan resides in the remainder of the document, this section is the most critical in terms of attracting capital and financing source interest. Basically, the capital/financing sources must be able to conceptualize, understand, and justify the business concept from the information presented in the executive summary. This section must excite readers, pique their interest, and move them with a sense of urgency to pursue the business opportunity at hand.

✔ **Market and industry analysis:** Without a viable market present, the only thing left to account for are losses (and we all know how much capital/financing sources love these). This segment of the business plan is often the most important in that it substantiates the need for a product and/or service that isn't being fulfilled within the current economic environment. Beyond providing information and support on the market size, characteristics, and trends, this section must also present a clear understanding of the businesses' competitive niche, target market, and specific marketing strategies. In addition, a summary of the marketplace competition is usually provided to identify and properly manage these associated risks.

Quantifying the size of the market in coordination with qualifying the market need supports the basis of the business concept but represents only half the battle (and often the easier of the two halves). Identifying the specific niche and target market and developing an effective marketing strategy to capitalize on the opportunity present is often more challenging and critical to the future success of the business. On top of all of these challenges, accumulating reliable and meaningful market data can be very difficult. Industry trade organizations, governmental agencies, the Internet, and regional business publications all represent good data sources that you can tap to accumulate market information.

✔ **Operational overview:** This segment of the business plan addresses a number of operational issues, including personnel requirements, technological needs, locations (for example, office, production/manufacturing, warehouse/distribution, and so on), company infrastructure requirements, international considerations, professional/expert counsel resources, and the like. Clearly, the market segment of the business plan drives various business operating elements in terms of the resources needed to implement and execute the plan. For example, if a company is planning on expanding into new foreign markets where the local government still "influences" the distribution channels, then the operating segment needs to address how the product will be distributed and what international partners will be essential to the process.

In addition, business plans quite often dedicate a large portion of this segment to providing an overview of the management team in terms of both its past credentials as well as its responsibilities with the new business concept moving forward. The market may be ripe and capital plentiful, but without a qualified management team, the business concept will more times than not sink.

✔ **Financial segment:** In a sense, this section brings all the elements of the business plan together from an accounting and/or financing perspective. Financial forecasts or proformas are prepared to project the anticipated economic performance of the business concept based on the information and data presented in the business plan. The market segment tends to drive the revenue portion of the forecasts because the information accumulated and presented here substantiates items, such as potential unit sales growth (in relation to the size of the market), pricing, and revenue sources by product and service. The expense element of the forecasts is often driven by the operating segment of the business plan because the business cost structure in terms of personnel, assets, company infrastructure, and so on are addressed here. When all the elements of the business plan are put together in this segment, not only is the forecast profit and loss or income statement produced, but, just as importantly, the projected balance sheet and cash flow statement are generated as well. With all this information now in hand, the capital required to execute the business plan should be readily quantifiable.

The management team responsible for executing the business plan is in effect the business plan. That is, financing and capital sources are lured in by business plans and can easily turn over any concept to a slew of professionals for further due diligence, reviews, evaluations, critiques, and so on. If investors are concerned about, say, a technological basis within a biomedical company, then you can hire medical or technology-based professionals to complete additional due diligence and either approve or can the idea. However, the management team standing behind the business plan and its execution is really where the capital and financing sources invest. The integrity, qualifications, experience, determination, passion, and commitment displayed by the management team are of utmost importance. This point holds true for the presentation of the business plan by the management team as well. The preparation taken by the CEO and his management team can give a glimpse to potential investors of how organized, meticulous, and focused a management team is. Any concerns here, and the capital and financing sources have their out.

In addition, you must sell your concept. In today's economic environment, new ideas and business plans are produced by the tens of thousands each and every year (and those are the ones that actually make it to somewhat of a formal presentation stage). Capital and financing sources are presented with these plans daily and are constantly challenged to focus on the best and brightest ideas. As such, selling or marketing the business concept to capital and financial sources becomes the most difficult task in launching the business concept. Its one thing to get people interested in the business plan and a good story. It's an entirely different story to actually get money committed to the concept. The lead parties responsible for securing the needed capital or financing will find that 110 percent of their time will be consumed with this process. Displaying passion, determination, confidence, reliability, commitment, knowledge, and experience are all essential to the process. Above all, however, is that the parties responsible for securing capital or financing must be able to handle rejection because capital sources have a far easier time saying no than yes. Selling your concept becomes the greatest sales challenge most business executives will ever face.

Finding Sources of Capital

In the movie *Jerry McGuire,* Cuba Gooding, Jr., playing a professional football player, uttered the now somewhat infamous line of "Show me the money." These four words sum up the capital-raising process as best as any because until you have the money in hand, a business concept is really nothing more than the paper the business plan is written on.

Fortunately, many potential sources of capital are available to launch your new business, open a new product/service niche within a corporate conglomerate, or acquire a pesky competitor. The sources listed in the following sections are by no means an all-inclusive list but rather an overview of the variety of avenues available to raise capital.

Family, friends, and close business associates

Family, friends, and close business associates (FF&CBAs) have been one of the primary capital sources to launch new business concepts since the beginning of time and will most likely continue to fill this role in the future. The range of capital-raising options from FF&CBAs stretches from the founders of a business tapping their own credit worthiness or resources (savings, home equity, or credit cards) to Mom and Dad or a trusted business associate stepping up with the needed seed money to launch the company. Generally, this type of capital tends to be for lower dollar amounts, geared toward equity as opposed to debt (given the uncertain nature of the business and higher risks present in terms of generating cash flow), and provided to closely held and/or family-operated businesses. However, debt can be effectively utilized with more mature businesses generating solid profitability with some type of security present (such as real estate).

The good news is that raising capital from FF&CBAs can often be completed quickly without a significant amount of legal paperwork and/or similar investor creditability issues being present.

The bad news is twofold:

- ✔ **The amount of capital available from these sources is often restricted.** It's one thing to pull together a couple of hundred thousand dollars, but when a business concept needs a million or two, not too many FF&CBAs have this type of liquidity available (unless your last name is DuPont or Getty).

- ✔ **Having unsophisticated FF&CBAs provide capital to a business carries with it unforeseen risks and emotional elements that can explode.** Reporting to a seasoned investor that a business concept didn't work and that their investment is worthless may not be the most pleasant task in the world, but at least the investor was aware of the risks. Telling your aunt and uncle that you've just blown through their nest egg and the business has failed is another story. The external costs of losing a family members' investment can be ten times the actual internal amount of capital invested.

Be very wary of FF&CBA capital sources and the subjective costs that are often attached. Approach and evaluate as capital sources only FF&CBAs that clearly understand the investment process and business in general and that can afford the potential loss. Nothing is worse than having a business fail and then watching the family disintegrate as a result.

Private capital

In the business world, a large number of private capital sources are available and include such sources as venture capitalists (VCs), investment bankers, angels or white knights, and similar types of private investment groups. Private capital sources come in a variety shapes, sizes, and forms, but all tend to gravitate toward a common set of criteria:

- ✔ **The dollar size of the capital commitment is generally much larger.** These groups are comprised of highly trained and sophisticated professionals responsible for managing large pools of capital and, as such, apply the concept of economy of scale frequently.

- ✔ **These groups tend to be more risk-based capital sources and look for higher returns from equity driven transactions.** These groups are comfortable with making equity investments in relatively early stage businesses without proven profitability (but with significant potential) or structuring risk-based debt facilities to support a "higher risk" business opportunity (in other words, the debt is secured by nothing more than goodwill). Just remember that higher investment returns will be expected for taking on the added risk.

✔ **These groups aren't looking to invest in a company with a revenue potential of $10 million after five years (similar to a solid regionally based construction subcontracting company).** With the types of capital these groups have available, the business opportunity must be relatively grand to pique their interest. While the next Microsoft isn't needed, these groups look for opportunities that produce in excess of $100 million in annual revenue (over a reasonable time) and generate strong profits or earnings. Companies that offer rather novel product or service concepts with serious market potential are favorites of these groups.

✔ **Private equity sources or groups tend to be very focused on the eventual exit strategy available to realize their ultimate return.** Reasonable timelines or horizons are expected from the point these groups invest to the time they realize their final return. The final return generally comes from the company being sold or by utilizing public investment markets to provide these groups with a readily available market to dispose of their holdings.

The good news with private capital is that larger capital amounts are available, the groups are generally very sophisticated and can provide invaluable management support, and the capital is often equity-based so that aspiring businesses in need of large capital infusions have a resource.

The bad news is that these groups tend to ask for (and receive) a higher ownership stake in the business and thus can exert a significant amount of management control and influence. In addition, these groups retain highly trained professionals who are very demanding when they're undertaking their investment review/evaluation process. If your case isn't ready to be presented, then don't, because private capital sources won't even give you the time of day without a business concept or plan that can stand a punishing evaluation.

Banks, leasing companies, and other lenders

Debt capital sources including banks, leasing companies, government-backed programs, asset-based lenders, factoring companies, and the like have evolved over the past 100 years into one of the most sophisticated capital source groups around. For almost any debt-based need, some type of lender is readily available in the market. These groups, similar to private sources, tend to look for a common set of characteristics when extending capital in the form of debt:

✔ **Security of some sort — an asset or personal guarantee, for example — must be present.** Lenders like a secondary form of repayment in case the borrower can't cover the debt service requirement.

- ✔ **Debt providers tend to look for more stable business environments where a company has been in business for an extended period of time and has a proven track record.** Businesses don't have to necessarily generate a profit to secure debt financing, but it certainly helps.

- ✔ **Debt capital sources are more conservative in nature.** Their goal is to ensure that the debt can be repaid while generating an adequate return. Maintaining solid financial returns and strong ratios is more important than watching the company double in size, placing too much pressure on its leverage ratios.

From a positive perspective, debt capital sources cover a broad spectrum of financing requirements ranging from as little as $50,000 (a niche factoring or leasing company providing capital to small businesses) to billions of dollars (the world's largest banks providing financing for a multibillion dollar public company buyout). In addition, management control isn't relinquished because debt providers generally don't have a say in an ongoing business.

On the flip side, security in some form is usually required, which places business (and potentially personal) assets at risk. Also, the debt must be repaid per the terms and conditions established, regardless of whether the company's performance allows for the repayment. Unlike equity investments, which tend to generate only a distribution of earnings or dividends when the company's performance dictates, debt repayment terms must be adhered to, and, if not, the company can suffer the wrath of its creditors demanding repayment.

Businesses often secure capital from more than one source on a periodic basis. For example, risk-based capital (in the form of equity) may be secured to develop a new product and support the initial launch into the marketplace, whereas debt-based capital may be secured to support an increase in inventory and to carry trade accounts receivable as customers purchase the products. Both forms of capital aren't only appropriate for this company's needs, but, in addition, the lenders may be more willing to step forward and provide the necessary capital knowing that another partner has made a commitment. The herd mentality holds true for capital sources because they view the opportunity in a more positive light (with a higher degree of success) knowing that the right amount and types of capital have been secured.

Public capital

Almost every business owner, professional, and manager is aware of the public markets available to trade stocks and bonds, including the New York Stock Exchange, NASDAQ, and similar venues. Both equity (such as the common stock of Microsoft) and debt (such as United States Treasury Bills) instruments are actively traded in these open markets.

While the allure of the public markets is very appealing to business owners and often is viewed as the end game, the reality of operating in a public market can be very different. As such, public capital sources have developed a unique set of qualifications in terms of making it the most appropriate capital source to pursue:

- ✔ **Think big.** Public markets are better suited for companies thinking in hundreds of millions or billions than millions.

- ✔ **Think public.** Basically, all your company's information, financial records, activities, and so on will be available for public viewing. You must not only be prepared to disclose the information, but also make sure that the disclosure is prepared in the proper format.

- ✔ **Understand risk.** Are the returns and rewards for being public adequate in relation to the risks you and your business assume?

- ✔ **Think expensive.** It's very expensive to "go public" and then maintain and support all the tasks necessary to stay public, including more frequent reporting requirements, federal government antifraud measures compliance, such as the Sarbanes-Oxley Act of 2002 (SOX), production of public reports and documents, and added professional fees.

Public capital market's positive attributes include having access to extremely large capital levels that can tap the widest range of sources available (stretching the globe). There really isn't any deal too big for public markets as the United States $9 trillion of outstanding debt clearly displays. The liquidity public markets offer the ability to establish fair market values almost instantaneously, as well as access to both debt and equity sources also represent positive attributes.

As you know, there is no utopia from a capital sources standpoint, so there must be downsides to public capital as well:

- ✔ **Cost:** Staying in compliance with all the public reporting requirements can be extremely expensive.

- ✔ **Added management exposure:** Even when no fraud exists, investors in public debt and equity instruments can turn into a company's worst nightmare when things aren't going as planned. The additional burden placed on the management team can be extensive and detract the company from actually running its business.

- ✔ **Misconception about liquidity:** Just because your company is publicly traded doesn't mean that liquidity is present. The stock of smaller companies — those with less than $100 million of market capitalization — are often not actively traded on the open market, which can make selling or buying a large block of stock difficult (not to mention the scrutiny insiders received when undertaking these transactions).

Although plenty of small companies are publicly traded, public markets are generally best suited for the big boys of corporate America.

Other creative capital sources

Sometimes you need to get a little more creative with identifying capital sources and tapping potential nontraditional capital avenues. The number of creative capital sources are endless, so rather than attempt to cover every trick of the trade, we offer a diversified list of creative ways to manufacture capital:

- ✔ **A company generates positive internal cash flow and reinvests this asset internally as needed.** Countless examples of this strategy exist, including a medical company, such as Merck, using positive cash flow from one line of pharmaceutical products to support research and development on a new drug to a gold mining company, such as Newmont, using its cash flow from a proven gold ore reserve to explore and develop a promising new gold ore reserve. Positive internal cash flow is a real source of capital available to finance business operations that is both readily available and, logistically, much easier to secure. However, it should be kept in mind that positive internal cash flow must be managed and invested appropriately within the best interests of the company and its shareholders.

- ✔ **A company utilizes creative forms of unsecured financing from vendors, partners, customers, and so on to provide a real source of capital.** For example, a company may require customers to prepay 20 percent of their order as a requirement to start the production and future delivery process. Or it may ask key product suppliers to grant extended terms from 30 days to 90 days during certain seasonal periods.

- ✔ **A company looks for gifts.** Governments, universities, and nonprofit organizations have resources available in the form of grants, low interest rate loans (with limited downside risk), incentive credits, and so on, which are intended to be used for special interests or purposes. The general idea is to provide this capital to an organization that will use it in the best interest of the general public. Biotechnology companies often secure research grants for work being completed on disease detection, prevention, and possible cures. Educational organizations may receive a grant that helps retrain a displaced group of workers or poorly educated work force. Under either scenario, the same concept is present in terms of committing the capital for a common good.

Other creative capital sources are available to companies as well, one of which we summarize in the following example.

A software company is developing a new fraud protection system for use in the banking system. Not only does the development of the system need to be capitalized, the initial marketplace launch requires additional capital to ensure that the end customers (mainly banks) can review, test, evaluate, and, when appropriate, implement the systems. Internally, the company doesn't have enough capital to support this project, so it completes an acquisition of a sister company that was producing strong internal cash flows to support the project. The company issues its equity in exchange for all the assets of the target company (which, in effect, was the future cash flow stream). This scenario provides the company with enough ongoing cash flow from the acquired business's product sales to both fund the system development and market it to the banks.

To a certain degree, managing the capital sources, after the capital is secured, can be even more challenging and difficult than raising the capital itself. Managing the capital sources tends to be more intangible in nature as it's geared toward relationship support and communication efforts as opposed to just presenting hard financial and accounting data.

Understanding Business Legal Structures and Raising Capital

You should clearly understand how your businesses legal structure may impact your ability to raise capital. Not only are significant tax, cost, and liability issues present when choosing what form of legal business entity to form, you must consider the impact the business legal entity has on securing capital. That is, certain business forms limit the type and amount of capital that you can secure, especially from an equity perspective. Chapter 9 provides an overview of the various legal structures available to form a business as viewed from a tax perspective. Table 10-1 summarizes the various pros and cons of each type of business from a capital-raising and formation perspective:

Table 10-1	Pros and Cons of Each Business Type	
Business Type	**Pros**	**Cons**
Sole proprietorships and partnerships	Inexpensive, easy, and quick formation possible. Structure is simple to understand and implement.	Doesn't provide for a liability shield for business claims against personal assets. Equity capital sources limited to FF&CBAs (at best).
Limited liability company (LLC)	New business form that combines liability benefits of a corporation with certain tax benefits. More flexible than a subchapter S corporation in that other legal entities may invest equity in the LLC.	Relatively new business type that is more complex and expensive to establish. Not ideally suited to attract large private equity investments looking for liquidity through a public offering.

(continued)

Table 10-1 *(continued)*		
Subchapter S corporation	Liability shield present due to corporate structure. Well established legal form for small businesses that offer various tax benefits.	Ownership limited to a maximum of 75 individuals. Other legal entities can't invest in the company. Corporate compliance and reporting issues more complex and expensive.
Regular C corporation	Liability shield present due to corporate structure. Equity capital sources may come from individuals and/ or businesses with no restriction on the number of types of investors present.	Corporate compliance and reporting issues more complex and expensive. Taxation structure not as advantageous.

Don't expect the legal structure of the business entity to protect you from personal claims, especially when the willful intent to defraud is present. The current political, social, and business environment is hell-bent on aggressively pursuing white collar criminals as a result of the high profile business failures from 2000 through 2003.

Putting Your Capital to Good Use

Understanding how capital impacts your company's performance, either in a positive or negative fashion, represents a critical component of managing your capital resources. Figure 10-1 presents the financial performance of a company where all elements of this business are exactly the same with the exception of how the business was capitalized.

Under the equity scenario, a total of $2 million of capital was raised, all in the form of equity. Under the debt scenario, a total of $500,000 of equity was raised, and $1.5 million of debt was secured (of which $300,000 was repaid during the year). The income statements are exactly the same with the exception of the fact that the debt scenario has interest expense present. The quick financial analysis highlights the key differences and indicates that by using debt, the company was able to generate better returns for the equity owners.

Keys to raising capital

Raising capital really does represent the ultimate sale in terms of convincing a capital source to actually believe in your business and then forking over the money. Terms such as nerve-racking, frustrating, euphoric, rollercoaster, and the like will become common place in addition to hair loss, stress, and joy. So, in order to capture the essence of the fund-raising process as quickly as possible, we provide the following tips:

✔ **Be prepared.** Like the Boy Scouts of America say, always be prepared. Capital sources expect and demand the highest quality information, plans, and underlying support when evaluating an investment opportunity.

✔ **Be persistent.** Capital sources are looking for reasons to say no. We can't emphasize enough the attributes of persistence and determination when pursuing and securing capital.

✔ **Be patient.** Raising capital often takes much longer to finalize than most people realize. You need to anticipate delays in the capital-raising process as rarely do deals close on time. Your business will need to be prepared to manage the inevitable delays that will occur.

✔ **Qualify the capital sources.** Make every effort to qualify your capital sources to ensure that the most appropriate avenue is pursued in relation to the operating status of your business. Don't waste your time or theirs and by all means make sure that the capital source is capable and accredited to support the request. Researching and understanding capital markets represent integral components of qualifying the capital sources.

✔ **Communicate.** Communication efforts are critical to successfully securing and managing capital. Keep the capital sources up to date with all relevant information, good or bad.

✔ **Document and disclose.** Don't underestimate the importance of properly documenting all capital-raising activities, from the initial communications to final agreements. Full and complete disclosures are a must in today's hostile economic environment.

✔ **Develop exit strategies.** All capital sources want their money back with a solid return at some point. Offer clear and reasonable exit strategies to provide the capital sources with comfort that a light is present at the end of the tunnel (and hope that it's not a freight train barreling down the other direction).

✔ **Risk rewards relationship.** To a capital source, equity investments carry more risk than debt investments, and, as such, the return realized on the investment must be higher. To a business, debt can expose the company to greater risks but also higher returns. The trick is to find the right balance.

The heart of raising capital lies in a business' ability to generate a profit and positive cash flow. Cash flow represents the ultimate lifeline of any business operating. Understanding how a business generates and consumes cash represents the single most important item in determining whether a company will be economically viable and gain the interest of capital sources, or die a natural death and be discarded to the mass grave of dead business plans.

Here's the financial statement analysis for Figure 10-1. (For more information on the analysis process, see Chapter 4.)

- ✔ **Returns:** The debt scenario produces a return on equity of 24.74 percent compared to a return on equity of 14.21 percent with the equity scenario. The return on assets is almost identical for both scenarios.

- ✔ **Earnings:** The debt scenario generates earnings per share of almost four times that of the equity scenario ($.82 per share compared to $.23 per share).

- ✔ **Leverage:** The only real downside to the debt scenario is that this scenario has a much higher debt-to-equity ratio — 1.45 compared to .38 — and a debt service coverage ratio of approximately 1.3 (total earnings of $410,983 divided by the company's total annual debt service including loan principal payment of $300,000 and interest payments of $72,000). While using debt was beneficial in terms of enhancing returns, it also has placed the company in a higher risk status due to the amount of debt leverage used. (See the next year's operating results in Figure 10-2.)

In 2005 (see Figure 10-2), the company is dealing with a recession that is driving sales and margins lower after having a robust year in 2004 with strong margins and profitability. While its selling, general, and administrative expenses were reduced as result of the difficult times, it wasn't enough to enable the debt company to generate a profit. Now the equity financed company is able to generate a small profit and produce positive returns on assets and equity, while the debt financed company incurs a loss and negative returns.

Making matters even worse is that the debt-financed company may now be in violation of certain debt covenants and in default of the loan agreement. For example, the loan agreement may read that the company needs to maintain a debt coverage service ratio of at least one and/or produce profitable results on an annual basis (both common covenants for lending sources). Because the company has violated both, it's in technical default on the loan, which will require a fair amount of management attention moving forward.

And just to add a little more insult to injury, the real damage may not be realized until 2006 and beyond. While the equity-financed company has a strong balance sheet and ample cash to expand after the recession ends, the debt-financed company is stuck with restructuring its balance sheet to please its creditors. Thus, it may miss significant growth opportunities in 2006 and beyond, costing the company sales and profits.

XYZ WHOLESALE, INC.
CAPITAL STRUCTURE COMPARISON

Summary Balance Sheet	Equity FYE 12/31/04	Debt FYE 12/31/04
Current Assets:		
Cash & Equivalents	$439,569	$94,929
Trade Receivables, Net	$1,272,083	$1,272,083
Inventory	$1,383,391	$1,383,391
Total Current Assets	$3,095,043	$2,750,403
Fixed & Other Assets:		
Property, Plant, & Equipment, Net	$1,250,000	$1,250,000
Other Assets	$75,000	$75,000
Total Fixed & Other Assets	$1,325,000	$1,325,000
Total Assets	$4,420,043	$4,075,403
Current Liabilities:		
Trade Payables	$1,037,543	$1,037,543
Accrued Liabilities	$51,877	$51,877
Line of Credit Borrowings	$0	$0
Current Portion of Long-Term Liabilities	$0	$300,000
Total Current Liabilities	$1,089,420	$1,389,420
Long-Term Liabilities:		
Notes Payable, Less Current Portion	$0	$900,000
Other Long-Term Liabilities	$125,000	$125,000
Total Long-Term Liabilities	$125,000	$1,025,000
Total Liabilities	$1,214,420	$2,414,420
Equity:		
Common and Preferred Equity, $1 Per Share	$2,000,000	$500,000
Retained Earnings	$750,000	$750,000
Current Earnings	$455,623	$410,983
Total Equity	$3,205,623	$1,660,983
Total Liabilities & Equity	$4,420,043	$4,075,403

Figure 10-1:
Business capitalization comparison — 2004.

(continued)

Summary Income Statement	Equity FYE 12/31/04	Debt FYE 12/31/04
Revenue	$15,265,000	$15,265,000
Costs of Goods Sold	$11,067,125	$11,067,125
Gross Profit	$4,197,875	$4,197,875
Gross Margin	27.50%	27.50%
Selling, General, & Administrative Expenses	$3,251,000	$3,251,000
Interest Expense	$0	$72,000
Other (Income) Expenses	$212,000	$212,000
Net Profit Before Tax	$734,875	$662,875
Income Tax Expense (Benefit)	$279,253	$251,893
Net Profit (Loss)	$455,623	$410,983

Quick Financial Analysis	Equity FYE 12/31/04	Debt FYE 12/31/04
Debt to Equity Ratio	0.38	1.45
Debt Service Coverage Ratio	N/A	1.30
Return on Equity	14.21%	24.74%
Return on Assets	10.31%	10.08%
Earnings Per Share	$0.23	$0.82

Figure 10-1 (continued): Business capitalization comparison — 2004.

Conversely, equity capital offers a chance to strengthen the balance sheet and help manage the company's operating risks through good times and bad. Maintaining a strong balance sheet can really provide a competitive weapon when expanding a business into new markets or exploring a unique business opportunity. However, having too much equity without being able to generate adequate returns can dampen investor enthusiasm and produce a rather rest-less group of shareholders and board members.

Equity-financing sources don't invest capital to watch it generate below-average returns. Equity capital, although representing a lower perceived risk to the company, is by its nature a higher risk capital source (to the providers) and must produce a satisfactory investment return. If not, the equity capital will find an opportunity that does provide the necessary return.

XYZ WHOLESALE, INC.
CAPITAL STRUCTURE COMPARISON

Summary Balance Sheet	Equity FYE 12/31/05	Debt FYE 12/31/05
Current Assets:		
Cash & Equivalents	$941,214	$263,094
Trade Receivables, Net	$1,081,271	$1,081,271
Inventory	$1,216,430	$1,216,430
Total Current Assets	$3,238,915	$2,560,795
Fixed & Other Assets:		
Property, Plant, & Equipment, Net	$1,000,000	$1,000,000
Other Assets	$75,000	$75,000
Total Fixed & Other Assets	$1,075,000	$1,075,000
Total Assets	$4,313,915	$3,635,795
Current Liabilities:		
Trade Payables	$912,322	$912,322
Accrued Liabilities	$45,616	$45,616
Line of Credit Borrowings	$0	$0
Current Portion of Long-Term Liabilities	$0	$300,000
Total Current Liabilities	$957,938	$1,257,938
Long-Term Liabilities:		
Notes Payable, Less Current Portion	$0	$600,000
Other Long-Term Liabilities	$125,000	$125,000
Total Long-Term Liabilities	$125,000	$725,000
Total Liabilities	$1,082,938	$1,982,938
Equity:		
Common and Preferred Equity, $1 Per Share	$2,000,000	$500,000
Retained Earnings	$1,205,623	$1,160,983
Current Earnings	$25,353	($8,127)
Total Equity	$3,230,976	$1,652,856
Total Liabilities & Equity	$4,313,915	$3,635,795

Figure 10-2:
Business capitalization comparison — 2005.

(continued)

Summary Income Statement	Equity FYE 12/31/05	Debt FYE 12/31/05
Revenue	$12,975,250	$12,975,250
Costs of Goods Sold	$9,731,438	$9,731,438
Gross Profit	$3,243,813	$3,243,813
Gross Margin	25.00%	25.00%
Selling, General, & Administrative Expenses	$2,990,920	$2,990,920
Interest Expense	$0	$54,000
Other (Income) Expenses	$212,000	$212,000
Net Profit Before Tax	$40,893	($13,108)
Income Tax Expense (Benefit)	$15,539	($4,981)
Net Profit (Loss)	$25,353	($8,127)

Figure 10-2 (continued): Business capitalization comparison — 2005.

Quick Financial Analysis	Equity FYE 12/31/05	Debt FYE 12/31/05
Debt to Equity Ratio	0.34	1.20
Debt Service Coverage Ratio	N/A	0.13
Return on Equity	0.78%	-0.49%
Return on Assets	0.59%	-0.22%
Earnings Per Share	$0.01	-$0.02

Chapter 11

Diagnosing Your Financial Condition

*Y*our small business earns profit year in and year out. You closely study your P&L statements. You've put in place effective internal controls to prevent embezzlement and other theft and fraud against your business. Your Controller assures you that your accounting system is reliable and has no errors. Your CPA says your financial statements follow generally accepted accounting principles (GAAP). The Internal Revenue Service hasn't challenged your income tax returns. You're on good terms with your bank. Therefore, your business's financial condition is in good shape, and you have no financial problems. Right?

Not so fast. Making profit doesn't necessarily mean that your financial condition is in good shape. Managing profit isn't the end of the story; you must also manage your financial condition. Making a profit doesn't automatically make your financial condition sound. In fact, your financial condition may be spinning out of control despite making profit. For example, rapid sales growth crimps cash flow, which can cause serious liquidity problems.

Instead of making a profit, suppose that you had a loss for your most recent year. In this situation, you'd probably be quite concerned about your financial condition. You'd think, "Hey, the loss hurts my financial condition, doesn't it? A loss means I'm worse off, and that my financial condition has suffered." This is true. But don't wait for a loss to be concerned about your financial condition. Managing financial condition is just as critical as making profit. If you fail to keep on top of your financial condition, your days of making profit may come to an abrupt end.

Connecting the P&L and Balance Sheet

Large business organizations appoint a full-time CFO whose responsibilities include controlling the financial condition of the business. (*Financial condition* refers to how your liabilities stack up against your assets, the liquidity of your business, and how efficiently you're using your assets.) The small business owner/manager doesn't have this luxury. You have to be your own CFO and manage the financial condition of your business yourself. You can call on outside experts for advice, of course, but the day-to-day management of financial condition falls in your lap. You have to know what to look for in your P&L in managing profit. Likewise, you have to know what to look for in your balance sheet in managing your financial condition and then determine whether these factors are under control.

Managing financial condition begins with understanding the connections between sales revenue and expenses and their related assets and liabilities. Not to toot our own horn, but John has written a book that has been in print more than a quarter century, *How to Read a Financial Report* (Wiley). The one compliment John hears more than any other is that he clarifies the connections between sales revenue and expenses in the income statement (P&L report) and their corresponding assets and liabilities in the statement of financial condition (balance sheet).

Financial reports don't show lines of connection between the P&L and balance sheet. Each financial statement is on a separate page in most financial reports, so drawing lines of connection would be awkward. Because you see no visible lines, you have to make connections between sales revenue and expenses and their related assets and liabilities. In other words, you have to know how to match up items in the P&L with items in the balance sheet.

Accountants who prepare financial statements presume that users know these critical links between the P&L and balance sheet. Accountants don't provide a roadmap of the arteries between the profit report and financial condition report. At the same time, many financial analysis ratios are based exactly on these connections. For example, the asset turnover ratio (see Chapter 8) hooks up sales revenue and total assets.

Figure 11-1 presents the P&L and balance sheet of a small business in a side-by-side format to show the lines of connection between sales revenue and expenses in the P&L and their interrelated assets and liabilities in the balance sheet. (We explain the P&L report in Chapter 2 and the balance sheet in Chapter 3.) As you may have surmised, we round off dollar amounts in the financial statements so that calculations are easier to follow.

The P&L statement in Figure 11-1 deviates from standard practice in one respect: Just one total amount for all operating expenses, excluding depreciation, is disclosed. The P&L reports of most businesses usually include several operating expenses in addition to depreciation. For the purpose of this chapter, however, we need just one total amount for all operating expenses excluding depreciation.

Say that you're the principal manager of the business whose P&L and balance sheet are shown in Figure 11-1. The business is organized legally as a corporation, and you own a sizable percent of its capital stock shares. The majority of shares are owned by outside investors who aren't involved in the management of the business, although they sit on your board of directors.

What do the financial statements presented in Figure 11-1 reveal about your business? The financial statements say that you made a profit for the year and that your business's financial condition is reasonably healthy. Your bottom-line net income equals 3.75 percent of sales revenue. Net income divided by owners' equity at year-end equals 26 percent, which is a respectable rate of return on owners' equity capital. These are two very important benchmarks of financial performance. You need to earn a satisfactory return on sales (profit as a percent of sales revenue) in order to earn a satisfactory return on equity capital (profit as a percent of owners' equity).

This chapter addresses a different financial management imperative: Is your balance sheet in proper alignment with your P&L statement? Are the balances (amounts) of your assets and liabilities consistent with the amounts of your sales revenue and expenses, which is another way of asking, Are you controlling your assets and liabilities? Or, are you letting them float around without close management attention?

Chapter 3 explains that changes in assets and liabilities during the period affect *cash flow from profit* (operating activities). The chapter also explains that depreciation is not a cash outlay in the period in which depreciation expense is recorded. Understanding cash flow from profit is extremely important. This chapter, on the other hand, examines the relationships between sales revenue and expenses and the assets and liabilities directly connected to the profit-making activities of a business. This chapter focuses on the *proper sizes* of the assets and liabilities relative to the sales revenue and expenses of the business. If you don't control the sizes of your assets and liabilities, then your financial condition can end up in deep dodo, as a former United States President used to say.

Your Business Name
P&L Statement
For Year Ended December 31, 2008

Sales revenue	$5,200,000
Cost of goods sold expense	$3,120,000
Gross margin	$2,080,000
Operating expenses	$1,664,000
Depreciation expense	$85,000
Operating earnings	$331,000
Interest expense	$52,500
Profit before income tax	$278,500
Income tax expense	$83,550
Net income	$194,950

Figure 11-1:
Connecting
the P&L and
balance
sheet.

Following are the key connections between the P&L statement and the
statement of financial condition:

- **Sales revenue,** being the overall size measure of a business, is an indicator of how much *cash* a business needs.

- Making sales on credit generates the asset **accounts receivable.**

- Products sold to customers, the cost of which is recorded in cost of goods sold expense, typically are from a stock of products held for immediate delivery to customers; the cost of unsold products awaiting future sale is in the **inventory asset.**

- Retailers and wholesalers use credit to purchase the products they sell; the liability for unpaid purchases is recorded in the **accounts payable account.**

- Certain operating costs are paid in advance, before being recorded as expense; the amount of these prepayments are held in the asset **prepaid expenses.**

- Many operating supplies and services needed to run a business are purchased on credit and aren't paid until later; the costs are recorded in the **accounts payable** liability account.

Your Business Name
Balance Sheet (Statement of Financial Condition)
At Close of Business December 31, 2008

Cash	$500,000	
Accounts receivable	$250,000	
Inventory	$720,000	
Prepaid expenses	$96,000	
Current assets		$1,566,000
Fixed assets, at original cost	$745,000	
Accumulated depreciation	($348,000)	$397,000
Total assets		$1,963,000
Accounts payable–inventory purchases	$260,000	
Accounts payable–operating expenses	$160,000	
Accrued expenses payable	$192,000	
Short-term notes payable	$300,000	
Current liabilities		$912,000
Long-term notes payable		$300,000
Owners' invested capital	$250,000	
Retained earnings	$501,000	
Owners' equity		$751,000
Total liabilities & owners' equity		$1,963,000

Figure 11-1:
Continued.

✔ Some operating expenses are recorded based on calculations and estimates of costs as they accumulate and accrue over time that will not be
paid until later; the amounts of these unpaid costs are recorded in an
accrued expenses payable liability account.

✔ The cost of **fixed assets** (except land) is allocated to depreciation
expense over their estimated useful lives.

✔ The amounts of **short-term and long-term notes payable** and the interest rates on these debt instruments determines interest expense.

Window dressing

To hide a cash shortage when releasing financial statements to outside parties (when requesting a loan or negotiating a line of credit with your bank), a business may engage in an accounting sleight of hand called *window dressing*. Cash collections from customers in payment of their accounts receivable owed to the business that are received after the balance sheet date (December 31, 2008 in the Figure 11-1 example) are recorded as if these cash collections were received on the last day of the year. Thus, the cash balance is higher than it actually was at the end of the year, and the accounts receivable balance is lower. For example, the business shown in Figure 11-1 may have held its cash collections journal open for a few days into 2009 during which $100,000 cash was received from its customers. As a result, your cash balance is overstated by $100,000, and your accounts receivable balance is understated by $100,000.

Engaging in window dressing to pump up your cash balance is misleading, of course. You may be somewhat surprised that an accountant would go along with this ruse, but it happens all the time. While in public accounting, we saw it frequently. As a matter of fact, many businesses regularly do some window dressing at year-end. Otherwise, they'd have to report a very low cash balance in their year-end balance sheet. Their reasoning is that they're getting by on a low cash balance, and that if they told the truth, lenders and outside investors in the business would be unduly alarmed by seeing such a low cash balance.

Accountants generally go along with a reasonable amount of window dressing if they judge it to be necessary. Even outside CPA auditors tolerate a reasonable amount of window dressing. What's reasonable? We can't answer this question definitively. Our best estimate is that most accountants and CPA auditors would draw the line beyond five business days of holding the books open on cash collections of accounts receivable.

The following sections explain each connection in more detail. The balance sheet presented in Figure 11-1 presents the financial condition of your business, as it should be assuming that everything is under control and in perfect relationship with your sales revenue and expenses. In other words, it's a normative, or ideal, balance sheet — as if all your assets and liabilities are in precise agreement with your sales revenue and expenses.

Sales Revenue⇨Cash

The argument is endless regarding how large the day-to-day working cash balance of a business should be. Some argue for a lean and mean approach; their main point is that only a minimal cash balance is really needed, and a low balance keeps the business on its toes. At the other extreme, some argue that a business manager is too busy to keep tabs on the day-to-day cash balance and has more important things to do. Some argue, as we do in Chapter 4, that you shouldn't isolate on cash alone, but focus on liquidity that includes more than just cash in the bank.

In the example shown in Figure 11-1, your cash balance at year-end is $500,000, which equals five weeks of your annual sales revenue:

$5,200,000 annual sales revenue ÷ 52 weeks = $100,000 sales per week

$500,000 year-end cash balance ÷ $100,000 sales per week = 5 weeks of sales

Most business managers would consider a cash balance equal to five weeks of annual sales quite adequate. In fact, many small businesses would love to have this much cash as a percent of sales. Many small businesses have trouble raising enough cash in the first place (see Chapter 4 on raising capital), or they don't generate enough cash flow from profit to provide enough cash.

Credit sales revenue⇨accounts receivable

Generally speaking, a business offers to sell its products (and services) on credit to other businesses. A credit sale is recorded as soon as the sale is consummated, which generally is when the customer takes possession and the title passes to the customer. Depending on the credit terms, the seller does not receive cash until later. Credit terms vary from business to business, as you probably know. In many cases, the seller offers an incentive to pay quickly, such as a 2 percent discount for payment made within 10 days. Generally, a business extends qualified customers a 30-day credit period. Of course, the seller expects to be paid at the end of the 30-day period. However, actual collection from some credit customers takes longer, as you probably know from experience.

In Figure 11-1, half the annual sales revenue is from sales made at retail for cash (net of credit-card discounts). The other half is from credit sales to businesses. The standard credit term for business customers is 30 days. However, some credit customers take more than 30 days to pay for their purchases. Some take advantage of your prompt payment discount. But other credit customers take 45 days or more to pay up. You send reminder letters to the slow payers, but you tolerate late payment in order to keep them as customers.

Based on your experience with credit customers and your credit-collection policies, you know that your business has about five weeks of sales on the books not yet collected. Therefore, the year-end balance of accounts receivable is $250,000:

$5,200,000 sales revenue × 50% credit sales = $2,600,000 credit sales

$2,600,000 credit sales ÷ 52 weeks = $50,000 credit sales per week

$50,000 credit sales per week × 5 weeks average collection period = $250,000 balance of accounts receivable at end of year

Your year-end balance sheet (see Figure 11-1) reports that accounts receivable is $250,000, so you're right on target. In other words, your accounts receivable is the correct size relative to your total annual credit sales based on your credit terms and collection experience.

Cost of goods sold⇨inventory

Generally speaking, businesses sell products *from stock* or *on order*. In other words, a business has an inventory of products ready for immediate delivery to its customers, or it takes orders for later delivery. (A business can do both, of course.) The business in Figure 11-1 sells from stock. Some products sit in the warehouse for many weeks before they're sold; other products move through the warehouse quickly. Based on the sales mix, your inventory equals 12 weeks of sales. Putting it another way, your *inventory turnover ratio* is four times per year (52 weeks ÷ 12 weeks average inventory holding period = 4 times).

Based on your average holding time for products before they're sold, your year-end inventory balance is

> $3,120,000 annual cost of goods sold expense ÷ 52 weeks = $60,000 per week
>
> $60,000 cost of goods sold per week × 12 weeks holding period = $720,000 inventory

Most of your products are purchased on credit, which leads to the next connection.

Inventory⇨accounts payable— inventory purchases

Business-to-business selling and buying is based on credit. If your credit rating is very poor, then your sources may ship products only COD (cash on delivery). If your credit rating is good, your vendors may give you 30 days credit, or one month, to pay for your purchases. You tend to pay in four weeks, just a couple of days shorter than the full 30 days credit period. For this example, your inventory balance equals 12 weeks of annual cost of goods sold expense. So, your liability for product purchases on credit is

> $60,000 cost of goods sold per week × 4 weeks credit period for inventory purchases = $260,000 accounts payable for inventory purchases

Your *net* investment in inventory is $460,000: $720,000 inventory − $260,000 accounts payable for inventory purchases = $460,000 net investment in inventory. You could make an argument that inventory should be reported net of the accounts payable liability, but you never see this in external financial statements. Accountants generally are conservative and would be concerned that a liability might get lost if it were netted against the inventory asset account. However, the small business manager should keep in mind that the amount of cash invested in inventory is net of the accounts payable for inventory purchases.

As you probably know, providing business credit ratings is a big business. Before computers came along, only a handful of companies collected information on businesses and sold credit ratings. Now it's mostly done over the Internet. If you have a few minutes, go to a search engine on the Web (Google or Yahoo!, for example) and enter business credit ratings. You may be surprised at how many hits you get. Some of the old names are still there (Dun & Bradstreet and Moody's, for example) but many new names — including Equifax and Experian — are out there. One credit ratings source indicates it has credit information on more than 15 million businesses, *including your business.* Do you know your business's credit score? Having a good credit score improves the credit terms you get from your vendors and for your bank loans.

Operating expenses⇨prepaid expenses

Businesses pay in advance for certain expenses. Insurance premiums, for example, are paid for before the cost is allocated to expense over the life of the insurance policies. A business stockpiles office, computer, and shipping supplies before they're actually used and charged to expense. In some locales, property taxes are paid at the start of the tax year, and the amount is allocated to expense each month or quarter. When prepaid, the costs are recorded in an asset account called *prepaid expenses* (see Figure 11-1). At any one moment in time, this asset account has a balance, which is the amount of prepaid costs that haven't been charged to expense yet. This particular asset is listed last in the current assets section of the balance sheet, as shown in Figure 11-1.

The size of the asset prepaid expenses relative to total annual operating expenses varies from business to business, which simply means that some businesses have to prepay more of their expenses than others. The year-end balance of your prepaid expenses equals three weeks of your annual operating expenses:

$1,664,000 annual operating expenses ÷ 52 weeks = $32,000 operating expenses per week

$96,000 year-end prepaid expenses ÷ $32,000 operating expenses per week = 3 weeks

In most situations, you don't have to worry about prepaid expenses too much. For one thing, this asset is typically much smaller than accounts receivable and inventory, so there is less dollar amount to get out of control. Second, many expenses that you have to prepay are on automatic pilot. For example, insurance companies notify you when policies need to be renewed, and when supplies drop to a certain level you replenish them.

Operating expenses⇨accounts payable–operating expenses

In contrast to prepaying some expenses (see preceding section), a business records many expenses before they're paid. Unpaid operating expenses are recorded in the liability account called *accounts payable*. In Figure 11-1, we use two accounts payable liability accounts: one for unpaid purchases of inventory and the second for unpaid operating expenses. The balance sheet in Figure 11-1 presents two accounts payable liability accounts: one for each category. In external balance sheets, most businesses report just one total combined amount of accounts payable. (For internal reporting for management analysis and control, you can instruct your Controller to separate the two sources of accounts payable.)

If your business has a good credit rating and you have a long record of paying your bills on time, you'll have no trouble buying services and operating supplies on credit. For example, say that you buy utilities (gas, electricity, telephone, Internet, and so on) on credit. Your lawyer and CPA extend 30 days credit to your business, as do virtually all your vendors and suppliers. One other point: Your business has invoices for the amounts recorded in accounts payable. As a matter of fact, the bills (invoices) received from your vendors and suppliers are the source documents used to record the expenses.

Although most of your trade credit is for 30 days, you have found from experience that your accounts payable tend to equal five weeks of annual operating expenses. Therefore:

> $1,664,000 annual operating expenses ÷ 52 weeks = $32,000 operating expenses per week

> $32,000 operating expenses per week × 5 weeks average time to pay accounts payable for operating expenses = $160,000 year-end accounts payable balance

In Figure 11-1, your accounts payable for operating expenses balance is $160,000 at the close of the year. (Keep in mind that we're dealing with rounded dollar amounts in the example, and in actual situations, the calculations don't come out in even digits, of course.)

Could the amount of accounts payable for operating expenses in the balance sheet ever be zero? Well, it is unusual, but we can think of two opposite situations in which it would be true, or almost true. One is when the credit rating and bill paying history of a business is so bad that no one will extend credit — the business has to buy everything COD. The opposite case is one in which a business has an excellent credit record, but is so conservative that it pays every invoice the same day the invoice is received.

Operating expenses⇨accrued expenses payable

Certain operating expenses accumulate, or accrue, in the background as it were. The business doesn't directly purchase these things and doesn't receive invoices for them. For example, your business gives employees two weeks vacation per year and pays for sick leave. Suppose that your real estate taxes are paid once a year in arrears, or at the end of the tax year. As you progress through the year, you're approaching the date when you'll pay the annual property tax. You sell products that have to be serviced after the point of sale under terms of the warranty and guarantee on the products. In short, the amounts of certain expenses pile up during the year, which will be paid sometime later.

A basic principle of profit accounting, known as the *matching principle,* is that the full amount of expenses should be recorded in the same period as sales revenue. It doesn't make sense to record revenue from sales of products in one period, but to delay recording some of the expenses of making the sales until the next period. This is good theory, without a doubt. But recording all expenses that should be matched against sales revenue for the period is easier said than done. The crux of the problem centers on those expenses that accrue like a thief in the night, as it were. The amount to record for utilities expense is simply the amount on the invoice from the gas and electric company for the month. Exactly what amount should be recorded for the cost of future vacation time earned by employees for the pay period just ended?

In short, your Controller makes estimates of those operating expenses that gradually accumulate during the year. These are real liabilities that will have to be paid sometime later. The liabilities for these expenses are accumulated in the *accrued expenses payable* account – see Figure 11-1. The actual titles for this liability vary widely from business to business. You see quite a range of titles. (In contrast, the title accounts payable is fairly standard for purchases on credit.)

The size of a business's accrued expense payable liability can range from relatively small to fairly large. Based on the experience of your business, this liability tends to run about six weeks of your annual operating expenses. Therefore:

$1,664,000 annual operating expenses ÷ 52 weeks = $32,000 operating expenses per week

$32,000 operating expenses per week × 6 weeks delay in paying accrued expenses payable = $192,000 year-end accrued expenses payable balance

Accounting for accrued operating expenses is very tricky and open to manipulation (not that you would even think of fiddling with your books, of course). We won't bore you by discussing technical details regarding estimating accrued operating expenses. If you have a free moment (not too likely, we assume), you can ask your Controller for a briefing regarding the main issues in estimating operating expenses for your particular business. One or two major issues may deserve your attention.

Frankly, many small businesses don't make much of an effort to record these types of expenses, given the difficulties in estimating the costs. Generally speaking, accountants tolerate not recording the accrual of such costs. The expenses are recorded on a when-paid basis, which is too late. Not recording the expenses on time causes somewhat of a mismatch between sales revenue and expenses, but as you've heard said, "It's close enough for government work."

Fixed assets⇨depreciation expense

Most businesses own at least some, and perhaps all, of the long-term operating assets they need to make sales, maintain an office, store inventory, deliver products to customers, and so on. These resources are informally called *fixed assets* (see Figure 11-1) because they're relatively fixed in place and aren't held for sale in the normal course of business. Examples of fixed assets include land and buildings, furniture and fixtures, land improvements (paved parking lots, landscaping, sidewalks, and so on), computers, delivery trucks, tools, computers, and many types of equipment. Interestingly, accountants generally don't use the term fixed assets in a balance sheet. Rather, the more common title for these assets is *property, plant and equipment*.

The cost of a fixed asset (except land) is allocated to depreciation expense over the estimated useful life of the asset, which can be as short as three years to 39 years (for buildings). The useful life estimates permitted for federal income tax are adopted by most businesses, instead of making more realistic estimates for the actual useful lives for its fixed assets. A building is depreciated over 39 years, whereas its actual use may run 50 years or more. Also, the income tax law permits front loading of depreciation; more depreciation expense is recorded in the early years than in the later years. This tilting of depreciation expense toward the early years is called *accelerated depreciation.* The main alternative is the *straight-line method,* in which an equal amount of depreciation expense is recorded in each year of the useful life of the fixed asset.

In recording depreciation expense, the accountant doesn't decrease the cost balance of the fixed asset account, which you may think would be the way to do it. The fixed asset is wearing out or losing its economic usefulness to the business. So why not decrease the fixed asset account by the amount of depreciation expense? Instead, depreciation expense is recorded in the contra account called *accumulated depreciation.* The balance in this account is deducted from the cost balance in the fixed asset account. The main purpose is to report fixed assets at their original cost in the balance sheet and to show how much of the original cost has been deducted over the years as depreciation expense.

The idea is that the original cost of fixed assets has information value to users of the financial statement. Deducting the balance of accumulated depreciation from the original cost balance gives the *book value* of the fixed assets. For the example in Figure 11-1, $348,000 accumulated depreciation is deducted from $745,000 original cost, which gives $397,000 book value for its fixed assets. The book value is added to the balances of other assets to determine the total assets of the business.

In Figure 11-1, you may suspect a missing link: There is no line of connection from sales revenue to fixed assets. To make sales and carry on operations, a business definitely needs fixed assets. There's no argument about this point. However, determining the size of fixed assets relative to sales revenue isn't practical. You can't develop guidelines for sizing fixed assets relative to sales revenue for several reasons.

For one thing, a business could, conceivably, lease all its fixed assets, including its real estate, computer system, office furniture, vehicles, and so on. In this extreme case, the business would have no fixed assets; it would have rent expense instead of depreciation expense. Usually, a business owns at least some of the fixed assets it needs to operate, so it would be unusual to find no fixed assets at all in a balance sheet. A business may have acquired many of its fixed assets years ago. (An indicator that its fixed assets are old is when the accumulated depreciation balance is a large percent of original cost.) In this situation, the business's sales revenue is in current dollars, but its fixed assets are in old dollars, making a comparison between the two misleading.

In any case, the cost of fixed assets drives depreciation expense. (In Figure 11-1, see the line of connection from fixed assets to depreciation expense.) You should keep an eye on this ratio. In 2008, your depreciation expense equals about 11 percent of the original cost of your fixed assets: ($85,000 depreciation expense ÷ $745,000 fixed assets cost = about 11%). The 11 percent ratio of depreciation to fixed assets indicates an average depreciation life of about nine years. If the depreciation ratio to fixed assets differs significantly year to year, you should ask your Controller for an explanation.

Notes payable⇨interest expense

The total amount of borrowings (typically on the basis of notes payable and a line of credit) and the interest rates on the debt drive the amount of interest expense. In Figure 11-1, interest expense is 8.75 percent of your company's short-term and long-term notes payable:

> $52,500 interest expense ÷ $600,000 total of notes payable = 8.75% annual interest rate

 Your 8.75 percent interest rate may appear high. Your small business may have to pay a higher interest rate just because it's small. Many lenders operate on the assumption that the risk in loaning money to a small business is greater than to a larger business, which has more financial management sophistication. Also, there is the size factor. Small business loans are smaller than large business loans, of course, which means the lender has a smaller base to work with relative to its loan-processing costs. So, the lender compensates for the smaller loan base by charging a higher interest rate. Also, the lender may tack on other loan costs, such as origination fees, and these tend to be a higher percent of the loan compared with a larger loan that is charged the same fee.

Being the principal manager of the business who negotiates the terms of your loans with the lenders, you're in the best position to judge whether the 8.75 percent interest rate is appropriate. If the amount of your debt varied widely during the year, ask your Controller to do a more precise calculation based on the weighted average debt balance during the year. If you thought your interest rate was 6 percent but the ratio of interest expense to notes payable is almost 9 percent, you should do a little more investigation.

Side-stepping around two other connections

At the end of the year, your business probably had a small amount of accrued interest payable on your short-term and long-term notes payable. Accountants calculate the exact amount of interest expense that has accrued to the end of the year since the last interest payment was made in order to record the full amount of interest expense for the year. The accrued amount of interest is recorded in the *accrued interest payable* liability account. Also, a small fraction of your income tax expense for the year may still be payable at year-end. The unpaid amount is recorded in the *income tax payable* account.

Accrued interest payable and income tax payable are in the same nature as the accrued expenses payable account discussed for operating expenses. In fact, many companies lump together all accrued expenses in one liability account — although financial reporting practices vary quite a bit in this regard. In most businesses, accrued operating expenses payable are much larger than accrued interest and income tax payable. (If a business is a pass-through tax entity, it doesn't have income tax expense; see Chapter 9.)

In Figure 11-1, we don't show the connections between interest expense and income tax and their liability accounts. In most situations, these amounts aren't consequential. However, suppose that you're seriously in arrears in making interest payments and that you haven't made the required install-ment payments on your income tax for the year. In this situation, these liabili-ties should be disclosed in your balance sheet. Actually, financial reporting disclosure standards say that you should explain the overdue nature of these liabilities in a footnote to the financial statements. Well, that's the theory. Whether you'd be willing to disclose these two overdue liabilities in your balance sheet is another matter.

The balance sheet in Figure 11-1 is for the ideal situation, in which you have every asset and liability under control at the right size relative to your sales revenue and expenses. Things don't always go so well, of course. One or more problems can develop, as you probably know from personal experi-ence. The first step is to know what the sizes of your assets and liabilities should be. These normative sizes serve as control benchmarks against which your actual asset and liability balances are compared.

Minor variances between actual year-end balances and the benchmark bal-ances usually are of no great concern. For example, if your year-end accounts receivable had been, say, $265,000, then you're $15,000 off target, because the balance should be $250,000. This amount of variance probably is in the noise level. But if the year-end balance had been much higher, you probably should look into the reasons for the deviation.

Spotting Financial Condition Problems

This section looks at alternative scenarios in which the financial condition of your business has one or more trouble spots. The statement of financial condition (balance sheet) in Figure 11-1 is the reference point. Your year-end asset and liability balances in this scenario are what they should be. In each alternative scenario, you have let one or more of your assets and liabilities get out of control. You should move quickly to correct the problem before it gets more serious.

In the following alternative scenarios, the P&L statement is the same as in the original scenario (see Figure 11-1). In other words, we don't change your P&L. Your total sales revenue for the year is $5,200,000, and you earned $194,950 profit (net income after income tax). However, making a profit doesn't necessarily mean that your financial condition is in good shape. The following scenarios illustrate how things can spin out of control if you don't keep a close watch on your assets and liabilities.

Finding the problem(s) – Case #1

Normally we make section headings clear to give you a preview of what's in the section. But doing this would telegraph the financial condition problem we want you to identify. For an alternative scenario, we want you to first read the balance sheet and find the problems.

So, at this point, scour the new balance sheet scenario shown in Figure 11-2 and find the trouble spots. We do *not* include lines of connection between the P&L and balance sheet in Figure 11-2. Financial reports do not show these lines of connections. Figure 11-2 is more realistic in this regard. You have to mentally draw lines of connection yourself.

In the alternative scenario shown in Figure 11-2, are some of your assets or liabilities out of kilter with your sales revenue and expenses? You should have identified one trouble spot. In the business example, half your sales are on credit, and your average credit sales per week equal $50,000. Therefore, your year-end balance of accounts receivable equals seven weeks of credit sales (see Figure 11-2 for data):

> $350,000 year-end balance of accounts receivable ÷ $50,000 average credit sales revenue per week = 7 weeks of sales in ending accounts receivable

Based on the 30-day credit terms you offer credit customers and considering how aggressive you should be in collecting overdue receivables, you should have only five weeks of receivables at year-end. So, something is wrong. How do you explain the bloated year-end balance of accounts receivable? You definitely should look into this matter.

One possibility is that one or two of your larger customers asked for additional time, which accounts for most of the accounts receivable overage. Or perhaps your collection efforts on past due customers' accounts has become too lax. Or perhaps someone in your business has diverted cash collections into his pocket and has attempted to cover up the embezzlement by not recording the credits (decreases) in customers' accounts receivable. Whatever the reason(s), you'd better find out. You may discover in your investigation that one or more customers' accounts should be written off as uncollectible and recorded as bad debts expense. In any case, you should have your Controller regularly prepare an *aging analysis* of your accounts receivable, which shows the amount of receivables that are current and the amount that are past due.

You should also notice in this scenario that your ending cash balance is $100,000 lower than in the benchmark scenario (see Figure 11-1). The ending balance of accounts receivable is $100,000 higher, which means you failed to collect this amount of cash from customers (which you should have), so your cash balance is $100,000 lower. In this scenario, your $400,000 ending cash balance equals four weeks of annual sales revenue, which is probably adequate.

Finding the problem (s) — Case #2

Figure 11-3 presents another year-end balance sheet scenario for your business. Treat this scenario independently of the scenario examined for Case #1. Did you identify the trouble spot in this Case #2 scenario?

In scrutinizing the balance sheet in Figure 11-3, you should have noticed that your year-end inventory balance is too high compared with your 12 weeks standard inventory holding period. As calculated in the section "Cost of goods sold⇨Inventory" in the chapter, your cost of goods sold expense equals $60,000 per week. Thus, your ending inventory equals 16 weeks of sales (see Figure 11-2 for data):

> $960,000 year-end inventory balance ÷ $60,000 average cost of goods sold expense per week = 16 weeks ending inventory

You should definitely look into why you're holding an extra four weeks of inventory (compared with your normal 12 weeks inventory holding period). There may be good reasons. For example, maybe a vendor offered a deeply discounted purchase price if you placed a very large order, and you made a very large purchase just before the end of the year. Or perhaps the purchasing manager goofed and bought several products that aren't selling. You should order up an *aging analysis* on your ending inventory — a schedule that classifies products according to how long they've been sitting in inventory. You may not be able to sell old products at regular sales prices. If this is the situation, you should write down the cost of the products according to the *lower of cost or market rule.* (We explain this accounting procedure in Chapter 6.)

Your Business Name
P&L Statement
For Year Ended December 31, 2008

Sales revenue	$5,200,000
Cost of goods sold expense	$3,120,000
Gross margin	$2,080,000
Operating expenses	$1,664,000
Depreciation expense	$85,000
Operating earnings	$331,000
Interest expense	$52,500
Profit before income tax	$278,500
Income tax expense	$83,550
Net income	$194,950

Figure 11-2:
Alternative scenario for balance sheet – case #1.

Your inventory is $240,000 higher than it should be, which means you spent cash to pay for the inventory increase or you increased your accounts payable for inventory purchases (or did some of both). Note that the year-end balance of accounts payable for inventory purchases is the same amount as in the Figure 11-1 benchmark scenario, which means you did not finance part of the inventory increase by increasing your accounts payable for inventory purchases. Therefore, your cash balance took a $240,000 hit from letting your inventory get out of control, which is seen by comparing the cash balances in the benchmark and alternative scenario:

> $500,000 cash balance in benchmark scenario – $260,000 cash balance in alternative scenario = $240,000 reduction in cash balance

As you see in Figure 11-3, your year-end cash balance is only $260,000, which is less than three weeks of sales:

> $260,000 ending cash balance ÷ $100,000 average sales per week = 2.6 weeks

Your cash balance is rather thin in this scenario. Most small business managers would be worried about a working cash balance equal to less than three weeks of sales. On the other hand, we must admit that many small businesses would love to have a cash balance equal to 2.6 weeks of sales. They live hand to mouth in terms of cash flow. They wait to see how much cash comes in during the day before deciding on the amount of checks they can write for that day. They have little or no buffer, or reserve of cash, to pay their liabilities on time when their day-to-day cash inflow is irregular. That's no way to run a railroad!

Your Business Name
Balance Sheet (Statement of Financial Condition)
At Close of Business December 31, 2008

Cash	$400,000	
Accounts receivable	$350,000	
Inventory	$720,000	
Prepaid expenses	$96,000	
Current assets		$1,566,000
Fixed assets, at original cost	$745,000	
Accumulated depreciation	($348,000)	$397,000
Total assets		$1,963,000
Accounts payable—inventory purchases	$260,000	
Accounts payable—operating expenses	$160,000	
Accrued expenses payable	$192,000	
Short-term notes payable	$300,000	
Current liabilities		$912,000
Long-term notes payable		$300,000
Owners' invested capital	$250,000	
Retained earnings	$501,000	
Owners' equity		$751,000
Total liabilities & owners' equity		$1,963,000

Figure 11-2:
Continued.

You need to keep a close watch on accounts receivable and inventory. These two assets, in particular, can drift out of control. You may be well advised to instruct your Controller to give you frequent *flash reports* on these two assets, so you can get a heads up on problems before they get out of control. We discuss flash reports in Chapter 7.

Finding the problem (s) – Case #3

Figure 11-4 presents another year-end balance sheet scenario. In Case #1, you allowed your accounts receivable to get too big, and in Case #2, you allowed your inventory to get too big (see preceding sections). In the new scenario, these two assets are the proper sizes (the same sizes as in the benchmark example shown in Figure 11-1). What trouble spots do you see in the new scenario (see Figure 11-4)?

Your Business Name
P&L Statement
For Year Ended December 31, 2008

Sales revenue	$5,200,000
Cost of goods sold expense	$3,120,000
Gross margin	$2,080,000
Operating expenses	$1,664,000
Depreciation expense	$85,000
Operating earnings	$331,000
Interest expense	$52,500
Profit before income tax	$278,500
Income tax expense	$83,550
Net income	$194,950

Figure 11-3: Alternative scenario for balance sheet — case #2.

Compared with the benchmark scenario shown in Figure 11-1, five balance sheet items are different in this new scenario (see Table 11-1).

Table 11-1	Differences Between Case #3 Scenario and Benchmark Scenario		
Account	**Case #3**	**Benchmark**	**Difference**
Cash	$250,000	$500,000	($250,000)
Loans to officers	$50,000	$0	$50,000
Accounts payable — inventory purchases	$360,000	$260,000	$100,000
Accounts payable — operating expenses	$240,000	$160,000	$80,000
Retained earnings	$121,000	$501,000	($380,000)

In this scenario, by not paying your bills on time, you've let the balances of your two accounts payable run up $180,000 higher than what they should be. Undoubtedly, your creditors aren't happy, but they probably haven't shut off credit because they want to keep your business. However, paying your bills late can hurt your credit rating. Your vendors and suppliers probably will remove you from their most favored customer list. You may have trouble getting quick delivery, special favors, and other special deals from them.

Your Business Name
Balance Sheet (Statement of Financial Condition)
At Close of Business December 31, 2008

Cash	$260,000	
Accounts receivable	$250,000	
Inventory	$960,000	
Prepaid expenses	$96,000	
Current assets		$1,566,000
Fixed assets, at original cost	$745,000	
Accumulated depreciation	($348,000)	$397,000
Total assets		$1,963,000
Accounts payable—inventory purchases	$260,000	
Accounts payable—operating expenses	$160,000	
Accrued expenses payable	$192,000	
Short-term notes payable	$300,000	
Current liabilities		$912,000
Long-term notes payable		$300,000
Owners' invested capital	$250,000	
Retained earnings	$501,000	
Owners' equity		$751,000
Total liabilities & owners' equity		$1,963,000

Figure 11-3:
Continued.

Given the $180,000 run up in accounts payable, one would expect that your cash balance would be higher, not $250,000 lower. How did this happen? Well, there are two reasons. First, note the new asset *loans to officers*. The business loaned you and another manager $50,000. This scenario happens all the time, although it's not a particularly good idea to use your business as a source for personal loans. A principle of business is that transactions should be at arm's length, which isn't possible when a business loans money to managers of the business. The loan probably isn't illegal; state business laws don't prohibit loans to insiders. But is it good business? That's another matter.

Note that the loans to officers is put outside the current assets category, which means the loan will not be paid back to the business in the short term (which generally means less than one year). A footnote to the financial statements should disclose the interest rate and other terms of the loan.

Your Business Name
P&L Statement
For Year Ended December 31, 2008

Sales revenue	$5,200,000
Cost of goods sold expense	$3,120,000
Gross margin	$2,080,000
Operating expenses	$1,664,000
Depreciation expense	$85,000
Operating earnings	$331,000
Interest expense	$52,500
Profit before income tax	$278,500
Income tax expense	$83,550
Net income	$194,950

Figure 11-4:
Alternative
scenario for
balance
sheet –
case #3.

However, the loan to officers is the least of our concerns in this new scenario. Note the $380,000 difference in retained earnings between the two scenarios (see Table 11-1 or compare Figures 11-4 and 11-1). *Retained earnings* is one of two basic owners' equity accounts. The investment of capital in the business by its owners is recorded in one type of owners' equity account. For a corporation, the account is called *capital stock*. (In Figure 11-4, the more generic *owners' invested capital* is used instead of capital stock.)

The amount of profit earned by the business is *not* comingled with capital invested by owners. Instead, a separate owners' equity account is used in which annual profit is recorded. (In Figure 11-4, this account is called retained earnings, which is the most common title for business corporations.) When the business makes a distribution to owners from profit, the amount of the payout is recorded as a decrease in retained earnings. In short, the balance in retained earnings equals the cumulative profit over the year minus the cumulative amount of distributions from profit.

The most troubling thing about the alternative scenario shown in Figure 11-4 is the extremely low balance in retained earnings. Compared with the benchmark scenario, your retained earnings balance is $380,000 lower ($501,000 balance in benchmark scenario – $121,000 balance in Figure 12-4 = $380,000 smaller balance). This means your business distributed $380,000 more from profit over the years than in the benchmark scenario, which is very disturbing for several reasons. Your cash balance is slim compared with annual sales revenue; your quick ratio and current ratio are alarmingly low; your debt to equity ratio is dangerously high; and you may be violating the rules of fair play with your creditors and lenders. These are very serious matters! As a matter of fact, in this scenario you may be in violation of loan covenants that

Your Business Name
Balance Sheet (Statement of Financial Condition)
At Close of Business December 31, 2008

Cash	$250,000	
Accounts receivable	$250,000	
Inventory	$720,000	
Prepaid expenses	$96,000	
Current assets		$1,316,000
Loans to officers		$50,000
Fixed assets, at original cost	$745,000	
Accumulated depreciation	($348,000)	$397,000
Total assets		$1,763,000
Accounts payable—inventory purchases	$360,000	
Accounts payable—operating expenses	$240,000	
Accrued expenses payable	$192,000	
Short-term notes payable	$300,000	
Current liabilities		$1,092,000
Long-term notes payable		$300,000
Owners' invested capital	$250,000	
Retained earnings	$121,000	
Owners' equity		$371,000
Total liabilities & owners' equity		$1,763,000

Figure 11-4:
Continued.

require your business to maintain minimum quick and current ratios (and perhaps other ratios as well). Loan covenant violations usually give the lender the right to *call* the loan (demand immediate payment).

Your year-end cash balance equals only two and half weeks of sales ($250,000 year-end cash balance ÷ $100,000 average sales per week = 2.5 weeks of sales). You're cutting it pretty close with such a low cash balance, although we have to admit that many small businesses operate with small working cash balances, even less than two weeks of annual sales in many cases.

Chapter 4 explains the analysis of *solvency,* which generally refers to the ability of a business to pay its liabilities on time in full. Two key tests of short-term solvency are the *quick ratio* and the *current ratio.* Generally speaking, the quick ratio should be 1.0 or higher, and the current ratio should be 2.0 or higher — although these are only rough guidelines and should be adapted for different lines of business.

In any case, your quick ratio and current ratio are computed as follows (see Figure 11-4 for data):

($250,000 cash + $250,000 accounts receivables) ÷ $1,092,000 current liabilities = .46 quick ratio

$1,316,000 current assets ÷ $1,092,000 current liabilities = 1.21 current ratio

Both these ratios are dismal and probably would set off alarm bells in the minds of your creditors and lenders. Also, the low ratios would harm your credit rating. Your quick assets (cash and accounts receivable) are less than half your short-term, or current, liabilities. Your current ratio (which includes all current assets) is not much better. You have very little cushion to pay your short-term liabilities. We're not saying that you're on the verge of bankruptcy, but you're walking dangerously close to the edge of the cliff with such low solvency ratios. If you were to default on the terms of your short-term notes payable, the lender could take legal action to push you over the edge. Your lender may take a look at your balance sheet and terminate your line of credit or not renew your note payable.

Also, your debt-to-equity ratio is out of whack (see Figure 11-4 for data):

($1,092,000 current liabilities + $300,000 long-term notes payable) ÷ $371,000 owners' equity = 3.75 to 1 debt-to-equity ratio

In other words, you're using $3.75 of debt (some non-interest and some interest-bearing) for every $1.00 of owners' equity (invested capital and retained earnings). Frankly, we'd be surprised if you could persuade lenders to allow your business to operate with such a high ratio of debt to equity. Most lenders would insist that you build up a much larger retained earnings balance or that the owners should invest more capital in the business.

The combination of negative factors in the Figure 11-4 scenario may indicate that you're playing fast and loose with the rules of business fairness. As you undoubtedly know, business is done on the basis of mutual trust between a business and its employees, customers, creditors, lenders, and owners. There are many rules of fair play. One such rule is that you shouldn't deliberately put your business in a financial situation that would cause losses to your creditors and lenders beyond the normal business risks they take in extending credit or loaning money to your business. In particular, the rule prohibits taking money of the business — loaning money to officers or paying out excessive distributions from profit — that puts your creditors and lenders at unjustifiable risk. Disreputable businesses do just this. You've probably had contact with some. They operate on the dog-eat-dog principle and have few scruples. Fortunately, most scumbag businesses don't last too long. The reputations of their managers make them pariahs in the business world.

Part IV
Looking at Service and Manufacturing Businesses

The 5th Wave   By Rich Tennant

KNOB BROS.
- Paint Drying Equip.
- TV Test Pattern Design
- Sap Buckets

"Maybe it would help our Web site if we showed our products in action."

In this part . . .

The main business example for most of the book is a retailer that sells products. In this part of the book, we look at two other main types of small businesses. Chapter 12 focuses on businesses that sell services and contrasts their financial statements with those of businesses that sell products. The service sector of the American economy is a huge percent of gross domestic product. The fundamental financial management functions and analysis techniques have to be adapted to the characteristics of service businesses.

Many small businesses are manufacturers that make the products they sell. Compared with a retailer that sells products made by other businesses, a manufacturer has certain additional financial management issues. Chapter 13 explains how to trace manufacturing costs into the calculation of product cost and how product cost flows into cost of goods sold expense, which affects the amount of bottom-line profit for the period of course.

Chapter 12

When You Sell Services

. . . .

In This Chapter

▶ Comparing financial statements of service and product businesses

▶ Contrasting expense behavior of a service and product business

▶ Analyzing profit sensitivity to changes in sales volume and sales prices

▶ Inspecting trade-offs between sales volume and sales prices

. . . .

A sk business consultants, and we'd bet most would say that one of the first things new clients tell them is "Our business is different" — which is true of course; every business is unique. On the other hand, all businesses draw on a common core of concepts, principles, and techniques. Take people. Every individual is different and unique. Yet basic principles of behavior and motivation apply to all. Take products. Breakfast cereals are different from computers, which are different than autos, and so on. Yet, basic principles of marketing apply to all products, and services, for that matter.

Applying basic business concepts and principles is the hard part, which managers have to do well. The manager must adapt the basic concepts and general principles to the specific circumstances of his particular business. The financial topics, tools, and techniques of analysis we explain throughout the book have to be adapted to fit the characteristics and problems of each particular business. This chapter focuses on service businesses and the fundamental financial differences of service and product businesses.

Comparing the Financial Statements of Service and Product Businesses

A *service business,* as the term implies, sells services. It may or may not sell products along with its services (popcorn in a movie theater, for example), but its primary stream of revenue is from selling services. Service businesses extend over a very wide range of activities in the economy – from airlines to freight haulers and so on. The service sector is the largest general category in the economy, although it's extremely diverse.

The financial statements prepared by your Controller are the financial anchor point and frame of reference of your business. To find out whether you're making a profit or incurring a loss you look to the P&L statement. To find out your financial condition, you look to the balance sheet. And to understand the amount of cash flow from profit or loss, as well as your other sources and uses of cash, you turn to the statement of cash flows. You should also develop a profit model for your business (see Chapter 8).

You don't have to be an expert accountant to manage your business. But you should have a tight grip on your financial statements. You should look forward to curling up with your financial statements, just as you do with your favorite novelist. Financial statements tell the story of your business, for good or bad. And there's a lot of drama in the financial statements, that's for sure. In short, you have to understand your financial statements to understand the financial performance and condition of your business. What's the alternative? Well, you could simply ignore your financial statements and hope for the best. Ignorance of the law is no defense if you're arrested, and ignorance of your financial statements is no defense if you get into financial trouble.

On the one hand, service businesses are very much the same as companies that sell products. On the other hand, the differences between the two types of businesses warrant a separate chapter. For one thing, there are certain financial statement differences between service and product businesses.

P&L reports of a product and service business

We take the P&L report example from Chapter 11 for a product business and adapt it to a service business that has the same annual sales revenue and profit. Figure 12-1 presents the side-by-side comparison of the P&L statement of the product business and the service business. Note the following differences:

- ✔ Because it doesn't sell products, a service business (that sells only services) doesn't have the cost of goods sold expense.

- ✔ Because it doesn't have the cost of goods sold expense, a service business doesn't have a gross margin (also called gross profit) line in its P&L.

- ✔ The cost of goods sold expense of a product business is replaced by higher operating expenses for the service business, which consists largely of higher labor cost (wages, salaries, and benefits).

Aside from the preceding three differences the P&L statements of service and product businesses are very much alike. And it goes without saying that both service and product businesses are subject to the same accounting standards. There is not one set of financial reporting rules for service businesses and another for product businesses.

Figure 12-1:
Contrasting the P&L of a product business and same size service business.

Product Business P&L Statement For Year Ended December 31, 2008		Service Business P&L Statement For Year Ended December 31, 2008	
Sales revenue	$5,200,000	Sales revenue	$5,200,000
Cost of goods sold expense	$3,120,000	~~Cost of goods sold expense~~	
Gross margin	$2,080,000	~~Gross margin~~	
Operating expenses	$1,664,000	Additional operating expenses	$3,120,000
Depreciation expense	$85,000	Operating expenses	$1,664,000
Operating earnings	$331,000	Depreciation expense	$85,000
Interest expense	$52,500	Operating earnings	$331,000
Profit before income tax	$278,500	Interest expense	$52,500
Income tax expense	$83,550	Profit before income tax	$278,500
Net income	$194,950	Income tax expense	$83,550
		Net income	$194,950

The accounting profession has taken action recently to exempt private businesses from certain of the highly technical and convoluted accounting standards mandated for large public corporations. And certain accounting standards (concerning the reporting of earnings per share, for example) have never applied to private businesses. But don't get the wrong idea: The essential core of accounting standards that govern the measurement of profit and the reporting of financial condition and cash flows apply to all businesses — public or private, and big or small.

Your Controller should be keeping up to date on GAAP developments. (For more on GAAP, see Chapter 5.) When John served on the board of directors of a local bank, he discovered that several of the bank's small business loan applicants presented financial reports that violated current GAAP. Evidently, their accountants hadn't looked at the GAAP rulebook for many years. In particular, many of the loan applicants didn't include a statement of cash flows in their financial report, yet this financial statement had been required, according to GAAP, for several years. The lack of a required financial statement raised a red flag that other accounting shortcomings and errors may exist in the financial report.

The balance sheet and statement of cash flows of service and product businesses

The *balance sheet* is a summary of the assets, liabilities, and owners' equity accounts of a business. A service business has many of the same assets and liabilities that you find in the balance sheet of a product business, except for two main differences:

- ✔ A service business doesn't have an inventory asset account unless it also sells products in connection with selling services.

- ✔ A service business doesn't have a liability for purchases of products on credit unless it sells some products along with its services.

In short, a service business has no inventory asset account and no liability account for purchases of products on credit, or these two accounts are substantially less than a product company. For example, compare the balance sheets of General Motors or Ford (product companies, of course) with the balance sheets of a wireless cellular service company (such as AT&T or Sprint) and United Airlines. Wireless cellular phone businesses do sell phones and other products, but they're not their mainstream sales revenue source. Product sales are a secondary revenue source for many service businesses.

Some service businesses, including airlines, gas and electric utilities, and railroads, make heavy investments in long-term, fixed operating assets. Some small businesses have to invest heavily in fixed operating assets that aren't held for sale; a good example is a rental business that rents everything from tents to backhoe loaders. These businesses are said to be *capital intensive*. The property, plant, and equipment section of their balance sheet is relatively large compared with their annual sales revenue.

In contrast, other service businesses, such as professional legal firms and movie theaters, make relatively light investments in fixed operating assets — unless they buy the building they operate in instead of leasing space in the building. Assuming that these service businesses don't own their buildings, their total assets are a relatively small percent of their annual revenue. So, they don't need a lot of capital to operate.

Product-based and service businesses have only minor differences in the statement of cash flows. For a product business, a major increase or decrease in its inventory during the year has a dramatic impact on cash flow from profit (see Chapter 3). A service business doesn't have to worry about the inventory factor, though all the other factors that affect cash flow from profit affect a service business, as well as a product business. In both types of business, depreciation (and amortization expense, if the business has any) doesn't require a cash outlay in the year it's recorded. Changes in prepaid expenses, accounts payable, and accrued expenses payable either help or hurt cash flow from profit for the year. (Chapter 3 explains cash flow from profit.)

Looking at the Expense Structures of Product and Service Businesses

Figure 12-1 reveals that a service business doesn't have the cost of goods sold expense, which is a variable expense that depends on the volume of products sold. (This comment assumes that the business sells only services, and no products.) Instead of selling products, a service business provides services for its customers. People perform services, of course. Therefore, a service business needs more employees for the same level of sales revenue compared with a product business. Service businesses have larger labor costs than product businesses for the same level of sales revenue.

Fixing on fixed costs

Generally speaking, service businesses are saddled with large annual *fixed* costs. Most service businesses pay their employees fixed salaries, or fixed hourly rates, based on a 40-hour workweek. By and large, their labor cost is fixed, unless they're willing to lay off employees. Also, a service business may make heavy capital investments in buildings, equipment, and other fixed assets and therefore record a relatively large depreciation expense each year. Depreciation is a fixed expense. Or a service business may sign lease contracts that call for relatively fixed rents per year.

Relative to sales revenue, service businesses generally have a much higher ratio of fixed costs to sales revenue than product businesses. Recall that the cost of goods sold expense of a product business is a variable cost. A service business doesn't have a large cost of goods sold variable expense, but it does have a lot of fixed operating costs.

Figure 12-1 compares the standard P&L reports of a product business versus a same-size service business. The design of these P&L reports is appropriate for *external* financial reporting and is in accordance with GAAP. (For more on GAAP, see Chapter 5.) External financial reports consist of the financial statements and other disclosures that are released outside the business, mainly to its lenders and shareowners. In external financial reports, the financial statement that reports sales revenue, expenses, and bottom-line profit is *not* called the P&L. Rather, the profit report is called the *income statement*.

Managers need a lot more detailed information about revenue and expenses than that reported outside the business. This additional management information is included in the body of the P&L or in supplementary schedules.

The P&L reports presented in Figure 12-1 conform to accounting standards and common reporting practices. However, they don't show the *expense behavior* of each business, which refers to how their expenses behave relative to changes in sales activity. Yet expense behavior information is extremely useful for management decision-making analysis. Figure 12-2 illustrates the expense behavior for the product and service business example.

Note that the P&L reports in Figure 12-2 are truncated at the operating earnings line. We don't need the interest and income tax expenses in the following discussion. The fixed costs of the service business are much higher than the product business. The variable expenses of the product business are much higher than the service business.

P&L Statement
For Year Ended December 31, 2008

	Product Business		Service Business	
Sales revenue		$5,200,000		$5,200,000
Variable costs:				
Cost of goods sold expense	$3,120,000		$0	
Operating expenses	$832,000	$3,952,000	$832,000	$832,000
Contribution margin		$1,248,000		$4,368,000
Fixed costs:				
Operating expenses	$832,000		$3,952,000	
Depreciation expense	$85,000	$917,000	$85,000	$4,037,000
Operating earnings		$331,000		$331,000

Figure 12-2:
The cost structures of a product and service business.

In Figure 12-2, the cost of the two companies are separated into variable and fixed categories. The product company's cost of goods sold is a variable expense; this expense goes up and down like a yoyo with ups and downs in sales. Half of its $1,664,000 annual operating expenses (from Figure 12-1) are variable and half are fixed. So, you find one-half, or $832,000, under variable costs, and the other $832,000 under fixed costs for the product business. To keep the service business example on a level playing field with the product business, the total of its variable operating expenses is also $832,000 (see Figure 12-2). All other operating expenses of the service company operating are fixed.

When a P&L report is formatted to disclose expense behavior (variable versus fixed costs), the usual practice is to deduct variable expenses from sales revenue to highlight *contribution margin*. The word margin is clear enough, but what does the word contribution mean? The idea behind this term is that the residual of sales revenue after deducting variable expenses contributes toward recovering the fixed costs of the business. Contribution margin goes first toward recouping fixed costs. After the fixed cost hurdle is cleared, the business breaks into the profit zone. If the business fails to earn enough contribution margin to cover its fixed costs, it suffers a loss.

Figure 12-2 reveals that the $4,368,000 contribution margin of the service business is more than three times the $1,248,000 contribution margin of the product business. The ratio of contribution margin to sales revenue is 84 percent for the service business versus only 24 percent for the product business:

> Service business: $4,368,000 contribution margin ÷ $5,200,000 sales revenue = 84% contribution margin ratio

> Product business: $1,248,000 contribution margin ÷ $5,200,000 sales revenue = 24% contribution margin ratio

On the other hand, the $4,037,000 fixed costs of the service business is more than four times the $917,000 fixed costs of the product business. The result is that both companies end up with the same $331,000 operating earnings for the year. So, you may ask, What's the big deal? Do the different expense structures make any difference to the mangers of the businesses? Is New York a big city? Is Mount Everest a tall mountain?

First off, consider the *breakeven point* of each business. Breakeven refers to that exact sales volume at which sales revenue exactly equals total expenses and profit is precisely zero. (In the example, profit is defined as operating earnings before interest and income tax). At the breakeven sales volume, total contribution margin equals total fixed costs and, therefore, profit equals zero. You can use the contribution margin ratio to quickly determine the breakeven point.

Suppose that your contribution margin is 50 percent. So, 50 cents of each dollar of sales is absorbed by the variable costs of making the sale, and the other 50 cents goes toward covering fixed costs. Suppose that the total of your fixed costs for the year is $100. You need $200 sales revenue to earn $100 contribution margin: $200 sales revenue × 50% contribution margin ratio = $100 contribution margin. The $100 contribution margin exactly equals your $100 fixed costs, so you would breakeven.

Using this method, the breakeven sales revenues for each business, at which operating profit would have been zero, are calculated as follows (see Figure 12-2 for data):

Product business:

> $917,000 fixed costs ÷ 24% contribution margin ratio = $3,820,833 breakeven sales revenue

Service business:

> $4,037,000 fixed costs ÷ 84% contribution margin ratio = $4,805,952 breakeven sales revenue

The breakeven point of the service business is about $1,000,000 higher than the product business. The service business, given its large fixed cost commitment, needs about $1,000,000 more sales revenue than the product business just to reach its breakeven hurdle.

As the manager of the service business, you should definitely understand the higher breakeven point caused by your high fixed costs. This is the bad news. The good news is that once you cross over the breakeven point, each additional $1,000 sales revenue contributes $840 to your profit line (operating earnings in the example):

> $1,000 incremental sales revenue × 84% contribution margin = $840 incremental profit

In contrast, each $1,000 additional sales revenue over its breakeven point adds only $240 to the product company's profit line:

> $1,000 incremental sales revenue × 24% contribution margin = $240 incremental profit

Calculating profit yield from sales over breakeven

Figure 12-2 contains a hidden message in, which every small business manager should understand. The product business needed $1,379,167 sales revenue over its breakeven point to earn $331,000 operating profit for the year. In contrast, the service business needed only $394,048 sales revenue over its breakeven point to earn $331,000 operating profit for the year. See the following calculations:

Product business:

> $1,379,167 sales revenue in excess of breakeven × 24% contribution margin = $331,000 operating profit

Service business:

> $394,048 sales revenue in excess of breakeven × 84% contribution margin = $331,000 operating profit

The lower fixed costs of the product business means that its breakeven point is lower than the service business, even though its contribution margin ratio is much lower. The higher fixed costs of the service business means that its breakeven point is much higher, even though its contribution margin ratio is much higher. Generally speaking, you find a pattern in the business world: The higher the contribution margin ratio, then the higher the fixed costs and the higher the breakeven point.

Measuring profit sensitivity to variations in sales

Suppose that each business had experienced $100,000 higher or lower sales revenue than its actual $5,200,000 sales revenue for the year. The profit impact of the $100,000 swing in sales revenue for each business is calculated as follows:

Product business:

> $100,000 change in sales revenue × 24% contribution margin ratio = $24,000 change in profit

Service business:

> $100,000 change in sales revenue × 84% contribution margin ratio = $84,000 change in profit

On the upside, you'd rather be in the shoes of the service business, with its higher contribution margin ratio. Your profit would be $84,000 higher than the $331,000 profit for the year, which is about a 25 percent increase. On the down side, you'd rather be in the shoes of the product business, with its lower contribution margin ratio. The $100,000 sales revenue decline would cause profit to decrease only $24,000, which is about a 7 percent decrease. Of course, you can't have it both ways.

Contrasting Sales Volume and Sales Price Changes Impact on Profit

In Chapter 8, we introduce and explain the uses of a profit model. A profit model is invaluable for understanding profit behavior and for analyzing the impacts of changes in the primary factors that drive profit. As we mention in Chapter 8, every profit factor is subject to change. The small business manager needs a quick method to size up the impact of changes. A profit model is essential for making the critical decisions regarding how to deal with the changes.

Adapting the profit model for a service business

As you probably expect, the profit model for a product business has to be adapted to fit the different expense structure of a service business. Figure 12-3 presents the profit model for the service business example in this chapter. The profit model in Figure 12-3 stops at the operating earnings line. (Stopping at earnings before interest and income tax speeds up the following discussion.)

Figure 12-3:
The profit model for a service business.

Net Sales Revenue	$5,200,000
Variable Operating Costs	($832,000)
Contribution Margin	$4,368,000
Fixed Operating Costs	($4,037,000)
Operating Earnings	$331,000

Chapter 8 explains that when sales revenue changes (caused by sales volume or sales price changes), the total assets of the business change in response. In turn, the change in total assets usually triggers a change in the amount of interest-bearing debt of the business. The change in interest expense caused by a change in sales revenue is explained in some detail for the product business in Chapter 8. We don't repeat this discussion for a service business. The effect on interest expense from changes in sales revenue for a service business is much the same as for a product business. In neither case is the interest expense change a very significant factor in the analysis – well, except in some unusual cases.

Also, we don't include the income tax factor in the profit model for the service business. One reason is that many small businesses are organized legally as a pass-through tax entity. They don't pay income tax as a separate entity.

The first line in the profit model — net sales revenue — is sales revenue based on list prices less all discounts, allowances, and other deductions against sales revenue at list prices. (For more on net sales revenue, see Chapter 8.)

The variable operating costs in the service business example (see Figure 12-3) are *volume driven*. The annual sales volume of a service business is expressed in *units of service*, whatever these units may be — billable hours for a law firm, number of tickets for a movie theater, or whatever. A service business may adopt a common denominator to measure the diverse services it sells. For example, a trucking company may run local and long distance routes, flatbed and trailer hauls, containerized and loose products — and adopt ton-miles as a common measure for measuring its overall sales volume.

Although the fixed costs of a service business usually are a high ratio to sales revenue, it doesn't mean that its *sales capacity* is infinite. Just like for a product business, the small business manager of a service business should gauge the sales capacity provided by the annual fixed costs of the business. For example, based on the number of employees, the manager can estimate the maximum number of units of service that could be performed by the workforce. Or a trucking business can estimate the total number of ton-miles that it could deliver with its present size of trucks, trailers, and drivers.

Analyzing sales volume and price changes

For a product business, there is quite a difference on profit from an increase in sales volume compared with equal percent increase in sales price. The sales price increase has a much larger profit impact. What about a service business? Is the impact on profit much different between a sales volume increase versus an equal percent increase in sales price?

Suppose that the service business's sales volume had been 5 percent higher than in Figure 12-2. Using the profit model shown in Figure 12-3, the higher sales volume would have caused the following changes:

> $5,200,000 sales revenue × 5% additional sales volume = $260,000 sales revenue increase
>
> $832,000 operating expenses 5% additional sales volume = $41,600 operating expenses increase
>
> $260,000 sales revenue increase – $41,600 operating expenses increase = $218,400 contribution margin increase

Contribution margin increases 5 percent because both sales revenue and operating expenses increase 5 percent. What would happen to fixed costs at the higher sales volume? Well, for many businesses there may not be enough slack to take on 5 percent additional sales volume without having to increase fixed costs. In this situation, operating profit would jump a whopping 66 percent:

> $218,400 increase in operating profit ÷ $331,000 operating profit before sales volume increase = 66% gain in operating profit

Why does profit go up by such a large percent, from only a small percent increase in sales volume? Have you been paying attention to the high contribution margin ratio of the service business? The contribution margin ratio is 84 percent. So, 84 cents of each additional sales dollar goes to contribution margin. Now, for a key question: Would a 5 percent sales *price* increase do even better?

Suppose that the service business's sales prices had been 5 percent higher than in Figure 12-2. Using the profit model shown in Figure 12-3, the higher sales prices would have caused the following results:

$5,200,000 sales revenue × 5% additional sales volume = $260,000 sales revenue increase

Operating expenses: no change because there is no change in sales volume

$260,000 sales revenue increase – no change in operating expenses = $260,000 contribution margin increase

In this sales price increase scenario, the operating expenses of the service business, which are driven by sales volume, do not increase. The entire $260,000 increase in sales revenue flows down to contribution margin. And, to further add to the good news, the company's fixed costs would not increase at the higher sales prices. Fixed costs provide sales capacity, or to be more precise, sales *volume* capacity. When sales prices change and sales volume stays the same, the company's fixed costs remain the same.

Therefore, in the 5 percent higher sales price scenario, the company's operating profit would increase even more than in the 5 percent sales volume scenario:

$260,000 increase in operating profit ÷ $331,000 operating profit before sales price increase = 78.5% gain in operating profit

Note that the difference in the increase in profit between the sales price increase and the sales volume increase is not all that wide: $260,000 for the higher sales prices versus $218,400 for the higher sales volume. Still, the higher sales prices alternative — if you actually had a choice in the matter — should be favored because the higher sales prices puts no pressure on the fixed costs of the business. Anytime you talk about raising sales volume, you should take a hard look at your fixed costs and sales capacity, in order to determine whether fixed costs would have to be raised to provide additional capacity for the higher sales volume level.

Exploring tradeoffs between sales volume and price for a service business

A classic marketing quandary facing a business is whether to trade-off sales price and sales volume — for example, cutting sales prices in order to increase sales volume. Cutting sales prices is always risky. (We discuss the risks of cutting sales prices in Chapter 8 for a product business, which apply with equal force to a service business as well.) Referring to the product business example in Figure 12-2, suppose that the business is considering an across the board sales price reduction of 10 percent, based on the expectation that sales volume would increase 20 percent at the lower prices. The manager of the business in charge of this decision judges that the business could take on 20 percent additional sales volume without increasing its fixed costs, which may be stretching things a bit. Offhand, this scenario seems an attractive tradeoff. But the analysis shows the following results based on the data from Figure 12-2:

$5,200,000 sales revenue × [90% at lower sales prices] × [120% at higher sales volume] = $5,616,000 sales revenue, or $416,000 increase

$3,952,000 variable operating expenses × 120% at higher sales volume = $4,742,400 operating expenses, or $790,400 increase

We need go no further. Variable expenses, consisting in large part of cost of goods sold, would increase considerably more than the increase in sales. Contribution margin would plummet, and despite the manager's sanguine prediction, the company's fixed costs may increase at the higher sales volume.

Would the 10 percent sales price cut with a 20 percent increase in sales volume work out better for the service company example in Figure 12-2? Sales revenue would increase $416,000, the same as for the product company. But the company's variable operating expenses would increase only $166,400 based on the data from Figure 12-2:

$832,000 variable operating expenses × 120% at higher sales volume = $998,400 operating expenses, or $166,400 increase

So, the trade-off for the service company is more attractive. But keep in mind that adding 20 percent to sales volume may require a step-up in fixed costs. Many businesses can't take on 20 percent more volume with their present level of fixed costs. So, until you do a careful study of your sales capacity provided by your present level of fixed costs, you should proceed with caution.

Selling Some Products with Services

By definition, a service business sells services and not products. Even so, products often are sold with services. For example, a copying business (such as Kinko's) sells pens and office supplies. Of course, the main thing is selling copying services, not the products. Airlines sell transportation services, but they also sell food and beverages in flight. Hotels aren't really in the business of selling towels, but they know that many guests take these with them on the way out. Many personal and professional service firm, such as CPAs and architect firms, sell no product at all. (Although, come to think of it, John's architect charged for blueprint copies for his home remodeling project.)

In short, many businesses sell both services and products. Selling services may be the main source of sales revenue, but the business sets out to make profit on the products it sells as well. The examples of a product and service business shown in Figures 12-1 and 12-2 could be two parts of one business, which sells an equal amount of products and services. When selling products as well as services, the business should establish separate *profit centers* for each source of revenue. We discuss profit centers in Chapter 7.

Financial analysis tools are essentially the same for both product and service businesses. Of course, the models and tools of analysis have to be adapted to fit the characteristics of the business. This chapter demonstrates techniques of profit analysis for service businesses. The profit consequences from a change in sales volume versus a change in sales price for service businesses are not nearly as divergent compared with product businesses. Sales price increases have an edge over sales volume increases for both types of businesses, but the advantage is not nearly so pronounced for service businesses.

Chapter 13

When You Make the Products You Sell

*T*his chapter is an absolute must-read if you're the owner/manager of a small manufacturing business because it explains concisely how manufacturers determine their *product costs*. Retailers and wholesalers (distributors) purchase products in a condition ready for sale to their customers. Product cost is purchase cost for retailers; it is found in the purchase invoice. Manufacturers, on the other hand, must assemble their product costs as the products move through the production process.

In short, manufacturing businesses have to figure out the costs of making the products they sell. Their product costs aren't handed to them on a platter (purchase invoice). For setting sales prices, controlling costs, and planning, a manufacturing business must know the costs of making its products. General Motors must know the cost of making a Silverado pickup truck, and Apple must know the cost of making an iPod. If your business makes shopping carts you have to know the cost of making each model you sell.

What if you're not a manufacturing business? You probably have your enthusiasm for this chapter well under control. (The chapter does get a wee bit technical here and there.) We want to point out that all business managers use product cost information, and all products begin life by being manufactured. Even if your business doesn't manufacture products, understanding how manufacturing costs are accumulated and assigned to products and how certain product cost accounting problems are dealt with by manufacturers is very helpful in dealing with the manufacturers you buy products from.

Setting the Stage

Manufacturers are producers: They make the products they sell. The manufacturing process may be simple and short, or complex and long. It may be either labor intensive or capital (asset) intensive. Products, such as breakfast cereal, may roll nonstop off the end of a continuous mass-production assembly line. These products are called *process cost systems.* Or, production may be discontinuous and done on a one-batch-at-a-time basis; these are called *job order systems.* For example, printing and binding 100,000 copies of a book is an example of a job order system.

A *production run* consists of a batch of products that go through the manufacturing process as a separate group or bunch. In a process manufacturing system, the batch is the total number of units produced during a certain time period, such as one month or one quarter. In a job order system, the batch is the total number of units produced over as long as it takes to complete the job, which may be just a few days or most of the year. Manufacturing a Boeing 777 jet aircraft takes years, in fact.

The cost of each step and each input of the production process is recorded for the batch being manufactured. There are literally hundreds, or thousands of these cost components. The cost components are pulled together into the total cost composite for the batch. (*Note:* During the production process manufacturing costs are accumulated in an inventory account called *Work-In-Process;* when production is completed the cost of products is transferred to a *Finished Goods* inventory account.)

Introducing a Manufacturing Example

In the world of manufacturing, you find a lot of production differences from one product to another. You probably have a good sense of the diversity of production processes in different industries. Think about the production of auto gasoline in an oil refinery versus the production of a laptop computer or a loaf of bread. Most manufacturing businesses make more than just one product, as you probably know. It would be quite time consuming to use a completely realistic manufacturing business example in this chapter. Instead, we use a simplified example that captures the essential aspects and problems of determining the product cost of manufacturers.

The small business example in this chapter is an established manufacturing business that has been operating several years. Its managers have assembled and organized machines, equipment, tools, and employees into a smooth running production process that is dependable and efficient — a monumental task to say the least. Plant location is critical; so is plant layout, employee training, materials procurement, complying with an ever-broadening range of governmental regulations, employee safety laws, and environmental protection laws. Being in the manufacturing business is no walk in the park.

In our example, the business manufactures one product, and its entire output for the year is treated as one production batch. (In a more realistic setting, the business manufactures several products and makes the product in several batches over the course of one year — but this would really complicate the example.) Figure 13-1 presents the company's P&L report for the year just ended down to its *operating profit* line, which equals earnings before interest and income tax expenses. The P&L report includes a supplementary section that summarizes the company's production activity and manufacturing costs for the year, showing how product cost is determined.

Manufacturing costs consists of basic cost components, or natural groupings:

- ✔ *Raw materials* are purchased parts and materials that become part of the finished product. For example, Dell buys hard disk drives from other companies for the computers it makes; most manufacturers buy the nuts, bolts, screws and other hardware items they need in their production process from other companies.

- ✔ *Direct labor* refers to those employees who work on the production line. Direct labor costs include the base wages of the employees, of course, as well as the costs of their fringe benefits, which typically add 30 to 40 percent to base wages. For example, employer Social Security and Medicare tax rates presently are 7.65 percent of base wages; also there are unemployment taxes, employee retirement and pension plan contributions, health and medical insurance, worker's compensation insurance, and paid vacations and sick leaves.

- ✔ *Manufacturing overhead* refers to all other production costs. *Variable* manufacturing overhead costs are separated from *fixed* manufacturing overhead costs:

  - • *Variable* manufacturing overhead costs fluctuate with total production output. For example, the cost of electricity and gas that powers machinery and equipment goes up and down with the level of production output during the period.

  - • *Fixed* manufacturing overhead costs are locked in place over the short run and don't depend on the level of production activity. Examples include property taxes, fire insurance on the production plant, and plant security guards who are paid a fixed salary.

In Figure 13-1, the company recorded $8,220,000 total manufacturing costs and produced 12,000 units during the year. Of this amount, $7,535,000 is charged to cost of goods sold expense for the 11,000 units sold during the year, and $685,000 remains with the inventory increase of 1,000 units. This $685,000 of the manufacturing costs for the year will not be expensed until sometime in the future when the 1,000 products are sold. (*Note:* The precise amounts of cost of goods sold expense and the inventory increase depend on whether the business uses LIFO, FIFO, or the average cost method; we discuss these accounting methods in Chapter 6.)

In Figure 13-1, the company's annual production capacity is 15,000 units. Its $2,100,000 total fixed overhead costs provide the physical facilities and human resources to produce a maximum of 15,000 units over the year under normal and practical conditions of operation. In the example, the 12,000 units actual production output for the year equals 80 percent of company's production capacity (12,000 units output ÷ 15,000 units capacity = 80 percent). Actual output falls somewhere in the range of 75 to 90 percent of production capacity in most manufacturing industries. Most manufacturers have some downtime during the year or, for other reasons, don't make full use of all their production capacity.

Your Manufacturing Business, Inc.
P&L Report Including Manufacturing Activity Summary
For Year Ended December, 31, 2008

Sales Volume = 11,000 Units

	Per Unit	Total
Sales Revenue	$1,400	$15,400,000
Cost of Goods Sold Expense	($685)	($7,535,000)
Gross Margin	$715	$7,865,000
Sales and Marketing Expenses		($4,235,000)
General and Administrative Expenses		($1,420,000)
Operating Profit		$2,210,000

Manufacturing Costs For Year

Annual Production Capacity = 15,000 Units

Actual Output = 12,000 Units

Cost Components	Per Unit	Total
Raw Materials	$215	$2,580,000
Direct Labor	$260	$3,120,000
Variable Overhead	$35	$420,000
Fixed Overhead	$175	$2,100,000
Total Manufacturing Costs	$685	$8,220,000

Disposition of Manufacturing Costs:

To Cost of Goods Sold Expense	$685	$7,535,000
To Inventory Increase	$685	$685,000
Total Manufacturing Costs		$8,220,000

Figure 13-1: Presenting a P&L report and manufacturing activity summary for the year.

Computing Product Cost (Per Unit)

Product cost, which more correctly means product cost *per unit,* is determined by dividing the total manufacturing costs for a production run by the total number of units produced in the batch. For the business shown in Figure 13-1, product cost (per unit) is determined as follows:

$8,220,000 Total Manufacturing Costs ÷ 12,000 Units Produced = $685 Product Cost Per Unit

Essential aspects of product cost computation

Three aspects of the product cost computation are important to mention:

- ✔ First, product cost is a *calculated* amount. It doesn't exist until it's computed. Clearly, both the numerator and the denominator of the computation must be correct, or else the product cost is wrong.

- ✔ Second, only *manufacturing* costs are included and not the nonmanufacturing expenses of operating the business, such as marketing (sales promotion, advertising, and so on), delivery costs, administration and general management costs, legal costs, and, interest expense. A so-called Chinese wall should be erected between manufacturing costs and nonmanufacturing costs. The proper classification and separation between costs is critical.

- ✔ Third, the entire amount of *fixed manufacturing overhead costs* is included in the total of manufacturing costs that is divided by production output for the year, even though the business in Figure 13-1 has 20 percent idle, or unused production capacity.

 Research and development (R&D) costs aren't classified as manufacturing costs, even though these costs may lead to new products, new methods of manufacture, new compounds of materials, or other technological improvements.

Raw materials and direct labor costs are clearly manufacturing costs. Direct materials and direct labor are matched with or traced to particular products being manufactured. Keeping track of raw (direct) material and direct labor costs is mainly a matter of meticulous recordkeeping — making certain that the correct costs are matched with the correct products being manufactured.

Indirect manufacturing overhead costs

You can't directly attach or couple manufacturing overhead costs with particular products as they move through the production process. For this reason, they're called *indirect* costs. The cost of the security guard that patrols the manufacturing plant is one of many indirect manufacturing overhead costs. Overhead (indirect) costs are just as necessary to the manufacturing process as direct costs. Therefore, indirect manufacturing costs are included in the calculation of product cost.

Because of their indirect nature, overhead costs must be allocated among the batches of products manufactured. Traditionally, before computer-based data processing methods were available, manufacturers used practical methods for allocating manufacturing overhead costs to products. One common traditional allocation method was based on the direct labor hours of manufacturing each product. If, for example, one product required twice the direct labor hours than another it was allocated twice the manufacturing overhead costs. Modern methods for allocating manufacturing overhead costs to products are more sophisticated compared with a simple, one-factor method. Nevertheless, any allocation method ends up being arbitrary to some degree. The methods of allocating manufacturing overhead costs can be quite complicated and contentious

Direct versus indirect manufacturing costs are compared in the example of a print order for the production of 10,000 copies of a book. The paper and ink cost (raw materials) can be identified to each production run. Likewise, you can identify the employees who set up and operate the presses (direct labor) and match their compensation cost to the job. However, you can't directly identify variable overhead costs with particular press runs; instead, these costs must be allocated. The cost of electricity to power the presses can be allocated on the basis of the machine hours of each print run, which is logical and objective. In contrast, allocating the fixed annual compensation cost of the vice president of production to different print jobs during the year is rather arbitrary and subjective.

Fixed manufacturing overhead costs, which include a wide variety of costs including property taxes on the production plant, depreciation of the production equipment, fixed salaries of plant nurses and doctors, and so on, are very difficult to allocate among production batches. Nevertheless, these indirect costs must be allocated according to some method for sharing these costs among the different products manufactured by the company. The company in Figure 13-1 makes only one product. So, all manufacturing costs are assigned to this one product. (This is a sneaky way to avoid discussing overhead allocation methods, which is beyond the scope of the book.)

Idle production capacity issues

Unless a manufacturing business's actual output for the year is far below its production capacity, no attempt is made to estimate the cost of idle (unused) production capacity. In Figure 13-1, the entire $2,100,000 cost of production capacity is included in the calculation of product cost. Therefore, each unit of product absorbs $175 of the total fixed manufacturing overhead cost for the year.

In exceptional situations, you should pull out the cost of excessive idle capacity from the calculation of product cost. For example, a manufacturer may have been shut down half the year because of a prolonged strike by its employees' union and wasn't able to scale back its fixed manufacturing overhead costs. In this case, the business should estimate the portion of its total fixed manufacturing overhead costs that went down the rat hole during the year and record this amount as a special loss. Product cost should not be burdened with this abnormal cost. Well, this is the theory; estimating the amount of fixed overhead cost that was wasted during the year is very difficult, and no one likes to record losses of this nature.

Generally speaking, the cost of a reasonable amount of idle capacity (up to 25 percent as a rough rule) is included in the calculation of product cost. Sales prices are based on product cost (plus other factors of course). Think about the cost of idle capacity included in the sales price when you buy your next vehicle. You may be helping General Motors or Ford to cover the cost of their idle capacity. Isn't that a nice thing to do?

Tweaking the Basic Product Cost

The basic manufacturing example in Figure 13-1 is an ideal model for illustrating the nature and computation of product cost. However, keep in mind the following assumptions that lurk behind the example's facade:

- Costs are properly classified between manufacturing and nonmanufacturing.
- The manufacturing process is reasonably efficient and not unduly wasteful of materials, labor, time, and production capacity.
- The inventory increase caused by producing more units than were sold during the year is justified by good business reasons.

In some situations, one or more of these critical assumptions may not be true. A business may deliberately misclassify its costs, experience serious inefficiencies in its manufacturing process during the period, or increase its inventory more than it should have either by mistake or on purpose. The following sections explore these deviations from the ideal situation.

Misclassifying manufacturing costs

Some manufacturers have been known to *intentionally* misclassify their manufacturing overhead costs. They record a certain amount of manufacturing cost in marketing expense or general and administration expense that should have been recorded in their manufacturing overhead accounts. Therefore, the amount of the misclassified costs isn't included in the calculation of product cost. The purpose is to maximize costs that are charged off immediately to expense in order to reduce the current taxable income of the business. By minimizing current taxable income, a business reduces its income tax for the current year, of course.

The Internal Revenue Code takes a special interest in the problem of manufacturing overhead cost classification. The experience of the IRS had been that many manufacturers were misclassifying some of their manufacturing overhead costs. Congress amended the tax law to remedy this tax-evasion technique. The income tax law now spells out in some detail particular costs that must be classified as manufacturing overhead costs and therefore capitalized. *Capitalize* means to record the cost in an inventory asset account by including the cost in the calculation of product cost. The cost of products held in inventory remains in the inventory asset account, and the cost is not charged to expense until the products are sold.

The following costs should definitely be classified as manufacturing costs: production-line employee benefits costs; rework, scrap, and spoilage costs; quality control costs; and routine repairs and maintenance on production machinery and equipment. Of course, you should classify depreciation of production machinery and equipment, as well as property taxes on the production plant (building and building and land improvements), as manufacturing overhead costs.

To illustrate the effects of misclassifying manufacturing costs, suppose that $960,000 of the company's fixed manufacturing overhead costs had been recorded in general and administrative expenses. Otherwise, other factors remain the same as in Figure 13-1. Figure 13-2 shows the effects of the misclassification error. Note the impact on the operating profit line, which generally approximates taxable income before the interest expense deduction. (*Note:* As you probably know the income tax law has many special provisions that affect the actual taxable income of a business for a year, which we don't discuss in this book.)

In Figure 13-2 the amount of general and administrative expenses is inflated $960,000 (from $1,420,000 in Figure 13-1 to $2,380,000 in Figure 13-2). Now, you may think that operating profit should be lower the same amount, or $960,000. No, this isn't the case. The large part of the $960,000 misclassified fixed manufacturing overhead costs would be charged to cost of goods sold expense if it had been classified properly. The business sold 11,000 units of the 12,000 units it produced during the year, so $\frac{11}{12}$ of its manufacturing overhead costs end up in cost of goods sold expense. For the $960,000 of misclassified overhead costs, $880,000 would have been included in cost of goods sold expense if it had been classified properly:

> $960,000 misclassified amount of manufacturing overhead cost $\times$ 11/12 ratio of units sold to units produced during period = $880,000 amount that would have been in cost of goods sold expense.

Your Manufacturing Business, Inc.
P&L Report Including Manufacturing Activity Summary
For Year Ended December, 31, 2008

Sales Volume =   11,000 Units

	Per Unit	Total	
Sales Revenue	$1,400	$15,400,000	
Cost of Goods Sold Expense	($605)	($6,655,000)	← $880,000 too low
Gross Margin	$795	$8,745,000	← $880,000 too high
Sales and Marketing Expenses		($4,235,000)	
General and Administrative Expenses		($2,380,000)	← $960,000 too high
Operating Profit		$2,130,000	← $80,000 too low

Manufacturing Costs For Year

Annual Production Capacity =   15,000 Units

Actual Output =   12,000 Units

Cost Components	Per Unit	Total	
Raw Materials	$215	$2,580,000	
Direct Labor	$260	$3,120,000	
Variable Overhead	$35	$420,000	
Fixed Overhead	$95	$1,140,000	← $960,000 too low
Total Manufacturing Costs	$605	$7,260,000	

Disposition of Manufacturing Costs:

To Cost of Goods Sold Expense	$605	$6,655,000	← $880,000 too low
To Inventory Increase	$605	$605,000	← $80,000 too low
Total Manufacturing Costs		$7,260,000	

Figure 13-2: Misclassifying costs to reduce operating profit and taxable income.

Therefore, the net effect on operating profit is only $80,000: ($960,000 overstatement of general and administrative expenses minus $880,000 that would have been in cost of goods sold = $80,000 net decrease in profit).

Take notice of the manifold mischief that misclassifying manufacturing costs causes — see Figure 13-2 again. Cost of goods sold expense is wrong, which means gross margin is wrong. And, of course, operating profit is wrong. The amount of manufacturing cost allocated to the increase in inventory is $80,000 too low. Operating profit, or taxable income before interest, is $80,000 less, which is the point of the misclassification. Therefore, income tax for the year is lower. However, be warned: Intentionally misclassifying manufacturing overhead costs is viewed as cooking the books by professional accountants, and, more importantly, by the IRS. If you're tempted to misclassify your manufacturing costs, don't forget that the IRS may select your business to audit and discover that you've committed accounting fraud.

Although it would be rather unusual, a manufacturer could feasibly begin and end the year with no inventory. In this atypical case, operating profit would be the same no matter how costs were classified — although for internal reports to managers, the proper classification of costs is always important. Target sales prices are determined by marking up product cost a certain percent. Thus, managers should be very certain regarding whether the correct amount of manufacturing overhead costs are included in the calculation of product cost. If not, the markup percent should be adjusted because it would be based on an understated product cost. The better course of action is to properly classify manufacturing overhead costs in the first place.

Dealing with manufacturing inefficiencies

A basic premise of determining product cost is that the production process is reasonably efficient and not wasteful of materials, labor, and capacity. The cost of excessive materials and labor should not be included in product cost. Most manufacturers have a good idea of the quantity of each raw material that goes into a product, and how much time it takes for each labor operation in the production process. In short, they develop benchmarks and standards for manufacturing a product. Manufacturers know that they should allow for some inefficiency because production systems are not perfect all the time.

For example, suppose that 100 gallons of a raw material is in the finished product of a liquid industrial cleanser that the business manufactures. The business knows from experience that it needs 102 pounds on average for every unit of product because 2 pounds is spilt or otherwise lost during the production process and does not end up in the finished product. The cost of 102 gallons of raw material is included in product cost.

Managers should keep a close eye on productivity ratios in their production control reports and take quick action to deal with any problems that develop. Occasionally, however, things get way out of control, which raises a serious issue regarding the calculation of product cost. To illustrate such a situation, suppose that the business had wasted raw materials during the year. The $2,580,000 total cost of raw materials in Figure 13-1 includes $660,000 of raw materials that were wasted. These materials were scrapped and not in the final products.

As the manager, you should have spotted this problem before it amounted to such a large amount; you should have taken quicker action to deal with the problem. In any case, assume that the problem persisted, and the result was that raw materials costing $660,000 had to be thrown away and not used in the production process. Ideally, the $660,000 should not be included in the computation of product cost, which would lower the product cost by $55 per unit:

$660,000 wasted raw materials cost ÷ 12,000 units output = $55 lower product cost per unit.

The $660,000 excess raw materials cost should be presented as a one-time extraordinary expense in your P&L report. However, exposing excess raw materials cost in a P&L report can be a touchy issue. Would you want the blame for this laid at your doorstep? You may prefer that the excessive cost be buried in product cost and let it flow against sales revenue this way instead of showing the loss as a naked item in the P&L report. But, to reemphasize, the costs of excessive materials and labor should be reported separately either in the main body of the regular P&L reports to managers or in a special flash report that focuses on the costs and causes of the problem. (We explain flash reports in Chapter 7.)

Boosting profit by boosting production

In the section "Misclassifying manufacturing costs," earlier in this chapter, we explain how a business can reduce operating profit in order to minimize taxable income. In contrast, a business may engage in some hanky panky to *inflate* its recorded profit. There are many ways to cook the books in order to boost profit. You can record revenue too soon or expenses too late; these are the two basic schemes for cooking the books by retailers, wholesalers, and service businesses. A manufacturer has one more gimmick for boosting profit; it can simply produce more output than it really needs.

Refer to Figure 13-1. In particular, focus on the $2,100,000 fixed manufacturing overhead cost for the year. The business sold 11,000 of the 12,000 units it produced during the year. Therefore, $1,925,000 of this total cost ends up in cost of goods sold expense for the year:

$175 fixed manufacturing overhead cost per unit × 11,000 units sold = $1,925,000 fixed manufacturing overhead imbedded in cost of goods sold expense for year.

The remaining $175,000 of fixed manufacturing overhead cost is included in the 1,000 units increase in inventory (see Figure 13-1):

$175 fixed manufacturing overhead cost per unit × 1,000 units inventory increase = $175,000 fixed manufacturing overhead included in inventory increase

Evidentially, the business had good reasons for increasing its inventory 1,000 units — or did it? If sales volume has been on the upswing and the business forecasts sales growth next year, then the business may very well need a higher inventory to support higher sales next year. No one would argue against the business building up its inventory level in this situation. However, what if sales have been flat and probably won't improve next year? If this is the situation, why did the business produce 1,000 more units than it sold during the year?

The overproduction may have been a simple management mistake. The manager may have been too optimistic in predicting sales for the year and, in good faith, ordered 12,000 units of output because he thought this number would be needed for sales. On the other hand, the manager may have been more devious and deliberately boosted production output in order to pump up operating profit for the year. The manager may have boosted production output to nudge profit up a little.

To examine the profit impact of producing more units than are sold during the year, suppose that the business had produced only 11,000 units during the year, which is exactly the number needed for sales in the year. Figure 13-3 presents the P&L and manufacturing activity summary for this scenario. In this situation, operating profit would be $2,035,000, which is $175,000 less than in the situation in which the business manufactures 12,000 units during the year:

$2,210,000 operating profit in Figure 13-1 — $2,035,000 operating profit in Figure 13-3 = $175,000 decrease in operating profit

By producing 1,000 units more than sales for the year, profit is 8.6 percent higher:

$175,000 higher profit ÷ $2,035,000 operating profit if production output had been equal to sales volume for year (11,000 units) = 8.6% higher profit for year

Now, we should mention that there are good business reasons for increasing inventory. For example, the manager may anticipate shortages of raw materials next year or is expecting a strike by production employees that will limit output next year. At the same time, however, we should alert you that increasing inventory gives profit a shot in the arm (an additional $175,000 in the example). If production is ramped up mainly to pump up profit, the business ends up with an excessive level of inventory.

An excessive inventory situation presents all sorts of problems. Where do you store the additional products? Will you have to reduce sales price to move the products? Will the business have to downsize its inventory next year, which means it will have to slash production output next year? And, what about the $175,000 fixed manufacturing overhead cost included in the additional 1,000 units of inventory? If only 11,000 units had been produced, cost of goods sold expense would have absorbed the entire $2,100,000 fixed manufacturing overhead cost for the year. By producing 12,000 units, the company *seems* to be making better use of its production capacity. But is it, really? Producing excessive inventory is a false and illusory use of production capacity.

As a practical matter, drawing a line between excessive and acceptable inventory increases is difficult. For the example in which the business manufactures 1,000 more units than it sells during the year, most accountants would not object to allocating $175,000 of fixed manufacturing overhead costs to the inventory increase — with the result that operating profit benefits by $175,000. A company's ending inventory would have to be extremely large relative to its annual sales before the Controller would step in and argue that the inventory increase should not be recorded at normal cost.

Your Manufacturing Business, Inc.
P&L Report Including Manufacturing Activity Summary
For Year Ended December, 31, 2008

Sales Volume = 11,000 Units

	Per Unit	Total	
Sales Revenue	$1,400	$15,400,000	$175, 000 higher because burden
Cost of Goods Sold Expense	($701)	($7,710,000)	rate (fixed manufacturing
Gross Margin	$699	$7,690,000	overhead cost per unit) is higher
Sales and Marketing Expenses		($4,235,000)	
General and Administrative Expenses		($1,420,000)	
Operating Profit		$2,035,000	$175,000 lower because cost
			of goods sold expense is higher

Manufacturing Costs For Year

Annual Production Capacity = 15,000 Units
Actual Output = 11,000 Units

Cost Components	Per Unit	Total	
Raw Materials	$215	$2,365,000	
Direct Labor	$260	$2,860,000	
Variable Overhead	$35	$385,000	Total fixed manufacturing overhead
Fixed Overhead	$191	$2,100,000	costs is the same, but the total is spread
Total Manufacturing Costs	$701	$7,710,000	over fewer units produced, which
			gives a higher burden rate per unit

Disposition of Manufacturing Costs:

To Cost of Goods Sold Expense	$701	$7,710,000	Production output equals sales
To Inventory Increase	$701	$0	volume, so there is no increase
Total Manufacturing Costs		$7,710,000	in inventory

Figure 13-3: Looking at profit if production output had equaled sales volume.

Looking at Cost Accounting Beyond Manufacturing

Determining the appropriate and relevant cost of anything — the cost of manufacturing a product, the cost of providing a service, the cost of educating a student, the cost of jailing a prisoner — is extremely important for making good business, social, and governmental decisions. Three principles of manufacturing cost accounting apply to most situations in which you need to know the cost of an activity:

✔ Classify costs properly, which means including only costs that should be attached to a particular activity and excluding costs that belong somewhere else.

✔ Distinguish between *direct and indirect costs;* indirect costs have to be allocated, or distributed among different activities.

✔ Separate between fixed costs that can't be reduced in the short term, and variable costs that can be reduced in short order.

Part V
Reaching the End of the Line

The 5th Wave   By Rich Tennant

"What made you think you were the one to own and operate a china shop, I'll never know."

In this part . . .

In Walt Disney stories, everyone lives happily there-after, except the wicked witch, of course. This scenario doesn't quite square with the fate of many small businesses. Either voluntarily or involuntarily, a small business eventually comes to an end. The end can be a success story, in which the principal owners sell the business at a good price. Or the end can result from the financial distress of the business.

Chapter 14 offers a succinct explanation of how to value an ongoing business that is under no pressure from its creditors to sell out. The owners simply want to cash in their chips and move on. Chapter 15 explains shutting down a business, including when the business is under financial pressure to end its operations. Bankruptcy is one option. Even if you avoid bankruptcy, you may decide to terminate the business. You don't just close the door and walk away from the business. There's a lot more to it than that!

Chapter 14

Putting a Market Value on Your Business and Selling

. . . .

In This Chapter

▶ Clarifying why you need a business valuation

▶ Valuing your business

▶ Supporting a successful business valuation

▶ Understanding business acquisitions types

▶ Structuring the sale of your business

▶ Managing the business acquisition process

. . . .

*Y*ou've toiled for years with managing your business. Through good times and bad, you've been able to not only survive, but prosper and build real value within your organization. Now it's time to bear the fruits of your labor and capitalize on the market opportunities present to develop and execute an exit strategy. Well, welcome to the club as each and every day throughout the world, hundreds of businesses are pondering this move. From megamergers handled by the power brokers on Wall Street to the local dry-cleaning operation being sold after 50 years of family ownership, selling and buying companies represents big business.

But how does this whole exit strategy thing work? Or more importantly, how are the values for these transactions determined? Is it similar to residential real estate, where appraisals are often used as the basis for the valuation? Or is it as simple as looking at a balance sheet to determine what the net owner's equity balance is? This chapter explores the basics of business valuations, as well as summarizes the most common business sale types and structuring issues and the risks associated with each.

Your business's financial statements represent the heart of the business valuation discussion. If you don't understand your financial statements and, more importantly, how much cash flow is generated from your business, then you won't understand the business valuation process. If you're unsure of how to read your financial statements, then check out Chapter 3.

Why You Need Business Valuations

Business valuations are critical to managing an operation. On the surface, they tell you how much a business is worth and (more importantly) how much you can make from owning all or a portion of it. Everyone has heard the stories about the young entrepreneur, starting a business in his garage, selling it years later for millions of dollars, and living the good life in sunny Southern California. There is no question that determining your potential windfall represents an important reason to calculate the value of a business but it's just one of the many uses of this all important piece of data.

Assuming that a business valuation is needed only to support the eventual sale of your company can be dangerous. Business valuations represent an essential part of the ongoing business management function in terms of properly protecting business assets.

The Why part of valuing a business (beyond the obvious) is often more important than the How for many reasons:

✔ **Business insurance:** All businesses utilize insurance to manage operating risks. The most widely used insurance types are general liability (to protect against a customer claiming damages from using the company's product or service), workman's compensation insurance (mandated by almost every state in the country to cover injuries suffered by employees), directors and officers (to provide additional liability coverage to the directors and officers of the business), and medical/life (coverage provided to employees for health, medical, and death-related claims). In addition, almost every business utilizes property and causality insurance to protect the company's assets from damage and/or loss of use. The basis for determining the property and causality insurance premium is a function of both tangible and intangible assets. Understanding the value of a business assists in securing the proper type, form, and amount of property and causality insurance, which includes the value associated with loss of use.

Companies often mismanage this issue in an effort to reduce expenses at the risk of exposing the organization to lost income and cash flow streams. Improper insurance coverage can cost a company mightily in terms of impairing its business value.

✔ **Life insurance and business planning:** Most businesses are privately held by a family, small group of owners, or individually. Quite often, a need arises to value the business for planning purposes. For example, a corporation may be owned by three partners, all of which are married. In the event one of the owners dies, the remaining owners may want to purchase the deceased owner's interest in the company from the surviving spouse rather than have the surviving spouse become a partner (which can often lead to significant management problems). Often, companies purchase term life insurance on each owner to provide enough coverage to purchase the interest held. Hence, if a company is valued at $10 million and the deceased partner owned 25 percent, term life insurance of approximately $2.5 million is required. Rather than utilize internal resources to purchase the interest (which the company may not have or would place it in a difficult operating environment), the partners can use life insurance to help protect all the parties' interests. Clearly, having a business value established becomes an essential part of the planning and management process.

✔ **Individual estate planning:** Estate planning is similar to life insurance and business planning. Large, illiquid individually held investments can wreak havoc with estate planning and taxation issues if they're not properly planned for and understood. Having a firm and fair business valuation available that supports the worth of the investment can assist with both the estate management process, as well as provides for a solid data point for financial planning purposes. Estate taxes that aren't planned for are not only a problem for the estate, but may even be more of a problem for the business itself as a result of a forced or premature sale. That is, if the estate can't secure the necessary funds to cover the estate taxes, it may have no other option but to sell its interests in the business, which may result in new partners/investors or, worse yet, a complete business liquidation.

✔ **Business management:** Business valuations represent an essential element of almost any employee equity participation plan. Businesses often provide long-term compensation incentives to their employees via various forms of stock option or equity participation plans. Basically, the goal is to provide employees with an opportunity to generate future income and compensation in exchange for committing their services to the company for an extended period of time. Business valuations are essential to ensuring the plans work efficiently. For example, SAIC, a multibillion dollar defense and technology company headquartered in San Diego, used to establish (before the company went public) a fair market value for its stock on a quarterly basis so that all its employees, investors, and other interested parties have a fair basis on which to base investment decisions. If an employee needs to liquidate shares owned and sell them back to the company, a fair value or per share price is readily available. Determining the business valuation in this case supports an invaluable management tool.

✔ **Strategic business decisions:** In today's economic environment, a change in business direction, for whatever reason, can occur almost overnight. A market that once looked like it held all the promise in the world can quickly change, resulting in the need to liquidate or terminate the business unit. As such, having a reliable business valuation available can greatly assist management with making quick decisions. Having a reasonable business valuation available to assist management with making these types of business decisions is always helpful.

Every business should have a board of directors, or at least an advisory board, to assist with managing its operations and provide guidance on more macro-level business issues. These boards can provide invaluable management advice and assistance to any size operation and/or organizational structure. Selecting board members that have had real-life experience in buying, valuing, and selling businesses brings an additional resource that you may not have ever thought about. In addition, advisory and board members can offer additional support with a vast array of business issues ranging from managing rapid growth to supporting the company during times of crisis.

The need to value a business goes well past just "looking to cash out" or determining what it's worth. Business valuations represent an extremely important piece of information supporting a company's strategic business planning process and management functions. The real question lies in why this information is needed and how it can be used to better plan for the future.

How Businesses are Valued

Business valuations are based on the present value of future cash flows. No matter what valuation model, methodology, logic, concept, technique, and/or principal is used, they all come back to the company's ability to generate cash flow. Even when a company is being liquidated, the end value is based on how much cash will be left over for the equity investors. Simply put, cash flow reigns as king when valuing a business.

EBITDA

If you're valuing a business, get use to the term *EBITDA* (pronounced just like it is spelled). In its simplest form, EBITDA stands for earnings before interest expense, income taxes, depreciation expense, and amortization expense. EBITDA represents the basis for determining a businesses' adjusted cash flow on which to base a business valuation. In addition, this term can be expanded to *EBITDAO*, which simply adds the term other expenses to the end. A number of businesses need to add other expenses to this equation to account for various one-time or owner preference expenses and income that are nonrecurring in nature. By accounting for these one-time and nonrecurring items, you can clearly support the calculation of a company's "adjusted" cash flow stream (EBITDA updated for other expenses and income that are nonrecurring in nature).

When placing a value on a business, you should become familiar with the time value of money concept (or the present value of future cash flows). Simply stated, the *time value of money concept* assumes that a dollar in your hand today is worth more than a dollar in your hand next year, two years from today, and so on. Figure 14-1 provides a simple example of what a stream of $1,000 payments received over a five-year period would be worth today if you were able to earn 10 percent per year on the payments.

	Payment Date	Payment Amount	Interest Rate	Present Value of Payment Today
	12/31/08	$1,000	10.00%	$909
Figure 14-1:	12/31/09	$1,000	10.00%	$826
The time	12/31/10	$1,000	10.00%	$751
value of	12/31/11	$1,000	10.00%	$683
money.	12/30/12	$1,000	10.00%	$621
	Totals	$5,000		$3,791

What Figure 14-1 really says is that the real value of the payment amounts, although totaling $5,000, would be worth only $3,791 today in order to earn a 10 percent return on an investment. Or conversely, an investor would be willing to pay you $3,791 today to receive a payment stream of $1,000 per year for five years.

Although many business valuation models exist, two valuation techniques are particularly common and the easiest to understand:

✔ **Cash Flow Multiple method:** This method is applicable to most small- to medium-sized business operations and is often referred to as the Main Street approach. Under this method, a cash flow multiple is applied to a company's expected/future adjusted cash flow stream. This adjusted cash flow stream is most commonly referred to as EBITDA (see sidebar).

Generally speaking, cash flow multiples range from 3 to 6 (but can be higher or lower) and are influenced by a company's perceived risk and growth factors. In addition, it should be noted that historical cash flow information tends to be used as a basis or starting point when calculating the expected/future "adjusted" cash flow stream. For example, if a company's average EBITDA for the past three years has been $750,000 annually and a multiple of 4 is applied, the businesses' value is approximately $3,000,000 ($750,000 × 4). This business valuation method is more widely utilized by Main Street due to the nature of how these companies operate (a high volume of relatively small and unsophisticated businesses compared to corporate America as represented by Wall Street).

✔ **Price Earnings Multiple method:** This method is most applicable to larger, publicly traded businesses and is often referred to as the Wall Street approach. Using this technique, a business valuation is derived from taking the net after tax profit of a company and multiplying it by a market driven factor. For companies that enjoy the prospects of high growth rates, dominant market positions, significant financial resources, and other positive business attributes — all of which translate into potential significant higher future cash flow streams — a multiple of 20 or more may be applied. For businesses that are more mature with relatively steady cash flow streams, a lower multiple, such as 10, may be applied. This is one (but certainly not the only) reason why a company such as Microsoft may be valued using a factor of 23 whereas Exxon may only be valued using a factor of 12. This technique is most prevalent with publicly traded companies listed on the New York Stock Exchange, NASDAQ, and other markets. The market quickly and efficiently establishes the total value of the company (its market capitalization) that is readily available at any point in time.

Figure 14-2 illustrates the different valuation techniques in use and how they both come to basically the same valuation conclusion.

As is evident from Figure 14-2, both techniques essentially value the company at approximately $3.5 million. Or, in other words, a potential acquirer would provide $3,500,000 of consideration to generate a potential operating cash flow of approximately $835,000 per year (net profit of $355,260 plus depreciation expense of $200,000, interest expense of $62,000, and income tax expense of $217,740). In addition, note the following key valuation issues:

- **Applying industry standards:** The valuation derived in Table 14-2 is approximately 1 times the company's gross profit generated of roughly $3.3 million. You'll often find that within certain industries, common valuation reference points are made, such as $X \times$ revenue, $Y \times$ gross profit, or $Z \times$ book value. For example, in the banking world, business valuations are often based in terms of what multiple on the bank's net book value (or net equity) is achieved. Although this valuation technique may appear to be different, if you look close enough and apply the lessons of valuing a business on its ability to generate cash flow, you'll quickly understand why one bank will sell for two times its book value and another at one times: its ability to generate cash flow.

- **Using EBITDA(O) as the valuation basis:** Business valuations tend to be based on a company's ability to generate real or comparable operating income and cash flows (between similar companies operating in similar markets). The idea is to identify how much cash flow can be generated from the basic business operation as opposed to how much debt the business has incurred (producing interest expense) and how much has been invested in fixed assets (producing depreciation expense) to support the business. As an example, interest expense is added back to account for the fact that similar businesses may have been financed differently (one using debt and another using equity). While one of the businesses would have interest expense that would produce lower net profits, the other would not, producing higher profits. External business valuations need to extract the impact of how a company has been financed to properly calculate a real value for the assets being acquired. After the real value has been determined, the parties can then structure how best to finance the potential acquisition. (Refer to Chapter 10 for further information on business capital sources.)

- **Valuing businesses with negative cash flow:** Quite often, businesses are assigned a value even when their cash flow stream is negative. For example, during the year after hurricane Katrina, a number of businesses lost significant amounts of money as they attempted to recover from the devastating affects of this natural disaster. Businesses would still be assigned a value given the fact that the market would anticipate an eventual return to being able to generate positive cash flow. Valuations take into consideration these situations in order to properly account for these one-time and/or extraordinary events.

Business valuations are really based on two critical pieces of information. First is the expected or future cash flow the company has the ability to generate. Second is the multiple applied to the expected or future cash flow stream (by the market).

XYZ WHOLESALE, INC.
BUSINESS VALUATION COMPARISONS

Summary Income Statement	Cash Flow Multiple FYE 12/31/00	Price Earnings FYE 12/31/00
Revenue	$12,000,000	$12,000,000
Costs of Goods Sold	$8,700,000	$8,700,000
Gross Profit	$3,300,000	$3,300,000
Gross Margin	27.50%	27.50%
Selling, General, & Administrative Expenses	$2,450,000	$2,450,000
Depreciation Expense — D	$200,000	$200,000
Interest Expense — I	$62,000	$62,000
Other (Income) Expenses	$15,000	$15,000
Net Profit Before Tax	$573,000	$573,000
Income Tax Expense (Benefit) — T	$217,740	$217,740
Net Profit (Loss) — P	$355,260	$355,260
EBITDA (Sum of D, I, T, & P)	$835,000	N/A
Cash Flow Multiple	4	N/A
Business Value	$3,340,000	N/A
Net Earnings (Just P)	N/A	$355,260
Price Earnings Multiple	N/A	10
Business Value	N/A	$3,552,600

Figure 14-2: Business valuation comparisons.

The Keys to a Successful Business Valuation

The hard thing about valuing a business lies in the great unknown of future cash flows and the risks associated with being able to generate future cash flows. While historical operations can provide a sound starting point to determine future cash flows, it can also be very misleading. For example, a biotechnology company in an early stage of clinical trials has no historical positive earnings or cash flows, but may hold an extremely high market valuation based on the promise of future cash flows from the eventual production and sales of a new drug. Or conversely, a cemetery operation may have a one-time event due to a liquidation of real estate holdings (held for a long time), which will be nonrecurring. Hence, future cash flows can be distorted by historical events that are nonrecurring (positive or negative). The key lies in the ability to calculate a core or operating cash flow figure on which to base the valuation.

The following examples, by no means all inclusive, provide a flavor for how cash flows can be adjusted to be used as a basis when determining the most appropriate business value:

- ✔ **Expense savings:** One company may be interested in acquiring a business that offers tremendous expense savings opportunities via implementing the concept of economies of scale. By combining the two entities, an unprofitable business now may actually produce a positive cash flow (which has value). The elimination of duplicate accounting functions, human resource tasks, distribution facilities, and so on are often cited in business acquisitions and can assist in supporting the valuation calculated for the business being acquired. Easy targets include duplicate business overhead functions, such as accounting and finance, because, generally speaking, two CFOs or even two accounting departments aren't needed in the combined entity moving forward.

- ✔ **Added expense removal:** Pushing through other or personal expenses in closely held businesses has been around as long as the IRS (actually longer). Generally, these expenses aren't necessary for the ongoing business to operate, but the owners take advantage of the tax break. Removing these expenses to increase cash flows can lead to higher business valuations. Examples of these types of items include retaining family members in various administrative or clerical positions that are more of a luxury, inflating owner salaries, or passing through various personal expenses associated with travel, autos, and so on. Of course, nobody is questioning the legitimacy of these expenses for tax purposes, but we have yet to find a company that does not test these waters somewhat.

- ✔ **Potential cost increases:** Certain companies may be at a stage where a significant reinvestment in capital equipment, assets, and so on is required to continue to support and generate cash flows. You need to factor in these one-time expenditures into a business valuation model to reflect the impact on future cash flows. While depreciation expense is added back to determine the proper EBITDA, this figure can also be reduced in the scenario where significant reinvestments in fixed assets are required to keep a company competitive, such as upgrading its facilities to meet new environmental regulations.

- ✔ **Hidden assets:** Certain assets may have a significant value present external to the core business. For example, a company may have purchased real estate years ago for future business expansion, but the property is no longer needed internally. To an outside party, the value may be substantial, and, as such, this hidden value needs to be reflected in the complete business valuation. Or conversely, this asset may be excluded from the business valuation and carved out from any potential analysis to capture the core value of the business.

- ✔ **Intangible assets and/or intellectual property:** Brand names, research in process, patents, trademarks, contracts for retail shelf space, and similar types of assets have the ability to generate significant cash flows if managed properly. While one company may struggle with generating adequate cash flows, another may prosper by applying its marketing or financial muscle to an intangible asset.

- ✔ **Lost future business:** In service organizations, a business valuation may decrease as a result of a key principal leaving or retiring. Anyone who has evaluated an acquisition within the service industry knows how critical this issue can be in terms of negatively impacting future cash flows. If a partner of 30 years leaves, chances are a portion of his accounts will also leave, which in turn produces reduced future cash flow.

This list could go on and on. When a business is valued, all elements and facts of importance must be evaluated in terms of determining what is the most reasonable future cash flow stream that can be expected. From a logic standpoint, it's relatively easy to understand why a seller of a business would want to maximize the cash flow stream, or EBITDA, because a higher valuation would be received. Conversely, it's also just as easy to understand why a buyer of a business would want to minimize the cash flow stream or EBITDA because a lower valuation would be provided to the seller.

To increase the value of a business, a higher multiple applied to the cash flow or earnings stream is desired. Conversely, in order to decrease the value of a business, a lower multiple is used. The following list, which isn't meant to be all inclusive, covers factors that influence the multiple applied to the cash flow stream:

- ✔ **Interest rates:** Interest rates, simply stated, represent the cost of capital. For our purposes, the most common reference point for interest rates is the prime rate as established by the country's largest banks. In today's relatively stable interest rate environment, you can expect reasonable cash flow multiples. However, when the Federal Reserve Board even mentions that rates may rise, it should come as no surprise that valuations may be pressured lower.

A simple business valuation concept to remember is that when interest rates rise, business valuations decrease. This concept is based on the premise that the opportunity cost for the funds used to buy a business will be higher, and, with all things being equal (including the EBITDA of a business), the valuation must be lower to produce the desired return.

✔ **Growth potential:** Higher growth opportunities translate into stronger future cash flow potential and demand higher multiples. Just ask the dot-coms of the late 1990s and early 2000s about how they received astronomical valuations based on the premise of extremely high future growth rates. From a business perspective, the more information, support, and data that you can provide a potential buyer about the growth prospects of your business, the higher business valuation you will receive.

✔ **Length of cash flow stream:** Cash flow streams that are longer and more secure or reliable produce higher valuation multiples than shorter, uncertain cash flow streams. If a company has patent production in place for the next ten years (supporting the cash flow stream) versus three years, it's safe to say the valuation multiple will be favorable. This concept is commonly referred to as an *Evergreen income stream.* Just as it sounds, if you can produce cash flow streams that are forever green, cash flow multiples will increase.

✔ **Liquidity of investment:** If an investment is readily liquid with multiple buyers available, a higher multiple is generally provided. Nonliquid investments with limited market appeal increase risks and drive down valuation multiples. This concept is especially true on Wall Street, where the most widely held and largest publicly traded corporations may receive a higher valuation given the ability to readily sell investments on the open market.

✔ **Management continuity:** Management resources, experience, talent, and continuity represent critical elements of the business valuation process. In the infamous words of Gordon Gecko played by Michael Douglas in the movie *Wall Street,* nobody wants to buy or invest in a company that represents a dog with a different set of fleas. If the management team isn't qualified to operate the business and produce continued cash flow, the multiple applied to the cash flow stream will suffer.

✔ **Concentration or diversification risks:** The higher the concentration or diversification risk, the lower the multiple. Two like companies with the same cash flow stream operating in the same industry may receive different valuations because one company may generate its revenue equally from 100 accounts and the other from just 10 accounts equally. The impact of losing one account in 10 is far greater than 1 in 100 and increases the concentration risk. While it may be nice to generate 35 percent of your revenue and earnings from the Home Depots of the world, increased operating risks are present that may actually deflate the value of your business.

✔ **Timing is everything:** Just about everyone has heard this phrase at one time or another. For business valuations, timing really is everything in terms of driving higher multiples and increased liquidity. You need look no further than the robust valuation period experienced in the late 1990s that crashed within a period of roughly 12 months with the start of the new decade. Capitalizing on or missing the window of opportunity can significantly influence the multiple received.

The determination of the multiple to be applied to the cash flow stream really boils down the risks present: actual and perceived. Actual risks are relatively easy to understand and quantify and, as such, can be applied to the determination of the cash flow multiple in a relatively logical fashion. Of greater uncertainty are the debates that inevitability occur about perceived risks. These risks are much more subjective in nature and, if not properly managed and presented, can significantly impact the value of a business. Needless to say, the higher the risks, the lower the valuation multiple received, which in turn drives a lower overall business value.

There are no set rules in the business valuation game. While a seller may want to maximize cash flows and lower the risks (thus increasing the value), the acquirer may want to deflate potential future cash flows and increase the perceived risks (thus producing a lower value). Or, conversely, an estate may want to justify a lower valuation to reduce potential estate taxes, whereas the IRS may be more aggressive and increase the valuation for obvious reasons. While the basic principals used in the business valuation process are relatively constant, cash flow and how the EBITDA(O) and multiples are managed or manipulated represent the real basis of valuing a business.

To realize the maximum valuation for a business, you must properly package, prepare, and present the business. This preparation goes well beyond getting your financial and accounting house in order because the business valuation and sales process involves a significant amount of subjective elements beyond just the numbers. You wouldn't expect to realize the highest value when you're selling a home that has a leaky roof, weeds growing in the yard, and clutter thrown about. Nor would you expect to receive a reasonable offer for your business with personnel or management shortcomings, excessive expenses, or improperly prepared and presented financial information. Timing, as they say, is everything, and, while important when valuing and selling a business, preparation and presentation are just as critical! To this point, external professionals are often used to assist with this function. Top realtors often generate higher values (even with their commissions) for real estate properties if they know how to market and sell the properties. The same logic holds true for selling a business as the top business brokers, investment bankers, and/or mergers and acquisition specialists can enhance the value of a business and produce greater returns for the seller.

Types of Business Acquisitions

It's impossible to discuss all the attributes associated with a business acquisition as documenting the legal issues alone would demand another book be written. So in this section, we highlight key elements of business acquisitions.

Business acquisitions tend to come in one of two types: asset deals or stock deals:

✔ *Asset deals* are generally based on purchasing only the business assets of value (to the acquirer). Under an asset deal, specific assets of a business are acquired with the remaining legal entity left intact to either wrap up its affairs or continue with another business opportunity. This process may include buying just the ongoing business operations, including inventory, property, plant, and equipment, as well as the intangible assets (customer lists, patents, trade names) and leaving the remaining assets, such as trade receivables, prepaid expenses, and cash, with the old legal entity. The acquiring company purchases the assets and then integrates them into their operation for the purpose of realizing economic gain. The selling company is left to finalize its business affairs by liquidating the remaining assets, paying off the creditors, and hopefully having a return available to the owners or shareholders.

In a variety of situations, the selling company may still have an ongoing operation intact as the sale may only involve one division or segment of the business. Hence, the selling business continues its operations as usual with the exception of having one less division to worry about. Asset deals tend to be associated with smaller businesses or companies looking to shed a specific business interest.

✔ *Stock deals,* on the other hand, are generally based on purchasing the entire business entity (including buying all assets and assuming all liabilities). Under a stock deal, instead of purchasing specific assets of the selling company, the stock or equity of the selling company is purchased at fair market value with all assets being acquired and all liabilities assumed. The acquired company usually survives as a legal entity and continues to operate as subsidiary of the acquiring company or is in some capacity merged into a new entity formed for the specific purpose of acquiring the target company. Generally, the equity holders of the acquired company sell their holders (stock, LLC membership interests, and so on) for cash, equity, or stock in the acquiring company, a note payable, or a combination of these items. Stock deals tend to be associated with larger, publicly traded companies (as well as the larger privately held businesses) that have ample liquid resources and freely traded stock to complete the transaction.

You can realize significant tax benefits and savings opportunities by structuring a business acquisition correctly. The most significant benefit is being able to realize a gain on the sale of a business using federal established long-term capital gains tax rates as opposed to short-term ordinary income tax rates or better yet, structuring a transaction that allows the gain to be deferred from income taxes. Long-term capital gains tax rates are roughly 50 percent lower than short-term ordinary income tax rates. Obtaining proper professional accounting, legal, and taxation advice during the acquisition process represents an essential element of any business acquisition or sale and should be included in the planning process from the very beginning.

Although a number of advantages and disadvantages are present with each form, the same premise usually holds under either transaction in that the general business interests of the acquired company are maintained on an ongoing basis because the acquisition was based on the premise that an economically viable operation is present.

Structuring the Sale of Your Business

You've reached a major milestone in that not only have you found a party interested in buying your business, but you've come to terms on the value and what deal type will be used. Now the real fun begins as you and your support team focus on structuring the deal. The following overview of key structuring issues provides some basic insight as to how business acquisitions are put together. This list isn't meant to be an all inclusive list, but instead highlights some of the key structuring points that are generally a part of any business buy-sale agreement:

- **Forms of consideration:** It should go without saying that the acquiring company will need to remit some form of payment or consideration to the selling company, usually in the form of cash, stock, or equity issued by the acquiring company, debt (such as a note payable), assuming debts or liabilities of the selling company, or a combination of these items. For sellers, the preference is to get cash or liquid stock/equity in hand in the beginning to help manage future unknown risks associated with deferred consideration. For acquirers, the tendency is to conserve cash and manage the financing element of the transaction with some debt or restricted stock/equity. Remember, negotiating the value of the transaction is one thing. Agreeing on what consideration will be received (and when) is something entirely different.

- **Minimum working capital:** When a company acquires another business, the acquiring company usually requires a minimum amount of net working capital to be retained in the business. *Minimum working capital* is defined as the amount of current assets less current liabilities that is required to support the ongoing business operations. In effect, the minimum working capital represents the permanent capital investment needed to support a given operating level. For example, if a business has $2 million in current assets and $1 million in current liabilities, the net working capital is $1 million. If you're selling a business, you may feel that this positive $1 million of net working capital is yours and should be added to the purchase price. The acquiring company, however, will state that this $1 million of net working capital is required to support ongoing operations. The key concept related to this issue is centered in determining what a reasonable net working capital amount should be. If the parties to this transaction agree that $750,000 is the appropriate figure, then the selling party would be entitled to receive another $250,000 of consideration.

✔ **Assuming long-term debt:** Another concept selling companies often get confused with is based in how long-term debt is treated in the transactions. For example, say that a business was valued at $3 million but had $2 million of long-term debt. A transaction to sell this business could be handled in one of two ways. First, the acquiring company could remit $3 million of cash and not assume any of the long-term debt. The selling company would then be responsible for paying off the long-term debt of $2 million, leaving $1million of net proceeds. Second, the acquiring company could remit $1 million of cash and then assume the $2 million of long-term debt. The selling company still nets the same amount of $1 million, but now it becomes the responsibility of the acquiring company to pay off the $2 million of long-term debt.

When business valuations are calculated, long-term debt is often reduced from the gross value to determine the net value of the assets being acquired to reflect the fact that future cash flow will be consumed to repay the debt.

When selling a business, pay attention to what types of consideration will be received in relation to the creation of potential income tax obligations. By accepting stock or equity in the selling company, potential income tax obligations that may have resulted from a gain realized from the sale may be deferred (but not avoided) until you actually dispose of the stock or equity. Of course, you absorb added risks if stock or equity is accepted because you have no guarantees that the value of the stock or equity will remain the same (or that a market will exist to sell the stock or equity). The potential benefits realized from accepting the stock or equity (including potential deferring tax obligations, realizing appreciation in the stock or equity, and so on) need to be carefully weighed against the additional risks accepted (including incurring potential losses in the stock or equity and others).

Sale of a technology-based company

In late 1999 and early 2000, Tage worked with a company in Southern California that was looking to sell its business interests. The company produced roughly $15 million in annual sales and generated EBITDA of approximately $800,000 plus or minus. The business was a distributor of high-technology based products, primarily throughout the western United States.

The company elected to sell its business interests because the marketplace for its primary products was becoming extremely competitive. The combination of larger competitors (with 50 times the revenue level) and the commoditization of the products via sales channels being developed over the Internet were beginning to place significant pressure on the company's gross margin. As such, the company elected to prepare and present itself for sale to a larger publicly traded competitor that wanted to secure additional customers and distribution resources in the western United States.

The transaction took approximately nine months to complete, from the day a decision was made to sell the business to the final closing date. In summary, the company was able to realize a gross value of roughly $3.5 million, representing a cash flow multiple on EBITDA of approximately 4.4. Cash represented 40 percent of the consideration received with the remaining 60 percent received in the form of stock in the publicly traded company. The value of the stock was determined based on the average price of the shares as established by the market during the previous 90 days. A one-year restriction was placed on selling the stock (in the open market) received from the date of closing. After this one-year period, the stock could be sold freely. In addition, the CEO of the selling company executed a three-year employment agreement with the acquiring company to manage its expanded operations in the western United States.

✔ **Restrictive agreements:** A number of restrictive agreements are usually required, the majority of which tend to fall on the seller. For example, the acquiring company will want to ensure that the selling company or its founders do not compete against it in the future. You usually have the use of a noncompete agreement for a set period of time within set geographical boundaries. When stock or equity is provided as consideration from the buyer to the seller, the acquiring company will often place a restriction period on when and how much of the stock can be sold after the fact to avoid too much of their stock being "dumped" on the open market at once (driving down the price). This step is also undertaken to ensure the seller is committed to seeing the acquisition through to a successful integration with the buyer's business.

✔ **Representations and warranties:** Both parties will be required to provide representations and warranties as to the viability of the business being acquired and that the acquiring business is of sound "mind and body." In this day and age of fraud, deceit, and misrepresentations, both parties want to ensure added legal protection is in place to prevent the "take the money and run" attitude from prevailing. Representations and warranties are a normal and customary part of any business acquisition and are usually supported by active involvement from legal counsel. At first glance, the representations and warranties may look burdensome, but it really comes down to one key point: Are you, as the seller, willing to stand behind all of the statements, information, data, reports, and so on provided to the buyer?

From a seller's perspective, you should only make representations and warranties that are, or will be, under your control. For example, if your business owns intellectual property such as a trade name that represents an integral part of the acquisition, the buyer may ask you to represent that your company has 100 percent ownership rights to the trade name, and that no other organization has the right to legally use the trade name. This representation is one that you should be clearly able to make. However, if the acquiring company wants you to represent that one of your key suppliers will continue to provide material at a set price and quality level and no current contract is in place, you should not represent this because you can't guarantee the performance of an unrelated third party.

✔ **Variable acquisition control features:** A number of business acquisitions place controls on the valuation and consideration paid by implementing such elements as variable debt payments (or earn-outs), continued employment agreements for key management, meeting future operating performance objectives, and so on. The general idea is that some future event needs to occur (for example, management needs to stay intact for three years, X number of stores need to be opened, or the acquired business needs to produce Y cash flow) before additional consideration will be remitted. This setup tends to favor the acquiring company, but can also benefit the seller in that added deal kickers can be put in place if the acquired business actually performs better than expected. As a general rule, the more risks within a transaction, the higher portion of consideration paid based on variable acquisition control features.

✔ **Management continuity:** It benefits both the business buyer and seller to ensure that a qualified management team is retained to operate the company moving forward. Structuring favorable employment agreements for key management team members helps the seller with securing a better valuation and provides the buyer with a certain amount of protection against attrition and creating a vacuum in leadership. If properly managed and structured, everyone stands to benefit from retaining key management.

The Business Acquisition Process

Every business acquisition is a unique process. The following overview outlines the basic business acquisition process, from start to finish:

1. **Come to terms with separation anxiety.**

   Before you even begin preparing and packaging your business for sale, you should ask yourself one critical question: Are you ready to let go? For most entrepreneurs, starting a business from scratch and building it over 20-plus years represents more of a quest than a financial goal. The business becomes a second home, a part of the extended family, and, if you will, one of the children. Don't underestimate the emotional element of the business acquisition process.

2. **Prepare yourself.**

   Properly preparing and packaging your business is of critical importance. All relevant business information, including financial data and reports, marketing collateral, product or service documentation, and just about any other piece of information you can think of, should be prepared for eventual review, evaluation, and examination. Being better prepared translates into a more efficient process with higher valuations received.

3. **Know your market.**

   You need to be aware of what is happening in your market. If you wait too long to sell, you may not have much value left. You should always be aware of how the market shapes your business environment, and when the "market stars" may all align to provide the ideal environment to sell your business. Timing can be everything when selling a business.

4. **Secure proper professional support.**

   For most businesses operations, internal expertise usually isn't readily available to support the business acquisition process. As such, whether buying or selling a business, you should secure proper external professional support to assist with the acquisition process. This support includes but is not limited to legal counsel, accountants and/or tax professionals, financing groups such as investment bankers, traditional banks, and/or other capital sources, and business professionals with significant expertise in merger and acquisition activity. In addition, having an active and well qualified board of directors or advisory board can be a real asset in the process.

   Selecting the right professional support is critical. Just as with other consultation services, numerous companies offer services to support the business valuation and acquisition process, but make sure that you know what you're buying before signing up.

5. **Engage in the courting process.**

Think of this process in terms of dating; love at first sight, while possible, rarely happens. This part of the acquisition process involves meeting with different parties, groups, and companies, who all have some type of interest in the acquisition. More times than not, the date will go okay, but you can tell from the initial discussions that a good fit and long-term relationship will not be feasible. The idea is to focus on big picture issues, visions, strategies, and/or common goals to make sure that both the buyer and seller are on the same page. While you can share some very preliminary information and discuss certain strategies, hold off on providing too much information and data until you've had a chance to court for a while. You need to make sure that you're comfortable with the other party before a more formal relationship is pursued.

You shouldn't rush to provide too much detail or confidential information because you should provide only the extreme basics, such as where the company operates, what its top line revenue is, its marketing information, and so on — in other words, information that, for the most part, is already publicly available via your Web site or from other public sources.

6. **Share preliminary information.**

The courting process should reduce the potential parties involved in the transaction and help eliminate the "looky-loos" and "wannabe players" from the process. At this stage, both parties in the acquisition process should be prepared to execute a *nondisclosure agreement (NDA)* and/or confidentiality agreement. Basically, this agreement legally binds both parties to not disclose any information to an outside and/or party who isn't essential to the process. Once the NDA is executed, you can exchange additional information that is somewhat more confidential but still fairly summarized in nature to avoid providing too much detail too early.

Exchange only basic information, such as audited or reviewed financial statements, financial information, projections, reports, a business plan overview or executive summary, marketing collateral/material, and so on. (See Chapter 7 to understand the importance of internally versus externally prepared financial information.) The goal is to provide enough information on which to generate a basic offer but not provide too much detail that is confidential to your business. The idea is to take a more prudent strategy in distributing vital company information to parties that are really serious. If the offer isn't even close to being in the ballpark, then there's no point in moving forward.

7. Create a letter of intent or term sheet.

The good news is that you've made it to a point where you have an offer. The offer is usually provided in the form of a *letter of intent* or a *term sheet*. These documents are generated for the specific purpose of clearly spelling out what terms will be present in the acquisition and what will be expected of the buyer and seller in order to complete the acquisition. Obviously, the terms address such items as the initial estimated value of the transaction, what types or forms of consideration will be used, when the consideration will be paid, what restrictions may be present, and all other key elements of the transaction.

The letter of intent or term sheet does not represent a legally binding agreement to finalize the acquisition. Rather, it represents more of an agreement to agree on how the "meat and potatoes" portion of the acquisition process will proceed. The idea is to use the term sheet or letter of intent as a basic framework for the final acquisition to ensure that all the parties have a basic understanding in place as you proceed.

8. Practice due diligence.

Up until this step, the amount of information distributed as well as the discussions and negotiations have most likely been extensive, but they're nothing in comparison to what you'll undertake during due diligence. In its simplest form, *due diligence* represents the stage during which "everything is bared" between the parties. You need to make available all accounting, financial, operational, customer, marketing strategies, vendor, legal, intellectual property, employee, and/or just about any other piece of vital company data to the acquiring party to examine and review.

Due diligence is generally managed by key company personnel rather than the CEO and/or presidents (of the respective companies) because the majority of work to be completed is centered on the everyday types of transactions, issues, reports, and/or other normal and recurring business events.

If properly prepared for with no significant skeletons in the closet, due diligence, although a very intensive process, should be completed with limited problems. On the flip side, if you're not prepared and/or are attempting to hide something, due diligence is when the deal falls apart. Consider the due diligence process similar to an independent CPA audit times three. Not only must all the financial and accounting data be examined, but, the acquiring party will want to see all other key operating elements of the business.

The concept of reserve due diligence is extremely important to understand. If you, as the selling company, will be accepting future payment from the acquiring company as part of the consideration received, you'll want the right to examine the acquiring company's financial and operational data in order to protect your interests. Legitimate acquirers understand this issue and generally do not have a problem with providing relevant data. If resistance is received, a red flag should go up.

9. **Conduct subsequent negotiations and prepare documents.**

   If you think your deal was done with the letter of intent (see Step 7), think again. In almost every business acquisition scenario, something arises during the process that requires subsequent negotiations and acquisition restructuring efforts. Often, the due diligence effort turns up something that results in a need to restructure the letter of intent. Most minor findings and issues are easily managed between the parties by making revisions to the final acquisition documentation. For example, if uncertainties are discovered surrounding a key customer continuing to purchase a given level of products or services, the acquiring company may want to provide for more of the consideration in the form of a future payment than with cash upfront. The total value may not change, but the structure of the consideration may change to compensate the acquirer for additional risks.

The key during this process is to keep the communication lines open (especially between the respective attorneys) and remain flexible and adaptable to changing deal conditions. A certain amount of give and take between the parties will be necessary to finalize the deal. In addition, properly managing the communication of the transaction to key employees and the market in general is extremely important. Obvious risks are associated with communicating the sale too early, and you have still more risks if key employees consider leaving after what may be perceived as bad news. Keeping the deal mum until well into the process or until the deal has been publicly announced may well be the best tactic. And, if word does get out, a communication plan should be in place to address employee, vendor, customer, and other parties' concerns and questions.

While the due diligence process can take anywhere from several months and even up to a year to complete, don't forget to run your business. Many business owners begin to bask in the glow of perceived riches and forget to continue running and growing their business. Dropping the ball can jeopardize the future of the business and may also kill the deal as the acquiring firm is monitoring the business's progress during due diligence.

Final thoughts on business valuations

Somebody once came up to us and raised the question as to why the equity or net book value of a business isn't equivalent to its fair market value. Valuing a business based on its net book value sounds simple enough and would seem to make sense because, if the assets and liabilities on the balance sheet are fairly stated, the business should be able to liquidate with the remaining cash equal to the net equity of the business.

But rather than look at it in this fashion, we suggest an alternative view. If you could receive a cash flow stream of $100,000 per year from assets that have a stated value of $50,000, not only would you be willing to purchase the assets for $50,000, you'd most likely be willing to pay ten times this amount. Or, if an investment generated $50,000 in annual earnings but was going to cost $2 million, would you (or any other entity) actually pay $2 million, or would an attempt be made to drive the price down to, say, $500,000 to better equate the return with the investment?

Valuing a business isn't based on supply side economics (if it costs X, it will return Y in cash flow). Rather, the cash flows and earnings of Y determine the value of X.

10. Close the deal.

This step is easy; just be prepared to give your hand a workout by signing lots of documentation. Most often, the closing date and time is defined in the final documentation, which is generally referred to as the *final acquisition definitive agreement.* This agreement represents the legally binding document and finalizes the acquisition process. At this stage, you've finalized all deal points and negotiations with only the closing formality remaining.

Integrating the acquisition after it's closed can be five times more challenging. A properly planned and structured acquisition considers the vast array of issues that must be managed after the deal closes.

Chapter 15

Hanging Up the Spikes and Terminating Your Business

. . . .

In This Chapter

▶ Terminating a business

▶ Evaluating bankruptcy

▶ Planning for the burial

▶ Managing assets to maximize value

▶ Understanding the pecking order of liabilities

▶ Staying on top of critical operational issues

. . . .

*O*n the surface, you may assume that terminating a business is as easy as locking the doors, shutting down the phone and utility services, and turning off the lights (without even leaving a forwarding phone number or address). Conversely, you may think that electing to pursue bankruptcy is a more viable option in terms of letting the lawyers handle the final company affairs. While both options are available to companies looking to formally terminate their business interests, the actual process of terminating and dissolving a business often takes on a life of its own, which you must address proactively.

In this chapter, we discuss why a business termination may occur and the termination options available. We also delve into how the termination process actually works. From the initial birth of the business to its almost certain death, you need to apply the same accounting, financial, and business principles. Otherwise, the ghosts of past business failures may return to haunt you.

Looking into Business Terminations

When a company is first launched, its founders generally don't want to think about the business's eventual demise. To be quite honest, we've yet to see a business plan discuss this issue; the focus is centered on how successful the business is going to be and how much money everyone is going to make. Cold hard facts, however, tell a completely different story; more than 50 percent of businesses fail within their first five years of operations thanks to poor planning, weak management, capital limitations, stiff competition, and general economic turmoil. The real issue isn't based so much in the fact that a business entity will cease to exist, but rather how the business will meet its final demise. In other words, will the business be terminated in a voluntary fashion, or will the business reach the end involuntarily?

Whether a business termination is voluntary or involuntary, the business owners, founders, entrepreneurs, and/or key executives often have a difficult time accepting the economic reality of the situation and that the end is at hand. These individuals often pursue any course of action to keep the doors open and not let their business concept die. The emotional state of these individuals may push them into decisions that, to external parties, are clearly crossing the fraudulent line, but that the owners view still within the bounds of acceptable accounting and business practices. What these individuals fail to realize or simply don't want to accept is that the business enterprises' cash flow (or lack thereof) doesn't support a competitive economic model. To an external party, a quick review of the business plan and/or economic model may clearly project an unviable operation. An internal party, however, may trick himself into believing that the economic model does work. How? By increasing revenue assumptions, reducing expenses unreasonably, and/or presenting information (actual or forecast) to capital sources that isn't supportable. Being realistic is just as important in the life of the business as in its death.

Similar to the launch of a successful business venture, a successful business termination is based in the same fundamental principals: development of a business plan, retention of qualified management, and securing the proper amount of capital. Even at the very end, these critical business functions must continue to operate properly to ensure that the final funeral service and burial are completed once and for all.

Voluntary terminations

Voluntary terminations, in which the selling parties have an interest or desire to liquidate their holdings in a fair market value transaction with the acquiring parties, occur primarily as a result of one of two events:

✔ **The business is sold with the original legal entity remaining intact.** (See Chapter 14 for more on selling a business.) Under a *stock sale,* the acquired company usually survives as a legal entity and continues to operate as subsidiary of the acquiring company or is merged into a new entity formed for the specific purpose of acquiring the target company.

In an *asset sale,* the assets acquired have some economic value to the acquiring company. Under an asset sale, the legal entity that sold the assets still remains and will either continue to operate as a business entity or will be formally terminated. Under either scenario, the general business interests of the acquired company are maintained on an ongoing basis because the acquisition was based on the premise that the business is economically viable.

✔ **The owners are closing the doors.** This situation occurs more often than you think and may result from a variety of factors ranging from a family-owned and operated company that has no relatives interested in carrying on the family business to changes in governmental legislation that effectively kills a market for a business's product or service. Under this type of voluntary termination, businesses generally have advance notice (quite often years) that the business will eventually need to be terminated and can plan accordingly.

The good news with voluntary terminations is that an orderly close of the business is undertaken with both creditors and equity investors usually on board with the process. Hence, the biggest hurdle to face is managing the administrative process of closing the business, which you can accomplish either internally by retaining a *termination management team* to finalize the business's affairs or externally by hiring professional support.

Involuntary terminations

On the flip side of the voluntary termination process (see preceding section) is the ever-so-popular (yet unfortunate) *involuntary termination.* Involuntary business terminations tend to get more of the headlines because they're usually centered on an unfortunate event leading to a high-profile failure (which, of course, the press lives for).

This type of termination is usually brought on by external parties, such as creditors, shareholders, and governmental agencies, protecting their interests in a failing business. Generally, the heart of the problem lies in the inability of the business to grasp the extremely important concept of positive cash flow and net income. As the dotcom darlings of the 1990s quickly learned, a business must actually produce net income and positive cash flow to stay in business for an extended period of time.

Most involuntary business terminations are managed under the context of bankruptcy proceedings or/and equivalent processes, such as an Assignment for the Benefit of Creditors (discussed in the "Delving into Bankruptcy Protection" section of this chapter). As such, the federal court system, trustees assigned or retained to support the process, or business creditors are the ones who generally manage and control involuntary business terminations.

The involuntary termination of a business usually proceeds down one of two paths:

✔ **Orderly liquidation:** Under this process, a general consensus of the minds is reached by all parties, including the business owners, creditors, and/or any other outside party, such as a governmental organization. An orderly liquidation is considered an involuntary termination as more times than not, not enough assets or resources are available to cover all the business's obligations and liabilities, as well as the investments made by the owners. When this situation occurs, professional counsel is usually retained to ensure that the orderly liquidation proceeds as planned and that the available assets are remitted to the proper parties in the correct order.

✔ **Forced liquidation:** Just by the name alone, you can probably surmise that a forced liquidation is not a very pleasant experience. Under a forced liquidation, the parties involved don't agree that the business needs to be terminated. Company creditors and/or investors with significant interests in the business and large dollars at risk usually pursue forced liquidations, which involve significant professional and legal counsel participation, very high costs, and lengthy delays. The end result of a forced liquidation is similar to an orderly liquidation because you have fewer assets to distribute to the creditors and owners of the company.

Figure 15-1 compares a sample business's termination options from the ideal scenario where the business is sold to a worst-case scenario where the business is forced to liquidate. Note that involuntary terminations almost always result in significantly reduced outcomes.

In Figure 15-1, keep in mind the following key points:

✔ In Sale #1, the business was sold with a premium received above the company's net equity. In addition to the company's net equity of $1,200,000, the acquiring company was willing to pay another $1,200,000 for a total value of $2,400,000, which included assuming all the liabilities and receiving all the assets. After a sales transactional fee is paid of $120,000, the owners realize net consideration of $2,280,000, and everyone is (hopefully) happy.

DESCRIPTION	AMOUNT AS OF 1/1/05	VALUE ADJUST	AMOUNT REALIZED SALE #1	VA AD
SAMPLE DISTRIBUTION, INC.				
BUSINESS LIQUIDATION ANALYSIS				
ASSETS:				
CASH & EQUIVALENTS	$750,000	100%	$750,000	
TRADE RECEIVABLES, NET	$1,250,000	100%	$1,250,000	
INVENTORY, LOWER OF COST OR MARKET	$650,000	100%	$650,000	
OTHER CURRENT ASSETS	$75,000	100%	$75,000	
NET FIXED ASSETS	$400,000	100%	$400,000	
OTHER ASSETS & INTANGIBLES	$375,000	100%	$375,000	
TOTAL ASSETS	$3,500,000	100%	$3,500,000	
LIABILITIES:				
TRADE PAYABLES & ACCRUED LIABILITIES	$1,150,000	100%	$1,150,000	
SHORT-TERM DEBT, BANK LINE OF CREDIT	$750,000	100%	$750,000	
OTHER SHORT-TERM LIABILITIES	$50,000	100%	$50,000	
LONG-TERM DEBT	$350,000	100%	$350,000	
OTHER LIABILITIES & CONTINGENCIES	$0	0%	$0	
TOTAL LIABILITIES	$2,300,000	100%	$2,300,000	
EQUITY:				
COMMON SHAREHOLDERS EQUITY	$100,000		$100,000	
RETAINED EARNINGS	$1,100,000		$1,100,000	
NET EQUITY	$1,200,000		$1,200,000	

Figure 15-1:
Business
liquidation
comparison.

✔ In Orderly #2, the owners of the company have elected to undertake an orderly liquidation because they can't sell or operate the business profitably. A plan is implemented to liquidate the business assets and repay the debts. Notice that the overall net amount realized for the assets is only 71 percent of the total book value with significant reductions in values realized with net fixed assets, other or intangible assets, and, to a lesser extent, inventory. The reason for these value reductions is simple; once a business begins to liquidate, market forces will automatically discount the value of assets with significant pressure placed on assets that are used (who wants to purchase two-year-old computer equipment?), outdated (older inventory items hold no more than a scrap value in the market), or have no future use (an intangible asset, such as a patent that has no future value). In addition, the orderly liquidation incurs additional liquidation expenses for professional support, the retention of staff to manage the liquidation, continued expenses for rent, utilities, and so on, and the need to pay off future rent obligations. All told, the owners will be lucky to realize any value from this orderly liquidation and, in fact, may come up short to the tune of $70,000 (which the unsecured creditors would have to absorb with reduced payments). On the surface, you may think the owners of the business are disappointed with this outcome, but it has been our experience that owners are often elated to just break even.

> ✔ Forced #3, the worst-case scenario, represents a forced liquidation. In summary, this scenario takes the orderly liquidation and simply compounds the asset valuation reductions as the vultures and bottom feeders begin to really pound down the asset values. In addition, trade accounts receivable values suffer as customers begin to take advantage of the opportunity not to pay as a result of the severe company problems (and the fact that the company has limited resources to pursue collections). After incurring liquidation expenses that have increased due to additional legal fees to manage creditor disputes, this scenario paints a very dark picture: It comes up short by roughly $900,000. Needless to say, the unsecured creditors are going to get pounded on their ultimate settlement, which may be less than 20 percent on the dollar, with the owners having no chance to receive anything.

Delving into Bankruptcy Protection

Bankruptcy filings by individuals and businesses have reached all-time highs during the past decade. In some cases, the bankruptcy filing results from an economic model that no longer is viable (think Kmart's inability to compete in a highly intense mass merchandising market) or a one-time event that burdens the company with an unreasonable monetary obligation (claimants being awarded huge sums of money against Johns-Manville for asbestos-related claims). In others, it results from outright fraud (Enron). Whatever the cause, bankruptcy filings by businesses have been, and will continue to be, utilized as an effective strategy to manage a company's affairs in difficult economic times.

The term *BK* is most often used when referring to a business that has entered into federal bankruptcy protection or is well on its way to entering bankruptcy.

Most of the high-profile bankruptcy filings are entered into under Chapter 11, the guidelines established by the federal government. Under Chapter 11, a company is provided time to reorganize its financial affairs and develop a plan to satisfy both the creditors and equity investors in the company. Creditors have priority claims against company assets over equity investors (see Chapter 10). Hence, most Chapter 11 bankruptcy proceedings require a significant amount of input and involvement from the creditors to manage the reorganization process.

The creditors have the majority of the rights and preferences in these proceedings to protect their financial interest first and as such, the investors are usually left "holding the bag." If successful, the company's creditors and to a lesser extent, its management team, in addition to the federal court, all approve the reorganization plan and the company then exits bankruptcy protection to operate as an independent business. I mention the management team only in the context that someone must be left to keep the business operating and going forward. Needless to say, neither the court nor the creditors have any interest in all the details of keeping the business going forward and as such, a committed management team is necessary to emerge from Chapter 11.

Under a Chapter 7 bankruptcy proceeding (the most common type of bankruptcy), the company's goal is not to reorganize, but rather to liquidate all remaining assets and pay off creditors to whatever extent possible (with the understanding that the legal entity will be formally terminated). Federal laws still govern this type of bankruptcy proceeding, but the focus turns away from developing an ongoing viable economic business model and moves toward liquidating remaining company assets as efficiently as possible. The remaining company's affairs are turned over to a court-appointed trustee who is responsible for managing all the necessary steps to formally terminate the business. These steps include everything from liquidating remaining assets, to repayment of creditors (to whatever extent possible), to processing final paperwork, such as tax returns, legal notifications, and the like. Similar to a Chapter 11 bankruptcy, a Chapter 7 bankruptcy also incurs significant legal fees and is usually implemented by larger or more high-profile business operations.

While no set rules are present as to when a Chapter 11 versus Chapter 7 bankruptcy proceeding should be used, one key issue should be kept in mind. Chapter 11 bankruptcy proceedings are generally reserved for businesses that can display an economically viable business model will exist moving forward. If a business doesn't have the ability to produce positive cash flows and profits moving forward, then it has little need to enter into Chapter 11 bankruptcy.

Another type of termination proceeding available to companies in dire straits is an *Assignment for the Benefit of Creditors* (ABC). For lack of a better term, an ABC is nothing more than a poor man's version of a Chapter 7 bankruptcy proceeding. The same goals and objectives are present in that a liquidation effort is undertaken to maximize the value of whatever company assets remain and repay creditors and equity investors in the proper order. In addition, an independent trustee is required to manage the final termination affairs, but rather than being controlled under the laws of the federal court system, the termination is left directly to the trustee to administer. This trustee is usually a law firm that specializes in these types of transactions or an independent consulting group with a niche expertise. Beyond the difference with how the trustee is secured, the cost of an ABC is usually far less than a Chapter 7 bankruptcy because the court process is bypassed (unless the ABC turns ugly).

Most ABCs do not generate a return to the equity investors and usually produce far less cash than is needed to repay the creditors. ABCs are generally utilized (and represent a more efficient termination strategy) when the business entity is relatively small, legal squabbles aren't anticipated, the different types of creditors and equity investors are limited, asset recovery potential is poor, and opportunities for fraud and/or other types of misconduct aren't significant. ABCs also tend to follow a common path in that the business owners know that the end is at hand and have communicated it to the creditors and equity investors without much resistance received.

Keep in mind the following issues when you're considering BK or an ABC:

- Chapter 7 or 11 bankruptcy proceedings are generally very expensive and may take a relatively long time to complete. A business actually needs to be prepared to enter into bankruptcy with ample liquid financial resources just to get through the process. It often can be very expensive just going broke.

- Chapter 7 and 11 bankruptcy proceedings need to be supported by the proper legal and professional counsel because the issues involved can get highly technical.

- Fighting, arguing, and bickering between the different creditors, as well as the investors, can get nasty, resulting in lengthy delays and increases in professional fees. Properly managing the expectations of each party, whether within a BK or ABC, and/or group involved in the process can greatly assist in reducing costs and ensuring that the process is completed in a timely manner.

- An ABC represents a viable option to a bankruptcy when the right conditions are met, resulting in significant savings and the ability to streamline the process.

- Investors' equity values usually get hammered under any of the preceding proceedings. The risk reward relationship definitely plays out here because you either gain the highest returns or get left holding the bag.

Planning the Burial

The biggest stumbling block to terminating a business is often centered in figuring out how to start. Just as a business plan guides the business during its formation and growth years, a *business termination plan* should lead the business through its final months. Although this plan has a slightly different objective, the basis remains the same in terms of optimizing the business's remaining economic value and establishing a course of action. And just like the initial business plan identified the capital required to execute the strategy, so, too, must the business termination plan ensure that the appropriate resources are available.

The termination business plan will most likely not be as formal as the business plan in its presentation of data; when a business is shutting down, it's not attempting to impress potential capital sources. Rather its goal is to outline a termination strategy that maximizes asset values, repays creditors to the fullest extent possible, and provides a potential return to the equity investors, all within the most efficient means possible.

A business termination plan should contain the following elements:

- A **simple executive summary** outlines the events, market conditions, and so on that led to the business termination. While some parties will already have an understanding of the reasons, proper documentation is extremely helpful to the slew of parties caught by surprise.

- A **forecast** provides the time frame in which the termination is expected to be carried out and the capital/cash needed to execute the plan. One of the biggest mistakes made when terminating a business is underestimating how much capital/cash is required to execute the plan correctly. Remember, nobody is going to extend the business credit when it will soon be out of business.

- A **concise summary** reveals the company's remaining assets and liabilities. It should contain a marketing plan listing all assets and how they'll be disposed. In addition, a listing of every liability by class (for example, secured, unsecured, priority level, and so on) is essential to ensure that creditors are paid in the right order. *Note:* Include a summary of the equity investors by investment class to identify potential liquidation preferences.

- A **summary** of the remaining employees and external personnel resources needed to carry out the plan. Most business terminations require the support of external legal/professional counsel, and as such, these resources and costs need to be managed at the start of the process. We can't think of too many professionals willing to extend payment terms in a business termination.

- A **proactive communications plan or script** should be prepared to ensure that employees, customers, vendors, creditors, and other parties are kept up to speed on the effort and major milestones. There's nothing that will upset these parties more than being left in the dark.

✔ Finally, an **overview of the various operating factors,** including insurance requirements, physical locations needed, outstanding operating leases and commitments, and similar business issues, that will need to be handled. Remember, at some point the lights will actually need to be turned off with proper notices provided on where the mail should be forwarded.

The business termination plan not only provides the company's management with a final road map. But the key parties — either the board of directors and company officers still in control of the business or the creditors who have taken control of the company to protect their interests — responsible for approving the termination can view it. Without formal approval, the business (and potentially the board members and officers) may expose themselves to potential risks, acquisitions, and eventual legal action. The company will want to make sure that all relevant parties have reviewed the plan, agree that no other economically viable avenues exist, and formally approve the termination plan.

Managing Assets to Maximize Value

Liquidating remaining company assets represents one of the most important components of the business termination plan. Not only is the cash raised critical to getting creditors paid off, but hidden values and risks lurk behind the scenes. Figure 15-2 presents an overview of the major asset types owned by a business and the hidden value and potential risk for each type. This overview is in no way meant to be all-inclusive, but highlights the issues present when a termination effort is underway.

Figure 15-1 only scratches the surface. Many other issues (both positive and negative) surround each major asset type. Because each business is unique, different issues will undoubtedly be present that offer additional value enhancement opportunities while opening up the company to potential risks.

Here's a checklist for asset liquidations:

✔ Ensure that the company has as complete and comprehensive asset listing as possible. This step ensures that management has a solid starting point on how to manage the disposition so that it can allocate resources to the most valuable assets (to increase values) and avoid wasting time on assets with little or no value.

✔ Remember that a number of intangible assets may be present, whether or not a cost is stated on the balance sheet. These assets may include customer lists, trade secrets, sales databases, a below-market transferable property lease, and even the company name or Doing Business As (DBA) names. Don't underestimate the potential to realize value from these assets.

Asset Liquidation Overview

Asset Type	Potential Hidden Value	Potential Risks
Cash & Equivalents	Old outstanding checks never clear the bank and possibly could be recovered back into the company's general account.	Unprotected blank checks may be stolen, forged, and cashed. Protection of all bank documents and items is extremely important in a termination.
Accounts Receivable	An old account written off as worthless via the customer's bankruptcy may still have some value. Assigning this to a creditor in exchange for a cash payment may be possible.	The company's customers become aware of the termination and elect to string out payment in hopes of having to avoid making full payment. Who's going to collect the money if nobody's around?
Inventories	The shelf space the company's inventory occupies may have value to another business looking for additional exposure in a certain retail environment.	Disposing of old, worthless, and/or unwanted inventory may be costly and contain potential hazardous material problems.
Property, Plant & Equipment	Packaging up a group of fixed assets at a discount may provide the opportunity for the company to rid itself of an office lease with a personal guarantee. That is, the assets are sold below value, but a significant liability is also eliminated (not to mention the company does not have to move the assets now).	Selling tangible property such as desks, furniture, fixtures, computers, and so on may trigger a sales tax obligation which needs to be remitted to the appropriate parties. Also note that property, plant, and equipment may have a secured lender attached thus restricting the ability to liquidate these assets.
Intangible Assets	Customer lists, databases, and similar types of information may have significant value to certain third parties. Marketing of these Intangible Assets holds the potential of raising additional cash.	Allowing management and/or insiders to acquire databases and other key information without consideration may trigger a potential claim of wrongdoing by creditors or equity investors.
Other Assets — Prepaid, Deposits, Loans Receivable, etc.	Prepayments for rent, insurance, advertising, and similar items offer an opportunity to recover cash for the unutilized time period.	Terminating insurance coverage too early may leave the company's assets exposed to potential third-party claims.

Figure 15-2:
Asset liquidation overview.

✔ The potential for fraud, theft, or misallocation of assets is high in a business termination. Certain items, such as new computers, tend to "walk away" when management isn't paying attention. Proper safeguarding, such as making sure that all items over $1,000 are locked in a separate area, needs to be a priority.

✔ Ensure that all material transactions to liquidate assets are based on arm's-length transactions with fair market value received. Company insiders sometimes have a tendency to secure certain assets (with the idea of starting a new business) without considering the legal and fairness requirements of the situation. You can be assured that if the dollar amounts are large enough, the creditors and equity investors will pursue any transaction that smells of a related party or insider deal.

✔ Take advantage of experts, such as liquidators, commercial real estate brokers, or investment bankers, to enhance the value of the assets being disposed. Even though added costs are present, the extra value obtained via their marketing knowledge and muscle may be more than enough to offset their costs.

✔ Document all asset sales transactions appropriately to ensure that future disclosures and accounting are completed correctly. For example, if inventory is liquidated to a reseller, then no sales tax is due because the sale is from one business to another business. However, if inventory is sold at a bargain price to company employees — a business to end-user sale — then you need to collect sales tax.

✔ The ultimate value of an asset is really based on nothing more than its future cash flow. If other businesses are willing to buy a used computer for $250, then that amount is the value of the computer. If a patent generates a small royalty each month, then the future value of this royalty stream (discounted at the appropriate rate) represents its value. Similar to valuing and marketing a business for sale, anything that enhances an asset's future cash flow increases its value today.

Officers, executives, and other parties retained to terminate the business have a fiduciary responsibility to the creditors and equity investors to maximize the value of the assets being disposed. In today's highly fraud- and corruption-sensitive environment, creditors and investors are looking for ways to recapture losses even if it means piercing the corporate entity and pursuing key parties at the individual level.

Satisfying Liabilities

You must provide a complete and comprehensive listing of all liabilities so that management can properly structure how the company's assets will be distributed to its creditors. Of course, you can't arbitrarily pay off those creditors you like the best; you must follow a set pecking order:

✔ **Priority creditors:** Priority creditors, to a certain extent, have preference over almost all other types of creditors and need to be identified and managed first to avoid potential problems. Certain liabilities represent priority obligations. These liabilities include limited wage and vacation obligations to employees, unpaid payroll taxes, sales/use taxes payable, and similar types of items. Basically, the government doesn't want to see the employees or itself take a loss, and as such, these types of obligations can often pass through to the officers or board of a company if they're not paid.

Many of these items, including payroll taxes and sales and use taxes, are considered to be held in trust for the recipient by the company's officers, board, and/or other key executives.

✔ **Secured creditors:** These types of creditors are usually banks, credit unions, equipment-financing groups, asset-based lenders, and the like. These creditors generally lend only on a secured basis with an underlying asset present to support the value of the loan extended. Hence, if the company ever gets into trouble, the value of the liquidated asset is hopefully adequate to cover the amount of the outstanding loan. These creditors have preference over the unsecured creditors of the company.

✔ **Unsecured creditors:** These creditors are typically your primary trade vendors of the company and include material suppliers (for inventory), utilities (phone, electric, water, and so on), professional service firms, and other general corporate vendors (office supplies, temporary staffing company, and so on). These creditors have a claim against the company, but the claim is generally not secured with a specific asset. Hence, these creditors generally take a beating when an involuntary company termination is undertaken; normally, not enough funds are available to cover the outstanding debt obligation. Unsecured creditors may or may not have a preference over subordinated debt, depending on how the subordinated debt agreement is structured.

✔ **Subordinated creditors:** Subordinated creditors of the company generally are the last to receive any repayment of debt. (They do proceed payments made to equity investors, in most cases.) Subordinated debt is often structured with some type of investment return to compensate for the risks. This compensation may be in the form of higher interest rates paid on the subordinated debt or a *debt-to-equity conversion option,* which allows the debt to be converted to equity if the company performs extremely well. Subordinated creditors may have a preference over unsecured creditors if a *second position* (the secured lender has the first position) is taken in various company assets.

Personal guarantees

Lenders, trade vendors, or suppliers may demand personal guarantees (PG) as a condition for extending credit when a company doesn't appear financially stable, such as when dealing with a new company with limited credit history or a poorly performing company where the ability to continue is an ongoing concern. (For more on this topic, see Chapter 10.) In a *personal guarantee,* a key founder, executive, officer, or legal entity (such as a parent company of a subsidiary) promises to satisfy the debt if the company can't. Generally, a personal guarantee allows the lender, vendor, or supplier to pursue individual assets if the company can't cover the obligation.

PGs should only be entered into when appropriate because they can create significant financial distress on those providing the PG.

If an unsecured creditor with a PG is paid in full over another unsecured creditor without a PG, paid at 50 percent on the dollar, problems may arise as to the equitable distribution of cash. PGs can produce some of the worst migraine headaches and expose the individuals providing the PGs to unforeseen risks and significant economic loss. You can't play "favorites" with creditors in the same priority class to ensure a creditor with a PG present receives more than a creditor without a PG (just to make sure that the party providing the PG reduces their exposure).

Other unrecorded obligations

In addition to PGs (see preceding section), you should also pay close attention to commitments, contingencies, and/or other contractual obligations that aren't recorded or disclosed in the balance sheet, yet represent future monetary obligations. Operating leases or rental agreements for office space or equipment represent perfect examples of these types of commitments. A business may conclude that the office space or equipment can simply be returned to the rightful owner with no further rent or lease obligation present. However, if the vendor is unable to realize an appropriate value from the returned property to satisfy its losses, then the vendor may become an unsecured creditor to the company for the losses incurred. For example, if office space is abandoned with 50 months left on the lease and the landlord is unable to re-lease the space or must re-lease it at a reduced rate, then the vender has suffered an economic loss and can make an unsecured claim.

To make matters worse, these types of contractual obligations may carry PGs for the future payment stream, which can enable the vendor to pursue the personal assets of the individual providing the PG in the case of a default. The critical issue to remember with off-balance sheet obligations is that every commitment, contingency, and/or contractual obligation executed by the terminating business needs to be accounted for and managed in a similar fashion to the stated or recorded liabilities.

Equity preferences

By its very nature, preferred equity gives equity investors a preference to any distribution of assets over common equity holders (assuming that assets are even available). The preferred stock agreements should spell out these preferences both in terms of distributions to common shareholders as well as other preferred shareholders. Companies will often issue different series of preferred stock with unique terms and conditions, including asset distribution preferences.

Thinking about Employees, Insurance, and Taxes

Once a decision has been made to terminate the business, the majority of the company's employees will no longer be needed. Management needs to coordinate the termination of the nonessential employees to ensure that it provides ample warnings, pays vacation and/or other accrued earnings, and transitions or terminates other employee benefit programs (such as a 401k plan or health insurance). In certain cases, the business many need to disclose large employee reductions or reductions in force (RIF) to government agencies.

Pay special attention to your employee benefit programs to ensure that the plan administrators and third parties, such as an external payroll service to process year-end W-2 forms, can support employee transitions. Although severance packages aren't usually offered in these types of situations, set aside money to ensure that the employees don't get stuck with direct costs from benefit plan administrators and third parties. The last thing the officers or directors of the terminating company want is a bunch of angry employees creating problems after the fact.

Even though the business may have stopped selling products or offering services to the market, it doesn't mean that the business can terminate insurance. Ironically, focusing on risk-management issues is more important now than ever. As such, you need to manage the following forms of insurance during the termination process so that the company is not caught short:

- ✓ **Workers' compensation:** As long as the company has employees, leave workers' compensation insurance in force (as required by state laws). Generally, most companies retain a few employees to close down the business and manage the administrative issues that come with the process.

- ✓ **Directors and Officers (D&O):** Directors and officers' insurance is designed to provide liability coverage to the directors and officers of the company for potential wrongdoings. This issue has become extremely hot over the past three years thanks to high-profile fraud cases, such as Enron and MCI/WorldCom, and as a result, D&O insurance premiums are high. D&O insurance is often secured for trailing periods (for example, one, two, or three years after the company ceases operations) to provide additional coverage for legal proceedings from investors, creditors, and/or other groups that finally get around to pursuing an issue.

Hidden tax traps with liquidating a business

In most terminating business situations, not enough funds are available to repay the creditors in full. Okay, this sounds simple enough as the creditors get 35 percent on the dollar with the rest written off as they can't pursue the company or its officers, board members, and so on as no personal guarantees are present, no assets remain, and so on. This is commonly referred to as *debt forgiveness,* which the IRS and numerous states view as income to the business.

The terminating business can actually produce positive taxable income in its final year as a result of the amount of debt forgiveness realized. For a regular C corporation where any income tax obligation will be treated as either an unsecured debt (and thus written off) or applied to a previous year net operating loss, this income shouldn't present too many problems. However, for pass-through taxable entities (S corporations, partnerships, and LLCs that elects to report taxable income on the accrual basis), the taxable income would be distributed to the individual owners who then must report their pro-rata share of the income on their individual tax returns (thus triggering an additional income tax obligation at the personal level without a distribution available from the company to cover the obligation).

✔ **General liability:** As long as your doors are open, someone may get hurt on your property. For example, if an employee of a company that acquired fixed assets comes to your premises to pack and move the items and then slips and falls, your company may be on the hook. Keeping the general liability insurance in force until the last day of business is often a prudent business idea.

✔ **Property and casualty:** Insuring your assets through their final disposition date provides the necessary coverage in case of theft, accident, damage, and/or other events that may impair the asset's value. Safeguarding the company's assets represents a top priority during the termination process.

Our advice when it comes to business taxation and regulatory mandated costs within a terminating business is the same as we'd give a new business or any ongoing operation: Comply with the laws and regulations, plan properly, and, when needed, secure appropriate external professional counsel.

The terminating business needs to file the final tax returns for payroll, sales/use, property, income, benefit plans, and so on. You should let all taxing authorities and governmental agencies know that the business will no longer be operating and thus is not required to file periodic returns. Although it may take a while for the authorities and agencies to actually acknowledge that the business has terminated, you need to notify all the appropriate parties as to the legal status of the entity. Complying with governmental organizations other than for taxes also holds true for all of the business licenses, fictitious name statements, and certificates of authority to conduct business the company has secured over the years.

Managing Logistics

When you're terminating a business, all company records, including accounting, human resources, and corporate minutes, should be current to help with both termination and post-termination issues. A little extra effort put up front can alleviate a number of problems down the road.

In addition, you should store certain critical company files, records, information, and past transactions in a secure location and in the proper format. The files need to boxed, indexed, properly packaged, marked, and moved to a physical location for storage over an appropriate period, which may range from one to five-plus years, depending on the termination environment present and the likelihood of legal action or other inquires.

The company's electronic files, records, information, and so on should also be backed up and given to appropriate parties for storage and future retrievals if needed. You may even need multiple backups. You can dispose of nonvital or duplicate company documents, destroying any confidential information. For example, don't dump copies of employee pay records in the local trash bin because identity thieves are looking for this type of confidential information.

Ideally, all termination issues are resolved prior to the end of the company's annual fiscal year, eliminating the work and costs of keeping the business open into another fiscal year. Provide plenty of time to execute a termination with a keen eye kept on the company's annual fiscal year end.

You also need to process final corporate paperwork with various federal and state governmental agencies, as well as other parties. This paperwork includes filing final business tax returns (including income tax, sales/use tax, payroll tax, property tax, and others) at both the federal and state levels, processing notifications to the secretary of state of the desire to formally dissolve the legal entity (in the case of a corporation or LLC), forwarding final creditor and investor dissolution letters (for their personal records and accounting), and, in general, being prepared to communicate with any other party about the final termination and dilution of the business.

Legal notification requirements

You may hear the terms *dissolution* and *dissolving* of a business when a corporation or LLC is being formally terminated.

For example, the California Secretary of State requires a *Domestic Stock Corporation Certificate of Dissolution* be prepared and filed with the secretary of state to formally notify the department of corporations of the business's intent to terminate and dissolve. Although this form may sound complex to complete, it is simply a one-page form that notifies California's corporate regulatory department that the business has legally ceased to exist and that the termination was properly approved by the company's board of directors.

Finally, don't forget to identify and retain pre- and post-termination management teams. You can use either internal remaining employees or external professionals for this function, but they should be qualified, reliable, and prepared for the long haul. Setting aside money for these individuals is usually not a problem because most trustees, courts, and boards of directors recognize the value these individuals bring and will prioritize funds to be allocated for this use. Generally speaking, these individuals need to be paid upfront, as well as offered some type of compensation incentive, to properly tend to the buried business.

Part VI
The Part of Tens

The 5th Wave

By Rich Tennant

"Our profit statement shows a 13 percent increase in the good, a 4 percent decrease in the bad, but a whole lot of ugly left in inventory."

In this part . . .

The Part of Tens contains two shorter chapters: one directed to general small business management rules and the other to more specific financial management tools and tactics. Our thinking is this: First you must be a good general manager of your small business, which includes a wide range of functions. Assuming that you have good general management skills and know-how, you still need specific financial management savvy.

Chapter 16

Ten Management Rules for Small Business Survival

In This Chapter

▶ Starting right with planning

▶ Managing capital resources

▶ Communicating your strategies and results

▶ Keeping the end in sight

Gaining a solid understanding of the financial side of a business is important to its successful management. However, the root source of most business failures isn't so much based in the numbers but rather what business strategies, market factors, management decisions, and so on occurred that ultimately produced the numbers. Or, in other words, the financial performance of a company represents a final output or product that is used to measure business management successes and/or failures. That's why this chapter highlights the ten business management rules that are more intangible in nature yet represent the root of most small business operating problems or challenges.

Remember That Planning Counts

Proper planning is essential to the launch, growth, management, and ultimate success of your business. Don't underestimate the importance of dedicating resources to planning. Having access to sound financial plans structured for different operating scenarios is an absolute must.

When planning, keep in mind these two critical elements:

✔ **Planning represents an ongoing and fluid process.** The business plan represents a living, breathing tool that is constantly changing as market conditions change. The ability to adapt and remain flexible to changing market conditions has never been more critical than in today's fiercely competitive global marketplace.

✔ **Financial plans start with identifying, obtaining, and evaluating reliable third-party market data and information.** Yes, it's hard to believe that the authors of this book (both being accountants) would acknowledge the importance of this issue, but we're not dealing with the "Chicken and the Egg" riddle. Reliable third-party market data and information represents the heart of the planning process. Chapter 10 expands on this topic.

Secure Capital

The proper amount, type, and structure of capital must be secured to provide your business with the necessary financial resources to execute its business plan. One of the most common reasons small businesses fail is that they lack adequate capital to not only survive difficult times but, more importantly, prosper during growth opportunities. Although having a war chest available to "tap" during down times is important, having the proper amount and type of capital available to support a rapid growth period is even more critical. Raising capital has been, and will continue to be, one of the most critical and time-consuming tasks business owners and managers will ever undertake. Don't ever underestimate the importance of raising capital.

One of the greatest losses a small business will realize is that of lost opportunity, which has its roots in not being prepared to properly capitalize on market opportunities. The harsh reality is that the greatest loss a company will ever realize is never accounted for or presented in any way, shape, or form in its financial statements. Rather, missed market and business opportunities lurk in the background, haunting the business owner, manager, or entrepreneur with one simple reminder: "Imagine what I could have achieved!"

Don't Overlook Management Resources

Identifying and retaining a qualified and experienced management team represents an essential form of capital that is often overlooked but that is just as important as financial capital.

Capital comes in many shapes, forms, types, sizes, amounts, and structures and must be proactively managed in order to properly execute a business plan. When operating your business, don't forget about the "soft" capital. If management isn't readily available internally, then don't hesitate to secure properly qualified external professionals to support your business.

Understand the Selling Cycle

From an accounting perspective, the start of the selling cycle basically begins with a sales order, which then leads to an invoice and eventually payment. The accounting cycle, while relatively easy to define, represents only one element of the entire selling cycle. This cycle starts with conducting proper planning and market research and doesn't end until the customer's needs are completely satisfied (to ensure that the customer returns). The length of the complete selling cycle is often much longer than the aspiring entrepreneur wants to believe and represents one of the most common reasons businesses fail. (As expectations aren't met, capital is depleted, and management's creditability is destroyed.)

Understanding the selling cycle goes well beyond selling a product or service and collecting the cash. Rather, you can apply the selling cycle to almost any business function, from raising capital to securing management to developing new products. Make sure that you apply the concept of the selling cycle to every aspect of your business to ensure that proper plans are developed and capital resources are secured to handle the inevitable bumps in the road that will come.

Don't Fail to Communicate

Failure to communicate your company's financial results, what market factors are influencing your business's operations, and how your business will respond to the economic conditions present quite often is at the center of a businesses' ultimate failure. A business must develop proper communication channels and tools to deliver critical financial information and results, whether good or bad, to the appropriate internal and external parties.

The financial and operating results of your business, whether positive or negative, need to be communicated in a proactive and timely fashion to all key parties, both internal and external. Remember, the goal is to distribute reliable information on which all parties can respond and act (to support the company's business interests). Quite often, by proactively communicating operating results, even if the results are relatively poor, you gain added credibility with key management team members and external relationships. Delaying, downplaying, or even hiding bad news is a recipe for a disaster.

Practice CART

If you remember one acronym from this book, remember CART: Complete, Accurate, Reliable, and Timely. Your company's financial and accounting information system needs to produce complete, accurate, reliable, and timely financial information, reports, data, and so on so that management can make informed business decisions. Without CART, a business can't function properly or make informed and timely business decisions. Information represents the lifeblood of every business and starts with your internal accounting and financial information system.

Having raw transactional data that is accurate and timely is only half the battle. Being able to take this raw transactional data and present it in a reliable format that tells the entire (or complete) story is even more important.

CART isn't a mutually exclusive concept but rather a highly interdependent function that starts well before data is ever entered into the accounting system and ends well after the reports are generated.

Remember to KISS

No, we're not encouraging you to be overly friendly. We're referring to an important concept in managing financial information: Keep it Simple Stupid. Most businesses operate within an economic model that relies on two or three key financial factors or realities that tend to produce significant changes with profits or losses (and the associated impact on cash flows). Identifying, understanding, and managing these key factors often leads to the ultimate success or failure of a business. As such, structuring accounting and financial information systems that capture these factors in easily understood financial projections and supporting flash reports can greatly assist you (and your management team) with generating profits and the eventual big payday.

Comply, Comply, Comply

Chapter 9 is dedicated to the various taxes and tax equivalents that businesses must comply with today. It should come as no surprise that this chapter was also the longest one in the book given the current economic environment present and need for governmental bodies to raise funds.

Keep in mind four critical concepts:

✔ Subchapter S corporations, LLC's, and partnerships are all considered pass-through entities for income taxation purposes. That is, the taxable income or loss of a business is passed through to the owners of the company who are ultimately responsible for any income tax obligations. A regular C corporation isn't a pass-through entity so its income tax obligation resides at the company level.

✔ Within a pass-through entity, no dividends are present. Rather, a distribution of earnings may occur, which in itself isn't a taxable event. Remember, a tax obligation is generated when a distribution of taxable income occurs (via the distribution of taxable income on a form K-1) and not from a distribution of earnings.

✔ Various taxes, including payroll taxes, sales/use taxes, and certain excise taxes, are held in trust for taxing authorities. If these taxes aren't properly collected and remitted on a periodic basis, the taxing authorities can pierce the corporate veil and pursue collections against the owners of the business and/or the responsible parties (at the personnel level).

✔ You can establish *nexus,* which is when you legally conduct business in another taxing jurisdiction, within another location by executing the simplest of transactions. Once nexus is established, be prepared to proactively comply with numerous taxation requirements; the last thing you want to deal with is "tax and compliance" auditors descending upon your business from every angle.

Execute Your Exit Strategy

Every business owner, manager, and/or key executive must keep in mind that at some point, the end of a business will be at hand. This ending doesn't necessarily mean that the legal entity will cease to exist as a business; it may simply move in a new direction and formulate an updated business plan (to adapt to changing market conditions). However, for those businesses that are looking to execute an exit strategy and retire to the good life in beautiful South Beach Florida, remember the following valuation and exit strategy concepts:

✔ Retain a qualified board of directors and/or advisory board to support the business as it evaluates opportunities to exit. Having sound and experienced parties actively involved with selling your business represents an invaluable resource that you shouldn't overlook.

✔ Remember that the value of a business doesn't equal the owners' net equity as stated on the balance sheet. The value is based in its ability to generate future positive cash flows in relation to the business's inherent risks present. The combination of higher cash flow and lower risk will lead to increased valuations.

✔ Remember these three P's and one M when selling your business: Planning, Preparing, Presenting, and Managing. Manage these four issues well, and you generally see higher valuations, more attractive deal structuring terms, and a quicker deal timeline (eliminating problems or issues that may create delays in closing the transaction).

Know When to Say When

In the event that the business as currently operating is no longer economically viable and no market is available to sell the business, a final termination plan should be implemented to liquidate remaining assets. Voluntary liquidations offer the best opportunity for financial returns to be realized whereas involuntary liquidations (whether orderly or forced) often result in very poor financial results (not to mention the emotional strain that usually accompanies these events).

The emotional strain associated with a business termination is often far greater than the financial strain. Burying a concept that a business owner has put all his heart, soul, and energy into (not to mention money!) is one of the most difficult decisions a business owner will ever have to make. You need to make this decision objectively and efficiently. Retain external professionals to administer the final rites to the business.

Chapter 17

Ten Hard-Core Financial Tools and Tactics

In This Chapter

▶ Knowing the mechanics of making profit

▶ Controlling sizes of assets and operating liabilities

▶ Stabilizing sources of capital

*I*n this chapter, we briefly summarize ten rules for achieving your financial objectives. There are no dark, deep secrets to financial management. The techniques are straightforward. Your accountant can help you in executing these ten financial management procedures. You can hire outside consultants to advise you on occasion. But it really comes down to you. You should understand and take the time to perform these critical procedures.

Understand Profit Mechanics

It may seem unnecessary to say so, but you must understand how to make profit. You need a good business model to make profit, of course. And you need a profit model that you see clearly in your mind's eye. Your regular P&L (profit and loss) report is indispensable for tracking your profit performance. But the P&L has too much detail for strategic level profit analysis. A good profit model is small enough to scribble on the back of an envelope.

Three key factors drive profit:

✔ **Unit margin (or, margin per unit if your prefer):** Equals the *net price* received from selling one unit of product or service, minus all *variable expenses* of selling the unit.

- *Net price* equals list price less all sales price reductions (discounts, rebates, and so on) and less expenses that come off the top of sales revenue (sales commissions, credit card fees, and so on).

- The main variable expense of a business that sells products is *cost of goods (products) sold*. A business may have other significant variable expenses, such as packing and shipping costs.

✔ **Sales volume:** Equals the total quantity sold during the period. Unit margin times sales volume generates the *margin* earned from each product and service sold. All sources of sales combined generate the *total margin* of the business for the period, which equals profit before fixed expenses are considered.

✔ **Fixed expenses:** Equals total amount of cost commitments that you can't escape or decrease during the period. Examples are rents paid under lease contracts, depreciation, employees paid fixed salaries and wages, property taxes, and so on. Fixed costs provide *sales capacity,* which is the maximum volume that you can sell during the period.

Increasing sales volume increases profit — as long as you don't sacrifice unit margins on the products/services you sell and assuming that you stay within the sales capacity provided by your fixed expenses. Of course, it's better to increase sales of higher unit margin items than lower unit margin items. Improving unit margin is challenging. You have to increase sales prices or reduce the variable costs of making sales, which are daunting tasks. But improving unit margin by say, 5 percent, may be more realistic than improving sales volume 5 percent. And, besides, you don't have to worry about crowding the limit of your sales capacity by improving unit margin.

Understand Cash Flow

Hypothetically, you can run your business so that cash flow equals profit (or loss) for the period. A dollar of profit would yield a dollar of cash inflow, or a dollar of loss would cause a dollar of cash outflow. You wouldn't own any fixed assets on which depreciation is recorded; rather, you'd have to lease all your long-term operating assets. You'd make only cash sales, or if you extend credit to customers, you'd have to collect all receivables by the end of the period. You'd carry no inventory of products for sale, or if you did, you'd have to sell all products by the end of the period. You wouldn't prepay any expenses. And you'd pay all expenses by the end of the period and have no accounts payable or accrued expenses payable on the books. In this theoretical case, cash flow equals profit (or loss).

Of course, you can't really restrict your business this way. You may have to carry inventory; you may have receivables from credit sales; you may invest in fixed assets; and you may have unpaid bills and other unpaid expenses at the end of the period. These factors cause cash flow to differ from your bottom line profit or loss for the period.

Here are two principal examples of why cash flow differs from profit:

✔ Suppose that your accounts receivable (uncollected receivables from credit sales) increases $50,000 during the year, and annual sales revenue is $1,000,000. Therefore, cash flow from sales through the end of the year is $50,000 less than sales revenue. In other words, profit includes $50,000 of uncollected sales revenue.

✔ Suppose that $85,000 depreciation expense is recorded for the year. The cost balance of your fixed assets was written down $85,000 to recognize the use of your fixed assets during the year, and the fixed assets moved one year closer to their eventual disposal. The fixed assets were bought and paid for years ago. Therefore, profit includes an expense that required no cash outlay during the year.

The bottom line on cash flow is this. Start with net income or loss for the period, *as if* this amount were your cash flow for the period (but remember that it isn't). Next, add back depreciation. Don't stop here. Deduct *increases* in accounts receivable, inventory, and prepaid expenses. Or, add back *decreases* in these assets. Add back *increases* in accounts payable and accrued expenses payable. Or, deduct *decreases* in these two types of operating liabilities. Now wasn't that easy? Of course, you don't do all this arithmetic; that's the job for your accountant. Your job is to understand why these adjustments are made to profit to determine cash flow.

Know Your Sources of Profit

Most small businesses consist of two or more parts. Our local cleaner, for example, does both laundry and dry cleaning, and the prices are very different between the two. Clothing stores have men and women's departments. New car dealers operate a service department as well as sell new and used vehicles. Many restaurants and coffeehouses sell T-shirts and other souvenirs. You get the point.

Your accounting system should be organized to provide information for each major profit center of your business. Basically, a *profit center* is a separate source of sales revenue that you can assign direct costs to, in order to determine the *margin* earned for each part of your business. Margin is a measure of profit before considering the fixed expenses of the business. (See the section "Understand the Mechanics of Profit," earlier in this chapter.)

You need a P&L statement for your business as a whole, of course, but it's just the tip of the iceberg. What's under the water line is just as important. You need to know the profitability of each location, each product line, and each department for each mainstream revenue source of your business. In a nutshell, you should know the margin ratios and the amount of margin earned for every significant part of your business. The problem is how much detail to delve into. A local hardware store carries more than 100,000 different items. The general manager doesn't have the time (or patience) to read through margin reports for all 100,000 items, of course.

Generally, profit centers reflect the organizational structure of the business. For example, if you have two locations, you should get a separate margin report for each. If you make both wholesale and retail sales, you should treat each as a separate profit center. Within each profit center, you need further breakdown by products, customers, or on some other basis of making sales (over the Internet versus in-store, for example). Dividing your business into the right categories of sales and profit centers for management analysis and control is never easy. Consider getting the opinion of an outside consultant on how best to organize the reporting of profit centers.

Analyze Year-to-Year Profit Change

Suppose that your profit decreased 50 percent this year compared with last year. Shouldn't you know why? Shouldn't you find out the exact reasons for such a large drop in profit? Did sales volume shrink in some profit centers? Did unit margins change significantly? What happened to fixed expenses? We don't mean that *you* should take the time to do the detailed analysis. Ask your accountant to sort out the big changes from the small changes and to prepare a neat explanation of the key changes that caused the significant change in your profit.

In our experience, small business managers don't ask their accountants for a detailed year-to-year comparative analysis of profit. They rely on their gut feeling regarding the main reasons for the profit change. But without a thorough analysis, you can't be sure what caused the profit change. Spending time analyzing the change in profit from period to period is quite valuable. For one thing, it encourages you and your accountant to develop an analytical profit model. Furthermore, doing a comparative profit analysis helps in budgeting next year's profit plan. (See the upcoming section "Budget Profit and Cash.")

Keep Sizes of Assets Under Control

Marketing types like to say that nothing happens until you sell it. Sales and marketing is the heart of every successful business. You make profit by making sales. But you can't make sales without assets. You need a *working cash balance*. You need *inventory* if you sell products and *receivables* if you sell on credit. You need to own a variety of *fixed assets* (although you can lease many of them). Your *short-term operating liabilities* (accounts payable and unpaid accrued expenses) supply part of your total assets. The rest comes from debt and equity capital.

Suppose that your total assets minus your total operating liabilities equals $500,000. So you have to raise $500,000 capital. The owners (the partners in a partnership, the shareowners in a limited liability company, or the stockholders of a corporation) can put up the entire $500,000 capital. However, you probably would go to debt sources for part of your total capital. Both sources of capital have a cost. The cost of debt is interest, as you know. The cost of equity capital is higher; it's the rate of return that you should earn on the equity capital invested in the business. If your interest rate on debt is 8 percent, the owners expect you to earn an annual profit equal to 10, 15, or an even higher percent of return on their capital.

Don't overindulge in assets. Keep the sizes of your assets to no more than they have to be to make sales and conduct the operations of the business. Like people, businesses tend to get fat if they don't watch their weight. Chapter 11 explains the diagnosis of asset sizes.

Budget Profit and Cash

Chapter 7 explains the reasons for budgeting, which we don't repeat here. But we want to remind you of the critical importance of forecasting and budgeting profit, cash flow, and financial condition for the coming year. We strongly urge you to give your accountant at least estimates of sales volume, sales prices, costs, and major changes you're planning in the coming year. With this information, your accountant can whip out an impressive set of *pro forma* budgeted financial statements for the coming year.

Your budgeted statement of cash flow for the coming year is especially important. It may reveal that you'll have to raise additional capital to finance your growth, and the earlier you get started on this task, the better.

Audit Your Controls

Chapter 5 explains the need for internal controls. Small businesses are notorious for having weak internal controls and, therefore, are vulnerable to errors and fraud. Your business may be the exception, but don't bet on it. You lock the doors at the end of the day, don't you? In like manner, you should institute protective procedures to prevent fraud and establish checks and balances to minimize errors. Our advice is to hire a CPA to do a critical examination of your internal controls. It is money well spent.

Choose the Right Legal Entity

Chapter 9 explains income tax and the small business. Certain types of legal organizations are treated as *pass-through* entities for income tax purposes. The business doesn't itself pay income tax. A pass-through entity must determine its annual taxable income. Its taxable income is divided up among its owners in proportion to the ownership shares of each, and the owners include their shares of the business's taxable income in their individual income tax returns.

In contrast, a regular, or so-called C, corporation doesn't have this advantage. It's subject to income tax on its taxable income. Distributions from its after-tax net income to its stockholders are subject to a second income tax in the hands of the individual stockholders. As you probably know, the income tax law is complex. You should get the advice of an income tax professional on the best legal form of organization.

Stabilize Your Sources of Capital

Chapter 10 discusses raising capital for your business, which is a challenge for most startup business ventures. Raising capital during the early days of a business may be done in fits and starts and often lacks an overall cohesion and sense of continuity. This situation may be unavoidable during the hectic startup period of a new business. Once your business gets traction, it's very important to settle down on a steady policy for your sources of capital. Your lenders and owners will demand that you develop a predictable capital strategy for operating and growing your business.

Don't Massage Your Financial Numbers

Business managers are under pressure to report financial statements that look good, even if the underlying business realities aren't as good. In this book, we generally avoid discussing how to *massage the numbers,* although, here and there we refer to how managers could manipulate factors that drive profit (such as in Chapter 13 on manufacturing businesses). We draw the important distinction between *cooking the books,* which amounts to accounting fraud, versus nudging sales revenue and expense numbers up or down.

CPAs are ethically bound not to manipulate the accounting numbers used to prepare financial statements. As you know, there are commandments against telling falsehoods and committing adultery. Human behavior falls short of these ideals, of course. Unfortunately, massaging accounting numbers isn't uncommon. We encourage you to resist the temptation and follow the advice of the late sportscaster Howard Cosell who said, "Tell it like it is." However, if you engage in some massaging of the numbers, you should be aware of the consequences. In most cases, the result is robbing Peter to pay Paul, which accountants call a *compensatory effect.* Your profit looks better in this year, but you'll have to pay the piper next year because of the counterbalancing effect.

Appendix

About the CD

*I*n this appendix, you find out everything you need to know about the CD that accompanies this book.

System Requirements

You should be able to open the files on the CD for our book using almost any personal computer platform, including the following operating systems:

✔ A PC running Microsoft Windows 98, Windows 2000, Windows NT4 (with SP4 or later), Windows Me, Windows XP, or Windows Vista.

✔ A Macintosh running Apple OS X or later.

Of course, you need a CD-ROM drive in which the CD is inserted. In the unusual situation in which you don't have a CD-ROM drive, you can send an e-mail to John, one of the authors, at tracyj@colorado.edu, and he will e-mail you the files:

All files on the CD were prepared using Microsoft's Excel spreadsheet program. Therefore, you need the Excel program installed on your computer.

If you need more information on the basics, check out these books published by Wiley Publishing, Inc.: *PCs For Dummies,* by Dan Gookin; *Macs For Dummies* and *iMacs For Dummies,* both by David Pogue; and *Windows 95 For Dummies, Windows 98 For Dummies, Windows 2000 Professional For Dummies,* and *Microsoft Windows ME Millennium Edition For Dummies,* all by Andy Rathbone.

Using the CD

After inserting the CD in your CD-ROM, drive you should have no trouble opening the files on the CD for our book (assuming that you've installed the Excel spreadsheet program on your computer). Open the CD as you would any CD that has only files (instead of software and programs).

As you probably know, Excel is one of the components included in Microsoft's Office suite of programs. Office is available for both PC and Mac platforms. It doesn't matter whether Excel files are prepared using a Mac or a PC. Excel files prepared using a Mac are seamlessly opened by the Excel program on a PC, and vice versa.

We created the files on the CD for our book using the latest version of Excel. Generally speaking, Excel files are backward compatible. In other words, it should not cause any problem if you're using an earlier version of Excel. Furthermore, the Excel files on the CD for our book use only basic functions and features of Excel that have been in the spreadsheet program for many years.

What You'll Find on the CD

The CD for our book contains more than 40 Excel files. Each file is a duplicate of a figure in our book. Although each is a stand-alone file, some files present alternative scenarios for the same example.

We have prepared the files so that you and your accountant can use them as *templates*. You can adapt and tailor-make the format and data to fit the circumstances and facts of your business. Also, you can use the file to explore alternative, what-if scenarios – in order to analyze the effects of changes in sales volume, sales prices, costs, and other financial variables. Doing simulations of alternative scenarios is an excellent method to test your understanding of the example and to study the impacts of changes in the variables that drive profit, cash flow, and the other financial parameters of your business.

For your convenience of reference the following is a list of the files on the CD:

Figure 2-1: An illustrative small business P&L report

Figure 2-2: P&L report for year just ended and preceding year

Troubleshooting

Based on our experience using Excel files created on another computer, about the only problem we have encountered is the following: When you open an Excel file, sometimes a column doesn't appear wide enough, and you may see "XXXXXXXX" in one or more cells instead of the actual numerical value. This is only a warning that the column isn't set wide enough. In this case, simply widen the column. If you use Excel, your probably know that you can place the cursor on the vertical line in the column heading and double-click it to automatically widen the column enough to see the values for all cells in the column.

We have taken care to ensure that you should have no problems in opening every file and using it right away. Of course, no matter how careful you try to be, mistakes can escape your attention. If you find a mistake, please let us know. Send an e-mail to John at tracyj@colorado.edu. If you have any suggestions for improving a file, please get in touch.

Customer Care

If you have trouble with the CD-ROM for our book, please call the Wiley Product Technical Support phone number at (800) 762-2974. Outside the United States, call 1 (317) 572-3994. You can also contact Wiley Product Technical Support at **http://support.wiley.com**. John Wiley & Sons will provide technical support for general quality control items.

To place additional orders or to request information about other Wiley products, please call (877) 762-2974.

Index

• *C* •

• *G* •

• *J* •

Notes

Notes

Notes

BUSINESS, CAREERS & PERSONAL FINANCE

0-7645-9847-3

0-7645-2431-3

Also available:

- Business Plans Kit For Dummies
  0-7645-9794-9
- Economics For Dummies
  0-7645-5726-2
- Grant Writing For Dummies
  0-7645-8416-2
- Home Buying For Dummies
  0-7645-5331-3
- Managing For Dummies
  0-7645-1771-6
- Marketing For Dummies
  0-7645-5600-2
- Personal Finance For Dummies
  0-7645-2590-5*
- Resumes For Dummies
  0-7645-5471-9
- Selling For Dummies
  0-7645-5363-1
- Six Sigma For Dummies
  0-7645-6798-5
- Small Business Kit For Dummies
  0-7645-5984-2
- Starting an eBay Business For Dummies
  0-7645-6924-4
- Your Dream Career For Dummies
  0-7645-9795-7

HOME & BUSINESS COMPUTER BASICS

0-470-05432-8

0-471-75421-8

Also available:

- Cleaning Windows Vista For Dummies
  0-471-78293-9
- Excel 2007 For Dummies
  0-470-03737-7
- Mac OS X Tiger For Dummies
  0-7645-7675-5
- MacBook For Dummies
  0-470-04859-X
- Macs For Dummies
  0-470-04849-2
- Office 2007 For Dummies
  0-470-00923-3
- Outlook 2007 For Dummies
  0-470-03830-6
- PCs For Dummies
  0-7645-8958-X
- Salesforce.com For Dummies
  0-470-04893-X
- Upgrading & Fixing Laptops For Dummies
  0-7645-8959-8
- Word 2007 For Dummies
  0-470-03658-3
- Quicken 2007 For Dummies
  0-470-04600-7

FOOD, HOME, GARDEN, HOBBIES, MUSIC & PETS

0-7645-8404-9

0-7645-9904-6

Also available:

- Candy Making For Dummies
  0-7645-9734-5
- Card Games For Dummies
  0-7645-9910-0
- Crocheting For Dummies
  0-7645-4151-X
- Dog Training For Dummies
  0-7645-8418-9
- Healthy Carb Cookbook For Dummies
  0-7645-8476-6
- Home Maintenance For Dummies
  0-7645-5215-5
- Horses For Dummies
  0-7645-9797-3
- Jewelry Making & Beading For Dummies
  0-7645-2571-9
- Orchids For Dummies
  0-7645-6759-4
- Puppies For Dummies
  0-7645-5255-4
- Rock Guitar For Dummies
  0-7645-5356-9
- Sewing For Dummies
  0-7645-6847-7
- Singing For Dummies
  0-7645-2475-5

INTERNET & DIGITAL MEDIA

0-470-04529-9

0-470-04894-8

Also available:

- Blogging For Dummies
  0-471-77084-1
- Digital Photography For Dummies
  0-7645-9802-3
- Digital Photography All-in-One Desk Reference For Dummies
  0-470-03743-1
- Digital SLR Cameras and Photography For Dummies
  0-7645-9803-1
- eBay Business All-in-One Desk Reference For Dummies
  0-7645-8438-3
- HDTV For Dummies
  0-470-09673-X
- Home Entertainment PCs For Dummies
  0-470-05523-5
- MySpace For Dummies
  0-470-09529-6
- Search Engine Optimization For Dummies
  0-471-97998-8
- Skype For Dummies
  0-470-04891-3
- The Internet For Dummies
  0-7645-8996-2
- Wiring Your Digital Home For Dummies
  0-471-91830-X

* Separate Canadian edition also available
† Separate U.K. edition also available

Available wherever books are sold. For more information or to order direct: U.S. customers visit www.dummies.com or call 1-877-762-2974.
U.K. customers visit www.wileyeurope.com or call 0800 243407. Canadian customers visit www.wiley.ca or call 1-800-567-4797.

SPORTS, FITNESS, PARENTING, RELIGION & SPIRITUALITY

0-471-76871-5

0-7645-7841-3

Also available:
- Catholicism For Dummies
  0-7645-5391-7
- Exercise Balls For Dummies
  0-7645-5623-1
- Fitness For Dummies
  0-7645-7851-0
- Football For Dummies
  0-7645-3936-1
- Judaism For Dummies
  0-7645-5299-6
- Potty Training For Dummies
  0-7645-5417-4
- Buddhism For Dummies
  0-7645-5359-3

- Pregnancy For Dummies
  0-7645-4483-7 †
- Ten Minute Tone-Ups For Dummies
  0-7645-7207-5
- NASCAR For Dummies
  0-7645-7681-X
- Religion For Dummies
  0-7645-5264-3
- Soccer For Dummies
  0-7645-5229-5
- Women in the Bible For Dummies
  0-7645-8475-8

TRAVEL

0-7645-7749-2

0-7645-6945-7

Also available:
- Alaska For Dummies
  0-7645-7746-8
- Cruise Vacations For Dummies
  0-7645-6941-4
- England For Dummies
  0-7645-4276-1
- Europe For Dummies
  0-7645-7529-5
- Germany For Dummies
  0-7645-7823-5
- Hawaii For Dummies
  0-7645-7402-7

- Italy For Dummies
  0-7645-7386-1
- Las Vegas For Dummies
  0-7645-7382-9
- London For Dummies
  0-7645-4277-X
- Paris For Dummies
  0-7645-7630-5
- RV Vacations For Dummies
  0-7645-4442-X
- Walt Disney World & Orlando
  For Dummies
  0-7645-9660-8

GRAPHICS, DESIGN & WEB DEVELOPMENT

0-7645-8815-X

0-7645-9571-7

Also available:
- 3D Game Animation For Dummies
  0-7645-8789-7
- AutoCAD 2006 For Dummies
  0-7645-8925-3
- Building a Web Site For Dummies
  0-7645-7144-3
- Creating Web Pages For Dummies
  0-470-08030-2
- Creating Web Pages All-in-One Desk
  Reference For Dummies
  0-7645-4345-8
- Dreamweaver 8 For Dummies
  0-7645-9649-7

- InDesign CS2 For Dummies
  0-7645-9572-5
- Macromedia Flash 8 For Dummies
  0-7645-9691-8
- Photoshop CS2 and Digital
  Photography For Dummies
  0-7645-9580-6
- Photoshop Elements 4 For Dummies
  0-471-77483-9
- Syndicating Web Sites with RSS Feeds
  For Dummies
  0-7645-8848-6
- Yahoo! SiteBuilder For Dummies
  0-7645-9800-7

NETWORKING, SECURITY, PROGRAMMING & DATABASES

0-7645-7728-X

0-471-74940-0

Also available:
- Access 2007 For Dummies
  0-470-04612-0
- ASP.NET 2 For Dummies
  0-7645-7907-X
- C# 2005 For Dummies
  0-7645-9704-3
- Hacking For Dummies
  0-470-05235-X
- Hacking Wireless Networks
  For Dummies
  0-7645-9730-2
- Java For Dummies
  0-470-08716-1

- Microsoft SQL Server 2005 For Dummies
  0-7645-7755-7
- Networking All-in-One Desk Reference
  For Dummies
  0-7645-9939-9
- Preventing Identity Theft For Dummies
  0-7645-7336-5
- Telecom For Dummies
  0-471-77085-X
- Visual Studio 2005 All-in-One Desk
  Reference For Dummies
  0-7645-9775-2
- XML For Dummies
  0-7645-8845-1

HEALTH & SELF-HELP

0-7645-8450-2

0-7645-4149-8

Also available:
- Bipolar Disorder For Dummies
  0-7645-8451-0
- Chemotherapy and Radiation
  For Dummies
  0-7645-7832-4
- Controlling Cholesterol For Dummies
  0-7645-5440-9
- Diabetes For Dummies
  0-7645-6820-5* †
- Divorce For Dummies
  0-7645-8417-0 †

- Fibromyalgia For Dummies
  0-7645-5441-7
- Low-Calorie Dieting For Dummies
  0-7645-9905-4
- Meditation For Dummies
  0-471-77774-9
- Osteoporosis For Dummies
  0-7645-7621-6
- Overcoming Anxiety For Dummies
  0-7645-5447-6
- Reiki For Dummies
  0-7645-9907-0
- Stress Management For Dummies
  0-7645-5144-2

EDUCATION, HISTORY, REFERENCE & TEST PREPARATION

0-7645-8381-6

0-7645-9554-7

Also available:
- The ACT For Dummies
  0-7645-9652-7
- Algebra For Dummies
  0-7645-5325-9
- Algebra Workbook For Dummies
  0-7645-8467-7
- Astronomy For Dummies
  0-7645-8465-0
- Calculus For Dummies
  0-7645-2498-4
- Chemistry For Dummies
  0-7645-5430-1
- Forensics For Dummies
  0-7645-5580-4

- Freemasons For Dummies
  0-7645-9796-5
- French For Dummies
  0-7645-5193-0
- Geometry For Dummies
  0-7645-5324-0
- Organic Chemistry I For Dummies
  0-7645-6902-3
- The SAT I For Dummies
  0-7645-7193-1
- Spanish For Dummies
  0-7645-5194-9
- Statistics For Dummies
  0-7645-5423-9

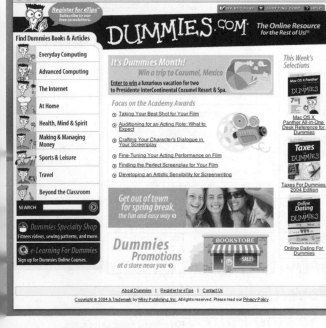

Get smart @ dummies.com®

- **Find a full list of Dummies titles**
- **Look into loads of FREE on-site articles**
- **Sign up for FREE eTips e-mailed to you weekly**
- **See what other products carry the Dummies name**
- **Shop directly from the Dummies bookstore**
- **Enter to win new prizes every month!**

* Separate Canadian edition also available

† Separate U.K. edition also available

Available wherever books are sold. For more information or to order direct: U.S. customers visit www.dummies.com or call 1-877-762-2974.
U.K. customers visit www.wileyeurope.com or call 0800 243407. Canadian customers visit www.wiley.ca or call 1-800-567-4797.